Archetypes of the Enneagram

Exploring the life themes of the 27 subtypes from the perspective of *soul*

Susan Rhodes

ACKNOWLEDGMENTS: I'm deeply grateful to all the people in the enneagram community from whom I've learned about this wonderful system, even those whose interpretation diverges from my own. I'm especially grateful to those who support an emerging vision of the system as a source of positive energy. Special thanks to Sheela Word for her film theme insights; to Deborah DiMichele for her thoughtful suggestions on book content and editorial help; and to Pamela Silimperi for her ongoing friendship and editorial support. My heartfelt appreciation goes out to my adopted family, the Thompsons (Norm, Adél, Norman & Hanna) for always being there when I need to talk, cry, or laugh.

978-0-9824792-1-6

All written content & graphics by Susan Rhodes
Cover design by Susan Rhodes

To order books, please contact the publisher:

Geranium Press
12345 Lake City Way NE #280
Seattle, WA 98125
geraniumpress@gmail.com

GERANIUM PRESS

This book is dedicated to all the people who have encouraged me to continue exploring the enneagram from a perspective that is joyful, spontaneous & open to new ideas

Contents

Part I: An Archetypal View

Part II: The Enneagram

Part III: The Subtypes

Part I

An archetypal view

The one thing

If Only One Thing Matters, Everything Matters
– recent documentary title

FIVE YEARS AGO, I had a dream:

I was enrolled in a girl's high school. Our work was to clean books. When I looked at the books I was assigned to clean, I realized that I didn't have to clean them all to the same degree. Most needed to get a grade of "C" or perhaps a "B." Surprisingly, some only needed a "D"! But a very small number required an "A." The cleaning on those books had to be meticulous, and this shocked and frightened me.

I woke up from the dream with a start, my head swimming with its energy. It was numinous—charged with meaning—so I knew it was important. But what did it signify?

"It's interesting," I thought, "that we're cleaning books, not reading them. Could it be that real learning is about refining our understanding of things we already know?" Okay, that made sense. I could grasp the idea that learning is about seeing things from a "cleaner" (finer and more subtle) perspective.

"But why don't we have to clean all the books well?" I wondered. "Is it really okay that some of the books only need to be cleaned well enough to get a barely passing grade? Don't we have to do pretty well in everything, at least average or a little above?"

Apparently not. It was a new idea for me to think that there were areas in life that just didn't matter that much—at least as far as my personal destiny was concerned. But here was the catch: I had to get an A in some areas; a B would not do. The shock this realization produced (even when dreaming) told me that the dream was challenging a deeply-held conviction. What could it be?

It took me a while to figure it out, but I slowly realized that I held the belief that it was possible to go through life without excelling very much as long as I stayed more or less in the average range. I could duck out on big plans and dreams (which were scary) so long as I didn't really screw up in a big way. Using that approach, I thought that I could stay safe and not hurt other people. But the dream was telling me otherwise. Clearly, if I did not excel in the areas that required excellence, all my other efforts would matter very little.

This dream reminded me of an intriguing Rumi passage:

> One thing must not be forgotten. Forget all else, but remember this, and you will have no regrets. Remember everything else, but ignore this one thing, and you will have done nothing. It is as if a king sent you on a mission to a foreign land to perform one special task for him. If you do a hundred things, but not this appointed task, what have you accomplished? Human beings come into this world for a particular purpose, and if they forget it they would have done nothing at all.

This passage conveys the message that we each have a unique destiny. This destiny involves the completion of some task that is quite specific to each individual. It's up to us to discover the nature of the task and to make sure that it gets done. If we can do this, we'll have no regrets.

Living without regret. What a wonderful idea—and a worthy goal. But is it really possible? Both my dream and Rumi say the answer is "yes," but neither tells us exactly how to do it. This is something we have to discover for ourselves. It's we who have to figure out which books to clean—which acts to perform. That's the "plot" of our lives, its *Cliff Notes* story line. But more basic than plot is *theme*: the archetypal thread that runs through our lives, subtly bending them to its hidden purposes. Theme is less obvious than plot, but it's what gives our life meaning and purpose.

It's when we begin to discern the themes that shape our lives that we begin to get an inkling of what Rumi's "One Thing" is all about. We begin to get a sense of our life's purpose, *dharma*, vocation, calling, or destiny—to make out the shape of the inner principle that governs our lives.

But this inner principle is a subtle thing that hides its face from the light of day. No scientific experiment can be done to prove its existence; no meditation, affirmation, or magic spell can force it to reveal itself to us in the absence of understanding. Nonetheless, it's always there, like the air we breathe, a subtle blueprint whose outlines gradually emerge as we move from childhood into young adulthood and beyond. When we look directly at it, it tends to disappear. (That's one reason that many self-help books are limited in their ability to tangibly help us. It's because they try to help too much. They try to boil things down into a simple formula, complete with exercises, questionnaires, and checklists for completion. In so doing, they lose touch with the very thing they're trying to explain.)

Sufi master Radha Mohan Lal likened the enigmatic nature of our path in life to that of the birds in flight. "Look at the birds in the sky. Can you trace the path of their flight?" One of his successors, Llewellyn Vaughn-Lee, said that those who seek this path "gradually we realize that this pathless path is none other than our own inner being calling out to ourself."*

How do we find this pathless path? How do we discern our invisible blueprint? There's no simple answer to this question. No matter how many self-help books we read, workshops we attend, or counselors we consult, nobody can hand us this answer on a platter. But there are tools we can use to become more attuned to its purposes, some of which (like yoga, meditation, prayer, introspection, breath work, and shamanism) have been practiced for millennia. Occasionally, new techniques are either invented or revealed; the scientific method is an example, because it gave us an entirely new way to look at ourselves and at life. Another is depth psychology, especially the Jungian and archetypal varieties. An even more recent addition is the enneagram, which is only now becoming widely-known as a tool for self-discovery. It's a powerful tool, especially when we use it for exploring individual differences in temperament, motivation, and orientation.

---

* Source: www.goldensufi.org.

The enneagram is said to have ancient roots. But its teachings were never revealed until the last century, when mystic G. I. Gurdjieff taught the enneagram as a system for describing nine steps in a transformational process. Later, Oscar Ichazo adapted it as a tool for discerning nine core motivations that give rise to personality differences. But Ichazo saw those differences as problematic, characterizing them as nine kinds of distorted thinking (cognitive fixations) that block spiritual transformation. Ichazo's student Claudio Naranjo, whose teachings have become widely dispersed, saw them as psychological pathologies driven by instinctual passions. The result is that the enneagram is now best known as a tool for describing how personality serves as a barrier to higher consciousness.

But that's not the only way to view the nine types. Because the enneagram is a universal system, I think it makes more sense to view the types as positive energy constellations—a point I've made in numerous *Enneagram Monthly* articles and in my book, *The Positive Enneagram.** While it's possible to misuse the energy of the types, there's no reason to think of them as inherently fixated or pathological.†

The geometry of the enneagram points us to the transformational nature of the nine types, because they're depicted as nine small circles (points) within a larger circle of wholeness (Fig. 1-1). The geometry also shows us the transformational role of each type (which can be discerned by looking at its position on the circle),‡ as well as its relationship with the other eight types, especially its wing points and connecting points —relationships that reveal additional transformational possibilities.§

The geometry also reveals something else: that we are not just our personalities, but part of something larger than ourselves (the larger circle)—something inherently whole and complete. We don't have to leave the small "circle of type" in order to participate in the larger circle of life.

---

* Available from Geranium Press at Amazon.com.

† See my book, *The Positive Enneagram: A New Approach to the Nine Types* (2009) for details (available from Amazon.com).

‡ See Chapter 7.

§ See Chapters 8 and 10.

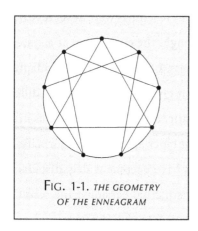

FIG. 1-1. *THE GEOMETRY OF THE ENNEAGRAM*

This last point is especially important because of the widespread belief in the enneagram community that ego is the enemy of essence, where *ego = our enneagram type* and *essence = the wholeness we are said to possess in the absence of ego*. If we think of ego as the small circle and essence as the larger circle, we can see that ego can never obscure essence (or vice-versa); both are always present. And neither is superior to the other.

But the "ego-versus-essence" paradigm is the basis for a lot of the work done in the field. It's a dualistic approach, because it relies on *either/or* thinking, which requires us to make a forced choice between two irreconcilable positions (either we chose ego or essence, not both). The alternative is *both/and* thinking, which says that we don't have to choose: we can embody ego and essence simultaneously. The geometry of the enneagram supports the *both/and* idea, freeing us up to see unity and diversity as complements, not opposites—and enabling us to see the enneagram, the types, and the subtypes in a more positive light.

The enneagram subtypes are the main focus of this book. They're the 27 personality profiles that we can generate by looking at how each of the nine types behaves in three diverse arenas of life: the personal (self-preservation) arena, the sexual (creative) arena, and the social arena. For a given individual, one of these arenas will usually be more dominant than the other two. To discover which one, we can ask ourselves, "Which of the following most attracts my interest?":

- ▸ My private world (*home, garden, family, solitary/personal pursuits*)?

- ▸ My intimate, creative, or spiritual life (*love affairs, dramas, intense experiences, transcendent spirituality, intense encounters*)?

- ▸ My role in social activities as either a leader or participant (*event planning, parties, charity work, causes, politics, fund-raising*)?"

The answer we choose will tell us our dominant subtype arena. Once we know both our type and subtype arena, we can figure out our dominant subtype.*

I didn't invent the idea of the subtypes; it's part of the corpus of original teachings on the personality enneagram as developed by Oscar Ichazo. However, my approach is quite different than that of most enneagram writers, because I view the subtypes the same way I view the types: from the "both/and" perspective mentioned earlier, not as instinctual drives contaminated by distorted ego passions and fixations.† In addition, I see the subtypes as pointers towards *dharma*, because they help us see the link between core motivation and the activities of real life—particularly when we use the framework of Jungian and archetypal psychology as the basis for our explorations. This is because archetypal psychology is the psychology of *soul*, and it's *soul* that leads us deep into the heart of life.

I base my ideas on the work of a variety of innovators, among them Carl Jung, James Hillman, Margaret Wheatley, Thomas Moore, Mark Epstein, Matthew Fox, Rupert Sheldrake, Arthur Koestler, Robert Johnson, Ken Wilber, Mihaly Csikszentmihalyi, Martin Seligman, and Stephen Nachmanovich.

My approach rests on three key premises. The first is that *personality is a good thing*; it's not something that separates us from our essential nature. This is why Carl Jung sees personality development as a key part of the individuation process: because it's by developing, refining, and stabilizing our personality that we transform ourselves.‡

The second is that *there's nothing about the psyche that is inherently unlovable.* According to Jung, even its darkest shadows are the *prima materia* for transformation.

---

* For the sake of brevity, I often abbreviate the arenas as follows: self-preservation arena = SP arena, sexual arena = SX arena, and social arena = SOC arena. I often refer to specific subtypes as SP Ones, SX Ones, SOC Ones, SP Twos, etc.

† By the way, one of the more confusing things in this kind of discussion is the different ways that people use the word *ego*. When I use it, I'm trying to describe psychic functioning on the level of everyday consciousness, not narcissistic (egocentric) thinking.

‡ I'm using the word *personality* in the same way that Jung uses it: to describe individuality at the level of everyday life. For his comments on personality and individuation, see Chapter 7 in *The Development of Personality* (1981), p. 169.

James Hillman goes further, saying that our unintegrated inner personas are of value for what they already are, not just what they can become.

The third is that *there are three different realms of consciousness* (spirit, ego, and *soul*) and that all three require nurturing if we are to live a fulfilling life. Secular culture favors the ego realm while religious culture favors the realm of spirit. But where does that leave the realm of *soul*—the realm of depth, feeling, imagination, and mystery—which is neither fish nor foul? In modern life, *soul* has become almost entirely invisible and thus devalued (although people like Jung, Hillman, and Joseph Campbell have been trying to revive our interest). So part of my purpose here is to contribute to that effort by introducing a three-realm approach to enneagram work.*

Part I (Chapters 1 – 5) introduces the world of archetypal psychology, a world in which life has meaning and we each play a particular role in the act of creation. The idea of introducing Rumi's One Thing is to raise the question that everybody wants to answer: *Why am I here?* Raising this question is the first step on a journey—a journey where we explore the nature of a path, what it means to be in the moment, the mystique of *soul*, and the power of myth. None of these explorations is designed to give a pat answer to the "Why-am-I-here?" question, but all provide clues about fruitful places to look for further answers.

More significantly, they "prime the pump" for our discussion on the enneagram in Part II.† It's necessary to start with a little pump-priming, because the enneagram is seldom if ever taught from a truly Jungian perspective. The current approach is instead based on Freudian psychology as amended by the kill-the-ego fervor of the 1960s. Chapter 6 explains how this works and where this approach originated; Chapter 7 focuses on ways we can link the personality enneagram with Gurdjieff's process enneagram, because this is the first step towards seeing the types from a transformational

---

* See Chapters 4 and 7.

† If you're the impatient type, you can skip right to Part II; it can stand on its own. It's just that Part I provides the context for my critique of enneagram theory in Part II.

perspective. Then there's a brief introduction to wing points, connecting points, and energy centers (Chapter 8), followed by a discussion of the theory that currently informs our understanding of the subtypes (Chapter 9). At the end of the chapter, I introduce an alternative framework for subtype work (and more broadly, enneagram work) that's simpler, more integrative, and more logically consistent than the current ego-versus-essence model. There's also a brief overview of the 27 subtypes.

Part III is where we explore the enneagram from an archetypal perspective, focusing on the archetypal roles we play in life and the archetypal themes that run like threads through the fabric of our lives. Each chapter focuses on one type and its three subtypes, using examples from life, film, and TV to bring them to life. After a brief epilogue, there are reference lists to books and films, along with a test for determining your type and subtype. (The test consists of short descriptions, so it's designed not so much to "nail" the type and subtype as to provide food for thought.)

¤ ¤ ¤

AT THE BEGINNING of her innovative book on living systems, *Leadership and the New Science* (1999), business consultant Margaret Wheatley remarks that "this book attempts to be true to...[a] new vision of reality, where ideas and information are but half of what is required to evoke reality. The creative possibilities of the ideas represented here depend on your engagement with them" (p. 9).

I would also like to be true to a new vision of reality that engages the reader. I hope to portray the types and subtypes in a way that's vivid enough to be both memorable and inspiring. I'd also like to leave some room for you, the reader, to walk into the world of the archetypes in your own way, so can imagine what they're like and reflect on the ways that they show up in your life.

Although this excursion is playful, it has a serious side. Archetypal energy is powerful. Its themes are powerful, which is why they're the stuff of great films and literature. While some archetypal images seem inspiring (the Social Idealist, Guardian Angel, or Horatio Alger), others may disturb us (the Dark Queen, Addict, or Vigilante). Yet other archetypes may seem disappointingly prosaic or trivial (the Loyalist, Fashion Plate, or Organizer).

Whatever their nature, they're all familiar to us. So they all belong in any exploration into the motivations behind human thought and action. But it's not always easy to look these archetypes squarely in the face, because they can evoke strong emotional reactions. Even positive images can arouse resistance if they make us feel that we're not living up to our potential.

Even so, I see advantages in working with all the archetypes. Inspirational archetypes give us goals towards which to strive. Shadow archetypes alert us to those areas of life that need our attention. And trivial archetypes often serve a not-so-trivial purpose: to help us ground the extraordinary in ordinary life by treating the trivial details of life as if they really matter.

And of course, they really *do* matter, just as *we* really matter. We don't live in a random world lacking any sort of overarching principle. Our lives mean something, and they're part of a larger context that also means something, although that meaning can become obscured by the busyness of modern life.

But every once and a while, we have an experience that cuts through that busyness and grabs our attention, often unexpectedly: Life becomes *It* and comes to find us, "ready or not." Something happens, and we're shocked into remembering—even if only for a moment—that life is a place of awe and wonder. There's a perfection about such moments, a "just so" quality, that enables us to stop and simply *be*—without trying to resist, exploit, or explain what is happening. In these "just so" moments, we see the world from a different perspective: the perspective of *soul*. I hope to breathe some *soul* into the pages of this book, because *soul* has the power to lead us into worlds we never knew were there and along paths that we never expected to travel.

What kind of path?

Do not follow where the path may lead. Go instead where there is no path and leave a trail.
– Harold R. McAlindon

WHEN WE PICTURE A PATH, what comes to mind? For me, it's a wilderness track, a trace made by animals, or some steps in the snow. It might even be a stream or an invisible crossing on the ice. It tends to have an elusive, mysterious quality that beckons, despite the dangers. And it often peters out and requires us to retrace our steps.

A path is clearly not the same thing as a trail. It is not well-marked, signposted, or paved. It does not have a clear beginning and ending. It does not include safety features like lights, handrails, or "You Are Here" signs. It is not safe but is intriguing nonetheless.

But a path sometimes *looks* like a trail, at least at the beginning. One day, I was walking through the forest with a friend on one of those days when you can't tell what the weather is going to do next. It was windy one moment and calm the next; the sun appeared and disappeared amid swiftly-moving clouds.

The place where we walked was along an ocean bay formed by the San Andreas Fault. The trail went along the beach and then steadily upwards, into the woods. There were several loops of varying lengths, most of which eventually returned to the beach.

The place had always had a mysterious quality but most of the time, I just saw it as a place to relax and enjoy nature's beauty. But on this day, it was different. Soon after we arrived, the wind picked up and it started to rain. We decided to walk, anyway;

it wasn't cold and the light rain didn't really bother us. As we ascended the path into the forest, it became darker. Soon the rain was coming down steadily. Somehow, my friend and I became separated. I couldn't find her and began to feel afraid. I found myself running down the trail calling out her name.

I saw a small path to the side, barely visible in the undergrowth. I thought, "Maybe I should go that way." Something about that path beckoned to me. I couldn't help thinking that my friend might have wandered down it, mistaking it for the trail. Maybe she's lost or injured, I thought. If she called, I wouldn't hear her because of the rain.

It was getting dark. I decided to take the path, but I couldn't see very well. I walked for a little ways, increasingly worried about my friend. The worry was distracting; I wasn't all that aware of my surroundings. I saw a narrow place in the path directly ahead that was bare and rocky. The rocks were shiny with rain.

I was about to step out when something stopped me—a sudden feeling of intense fear. It came out of nowhere. I looked up and squinted, trying to make out the surroundings. Suddenly, I realized where I was: on the brink of a rocky ledge 50 or 60 feet above the water. The "path" ahead was not really a path at all. It was just a dark vein of loose rocks along the sheer side of the cliff. One more step and I could well be over the edge.

I didn't take that step. I gasped and stepped back. Trembling with cold and fear, I slowly retraced my steps. When I came to the main trail, there was my friend, waiting for me.

"Where were you?" she asked, in an irritated voice. "I've been looking all over for you."

Still stunned from my experience, I didn't know what to say. I shrugged, and turned to walk back to the car. I mechanically noted that the sky was lighter. It was barely raining now. But we were soaked to the skin. When we reached the car, we turned the heater on full blast, grateful for the warmth. We were back in civilization again.

I didn't realize it right away, but this event foreshadowed the beginning of a very difficult period in my life—a time that seemed to me very much like walking along the edge of a dangerous precipice. But this experience indelibly imprinted something in me that helped get me through: the certain knowledge that I was not alone. Whatever the challenges I might encounter, there was an "invisible something" that would guide and protect me when the danger was greatest.

¤ ¤ ¤

Our path in life is a lot like that path in the woods. We feel compelled to seek it out but never know where it will lead. We often give ourselves a rational reason for following it (like searching for a lost friend), but is that the real reason? I doubt it. We follow it because it calls to us, leading us to some interesting scenery, new vista, dangerous precipice, or even a dead end. (Just because it dead ends doesn't mean it's worthless, although people living in a results-oriented culture might certainly think so!)

When we speak of finding our path in life, it is of course a metaphor. But it's a powerful metaphor because it evokes something deep within us, a yearning to be reunited with something we feel we've lost. To regain it requires a personal journey and hence a path. In the West, it's called the Hero's Journey or the Quest for the Grail. In the East, it's symbolized by the Zen Ox Herding pictures, which depict the stages of seeing the ox, taming the ox, and finally befriending it.

Such archetypal themes seem larger-than-life, which is why such stories are often associated with the mystical path—the path walked by the great spiritual explorers and saints throughout the ages. It's hard for most of us to picture ourselves embarking on such a path; it seems so arduous, exotic, and removed from ordinary life. It's hard to imagine a way to bridge the gap between the exotic world of the archetypes and the ordinary world of spilled milk, flat tires, and lousy bosses.

But maybe the gap isn't as great as it seems—or as great as it may have been in the past. Maybe the time has come when it's possible for ordinary people to be present in both worlds—or to see both worlds as two aspects of one world. Maybe it's possible to look at Rumi's remarks about the One Thing (Chapter 1) as an invitation to anyone who would like to live a life with "no regrets."

But if it's an invitation, it seems to be an invitation with strings. Because the One Thing we need to do is not something we picked ourselves; it's something mandated by the "king." Who is this king? And why is he in charge? Rumi gives us a clue when he says, "Human beings come into this world for a particular purpose." He's plainly implying four things:

1. Life has a purpose (it's not random or meaningless)
2. Human beings come into the world with a purpose (our lives matter)
3. Each of us have a unique and individual purpose (a specific task to carry out)
4. The fulfillment of our life's purpose (our task) will bring us a sense of personal fulfillment

It's good to hear from a sage like Rumi that our lives have purpose, because this gives us a greater sense of dignity and self-worth. And it's good to know that each of us has a *particular* purpose because this reaffirms our value as unique human beings. However, when it comes to the idea that we must fulfill our life's purpose in order to find fulfillment, this might give us pause.

Why? Because it implies that life actually expects something from us—that we're not 100% free to do as we like. Raised in a country dedicated to the proposition that life is about the pursuit of happiness—and believing very much in the idea that we have the right to exercise our free will when deciding how to pursue that goal—we may not be too enthused about the idea that we're under any sort of obligation simply because we exist. It brings to mind a favorite accusation of American children during fights with their parents: "I didn't ask to be born!"

Just why are we born? Why are we on this planet? Could it be that life somehow needs us, in order to realize its purposes on the earth?

That's what psychologist Robert Sardello believes. He makes the case that "the supposedly independent world is at every moment being supported by the presence of every individual in the world, whether or not the individual has any inkling that this is the case or not" (*Love and the Soul,* p. 43). The same idea is implied by Rumi when he speaks of doing a task for the king. If it is the king who sends us to do something, it's probably something that needs doing.

But look at the bright side. If we have an obligation to life, it probably means that life also has an obligation to us. If so, then we must have a genuine relationship with life—a relationship of mutuality and support. This brings to mind a story where Albert Einstein was asked by a reporter, "What is the most important question in life?"

Einstein could have said a lot of things. Perhaps the reporter was expecting something abstruse, as befits a world-class physicist. But what Einstein said was this:

"Is the universe a friendly place or not?"

Einstein's reply is touching, in that it speaks to the secret hope of all human beings: that we live in a universe which is essentially benevolent, not indifferent or evil.

A friend and I were having a discussion about this topic one day. She spoke of various fears she had, especially the fear of letting go. Several nights later, she had a dream in which a brass band was marching down the street, its members happily singing as they played. The lyrics were impossible to miss: "The universe is safe! The universe is safe!"

She woke up laughing.

How many of us believe that the universe is a friendly place? That life itself is friendly? How many of us ever consider the possibility?

Einstein was a fervent believer in the orderly nature of life ("God does not play dice with the universe"), which is why he found some of the paradoxes introduced by the new physics hard to accept. The author of *The Re-Enchantment of Everyday Life* (1996), Thomas Moore, also believes that life is a place of mystery, magic, and beauty. And he believes we are hungry to bring them into our lives, whether we realize it or not: "The soul has an absolute, unforgiving need for regular excursions into enchantment" (p. *ix*).

In *The Physics of Angels* (1996), theologian Matthew Fox laments the way that people in modern cultures have lost the thread of what life is really all about. In a conversation with field theorist Rupert Sheldrake, he remarked that "it's because we've lost the sense of the sacred in the heavens and on earth that we're in the trouble we're in" (p. 36). He goes on to affirm the idea that there's a positive relationship between heaven and earth, between spiritual beings and human beings, and that the relationship isn't one-sided: "It's a give-and-take, and human beings aren't just here to take" (p. 170).

If these individuals are right, then human beings have a real and tangible relationship with life—it's not just metaphorical. Such a relationship is like any relationship: it entails obligations but brings joy and shared pleasures. But this relationship can only blossom to the extent that we can overcome the legacy of logical positivism and reductionist science, which tells us that life is a series of random events, that God is nonsense, and that when we die, we cease to exist. Positivism equates the meaning of a statement with its method of verification, which means that anything that can't be verified using an acceptable method of verification (think "empirical science") is nonsense.

Ironically, the single person most associated with promoting this view, A. J. Ayer, had a powerful near-death experience towards the end of his life. In 2001, his attending physician Dr. Jeremy George, said that Ayer had once confided to him, "I saw a Divine Being. I'm afraid I'm going to have to revise all my books and opinions." (Stories like this make us realize that life is not only alive, but has a sense of humor!)

Alas, Dr. Ayer didn't get around to revising his books before he died. So his positivist legacy stands. Today, logical positivism has gone out of fashion but its ideas remain influential. These ideas are now embedded in the bulwark of materialist science (e.g., as represented by diehard Darwinians and those defending atheism on scientific grounds) and its war on scientists who dare to embrace alternative approaches on spiritual and religious grounds (e.g., transpersonal psychological researchers, parapsychologists, neuroscientists researching the effects of meditation on brain function, and scientists open to the idea of intelligent design).

Being more bookish than political, I wasn't aware of the controversy over intelligent design when I wrote a paper, "The Enneagram from a Systems Perspective," in which I mentioned four principles that guide my approach: the idea that (a) life is intelligent, (b) everything is connected, (c) openness facilitates flow, and (d) creative tension leads to evolution.* To me, the idea that life is intelligent seems self-evident,

---

* Available on my website: www.enneagramdimensions.net.

however controversial it may be. But this wasn't always what I believed; it's taken me a lifetime to put a dent in ideas I picked up from the collective—like the idea that human beings are powerless and alone, that life is indifferent to human needs, and that the only way to survive is to put myself first and others second. To think of life as basically supportive took a long time.

It also took actual life experiences, quite a few of them, to bring me around to this way of thinking. I was open to the idea but found it difficult to allow myself to rely on it sufficiently to really test out its premises. But as cosmologist and meditator Ken Wilber has observed, there are a great many things in life that can only be apprehended via direct experience, not study (which is why it's impossible to prove that life is benevolent by argument alone).

It doesn't help that modern culture is excessively impersonal, secularized, and efficiency-minded. It seems to discourage us from seeing life from a soulful perspective. In *The Soul's Code* (1996), depth psychologist James Hillman asks, "Why is it so difficult to imagine that I am cared about, that something takes an interest in what I do, that I am perhaps protected maybe even kept alive not altogether by my own will and doing?" (p. 12).

Author Margaret Wheatley provides this answer: "In the West, we didn't grow up learning about non-material forces. But this has become a critical curriculum. We must learn how to work with life in all its dimensions, seen and unseen."*

Modern culture makes it hard to retain the sense of being in communion with life. It diminishes our ability to decipher life's subtle messages—the ones that come to us as dreams, intuitions, hunches, riddles, gut feelings, instincts, or even songs on the radio. We all experience synchronicities but tend to write them off as curious coincidences. And we're often oblivious to other subtle environmental signals from which we might benefit (for example, the sudden sense of danger I felt when approaching the cliff's edge). Unaware that life is actually *alive* (i.e., conscious), we find it hard to really grasp the notion that human beings could be part of not only a

---

* *Leadership and the New Science: Discovering Order in a Chaotic World* (1999), p. 166.

physical ecosystem, but of something much more vast—or to grasp the notion that this "something" actually cares for us.

We sense that traditional cultures were more in touch with this "something," because they lived in a world where life was slower and people were closer to nature. This makes us tempted to romanticize the past (especially the culture of the "noble savage"). But a return to the past would involve tradeoffs that most modern people would find unacceptable. Most people who try to live without modern conveniences find it... well, *inconvenient* (to say the least). The same is true of individuals who look to the rituals of primitive cultures to restore their sense of belonging in the world. Those who look hard enough are often disturbed by what they find; many practices seem brutal to modern sensibilities (especially if we don't "pick and choose" the ones we like, but take them as we find them).*

As Ken Wilber has been at pains to point out, rationality and the modern world are not the enemy of consciousness, but an important advance over ignorance and superstition. But he also points out that each advance requires us to find new ways to relate to life, new ways to be in the world. The solution is not to revert to the past, but to find ways to relate to the future.† However, in *Integral Spirituality* (2006), Wilber notes that one of the reasons for our inability to establish a working relationship with the divine is that the great religious traditions from the mythic age (the era preceding the current rational era) have not managed to modify their theology in a way that allows them to satisfy the needs of modern practitioners. He suggests that these traditions need to differentiate core spiritual teachings from cultural traditions. Otherwise, he says, we're going to continue to have mythic-level religion (which is dogmatic) paired with rational-level science (p. 184). And science will continue to leave religion in the dust.

---

* For a discussion, see pp. 34–36 and 112–116 in *Deeply into the Bone: Re-inventing Rites of Passage* (2000), by Professor Ronald Grimes, an expert in religious rites.

† For a more thorough summary of his position, see my article "The Enneagram & Ken Wilber's Integral Kosmology," published in the *Enneagram Monthly* (Nov. & Dec. 2006) and available on my website (www.enneagramdimensions.net).

But this is not an easy transition to make. As a result, there's been an ever-widening schism between traditional religious practice and popular culture. I still remember the headline in the April 6, 1966 issue of *Time*, which asked us, "Is God Dead?" It was a shocking question (especially four decades ago). It conveyed the sense, not so much that God never existed, but that we no longer knew how to relate to Him. Or perhaps that He had somehow gone away, abandoning us to our fate—an understandable conclusion, given the turbulence of the 1960s.

But we might ask ourselves whether God went away or whether *we* did. Is it possible that we became spiritually disconnected because we bought into the proposition that most of us lack the ability to have a direct relationship with the divine?

That's what James Hillman believes. He says that, a long time ago, we divided the world into spiritual "haves" and "have-nots," and proceeded to create a small elite of people who were qualified to have a relationship with the sacred—people who seemed holy (like priests, popes, or saints), elite (like kings or nobles), or endowed with genius (like artists or intellectuals). We came to believe that such people were different from the rest of us. We looked to them for inspiration and guidance, believing we were too ordinary to have a relationship with the *daimon*, the muse, or the divine. We thought of ourselves as what Archie Bunker called "meatheads": ordinary people living ordinary lives—people whose ordinariness doomed us to a life of mediocrity.

But is the ordinary or average really mediocre? Biochemist Roger Williams doesn't think so. In 1971, he wrote an amazing little book entitled *You are Extraordinary* (which Aldous Huxley described as "marvelous!"). In this book, written almost 40 years ago, Williams made the case that we are each completely unique, even biologically. He predicted that in the future, psychology and psychiatry will recognize that every individual possesses "a high degree of inborn individuality" (p. 197). He asserted the dignity of the individual and expressed skepticism towards the scientific tendency to describe individuals by reference to statistical norms, such that their uniqueness becomes obscured.

His comments bring to mind something I recall from graduate school, where I and my colleagues were well aware of the amusing finding—replicated repeatedly—that virtually nobody ever describes himself as average, no matter what trait is being measured. This finding holds true despite the fact that the very idea of an average is to describe the place where most of the data points can be found. (I guess nobody likes to be a statistic.)

In *Free Play: Improvisation in Life and Art* (1990), musician Stephen Nachmanovich describes life itself as a creative venture and sees our challenge as human beings to discover how to live more creatively: "We block creativity by labeling it as unusual, extraordinary, segregating it into special realms like art and science. We segregate it further from ordinary life by establishing systems of star performers" (p. 121).

James Hillman also rejects this concept of "ordinariness as mediocrity." Traditionally, the idea of having a calling or vocation is associated with people who have special talents or qualities that separate them from us ordinary folk (which is why the word *calling* is often preceded by the adjective *special*). But Hillman says we all have a calling in life. It is indeed special, but special only in the sense of being unique. Our calling is encapsulated in seed form as *character*—the inborn potential to lead a meaningful life:

> *Character forms a life regardless of how obscurely that life is lived and how little light falls on it from the start. Calling becomes a calling to life, rather than an imagined conflict with life.* Calling to honesty rather than to success, to caring and mating, to service and struggle for the sake of living. This view....offers another idea of calling altogether, in which **life is the work** [emphasis mine].†*

If life is the work, then no one is left out. We all have potential to discover the *dharma*—and to fulfill it. We all have a path to walk, a task to perform, a life to live. We all have *soul*—a depth of being that calls out to be actualized in life. And as Hillman notes, "there is no mediocrity of *soul*" (p. 256).

---

* Here Hillman is referring to an earlier discussion where he speaks of the glorification of the anti-hero, the person who stands out because of his inability to come to terms with himself or with life.

† *The Soul's Code: In Search of Character and Calling* (1996), p. 255.

But soul work is not without its attendant dangers. If we're not careful, focusing only on *soul* can lead to a sense of grandiosity. We get carried away and begin to identify with (and take credit for) qualities that are designed to connect us with life, not to make us feel superior to others. Soul work can be destabilizing; it can take a person too far too fast, creating psychic disturbance and disorientation.

The antidote for both of these ills is a firm anchoring in life, such that it becomes impossible to be "swallowed whole" by the unconscious. That's why, in *Love and the Soul* (1995), Robert Sardello reminds us that *soul* only fulfills itself when it includes the outer world in its imaginings. Interiority can be deeply fulfilling, but "the world cannot be left out without interiority being captured by egotism" (p. 170). Thus, the call to *service* acts as a counterbalance to the call to *soul*.

So perhaps we can now see how Rumi's reminder that we are called to "serve the king" also serves *us* as individuals, because it helps keep our inflationary tendencies in check. To be really free, we have to voluntarily submit ourselves to the requirements of some other part of life. That to which we submit is always bigger than us; we make it so by the very act of submitting.

Here discrimination is called for, because we can't submit ourselves to just anybody or anything. We need to submit ourselves to something that is worthy of our efforts—hence, Rumi's reference to the king. Submission is only worthwhile when the object of our devotion is deserving of that devotion. Otherwise, this submission becomes trivialized; we become like groupies who idolize the latest superstar celebrities regardless of their actual merits either as artists or human beings.

It's when we understand the need for submission and select a suitable object of devotion that things begin to click. Although the words *submission* and *devotion* may suggest a specifically religious calling, they are only meant to suggest the kind of attitude that enables us to experience a sense of deep absorption and ongoing engagement—a state that psychologist Mihalyi Czikszentmihalyi calls *flow*. I would suggest that flow is the modern equivalent of submission and devotion, because flow is experienced only when we're really in sync with life. When we're in a state of flow, we have the "just so" feeling I spoke of earlier: everything comes together in the perfect moment. Joy arises, *soul* resonates, spirit soars.

Because it's a dynamic state, the sense of flow comes and goes. The idea isn't to hang onto it for dear life (although it's certainly tempting). The idea is to stay in the moment, being open to what is arising.

The path is in the moment; it unfolds as we put our foot out to take the next step. We think we know what's coming next, but every once in a while, the next step we take completely changes our life. That's what happened to Robert Johnson, a Jungian therapist. One day as a boy, he left his house buy a Coke from the corner store. Just as he stepped into the store, two cars collided in front of it. His left leg was inside the store, but the right one was still outside on the step. A second later, that leg was hit hard by one of the cars.

Johnson went unconscious. But he soon awoke in a very different place—a place that he later called the Golden World.* It was so magnificent that he didn't want to leave. But he couldn't remain there. Instead, he awoke to find that his life had been saved but his leg was missing.

In his autobiography, *Balancing Heaven and Earth* (1998), he says of that experience that although losing his leg was hard, "it was the loss of the Golden World...that was the most difficult" (p. 4). One step created two big changes, both of which were to shape his life in profound ways. It took him years, but he eventually integrated these events into his life in a way that enabled him to stop looking backwards, to the fateful moment of impact.

A single step also changed Suzanne Segal's life. She was waiting for a bus. It was an ordinary day, like any other. Newly-married and several months pregnant, Segal had left her previous life as a dedicated spiritual practitioner and started a new life with her husband in France. But in the second that elapsed between the time her foot left the curb and the moment that she stepped onto the bus, her world irrevocably changed. In

---

* Based on the readings of the mystic Mircea Eliade.

that moment, something shifted. She suddenly lost her sense of self. It initially left her body but remained nearby, just behind her left shoulder;*a few months later, it left for good and never came back.

Although Segal found she could function in life, she wasn't conventionally happy. She felt totally weird, unlike herself. It was terribly unnerving. So she sought relief from mental health professionals. But nobody could help her; they thought she was delusional. She knew she wasn't, but what could she do? To whom could she go?

It took her a decade before she finally gave up and resigned herself to living without a sense of self. Soon after, she encountered spiritual teachers who told her she wasn't crazy but was in a state of enhanced awareness. Several of them congratulated her for having achieved a state of cosmic consciousness.

Segal was dumbfounded. "How could I possibly be in a state of cosmic consciousness and not know it?"

She also wondered why the experience was hellish instead of blissful. She was told it's because her mind was in the way. Not knowing what was going on, her mind kept looking backwards for familiar referents. Not finding them, it gave out signals that something was wrong. Finally reassured, Segal was able to calm her racing mind. She gradually began to feel the terror recede, giving way to feelings of bliss and joy.†

My life also changed when I found myself on a path to nowhere, when one more step could have taken me over the cliff's edge. I'd been throwing myself into the future, anticipating what was to come. It was only when my attention was suddenly brought back to the moment that I saw the danger and stepped back from it.

What was it that brought me back to the moment, and just in the nick of time? Was it intuition? Instinct? Luck? I don't know. But I do know how I felt in that moment—how alive, alert, and aware. Even in my terror, I felt the magic of the moment.

---

* Although this description sounds strange—as Segal herself attests—this is how she describes her experience.

† Suzanne Segal died of a brain tumor a few years later, but not before recording her story in *Collision with the Infinite* (1998).

The magic of the moment

Stay fully present in the now—your whole life unfolds here.
– Eckhart Tolle

THE MAGIC OF THE MOMENT: these words remind me of all the magical moments I've had in my life, especially in my childhood. Moments like seeing the descent of the first few snowflakes in winter. Or riding my bike without training wheels. Or running downstairs on Christmas morning to find something wonderful under the tree.

In a very real sense, the path is a *potential that exists in the moment.* It's dynamic and pregnant, full of unimagined possibilities. At the same time, it has a certain "shape" to it, a certain innate character that gives it a fateful quality. But not until later. In the moment, the path does not look like a path. It only looks that way in retrospect, when we glance back at where we've been.

This "in the moment" quality of the path is well-captured by a story penned by Lee Carroll, but inspired by his alter-ego, Kryon, entitled *The Journey Home* (1997). It's the parable of a young fellow named Michael who is entirely ordinary in his disposition, except that he has a gnawing sense of discontent. In the aftermath of a serious accident, Michael has a visitation by an angel, who asks him what he most wants in life. Michael says he would like to go home, and that's how his journey begins.

As Michael sets forth, he does not know where he's headed. But fortunately, the first house he encounters is the House of Maps. This reassures him. The angel of the house addresses him as Michael of Pure Intent and tells him that this is the place where all the contracts for all the human beings on earth are kept. Michael doesn't know what that means; he's just interested in getting a map. But he soon finds out that the contracts *are* the map: the life maps for those making the journey.

Michael is given his life map and unwraps it, only to find that it's just a blank sheet with very little on it: only the path by which he'd arrived at the House of Maps, plus the words YOU ARE HERE next to a big X.

He's annoyed. "What kind of a map it this?" he wonders. "It's no good for anything." The angel informs him it's a gift, and he should kept it with him. So even though it seems worthless, he takes it and puts it in a safe place.

As he sets out towards the next house, Michael notices that something or somebody seems to be following him. He becomes increasingly agitated; something is clearly not okay. He catches sight of a dark shape, and this kicks his anxiety into high gear. By the time he arrives at a fork in the road, he's beginning to panic. He doesn't know which way to go.

He finally calls to the angel for help. But the angel tells him to look at the map. He sees that the map is now filled in to the fork. And what's more, it has an arrow showing which way to go! He takes off down the indicated path. Around the bend is the next house. He's reached a place of refuge.

By then, Michael realizes that the only way to use such a map is to stay in the present moment, because it only shows us what we need *right now*. This understanding forms the basis for the rest of his journey.

¤ ¤ ¤

MICHAEL'S DILEMMA is like the dilemma we all face in life: wanting to know what to do, which way to go—and wanting to know it in advance, so we can make plans, avoid problems, and generally exercise control over our lives. The habit of plan-making is so ingrained in modern culture that it's hard to imagine living without our plans and schedules. There are a lot of people that would never dream of leaving home without their calender or some high-tech scheduling device. Venturing forth without it would be like walking out of the house without shoes or a wallet.

But in this story, the angels are trying to show Michael another way to live: in the moment, not in the future. It's a good story not only because it teaches us lessons about life, but because it makes us feel that we can make the same journey that Michael did. And that's no small thing, because we live in a world that makes it hard to imagine such a possibility. Cynicism is rampant, and many people see life as nothing more than a game. Psychiatrist Eric Berne put his finger on the problem in his celebrated book, *Games People Play,* which became a raging best-seller when it was first published in 1964. Even though it's decades old, the book is still fresh, offering humorous though disturbing insights about the nature of the destructive social games into which we are so often drawn, even against our will—games like "Let's You and Him Fight," "Ain't it Awful?," and "Why Don't You – Yes, But."

Being in the moment is the opposite of game-playing. We don't play games when we're in the moment because we're tuned into something else. We don't even *want* to play games, because games block our ability to attune. The tricky part is figuring out how to fully participate in life (and interact with other people) without getting caught up in games that really aren't all that much fun to play.

The topic of un-fun games reminds me of my recent trip to Las Vegas for the International Enneagram Association conference. I find casinos depressing places and avoid them whenever possible. But of course the casino in the hotel was unavoidable; I'm told they design the hotels that way on purpose. Every time you have to go anywhere, you have to walk through a crowded and smoky casino full of people who look like they haven't seen the light of day in years. This particular casino was so big and confusing that I repeatedly got lost and found myself circling the banks of noisy, flashing slot machines, unable to find my way out. What a good metaphor for the maze we call modern life!

So how do we get out of that sort of maze? How do we manage to find ourselves—and find our path—when life is so full of confusion and distractions?

The Journey Home provides us with the answer to this question: we get out of the maze by cultivating pure intent. It was Michael's pure intent that saved him again and again—not his powers, talents, or social connections. With the right intent, anything is possible. The great thing about intent is that it's highly democratic; anybody can cultivate it. All it takes is desire. Of course, from a spiritual perspective, desire is something that is, well, *undesirable*. In Christianity, desire is associated with lust and sins; in Islam, it creates opportunities for Iblis (the devil); Buddhism, it's said to be at the root of all suffering.

However, Buddhist meditator and psychiatrist Mark Epstein started noticing that a lot of people attracted to meditation were trying to use it to eradicate desire. But he noticed something else: that it wasn't working. The desire people pushed away so assiduously—because it was "unspiritual"—refused to leave; it instead became unwanted Shadow material, popping up in disguised form whenever the opportunity arose.

He started realizing from a therapeutic point of view how important it was to "own" our desires, not treat them like unwanted intruders. But how could he square this sensible idea with the Buddhist notion that desire is the cause of all suffering?

He did it by looking more deeply into a variety of spiritual teachings. What he discovered is that, although some teachings discourage desire, others do not. Both Tantric and Sufi teachings not only fail to discourage desire, but actually cultivate it. In such traditions, he notes, desire "is a yoga in its own right...it is embraced as a valuable and precious resource" (p. 8). Looked at from this perspective, what we have to do is not to eradicate desire, but to relate to it differently. He cites the example of Sri Nisargatta, an Indian spiritual teacher, who once remarked that "the problem is not desire. It's that your desires are *too small*" (p. 8; emphasis mine).

Sufis too know about the power of desire; Sufi poets speak of our longing for the Beloved, and strive to *increase* our longing, not diminish it:

Oh Lord, nourish me not with love but with the desire for love.

– Ibn Al Arabi

Love's branches are buried in the heart and bear fruit accordingly.

– Ibn Ata

Love tears veils and reveals secrets.

– Nuri

Rumi is even more blunt when speaking of the transformative power of desire:

Passion makes the old medicine new, passion lops off the bough of weariness. Passion is the elixir that renews: how can there be weariness, when passion is present? Oh, don't sigh heavily from fatigue: seek passion, seek passion, seek passion!

From this perspective, passion is not a problem to be solved but a path to be followed, a means to find what is missing in life: our heart's desire.

Jean-Christophe Novelli, a Michelin award-winning chef, says that what he looks for in a culinary student is not so much skill or experience but passion:

What matters to me is the pleasure and the love of cooking—because at the end of the day, it's about passion...I'm willing to teach anybody anything, but if there is no passion, they are not welcome.

Whatever we call it, desire is a quality that's highly-prized (at least in some circles). Mark Epstein says that desire is something we can no longer afford to ignore as spiritual seekers. Instead, we need to discover a new way to hold desire. He reminds us that this is the very essence of Buddhist teachings, because it is the Middle Way (the path between extreme materialism and extreme asceticism).

In his original teachings, Buddha taught that the wheel of *dharma* (which is literally translated as "truth") upholds something, and that this "something" is desire. That's why Buddhism can actually be seen as a body of teachings designed to help us work with desire in a balanced way.

Even the Dalai Lama is not an enemy of desire. In a conversation with Dr. Howard Cutter, he remarked that there are many desires he embraces, like the desire for happiness: "It's absolutely right. [Also] the desire for peace. The desire for a more harmonious world, a friendlier world."* He also said that when Buddhists speak of cultivating a calm state of mind, they're not talking about becoming emotionally insensitive or apathetic: "Peace of mind...is rooted in affection and compassion. There is a very high level of sensitivity and feeling there" (p. 26).

---

* *The Art of Happiness* (1998), p. 27.

When The Dalai Lama was asked, "What is *dharma*?," he said it is to find the right path, the path that enables us to live a life of happiness and peace.* When Anagarika Munindra, an influential Buddhist teacher, was asked the same question, he replied, "*Dharma* is living life fully."†

If *dharma* is living life fully, then it's for all of us, not just for spiritual seekers. And it's not something we find by giving up desire. Just the opposite is true: we find the *dharma* by wholeheartedly pursuing our desires.

It's desire that brings us more fully into the moment because it's desire that motivates us to truly commit ourselves to whatever we're doing. And it's desire that keeps us in the moment, sharpening our senses and intensifying our experience. Desire gives us the incentive to allow life to be more dynamic and unpredictable, the way it is when we're in love. Maybe that's why, in Buddhist teachings, the idea of desire is often symbolized by the figure of the *dakini*, an Indian fertility goddess whose name means "sky dancer."

Tibetan Lama Chögyam Trungpa was once asked, "What is a *dakini*?"

"One never knows," was his whimsical reply.

But the fact that we don't know doesn't make *dakinis* any less intriguing. In fact, just the opposite is true. We don't need to analyze a *dakini* in order to appreciate her mystery and beauty—the way she can enthrall our hearts and mesmerize our senses. Where she goes, we follow.

Of course, this idea can be unsettling from a rational point of view. If one never knows how the dakini will come, one can't really control her. That's probably why desire is viewed with such suspicion.

Desire is the wild card in any situation, the unknown variable which can utterly change what's going on. That is why it's associated with liveliness and change. Without desire, life becomes arid; relationships dry up. Epstein says that it's desire that provides

---

* Source: "Laws of Dharma, as told by the Dalai Lama," available at www.indianexpress.com/ ie/daily/19971225/35950683.html.

† *Open to Desire* (2005), p. 148.

the spark in an intimate relationship, because it introduces a "quality of unpredictability" that keeps the relationship alive. If we're too focused on control, we become too scripted in playing our role—and this eventually kills the relationship.*

That's just what Jack Kornfeld discovered when he returned from several years of rigorous training as a Theravadan monk. He'd spent a lot of time cultivating spiritual discipline and often experienced high states of consciousness. But as soon as he returned to his life in the United States, he found himself once again enmeshed in the same relationship difficulties he'd been mired in prior to leaving (much to his dismay). He gradually realized that it's not enough to find a path that is purely transcendent, not if you want to "ground" your insights in everyday life. For this reason, he eventually wrote a book called *A Path with Heart* (1993), in which he encourages spiritual seekers to look less for a path that promises "glamorous and extraordinary aspects" and more for a path "that allows us to live in the world wholly and fully from our heart" (p. 12).

As many people know, the idea of a path with heart originated not with Kornfeld, but with Don Juan, the Yaqui shaman who taught Carlos Castaneda. When Carlos first approached Don Juan to inquire about being trained as a *brujo* (a Man of Power), Don Juan flatly turned him down. Carlos begged and pleaded, to no avail. When he asked why Don Juan wouldn't teach him, Don Juan told him it's because he didn't know his own heart. Finally, Don Juan agreed to teach him on one condition: he must find his "spot" (*sitio*)—the place where he could feel "naturally happy and strong."†

Carlos became puzzled. He had no idea what Don Juan was talking about.

Don Juan informed him that somewhere on the porch was just the right spot for him to sit. If he could find it, Don Juan might reconsider his decision.

Carlos was stumped. He had no clue how to proceed. He tried all sorts of things, picking one or two wrong spots, but gradually getting a sense of how to use his

---

* *Open to Desire*, p. 92. James Hillman expresses the same idea when he laments the lack of either love or fantasy in too many modern families. He says that the objective, neutral environment creates a vacuum "with nothing blowing through": "This sentence, 'I love you,' parroted back and forth by child and parent…may mean many things, but it definitely does not mean love, for when you love someone you are filled with fantasies, ideas, and anxieties" (*The Soul's Code*, p. 166).

† *The Teachings of Don Juan: a Yaqui Way of Knowledge* (1998), p. 82.

intuition as a guide. Eventually, he found the right spot, and became accepted as a student. And so began his training (as well as his literary career as a writer of books on Don Juan's techniques).

At the beginning of his journey, the hapless Carlos was always getting into one sort of trouble or another. He was eager to learn, but for all the wrong reasons. Don Juan tried to teach him the true nature of the path:

> *You must always keep in mind that a path is only a path; if you feel you should not follow it, you must not stay with it under any conditions....Does this path have a heart? If it does, the path is good; if it doesn't, it is of no use. Both paths lead nowhere; but one has a heart, the other doesn't. One makes for a joyful journey; as long as you follow it, you are one with it. The other will make you curse your life. One makes you strong; the other weakens you* (p. 210).

There are three very interesting statements here. One is that "the path is only a path"—that is, it offers us only a starting point, nothing else. (We provide the rest.) The path develops according to our unique nature and efforts. If we approach the path with the wrong attitude, it never really materializes; we are stopped even before we start.

The second is that "both paths lead nowhere." This is an enigma: why walk a path that leads nowhere? The only reason is to have the experience of walking it. So the focus is not on where the path will lead us (because it gives us nothing and takes us nowhere). The focus is on the experience itself: the experience of being present in the moment.

The third statement is that only a path with heart "makes for a joyful journey." The path with heart is the path that calls to us—the path that is right for us as an individual. If we take the wrong path (a path that's not in alignment with our true nature), it will make us "curse our lives." So it's important to know ourselves well enough to recognize our true calling.

¤ ¤ ¤

MICHAEL'S PURE INTENT, Epstein's desire, and Don Juan's path with heart all take us to the same place: the present moment where the path begins. Desire motivates us to discover our dreams, pure intent gives us the will to follow through on them, and an open heart lets us learn from our experience.

But we aren't the only actors in this drama; life also acts. And this is why there's magic in the moment: it's the magic of life. It's the invitation to life's dance. Once we get that invitation, it becomes our *dakini*, beckoning to us, pulling our attention into the "now."

And what do we find when we get there? A sense of aliveness, alertness, and flow. An opportunity to experience what Carl Jung called *synchronicity*: the sensation of connecting with life in a way that is as meaningful as it is inexplicable. Synchronicity has been described in many ways, most of them technical (Jung was concerned no one would take his ideas seriously if he described them too fancifully). So he described synchronicity variously as an "acausal connecting principle," "meaningful coincidence," and "acausal parallelism." His book, *Synchronicity: An Acausal Connecting Principle* (1973), is the definitive book on the topic. However, Carol Adrienne defines synchronicity less technically as "an apparently chance encounter that nevertheless seems cosmically orchestrated."* I think of it as evidence that magic is real, not imaginary.

What causes synchronistic events to occur? Nobody knows. But when we are in sync with life, these meaningful coincidences seem to occur more often than not, sprinkling a little fairy dust that brightens up our lives. The most famous example of synchronicity is probably Jung's story of the scarab beetle:

> *A young woman I was treating had, at a critical moment, a dream in which she was given a golden scarab. While she was telling me this dream I sat with my back to the closed window. Suddenly I heard a noise behind me, like a gentle tapping. I turned round and saw a flying insect knocking against the window-pane from outside. I opened the window and caught the creature in the air as it flew in. It was the nearest analogy to a golden scarab that one finds in our latitudes, a scarabaeid beetle, the common rose-chafer (Cetonia aurata), which contrary to its usual habits had evidently felt an urge to get into a dark room at this particular moment.†*

Journalist and philosopher Arthur Koestler spent many years collecting examples of interesting synchronicities. He includes a number of them in his book

---

* *The Purpose of Your Life*, 1998, p. 108.

† *Jung: Collected Works (The Structure and Dynamics of the Psyche)* (1970), p. 843.

The Challenge of Chance (1973).* One of them, submitted by mathematician Warren Weaver, came from Weaver's neighbor, George D. Bryson. It seems that Mr. Bryson was traveling by train from St. Louis to New York when he decided it would be fun to stop in Louisville, Kentucky, for the weekend. When he arrived, he asked at the train station about the leading hotel in town and was directed to the Brown Hotel. After checking into Room 317, he asked on a lark, "Is there any mail for me?" To his surprise, the clerk checked and then handed him a letter addressed to "George D. Bryson." Needless to say, he was amazed. Upon inquiry, it turned out that the previous resident of Room 317 was indeed George D. Bryson.

Koestler lists numerous other examples of synchronicities, but the reader can probably think of a few, as well. An example from my own life is the time my shamanically-oriented friend dared me to stroke her coyote pelt, which she felt held a trickster energy. I said okay and did it. Then we left for breakfast at a local diner.

The diner was the old-fashioned kind, not a modern facsimile. And the waitress was a crusty old broad who looked like she'd seen it *all* in her decades of waitressing. I ordered poached eggs that day. When the eggs arrived, the waitress somehow managed to dump them in my lap! Amazingly, they did not break. But they were hot, so I was torn between the Scylla of burning eggs and the Charybdis of eggs yolks all over my lap. Neither prospect seemed inviting.

The veteran waitress panicked. She was so undone that she was absolutely no help. I was afraid she'd break the eggs, so I waved her off and tried to deal with them myself. At this point, the situation was complicated by the fact that I started laughing so hard that I could barely concentrate on the task at hand. But somehow, I managed to get both eggs back on their plate without breaking either one, even though they were soft-poached!

The whole incident was very funny. I couldn't believe the eggs hadn't broken; I used to be a fry cook, so I knew how easily soft-poached eggs can break. And of course, I couldn't help but remember how I'd stroked the coyote pelt just a half an hour before. The two events seemed related.

---

* Alister Hardy and Robert Harvie are the co-authors.

I was even more convinced that this was a true synchronicity after my friend—who had dared me to stroke the pelt in the first place—managed to rack up two separate parking tickets that same day. She was not happy! She said she'd parked all over this town for many years and had never gotten a single ticket, and here she'd gotten two in one day. Coincidence? I couldn't imagine so.

The eggs-in-the-lap experience brought my attention right into the present moment, as these events usually do. They're particularly compelling when they happen to *us*, not somebody else (like A. J. Ayer's near-death experience in Chapter 2). They won't convince a total skeptic, but when it comes to that, nothing will. For those who have eyes to see—and are open to new experiences—the world is full of miracles, big and small. They're most easily noticed when we're in the moment.

Of course, synchronicity is possible only in a world in which everything is energetically related, which is why Combs & Holland observe that

> *synchronicity implies wholeness, and therefore, meaningful relationships between causally unconnected events. In quantum physics, we recover the view of a world as an unbroken fabric in which seemingly separate events do not occur in isolation but, in fact, form pieces interwoven into a common tapestry.**

These authors also say that synchronicity is closely related to creativity, observing that synchronicities often have "more the feeling of poetry than of physics" (p. *xxxiii*). Perhaps that's why they often have a peculiar, funny, or quirky quality to them. Synchronicities show us the interrelatedness of all things, and often in a way that reminds us to lighten up and laugh (as with my eggs-in-the-lap experience).

Dreams, rituals, and sudden shocks are also vehicles through which to experience the present moment. Dreams occur at night, when we are asleep. During the day, we're busy, so we can easily move out of the moment. But when we dream, we don't have that escape! We're right there in our beds, with nowhere to go. Our defenses are down, so messages that can't get through in the day can often sneak through at night. (Of course, we can still manage to "forget" our dreams, if they don't tell us what we want to hear. Dreams are messengers, not dictators.)

---

* *Synchronicity Through the Eyes of Science, Myth and the Trickster* (1996), by Allan Combs & Mark Holland, p. *xxxi*..

Rituals and rites of passage can also bring us into the moment, assuming we take them seriously. As ritual expert Ronald Grimes observes in *Deeply Into the Bone* (2000), "ritual is not just a way of acting, it is also a kind of awareness, a form of consciousness" (p. 71).

Sudden emergencies, shocks, and other traumas bring us into the moment by catapulting us out of ordinary consciousness into a heightened state of awareness. In *The Gift of Fear* (1997), Gavin de Becker relates many stories of people who suddenly find themselves in potentially dangerous situations (e.g., interacting with a potential attacker). They are afraid, but their fear is rational. So it propels them into a state of acute clarity where their instincts are kicked into high gear and time slows down. As a result, they're able to act instinctively—either to avoid a dangerous situation completely or to escape when a moment of opportunity arises.

I also experienced a moment of clarity as the result of a shock. It happened after I'd just received several blows in a row. The last straw was getting a phone message that my father had advanced cancer. I was sitting in my car, too stunned to drive. Then I looked up. There was a blue sky with clouds, some sneakers hanging over a wire, and several eagles circling overhead. Glancing downward, I saw a laughing crowd of people congregating in front of the local bakery. Suddenly, I was seized with a feeling of inexplicable happiness. Everything was exactly right with the world. It was *just so*.

This was a moment of perfect clarity. What was clear? I can't say. I just know I was present to life in a remarkable way.

Although it was a very brief experience, it opened me up in a way that changed my relationship with my father. When I went to see him, for the first time, I was able to speak to him honestly about the problems in our relationship. When he died a month later, I missed the "new dad" I'd just discovered. But I was happy in the understanding that we'd made an emotional connection after many years of small talk. What began as an awareness in the moment became an experience that changed me for good. It reached inside of me and resonated at the level of *soul*. It helped me know myself in a new way, to more deeply embody the essence of who I am. In this way, it initiated a new chapter in my life.

The domain of *soul*

Life is a pure flame, and we live by an invisible sun within us.
– Sir Thomas Brown

SOUL IS THE WORD that archetypal psychologists use to describe our embodied self. Embodied not just in the sense of being encased in a physical body, but in the sense of being deeply engaged with the self and the world—being *ensouled*. Soulful encounters marry the two, allowing us to bring the resources of the psyche into everyday life, where they can revitalize and heal.

Soul is the quality that develops in response to the experiences we encounter in real life. It creates the path and is in turned created by it. It develops not only as the result of right choices and good map-reading but also mistakes, wrong turns, and dead ends. If spirit says, "Let there be Light," *soul* says, "Let there be darkness." *Soul* thus destroys the false dream of living an idealized life by shattering the illusion that the ideal is better than the real. *Soul* embraces all the aspects of the self—even its shadowy aspects—thus allowing us to feel whole, despite the fact that we're not perfect.

Carl Jung, of course, appreciates the need to connect with *soul* and to understand the potential of the Shadow:

> *What our age thinks of as the "shadow" and inferior part of the psyche contains more than something merely negative. The very fact that through self-knowledge, i.e., by exploring our own souls, we come upon the instincts and their world of imagery should throw some light on the powers slumbering in the psyche...**they are potentialities of the greatest dynamism**" (The Undiscovered Self, 1956/2006, p. 107, emphasis mine).*

That Jung considers the deep psyche to contain "potentialities of the greatest dynamism" should give us pause. He's saying it contains something very special and singular, something we can't get from any other source.

Zen teacher John Tarrant also appreciates the potential of the soul. He reminds us that the wish to be more spiritual is often best-served by first becoming more attuned to *soul*, which is why "the way up—into true life—begins with the way down."*

Depth psychologist James Sardello concurs, observing that people are increasingly hungry for the qualities we associate with *soul*: imagination, meaning, story, art, mystery, and myth. He believes we are entering the age of soul consciousness, where people "will not tolerate living in a world devoid of...soul."†

But perhaps the most passionate writer on the topic of *soul* is James Hillman, the founder of archetypal psychology. From his perspective, depth psychology is synonymous with *soul*. His *magnum opus* on the topic is *The Soul's Code: In Search of Character and Calling* (1996). Here is its first paragraph:

> *There is more in a human life than our theories of it allow. Sooner or later something seems to call us onto a particular path. You may remember this "something" as a signal moment in childhood when an urge out of nowhere, a fascination, a peculiar turn of events struck like a annunciation: This is what I must do, this is what I've got to have. This is who I am* (p. 3).

For Hillman, *soul* attunes us to our calling in life, a calling shaped by our innate individuality or character. I'll return to the topic of character shortly, because it's central to our discussion of the enneagram subtypes (in that an understanding of the subtypes can contribute to the development of character). For now, it suffices to say that Hillman, following Plato and Plotinus, believes that we are all called by life in some way, called to embody a "defining image...and this form, or image, does not tolerate too much straying" (p. 11).

---

* *The Light Inside the Dark* (1998), p. 24.

† *Love and the Soul: Creating a Future for Earth* (2001), pp. 1-2.

The idea that we have a calling directly refutes the psychoanalytic notion that people achieve great things in life in order to compensate for some weakness in childhood. Hillman emphatically disagrees with this position; he finds it not only inaccurate, but degrading. He's likewise unimpressed with the notion that transformation is all about moving upwards towards transcendence, whereas moving downwards takes us into error, darkness, or evil, as reflected by expressions like, "My computer went down," or "It's a downer."*

From Hillman's perspective, in our focus on "growing up," we have forgotten the importance of "growing down"—of allowing ourselves to sink roots deep into the earth. He observes that from the moment of birth (which he reminds us, is done facing downwards), we begin to grow down, and that "we need a long life to get on our feet [to get really grounded in our being]" (p. 42).

In *Ego and Archetype* (1992), Edward Edinger echoes other depth psychologists in saying that "modern man urgently needs to re-establish meaningful contact with the primitive layer of the psyche...the primitive mode of experience that sees life as an organic whole" (p. 100). He also observes that "meaning is found in subjectivity... But who values subjectivity?" (p. 108).

Edinger's point is well-taken: that in modern life, it's objectively verifiable knowledge that's valued, not subjective impressions. Even people who see the value of a subjective point of view can't help but notice how it's devalued by society. In most versions of the Hero's Journey, the hero ventures forth into the darkness so he can eventually return triumphant to the light—not so he can learn to appreciate the marvels of the Deep.

It's around this point that Jung and Hillman part company, at least to some extent. Although both value the domain of *soul* and the Shadow work that takes place there, Jung appreciates Shadow work for its power to facilitate psychic unity while Hillman values Shadow itself—its chaos, mystery, passion, and beauty. For Hillman, the journey is less about "arriving" than about the experiences we have along the way.

---

* See George Lakoff and Mark Johnson's *Metaphors We Live By* (1980) for a discussion about how the metaphors we use reveal important things about our beliefs and culture.

This is an interesting difference, because it makes us ask ourselves whether *soul* has intrinsic value or has value only because it eventually leads us to spirit. If the passion of *soul* serves only as a device for accessing spirit, then *soul* is not the equal of spirit but only its handmaiden (and a much-maligned handmaiden, at that). If we believe that soul qualities really matter, we need to re-dignify the idea of *soul*, so that we no longer exploit its powers without recognizing its worth.

While I was writing this chapter, I synchronistically tuned into *America's Next Top Model*, a TV modeling competition hosted by Tyra Banks. At the end of every episode, one of the contestants is eliminated from the competition. As Tyra was eliminating one young hopeful, she looked at her with compassion (the girl was crying) and took her by the shoulders and firmly told her, "You have the ability to model. But you've got to get out of your own way. You've got to push, you've got to focus, you've got to want it—because this industry is about wanting it. Not all girls may have your amazing looks—if a girl *wants* it more, she's going to *take* it."

How does that scene strike you? Does it make you think, "It's only a silly modeling competition"? Or that, "It's too bad that America is such a cut-throat, competitive culture?" Or do these remarks strike a deeper chord?

In me, they struck a deeper chord. I felt I was watching not just a modeling competition but an archetypal drama in which the prospective heroine is confronted with her lack of ardor and told that a lukewarm attitude isn't going to get her anywhere. If she wants to do something, she's going to have to want it more than anything else (or to use Tyra's favorite expression, "to get *fierce* about it"). If she holds back, she'll never fulfill her dreams.

This is what *soul* is all about: allowing ourselves to *really want something* in life—and wanting it so bad that it just has to happen. In horse jumping, the same idea is captured in the expression, "Throw your heart over and your horse will follow." *Soul* gives us the intensity of purpose needed to fully commit ourselves in life. When we denigrate desire—and denigrate *soul*—we dim the spark that makes our world go round.

The widespread denigration of *soul* may explain the plaintive tone we often notice in the writing of *soul's* champions. The great wisdom traditions have for centuries focused on the transcendent realm of life (the realm of spirit) while at the same time denigrating, suppressing, or ignoring its immanent opposite (the realm of *soul*).* This is because the immanent has so often been seen as a barrier to the transcendent.

And there's actually some truth to this idea. *Soul* is a barrier to spirit in the same way that children are a "barrier" to parents. Children impose tremendous limitations on those who care for them. But they also force us to be present in life, whether we like it or not. Best of all, they amaze and delight us, waking up our senses and refreshing our jaded sensibilities. Similarly, *soul* qualities—especially its pathologies—demand our attention in ways that force us to see our weaknesses and emotional vulnerabilities. But they also support us by giving us the ability to love ourselves in spite of our faults. So *soul* delays us in ways that we ought to appreciate, because it alerts us to our arrogance, indifference, and sense of spiritual superiority.

If we cut *soul* out of our lives, life may initially seem simpler, but there's a price to pay. It turns out that soul qualities are hard to restore once we've killed them off. In an inner child workshop, I met a middle-aged man who'd been forced to toughen himself up at a young age in order to earn a living for his wife and kids. Now it was 20 years later, and he was trying to get in touch with his playful, vulnerable side, to no avail. No image or emotion came to him; he'd buried his feelings so completely that he just felt blank. In another workshop, I heard a woman casually talk about a man breaking into her home and attacking her. She told the story without emotion, like she was discussing the weather. She said she'd moved on, but I doubt that anybody really believed her (or that she really believed this herself). But what could we say?

The price of wallpapering over unwanted feelings is a loss of humanity: the inability to deeply love, care, or even feel. And in the end, our efforts aren't really successful.

* Disciplines oriented towards transcendence emphasize how we can ascend to heaven (or some other high state); those oriented towards immanence stress how we can anchor spiritual energy here on earth.

What is banished and rejected always seeks to be recognized and included. When we banish mystery from life, it returns to "haunt" us, creating what modern people call neurosis. We get the kind of symptoms that are now associated with mental illness. But these are not so much symptoms of illness as symptoms of *health*—symptoms created by the denied and rejected parts of the psyche seeking reintegration.

The rejected part is mainly feminine in nature, because it's the feminine that is associated with the earth, the subjective, and the mysteries of embodiment. The widespread denial of the feminine is now taking its toll on a world where the physical pollution of the earth serves as a mirror for the spiritual pollution of the feminine (at the hands of a culture that seeks to banish from view all things dark, messy, inconvenient, incomplete, indirect, immature, and yielding). This denial also denigrates our chief source of motivation: desire, because desire is a feminine virtue. Desire brings us into the realm of *soul*, stirring up our creative juices and plunging us into the passionate side of life—not to trap us in endless embodiments or force us into a life of sin, but to allow us to fully experience what it means to be human.

Of course the realm of *soul* has a shadow side, but so does the realm of spirit, as Mark Epstein, Jack Kornfeld, and Ken Wilber all point out. Wilber observes that if we try to move towards spirit mainly to escape *soul*, we simply take our shadows with us, to the next level, "which is why even advanced meditators often have so much shadow material that just won't go away."* Spiritual teacher Andrew Cohen has also commented that advanced meditators can be the hardest students for a teacher to guide (because they're so dispassionate that it's hard to penetrate their aura of calm). And in *Halfway Up the Mountain*, Marianna Caplan notes that people can get stuck in "spiritual cul-de-sacs," mentioning the work of the Indian saint Meyer Baba, whose mission in life was to assist "masts" (people stuck in states of spiritual absorption). His goal was to produce some sort of movement in these practitioners. Caplan comments on how this worked:

* *Integral Spirituality* (2006), p. 113.

"Sometimes they went up, and sometimes they went down, but...what mattered was that they entered into the process of spiritual work once again" (p. 185).

Does this sound strange—that someone can transcend ego and still get spiritually stuck? If it does, perhaps it's because we're in the habit of seeing ego as the only obstacle to spiritual development. But Meyer Baba's work shows us that there are many ways to get stuck—and also, what matters is not so much which direction we're headed (up or down), but that we're moving, not standing still.

Spirit gives us light, justice, and the ability to see; *soul* gives us passion, empathy, and ability to love, and to love passionately. We need both to be fully human. That's why John Tarrant says that "every journey towards wholeness involves the interplay of spirit and *soul*, observing that

> *soul knows where spirit is too dominant, [where] we are greedy for pure things: clarity, certainty, and serenity...Spirit forgets the necessity for imperfection, and that within our very incompletion is the opening where love appears.**

We need both spirit and *soul*; one without the other doesn't work. But if we're to bring the two together, we must find a place for them to meet. Tarrant speaks of this place as the realm of *character*, noting that if we have character, we're not overwhelmed by either spirit or *soul*. Character is what enables us to hold the opposites of spirit and *soul* in close proximity without allowing either one to dominate.

Character is what develops in the realm of action—the realm of ordinary, everyday life. This is also the realm of ego, because ego is what directs our actions. So spirit and *soul* meet on the plane of the ego, which becomes the balance point between the heights and the depths.

So we can think of life as having three realms: the realm of spirit, the realm of *soul*, and the realm of ego (ordinary consciousness). The *realm of spirit* includes clarity, the light, the heavenly gods, the intellect, and the masculine principle. The *realm of soul* includes mystery, the darkness, the gods of the Deep, the passions, and the feminine principle. The *realm of ego consciousness* includes everyday consciousness, the

---

* *The Light Inside the Dark* (1998), p. 19.

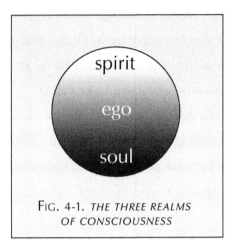

FIG. 4-1. *THE THREE REALMS
OF CONSCIOUSNESS*

commonplace, ordinary people, physical action, and the *yin-yang* principle of achieving a balance between all extremes (Fig. 4-1).*

All three realms must be acknowledged and "given their due"; none should be considered better than either of the others because all are necessary for a balanced life (and a balanced world).†

Spiritual explorer Drunvalo Melchizedek found this out when he was teaching people to connect with their Higher Self. While he was able to make this connection himself, he wasn't as successful in teaching others to do the same. But he didn't know why. One day, a man showed up at one of his workshops, someone who didn't look like a typical workshop participant.

Drunvalo asked him why he was there. The man shrugged and said, "I don't know." He obviously felt he ought to be present, but why?

A few days later, Drunvalo asked the man what he did. He said he was a *kahuna* (Hawaiian shaman). He added, "I teach people how to connect with the Higher Self."

---

* See, e.g., Chapter 9 in J. Nigro Sansonese's *The Body of Myth* (1994) for a discussion of the three worlds.

† By a balanced world, I don't mean some sort of idealized utopia in which there's no conflict, limitation, or pain. That would bore people stiff! What I mean is a world in which we can experience not only conflict, but communion; not only limitation, but freedom; not only pain, but joy. (Of course, all these experiences are already possible, but most of us would like to see a little less pain and a little more joy.)

So when it came to that part of the workshop, Drunvalo turned it over to the *kahuna*, who told everybody that in order to contact the Higher Self, it's necessary to first contact the *Lower Self*—the self that's akin to Mother Earth. To do this, he said, we have to become more open, receptive, and playful, like a child.

After Drunvalo's experience with the *kahuna*, he started including workshops designed to help people shift gears, so they could once again experience life from a child's perspective—not in the sense of regressing (becoming childish, immature, or unthinking), but in the sense of become more spontaneous and open-hearted.

Contacting the Lower Self is about retraining the ego to step aside so that we can experience the self on the level of *soul*. Some people, like Drunvalo, do this intuitively. But many of us do not. And because Drunvalo was consciously unaware of what he was doing, he could not teach it to others. Once he was informed by the *kahuna*, he realized it was necessary to focus specifically on the Lower Self.

This story illustrates the problem we have in modern society, where the lower world*—the primal, mysterious world of *soul*—has been neglected for so long that it's virtually disappeared from our collective awareness. This makes it very hard to see *soul* as valuable, or even real. A serious consequence of the invisibility of *soul* is that we've lost the ability to distinguish it from spirit. As Hillman points out,

> the three-fold division [of mind, soul, and spirit] has collapsed into two, because soul has become identified with spirit. This happens because we are materialists, so that everything that is not physical and bodily is one undifferentiated cloud (p. 68).

What's worse is that, when we lump soul in with spirit, soul loses out, because it is misunderstood. As Hillman points out, its pathologies are seen as "evidence of the lower, unactualized rungs of the ladder." And of course people want to climb the ladder, not languish on its lower rungs. Hillman tells us that "spirit is after ultimates and it travels by means of a *via negativa*. "Neti, neti," it says, "not this, not this." Strait is the gate and only first or last things will do...soul must be disciplined, its desires

---

* By the way, I don't think that the use of the term *Lower Self* was meant by either the *kahuna* or Drunvalo to suggest that it's "less than" [worst than] the Higher Self. But the reason this bears mention is that the idea that "higher is better" has become so much a part of our thinking.

harnessed, imagination emptied, dreams forgotten, involvements dried" (p. 69).*

Even those who know *soul* is real may be reluctant to seek it out, because of the prejudice in our post-Enlightenment world against irrationalism—a prejudice that led to difficulties for Carl Jung at a crucial point in his life. Soon after his break with Sigmund Freud, Jung reached the point where he knew it was critical to reconnect with the child inside him. But he didn't want to do it. (He says that as a grown man, he found the prospect "painfully humiliating.")

But he realized he had no choice, not if he wanted to rejuvenate his inner life. So he took up his childhood passion for building little cottages and castles, eventually constructing an entire village out of stones by the lake. He worked on this project every day after lunch and sometimes during the evening. As he become more and more absorbed in the work, something began to shift. And Jung began to fully appreciate the value of this activity, noting that it became "the turning point in my fate...I was on the way to discovering my own myth. The building game was just a beginning."†

Jung intuitively grasped the importance of this kind of inner work. But how many other people realize it? When the culture is so divorced from the world of *soul*, how do those of us not blessed with Jung's sensitivity manage to do the work required to achieve inner balance?

Many of us never do. We do the best we can, living mostly on the level of ego (the realm that Ken Wilber calls Flatland). Some of us try to escape Flatland via spiritual transcendence. But as Drunvalo discovered, it's not so easy to connect with what is higher when we lack a connection with what is lower. Even if we somehow manage to reach the world of spirit, we're likely to retain unwanted psychic baggage, as Wilber and others have pointed out.

Ego alone—or even ego combined with spirit—is unbalanced. We need to develop all three aspects (ego, spirit, and *soul*) to create a stable psyche. This is because

---

* See Chapter 5 for a discussion about the value of pathology.

† *Memories, Dreams, Reflections* (1963), p. 174.

of the principle of triangulation (akin to Gurdjieff's Law of Three)*which says that in order to locate ourselves in time or space, we need to have ourselves and two additional reference points. So ego needs both spirit and *soul* to gain a sense of how to function in life. If either are missing, it can't properly do this.

Lacking a proper set of reference points, ego uses the only one it knows: itself. This is how the self-referencing ego is born. From that point onward, ego becomes the sole arbiter for determining what is good and what is not. It imposes psychic order by using its own preferences as the standard for goodness. While this approach is obviously self-limiting, it's still better than chaos (especially during childhood). However, because the self-referencing ego lacks support from either spirit or *soul*, the order it creates is always in danger of collapsing. That's why it's so rigid and inflexible: rigidity is the only thing that allows it to maintain some semblance of integrity.

At some point in life, an opportunity may come along to connect with something beyond the world of ego. But the rigid ego tends to block out signals from other sources, both higher and lower, because that's part of its survival mechanism. Over the years, it acquires the habit of trusting only itself, which is how it comes to be trapped in Flatland, the world of surface appearances. But this entrapment occurs not because ego is bad, but because it lacks balance. As a result, it fears all the terrible things that might happen if it's not there to run the show.

The joke is that ego is never really running the show, at least not entirely. It's always supported by other psychic processes, some of which are considerably more subtle and profound. If ego can be coaxed to relax at little, it will begin to notice other inner resources upon which it can draw. The more it connects with spirit, the more it has access to lightness, clarity, and subtlety. The more it connects with *soul*, the more it has access to mystery, creativity, and passion.

---

* See Chapter 9 of *The Positive Enneagram* for a discussion. Briefly, the Law of Three is the idea that everything in existence comes in threes. In *The Positive Enneagram*, I talk about it as the basis for justifying an integrative (rather than dualistic) model of the enneagram.

Myths we live by

Old myths, old gods, old heroes have never died.
They are only sleeping at the bottom of our mind, waiting for our call.
– Stanley Kunitz

IN THE AUTUMN OF 1931, two scholars were walking along one of the paths at Madalen College in Oxford. One was arguing that myths are more powerful than facts; the other remained unconvinced. Just then, a gust of wind picked up the leaves at their feet and swirled them around in a way that seemed peculiarly meaningful "as if to authenticate what had just been said." The second gentleman never forgot that moment. It changed the way he looked at life. He later tuned into the mystical side of Christianity and began to write books that reflected his mythical understanding of that faith.*

The first gentleman was J. R. R. Tolkien; the second was C. S. Lewis. Both are veritable icons of modern mythic literature. But as we can see from this conversation, C. S. Lewis was originally more of a rationalist than a mythologist. He had to be convinced that myths were of value.

Rationalism has now become so entrenched as a standard for truth that to call something a myth is akin to calling it a fantasy or false belief. Hence, we see *Reader's Digest* articles with titles like "Ten Myths about Heart Disease" or books like *The Myth of Mental Illness*. As Jungian psychologist Edward Whitmont notes, "in ordinary

---

* Source: Professor Beldon C. Lane; "The Power of Myth: Lessons from Joseph Campbell," available at http://www.religion-online.org/showarticle.asp?title=171.

language, a myth carries the meaning of something untrue."* So when mental health professionals talk about our personal myths and stories, they're usually thinking of the stories we devise to make sense of our lives. The idea that these stories might possibly have a life of their own is not usually considered.

But there are other people—like Tolkien—for whom the world of myths and archetypes is very real indeed. Mystics have long understood the power of myths and mythic images. Rumi wrote a poem in which he tells us "not to be satisfied with stories" but to "unfold your own myth."† Theosophist B. P. Wadia notes that, "ideas in archetypal [mythic] regions produce idols in concrete worlds."‡ Llewellyn Vaughn-Lee says that archetypes are real, noting that "our Western rational culture [has] dismissed the world of symbols as superstition, though recently, as we hunger for meaning in our surface lives, we have begun to revalue these archetypal images."§

And Mircea Eliade says that myths and images are so important that, no matter how much we denigrate them or pretend not to take them seriously, we'll never actually succeed in forgetting them: "Man is free to despise mythologies and theologies but that will not prevent his continuing to feed upon decayed myths and degraded images."¶ In other words, even those who deny the reality of mythic themes and archetypal dimensions of life still find themselves getting caught up in the energy of such archetypes in some form, because we can't really live without them; they are literally "food for the soul."

Despite our sophistication, secularity, and scientific understanding, we still seem to need myths to live by and heroes to worship (even if the myths are no longer epics and the heroes have become somewhat tarnished). Whether we watch mythic themes

---

* *The Symbolic Quest* (1969/1991), p. 76.

† *The Essential Rumi,* p. 40, Coleman Barks, trans., with John Moyne (1995).

‡ "The World of Archetypes." Available at www.teosofiskakompaniet.net/BPWadiaSecretDoctrineStudies4.htm.

§ "Dreams: Reconnecting Us To The Sacred." Available at www.huffingtonpost.com/llewellyn-vaughanlee/dreams-reconnecting-us-to_b_427339.html.

¶ *Images and Symbols*, p. 19; cited in Whitmont, p. 99.

enacted in soap operas on TV, participate in rituals like tailgate parties before the Big Game, or get immersed in the Lives of the Rich and Famous, we're still seeking out experiences to feed the soul. (We might be feeding it junk food, but we're feeding it, nonetheless.)

Jungian and archetypal psychologists speak of discovering our own myth as a pivotal task in life, as we saw from Jung's experience building cottages (Chapter 4). Jung felt that myth was a better vehicle for describing human consciousness than science, because science deals only in averages while myth can describe our individual nature: "What man appears to be...can only be expressed by way of myth [because] myth is more individual and expresses life more precisely than does science."*

Whitmont observes that "Jung felt that the central meaning of our lives can only be grasped through a realization of our individual myths. These myths demand to be realized and translated into actual living...they must not remain mere fantasy or daydreaming."† So our personal myth is not something we make up; it's something with a life of its own.

Whitmont goes on to say that confronting the archetypal myth that is at our psychological core is how we find meaning in life. To liberate its meaning, it's necessary to determine its *intent*. This, he says, is how we transform "disturbing complexes" into something that gives our life new direction.

Robert Johnson observes that our personal myth "determines much of our experiences of life [sic]," which is why it needs to be understood. While it's possible to ignore it or pretend that it doesn't exist, "life is easier if we cooperate with that myth rather than continually pull against it."‡

To James Hillman, the idea that myths and archetypes might be just made-up stories is unthinkable. He would tell us that, without those stories, life as we know it could not exist. He observes that "myths talk to the psyche in its own language; they

---

* *Memories, Dreams, Reflections* (1965), p. 3.

† *The Symbolic Quest*, p. 84.

‡ *Between Heaven and Earth* (1998), p. 191.

speak emotionally, dramatically, sensuously, fantastically."* Myths are what make "concrete particulars" into universals, so that we can find meaning in the events of our daily lives. At the same time, unlike religion, myths don't tell us how to live; they're not moral lessons. Rather, they give us a way of looking at the world that enhances our ability to imagine, question, and look beyond surface appearances.

Mythologists like Joseph Campbell also believe in the tangible power of mythology, an idea which he introduced to the American public in the PBS series, The Power of Myth. The first question asked by interviewer Bill Moyers is, "Why should we care about myths?"†

Campbell says that we don't have to care—not if we don't want to. But then he piques our interest by saying that sometimes myths just "catch" people, "and once the subject catches you, there is such a feeling…of information of a deep, rich, life-vivifying sort that you don't want to give it up."‡

I first became aware of the power of mythology when reading Sansonese's *The Body of Myth* (1994), where the author convincingly describes the link between yoga and mythology. For the first time, myths began to come alive for me. Soon after, I started working with dreams and dialoguing with dream characters (doing what Jung calls active imagination work). The more I opened to the archetypal world, the more it opened up something in me. Over time, I became convinced that it's the mythic dimension of reality that gives rise to our mental, emotional, and physical reality, not the other way around. I also saw how the more attention we pay to our mythic experiences, the more they inform our lives in meaningful ways.

For example, I once had a dream in which I was on the plane of the archetypes. I was walking along a street where other figures were also walking. I couldn't see them clearly but I could feel the intensity and clarity of their presence; the experience was

---

* *Re-Visioning Psychology* (1977) p. 154.

† The question itself is illuminating, because it reflects Moyers' belief that most of the TV audience will be wondering the same thing. The assumption behind the question is that in a scientifically-oriented world, myths are no longer relevant. It is obviously up to Campbell to prove otherwise.

‡ *The Power of Myth* (1988), p. 4; this book contains the transcript of the TV interviews.

like trying on glasses that are way too strong. I knew the place was real and that it had the power to affect my life.

It's experiences like these that make me take myths and archetypes seriously.

But the modern world seldom takes myths seriously, especially the idea of having a personal myth. We are too busy for such musings. When we have dreams we don't like or imaginings that distress us, we try to ignore them. If that's not possible, we banish them with medication or therapy.

Redeeming these images and the mythic themes enables us to redeem our inner life and to remember our life's calling. And that's where the enneagram can be of assistance, because it helps us become aware of the images, archetypes, and themes relevant to people of a particular temperament. The enneagram presents us with nine ways of being in the world, each of which is associated with a "family" of archetypes and mythic themes. When we subdivide each of the nine types into three subtypes—based on arenas of interest—the archetypal patterns become even more sharply-defined.

But as I mentioned in Chapter 1, not many authors describe the types or subtypes in terms of mythic motifs. Instead, they use an interpretive framework that is not particularly myth-friendly.* The nine types are usually seen as nine kinds of character pathology that block our development both psychologically and spiritually; the subtypes are portrayed as pathological variations linked to emotionally-distorted instinctual demands.

This way of thinking is so alien to my own experience that I initially found the enneagram teachings disorienting. So I started writing articles describing alternative ways of working with the system, refining my ideas in the process. In 2006, I

---

* Exceptions include Michael Goldberg's fascinating *Travels with Odysseus* (2005), which maps *The Odyssey* onto the enneagram; Judith Searle's *The Literary Enneagram* (2001), which looks at the literary themes that exemplify each type; and Tom Condon's *The Enneagram Movie & Video Guide* (1999), which explores the types as portrayed in films. I should also mention *The American Book of Dying* by Richard Groves and Henriette Anne Klauser (2005), which presents nine true stories about dying individuals, each of whom is a different enneagram type. The stories are mythic by virtue of the subject matter (death) and how it is treated (as a personal journey into the Unknown).

published my first article, "Let's Depathologize the Enneagram,"* in which I made the point that seeing the nine types as character disorders was not a good way to unlock our inner potential. All the articles I've published since then have emphasized the advantages of a depathologized perspective for enneagram work.

But after listening to archetypal psychologists like James Hillman, I've considered writing an article called, "Let's Re-pathologize the Enneagram." The idea isn't to villainize the nine types but to ask the question, "Is pathology such a bad thing?" We tend to assume it is, which is why we want be rid of it. But in *Re-Visioning Psychology*, Hillman tells us that psychopathology is "central to the experience of *soul*" (p. 55),† echoing Jung's sentiment that "God enters through a wound." If this is true, then we miss the mark if we seek God only in the realm of spirit; perhaps He can also be found in the realm of *soul*, a sentiment captured in Keats' proposal to think of life not as a *vale of tears* but as a *vale of soulmaking*.

Acknowledging the missing realm of *soul* and the value of mythology for rejuvenating the psyche can tangibly improve our quality of life. This is what Moore is trying to tell us in *The Re-Enchantment of Everyday Life*, what Campbell is saying when he speaks of getting "caught" by mythology, and what Jung, Whitmont, and Johnson speak of when they allude to our personal myth. They're all hinting at the same intriguing possibility: that life is not dumb, but *intelligent*; not gross, but *subtle*; not mechanical, but *magical*.

Discovering our myth is how we bring magic back into life—but only to the extent that we hold it lightly and let it lead us where it will. If we bring the same mechanistic attitude to living our myth that we do to filing our taxes, we're going to miss out on most of the fun. Thus, Hillman cautions us about the dangers of globbing onto our personal myth in a way that turns it into something quite un-myth-like:

> *Living one's myth doesn't mean simply living one myth; it means mythical living. As I am many persons, so I am enacting various myths. As all myths fold into each other, no single piece can be pulled out with the statement, "This is my myth"* (p. 158).

---

* *Enneagram Monthly*, Oct. '06.

† All Hillman quotes in the remainder of the chapter are from *Re-Visioning Psychology* unless otherwise noted.

For Hillman, *mythos* is more like a perspective than a program for reform; if we get too invested in a particular myth, we run the risk of creating a heroic ego "learning how to do his deeds correctly" (p. 158). Myths, he says, do not tell us how to live our lives; they just give us another perspective from which to view them. And it's not a perspective that stands still or even one which moves, like the Hero, on a resolute course towards some preordained goal. From *soul's* perspective, it's the journey that matters, not the goal. So our *mythos* is more like the meanderings of a wanderer or Knight Errant, "picking up insights along the way" (p. 159).

With Hillman's comments in mind, let's reflect for a moment on what Rumi said about the One Thing (the thing we must do in order to fulfill ourselves in life; Chapter 1). At first, it looks like Rumi must be pointing to a specific task we must complete or a journey upon which we must embark. And for some of us, this may literally be true: we may well have an appointed task to complete or place to go. But it seems to me that the One Thing can't just be about what we *do*, but about *how we do it*—about our attitude, disposition, and relationship with life.

When we're in sync with life, we're present in the moment—and not in some kind of idealized, spiritualized way, but in a way that allows us to feel *emotionally invested*: excited, alert, happy to be alive. Of course, if's it's a bad moment, maybe we're feeling torn, guilty, afraid, or angry! But at least we're *present*.

The enneagram supports our ability to be more present by offering a vehicle for understanding what is actually going on in the moment: what motivations are behind our actions and those of other people. The more refined our understanding of the enneagram types and subtypes, the more insight it can provide.

But using the enneagram to understand motivational dynamics requires us to adopt the kind of enneagram model that can account for the diversity and complexity of human motivation (rather than reducing it to a set of nine ego fixations). So my focus in Part II is to describe the enneagram and how people currently work with it, as well as presenting a more myth-friendly model for enneagram work.

Part II

The Enneagram

6

Evolution of the enneagram

Most of the shadows of this life are caused by our standing in our own sunshine.
– Ralph Waldo Emerson

THE ENNEAGRAM is a wonderful system. It doesn't look like anything out of the ordinary—just a geometric figure with some dots and lines—but it's a system unlike any other. Those who really take the time to learn how it works will discover a great deal of practical information about themselves and other people.

The enneagram is now used for two main purposes: (a) describing nine kinds of personality types and (b) describing nine steps in a transformational process. Both of these approaches are relevant for exploring our potential roles, paths, and themes in life. The *personality enneagram* shows us what makes our path unique; the *process enneagram* shows us how to see it from a transformational perspective. When we bring the two together, we have a powerful tool for individuation.

Although I speak as though there are two separate enneagrams, there is really only one enneagram, because there is only one enneagram figure (Fig. 6-1). The figure is composed of a circle with nine numbered points on its perimeter. Each point is linked to two other points via crisscrossing lines in the middle; the crisscrossing lines are composed of two figures: a triangle and hexad. The hexad is an unusual figure that resembles two people kissing, one on each side of the circle. There's actually a third figure, as well: the enclosing circle.

Despite its simplicity, the enneagram is a powerful system. Although it is said to be ancient, it was not openly taught until the early 20th century, when the esoteric teacher G. I. Gurdjieff unveiled it as a system for describing transformational processes. The most well-known description of Gurdjieff's teachings on the enneagram is in Chapter 14 of Ouspensky's *In Search of the Miraculous* (2001).

However, around 1970, Oscar Ichazo introduced a new way of working with the enneagram based on the idea that each point can be likened to an "ego type," where ego is considered to be a barrier to spiritual transformation. Ichazo focused particularly on the nine points as nine dysfunctional ways of thinking (cognitive fixations) that separate us from our true or essential self. Although his teachings were originally

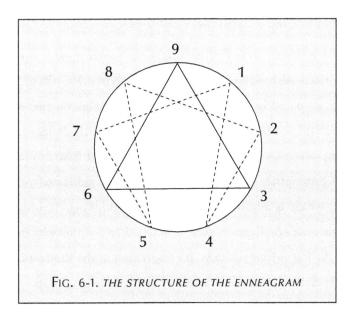

FIG. 6-1. *THE STRUCTURE OF THE ENNEAGRAM*

intended only for his students, they leaked out and became popularized as a system for describing nine personality types. The biggest leak occurred when one of Ichazo's students, Claudio Naranjo, started imparting them to his own students in Berkeley, California. His students in turn began to teach the enneagram, and the teachings soon spread to the four corners of the globe. After the first books began to appear in the late 1980s, the enneagram became even more widely-known.

What the enneagram initially became known for was its ability to describe the ways that personality blocks spiritual development. As a result, the first students were mostly spiritual seekers. As the system became better known, it began to appeal to a wider variety of people—people who saw the possibility of using it to become more aware of their personal potential, relationship dynamics, learning style, or career path.

But anyone seeking to use the enneagram for a broader purpose had to either ignore or gloss over the core paradigm underlying the Ichazo-Naranjo approach, which can be summarized as follows:

▶   *We are born in essence*
▶   *We gradually develop ego-personality, which cuts us off from essence*
▶   *To return to a state of essence, we must divest ourselves of ego-personality*

This is the ego-versus-essence paradigm on which most current enneagram teachings are based. Although most widely discussed in the works of A. H. Almaas,* this paradigm is rooted in the Ichazo-Naranjo teachings on the enneagram. It's based on a dualistic model of human consciousness which divides the psyche into two competing selves: an authentic ("essential") self and false ego self. This model embodies the assumption that our actions in life are motivated primarily by the false ego self, which is associated with distorted thinking, feeling, and instinct.

The idea that the ego displaces essence is based on a philosophy that cosmologist Ken Wilber calls Retro-Romanticism. It's a variation of the Romantic philosophy in which both pre-rational states (like infancy) and post-rational states (like superconsciousness) are viewed as superior to rationality (ego consciousness). The reasoning underlying this position is that only non-egoic states allow us to remain in touch with essence. But Wilber strongly disputes this argument, saying it's based on a form of

---

* A. H. Almaas is the pen name of Hameed Ali, one of Claudio Naranjo's original students. Ali later founded the Ridhwan School/Diamond Approach, which uses the enneagram in its transformational work. For a detailed critique of the "ego versus essence" paradigm as explicated in the works of Almaas, see Ken Wilber's brilliantly incisive argument set forth in an 11-page footnote in *The Eye of Spirit* (2001), pp. 365–377.

fallacious reasoning, because it fails to make any distinction between undeveloped (pre-rational) consciousness and highly developed (trans-rational or post-rational) consciousness. This false reasoning is what he refers to as the *pre/trans fallacy*.

Wilber also objects to the idea that we can ever truly be cut off from essence (because otherwise, it wouldn't be essential!). He argues that while it's possible to be cut off from essence in the relative sense (such that we feel basically "out of sync" during a given stage in development), the solution is not to blame the ego but to approach whatever blocks our awareness with non-judgmental acceptance, so that our defenses become lessened, thereby creating greater openness to experience. Table 6-1 contrasts Wilber's "transcend and include" position with the Retro-Romantic ego-versus-essence position.

Wilber's approach is not only more positive and better reasoned, but dovetails nicely with Jung's position that our personality requires development for us to individuate.

TABLE 6-1. TWO MODELS OF CONSCIOUSNESS DEVELOPMENT		
Pre-rational phase	**Rational phase**	**Trans-rational phase**
~ birth – 6 years	~ 7 years – adulthood	adulthood (if achieved)

	Pre-rational phase	Rational phase	Trans-rational phase
Ken Wilber's model	---------------------------- essence is ***present*** ---------------------------->		
	consciousness is present in seed form	ego-personality becomes the foundation for transcendent awareness	transcendent awareness "transcends but includes" earlier stages of consciousness
	Implications: ego consciousness is a stepping stone to transcendent awareness		
Retro-Romantic model	essence is ***present*** ---->	essence is ***lost*** ---->	essence is ***present***
	consciousness is present as essence	false ego-personality displaces essence	consciousness is present as essence
	Implications: false ego blocks out essential states of awareness ("pre/trans fallacy")		

It's also in accord with G. I. Gurdjieff's position that ego-personality and essence develop *independently* (and that essence does *not* therefore displace ego). Gurdjieff says that we need both ego and essence in order to work on ourselves.*

Interestingly, Gurdjieff's enneagram work never focused on the relationship between personality and essence; it focused on the nature of life and life cycles, especially transformational cycles. It directs our attention to the process by which transformation takes place, whether it's the transformation of food into a meal, sunlight into plant energy via photosynthesis, or an unformed personality into a vehicle for individuation. So Gurdjieff's transformational enneagram is a natural touchstone for anybody who sees personality development as a transformative process.

Just as Gurdjieff never saw personality as interfering with essence, he never envisioned the nine enneagram points as nine personality types (or if he did, he never publicly talked about it). Oscar Ichazo was the one with the vision to see the nine points in this new light. However, because of Ichazo's belief in ego-personality as an enemy of essence (and his interest in identifying each point on the enneagram as a point of fixation), it was to his advantage to look for correspondences between the two systems, because Gurdjieff's enneagram is entirely transformational.

If Ichazo had elected to compare the two approaches, he would doubtless have noticed their underlying unity. But because he did not, we have two separate enneagrams—and a decisive schism between those who work with the enneagram from a transformational perspective (Gurdjieff's inheritors) and those who work with it from a personality perspective (Ichazo's inheritors). The former regard the personality enneagram as a debased teaching that has little relationship to Gurdjieff's original vision, because they correctly perceive it as placing 100% of the emphasis on energy *blockage* instead of energy *transformation*.

If we drop the idea of seeing the nine types as forms of blockage, we can easily detect the parallels between the two systems. We can begin to notice ways in which

---

* See pp. 161-165 in *In Search of the Miraculous* for a discussion.

each point of view offers us unique opportunities for transforming ourselves (and for allowing life to transform us). We can begin to understand that transformation happens not in spite of our type peculiarities, but *because* of them—because of the way they pull us into the world, where we have the experiences that become the *prima materia* for transformation.

Seeing the types as opportunities instead of barriers has many advantages, not the least of which is the relief that comes from knowing that *we're basically okay as human beings.* Whatever shortcomings we possess, we're in no way defined by them. We're not stuck being an "ego type," because our type is not a creation of ego, especially the kind of monster ego envisioned by Ichazo and Naranjo.

In Chapter 7, we'll look more closely at the idea that the nine types are actually essence types or transformation types (not fixation types). But first, let's look at both enneagrams from a historical perspective, so we can get a better idea of why they developed in such different directions.

¤ ¤ ¤

When asked by a student about the roots of the enneagram, Sufi teacher Idries Shah replied that it's not a new system, but has existed for a long time in esoteric circles:

> *Memorize, therefore, this information, for it is of the greatest importance. The enneagon, or nine-pointed figure, is by no means unknown in 'occult' circles in the West...the nine-pointed figure is represented in many ways.**

He goes on to mention several veiled references to the enneagram. From his remarks, it's clear that he considers it to be a symbol of great significance, not some sort of self-improvement gimmick or flash-in-the-pan phenomenon.

When G. I. Gurdjieff introduced the enneagram teachings, he also said they were ancient.† He told his students that the enneagram is a universal symbol whose

---

* *The Commanding Self* (1994), p. 286.

† The most recent effort to trace the origins of the enneagram is "Hidden in Plain Sight: Observations on the Enneagram," by Virginia Wiltse & Helen Palmer, in *The Enneagram Journal* (2009), available from the International Enneagram Association.

teachings had been preserved in secret but that the system was now "available to all," although its usefulness, he said, depended upon instruction from "a man who knows." He further characterized the enneagram in a way that leaves little doubt as to its significance:

> *Everything* can be included and read in the enneagram. A man can be quite alone in the desert and he can trace the enneagram in the sand and in it read the eternal laws of the universe. Every time he can learn something new, something he did not know before (p. 294).*

Anyone who has worked with the enneagram will understand how it can continually yield up new insights. Although the enneagram is fairly simple to describe, it is not a simple system. It has countless dimensions, as Gurdjieff affirms, observing that it "has as many different meanings as there are different levels of men." He goes on to describe the dynamic nature of the enneagram, observing that "the enneagram is perpetual motion, the same perpetual motion that men have sought since remotest antiquity and could never find…A motionless enneagram is a dead symbol; the living enneagram is a system in motion" (p. 294).

After Gurdjieff's death, J. G. Bennett wrote *Enneagram Studies* (1983), where he speaks of the enneagram along similar lines, saying that it can be used to represent "every process that maintains itself by self-renewal…[including] the life process of any plant or animal, including man" (pp. 3–4). He uses the analogy of food preparation to describe the process by which raw energy is converted into something more refined. When we prepare someone's meal in a restaurant, he observes, we start and end with a clean kitchen, but in between, the kitchen is the setting in which transformation takes place—the place in which raw ingredients are transformed into a refined product suitable for consumption.

Observing that people have three aspects to their nature—body, soul, and spirit— he likens the kitchen to the body, the food to the soul, and the customers to spirit:

---

* All Gurdjieff quotes are from Chapter 13 of *In Search of the Miraculous* (2001); see especially pp. 293–294.

- ► *Body* is the place where the transformation takes place
- ► *Soul* is the energy that we embody (and which gets transformed)
- ► *Spirit* is the consumer of the energy that we transform*

Fig. 6-2 shows one way to graphically represent these ideas. Notice how Bennett's three aspects of human nature recall to mind the three realms of consciousness discussed in Chapters 4 and 5. Although I developed my model prior to finding this passage in Bennett's work, I was pleased to discover an enneagram-related model with very similar propositions. But it's not that surprising, since the enneagram is based on Gurdjieff's Law of Three: the idea that *for every duality we can imagine, there exists a third point which allows us to move out of duality and into a place of integration or synthesis.*

It's the existence of this third point that enables us to move away from dualistic deadlocks towards integrative problem-solving. We find the third point by being willing to "sit with the opposites" until we realize what is missing in our thinking—what we overlooked that needs our attention.†

In his book *The Intelligent Enneagram,* A. G. E. Blake also focuses on the importance of the Law of Three as a model for integrative problem solving, observing that nothing can happen without the presence of three forces (active, passive, and neutral). It's these three forces, he says, that confer upon life a sense of meaning. So for Blake, the enneagram is not just a model of all that we say and do, but "a stubborn cry of desire for meaning" (p. *xviii*). Blake likens the intelligence of

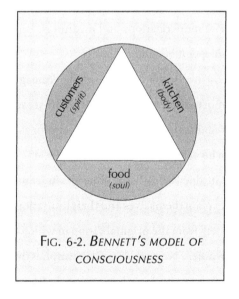

FIG. 6-2. *BENNETT'S MODEL OF CONSCIOUSNESS*

---

* Bennett also notes that in addition to being the consumer of transformed energy, spirit is also that which brings about the transformation; see pp. 10–15 for a discussion.

† See Chapter 9 of *The Positive Enneagram* (2009) for a longer discussion.

the enneagram to the intelligence that Sufis call *baraka*: Divine Grace. So being intelligent is not about having a high IQ but about our ability to cultivate *receptivity*—receptivity to the intelligence that exists in life. The enneagram provides us with a model of life's intelligence.

Another significant follow-up to Gurdjieff's enneagram legacy is *The Enneagram: Symbol of All and Everything* (2003) by Nathan Bernier. The author avows that "an original intelligence shapes and maintains this universe...However, the distance between man and the Absolute is such that the model of existence does not fit our logic and understanding" (p. 53). The enneagram, he says, is a symbol that helps people bridge this gap. Even so, Bernier says that he was initially reluctant to write about the enneagram, for fear that the act of writing would impose a limitation on the system that would tend to crystallize it in the mind of the reader. His reluctance was overcome by his reflection that the enneagram "is so special that the more we study it, the more interpretations flourish from it. It is like a cornucopia, always flowing with more and more relations and meanings. It is like a bottomless well[:]...the more we dig, the deeper it becomes" (p. 12).

I consider the personality enneagram to be one of those interpretations, although most people who follow Gurdjieff's teachings would say otherwise. For example, Bernier regards the personality enneagram as a false enneagram and cites other Gurdjieffians who take a similar position (pp. 45–47). Blake is less negative, observing that after Gurdjieff's death, the enneagram "came under the attractor of human beings wanting to explain themselves and their limitations to each other. This can be described as a 'deviation' from the original vision in which the psychological and the cosmological were one whole."*Nevertheless, Blake implies that it might be possible to use the enneagram for the purposes he describes, noting that it has long been an interest of human beings to understand how we can play various roles in life without becoming over-identified with them.

---

* *The Intelligent Enneagram* (1996), p. 256.

¤ ¤ ¤

NOW THAT WE HAVE a general picture of the transformational enneagram, let's take a look at the personality enneagram. To understand how the enneagram came to be used for describing ego types, we need to understand the culture that incubated it— the culture of the 1960s, especially that of the San Francisco Bay Area and the coastal retreat center, Esalen Institute.

Located in Big Sur, California, Esalen was established in 1962 by Michael Murphy and Richard Price as a place for exploring consciousness-expanding techniques and ideas. During the 1960s, it become a mecca for young people seeking a different way of life, a way of life free of the inhibitions (and prohibitions) of mainstream culture. Esalen's beautiful location and natural hot springs overlooking the Pacific Ocean attracted the interest of spiritual adventurers from far and wide.

In *Esalen: America and the Religion of No Religion* (2007), historian David Kripal speaks of Esalen's focus on promoting a new kind of secular mysticism without a base in any established religious tradition—what Kripal calls a "religion of no religion." Kripal says that, while many people think of Esalen as being Jungian in orientation—because it fits well with our image of the Sixties as a time of *mandalas* and the emergence of Eastern philosophy—it's actually more Freudian in outlook, especially Freud as interpreted through the lens of people seeking to "liberate the instincts" by breaking down emotional defenses and moral inhibitions. Gestalt psychologist Fritz Perls was the radical innovator who first popularized this approach; Claudio Naranjo was his chief disciple.*

Psychedelic drugs had introduced seekers to the possibility of experiencing ecstatic states of bodily awareness; the only problem is that such drug-induced states didn't last. People sought other methods for achieving what Kripal calls the "en-

---

* See especially pp. 141–144 for a discussion about the influence of Freudian thought at Esalen.

lightenment of the body."* Kripal points to Claudio Naranjo as being a key figure in promoting a way of thinking that combined "the wild, sexualized, and violent ecstasies of Dionysus...and the cool, cerebral, and rational contemplations of Apollo" (p. 21). Later, Kripal characterizes this enlightenment of the body as something that is achieved "through the surrender of the social [egoic] self" based on the Freudian idea that instinct is a form of "organismic wisdom" that can "progressively mutate both flesh and spirit once it is truly freed from ego" (p. 177).† So the idea of seeing ego as something that interferes with instinctual functioning (and more importantly, with the ability to experience enlightenment) was actively promoted at Esalen, especially by Perls and Naranjo.

By 1970, Naranjo had learned of a mysterious teacher who was rumored to be a member of the Sarmouni Sufi order and to teach a shortcut method to spiritual awakening (the Shattari Method of Sudden Enlightenment). This idea apparently created quite a stir among Esalen regulars. But to get the teachings, it was necessary to attend a 10-month retreat in Arica, Chile, something which was impractical for many people. Of the 54 who eventually attended the retreat, about a third were brought from Esalen by Naranjo.‡

Naranjo's mysterious teacher turned out to be Oscar Ichazo. And the place where the retreat took place—Arica, Chile—became the namesake for the organization that Ichazo henceforth established to spread his teachings (the Arica Institute). Retreat attendees included Claudio Naranjo, dolphin researcher John Lilly, and liberal arts professor Joseph Hart. The personality enneagram (known then as the *enneagram of fixations*) was among the key teachings.

---

* See pp. 21–24 and 456–459.

† It should be noted that the idealization of instinct is an idea embraced by Freud relatively early in his career—an idea which he later abandoned in favor of the position that unregulated instinct must be curbed by a reality-based ego. So it's strange that Sixties-generation neo-Freudians should embrace a theory specifically refuted by Freud himself.

‡ Looking back, we might ask whether anybody ever stopped to ask whether a method purported to confer instant enlightenment might be dangerous; but given the times, few people seemed inclined to "look before they leaped."

What we know about the early enneagram teachings comes mostly from two sources: Lilly and Hart's report in Charles Tart's *Transpersonal Psychologies* (1975) and Sam Keen's 1972 interview with Oscar Ichazo (published in *Interviews with Oscar Ichazo*, 1973). The title of the chapter containing the Ichazo interview ("Breaking the Tyranny of the Ego") tells us that the ego-as-enemy philosophy was definitely an idea he embraced. When asked whether it's possible to save the ego (rather than get rid of it), Ichazo replied, "We have no desire to save the ego or make it happy. Short of enlightenment, there is no way to harmonize or unify the psyche" (pp. 15–16).*

The enneagram of fixations was seen as a key tool for identifying ego fixations that stood in the way of our ability to be "in essence." If these could be eliminated, it was said, we would return a state of pristine essence or being, which was likened to the consciousness of a Samurai warrior, Zen master, or enlightened man.†

Such statements demonstrate the common thread running through both the Esalen program for promoting instinctual liberation and the Ichazo teachings on the enneagram: the idea that ego is the main barrier that stands in the way of spiritual liberation.‡

Within a year or two after receiving the enneagram teachings, Claudio Naranjo began to share them with his SAT (Seekers After Truth) group in Berkeley. Like Ichazo, Naranjo planned to keep the teachings confined to a select group. But after he was unsuccessful, he began to publish books on the enneagram as seen mainly from a Neo-Freudian Object Relational perspective.§ While Oscar Ichazo emphasized the

---

* The ego envisioned by Ichazo is obviously not the same ego envisioned by Freud, who saw ego as the guardian against the undisciplined incursions of *id*—a fact that Claudio Naranjo makes clear on p. 10 of his book, *Character and Neurosis: an Integrative View* (1994).

† Source: "The Arica Training," by John Lilly and Joseph Hart, in *Transpersonal Psychologies* (1975), Charles Tart, ed.

‡ It's interesting that both of the examples cited—Samurai training and Zen Buddhism—require years of training and severe spiritual discipline. Does this mean that only individuals willing and able to undertake such a severe regime can hope to experience "essence"?

§ *The Enneagram of Society* (1991); *Ennea-types in Psychotherapy* (1993); *Character and Neurosis* (1994).

role of delusional belief (fixated thinking) in creating the ego, Naranjo emphasized the role of emotional *passions*: nine forms of emotional imbalance that give rise to nine categories of psychological dysfunction, one for each enneagram type. His scholarly book, *Character and Neurosis*, describes each of them in detail.

In theory, each of the nine passions can be transformed into virtues and each of the nine fixations can be transformed into Holy Ideas. So at the core of the current enneagram model is the idea that we can describe each type in four main ways: in terms of its passion, virtue, fixation, and Holy Idea (see Table 6-2, based on the enneagrams in *Interviews with Oscar Ichazo*).

One thing I noticed soon after I became acquainted with the enneagram is how "loose" these descriptions are, both conceptually and linguistically. If we look at the passions, for example, we'll notice that they're based on the seven deadly sins (plus two: *deceit* and *fear*). Nevertheless, it's hard not to notice how the passions are just brimming with vitality while the virtues are not. Among the passions, we have powerful motivators like *gluttony, avarice, anger,* and *envy.* Conversely, the virtues are curiously denuded of vitality. Although virtues like *detachment, serenity,* or *innocence* are not undesirable, it's hard to see them as energizing. (It's also hard to see some of them, like *serenity* or *equanimity,* as qualities that can actually be cultivated.)

Also, some of the passions just don't seem that bad (e.g., *fear* and *anger*). Both fear and anger serve useful purposes; they're not intrinsically problematic. Others (*deceit, pride,* and *laziness*) don't seem very passionate (i.e., emotional): *deceit* is always connected with action (and often action that is coldly calculated), and *pride* seems more like a fixation than a passion, since it's clearly the product of wrong-headed thinking. And whatever laziness may be, it's hard to see it as a passion!

When we turn our attention to the fixations, we see similar problems. For starters, many of them don't look like mental qualities. Some (like *melancholy*) are mood states; others (like *flattery, planning,* and *cowardice*) are acts. If we contemplate transforming the fixations into Holy Ideas, we have two problems. The first problem is that many of the fixations seem so different from the corresponding Holy Idea that it's difficult to see how the two are related. What is the relationship of stinginess to Holy Omniscience? Or flattery to Holy Harmony? Or resentment to Holy Perfection? Few of the fixations seem to bear a discernible relationship to their Holy counterpart. (No wonder it took A. H. Almaas an entire book to try to explain the Holy Ideas!).*

The second problem is the ethereal, otherworldly quality of the Holy Ideas. They look so idealized (complete with Capitalized First Letters) that it's hard to relate to them as modes of thinking that we could actually use in everyday life.

Some of the problems with the passions and fixations could be solved by paying closer attention to the concepts involved and generating more precisely-worded terms. But the problem that can't be solved quite so easily is the dualism that permeates the entire model: the idea of *false self vs real self, ego vs essence, sin vs virtue, fixation vs Holy Idea*. If we accept this kind of model as valid, we'll never get out of the maze of dualism—a maze that has very real negative consequences for our lives. If we really believe that we literally have two selves—one real and one false—this belief will undermine any effort

TABLE 6-2. **THE PASSIONS AND THE VIRTUES**				
Type	**Passion**	**Virtue**	**Fixation**	**Holy Idea**
1	anger	serenity	resentment	Holy Perfection
2	pride	humility	flattery	Holy Will
3	deceit	truthfulness	vanity	Holy Harmony
4	envy	equanimity	melancholy	Holy Origin
5	avarice	detachment	stinginess	Holy Omniscience
6	fear	courage	cowardice	Holy Strength
7	gluttony	sobriety	planning	Holy Wisdom
8	excess (lust)	innocence	vengeance	Holy Truth
9	laziness	action	indolence	Holy Love

---

* *Facets of Unity: the Enneagram of Holy Ideas* (1998).

we might make towards self-improvement, because we'll never know which self we are improving, the real or the false. If we say we only want to be rid of the false self, we have the same problem: How do we distinguish it from the real self?

Dualism promotes doubt, and doubt will make us second-guess our actions. It will also encourage us to seek out authority figures who can tell us how to tell the difference between truth and falsehood. From there, it's all too easy to become sinners in need of a savior—or in modern times, seekers in need of a guru. And while there seem to be plenty of people willing to take on the guru role, we have to ask ourselves how we can know whether the teacher is really knowledgeable. After all, if it's our false self that's in charge, wouldn't it lead us to a false teacher?

My point here is that this whole way of thinking is counterproductive, both for students and teachers. It makes students lack confidence and makes teachers overly responsible for imparting wisdom that they may or may not possess. When we buy into a dualistic model of the psyche, we set up two big mental categories—good and bad—and then spend all our time trying to categorize what is happening in every passing moment. (Am I in ego or essence? Is this my real or false self speaking?)

Spiritually, dualism sets up a model whereby spirit is divorced from matter and the former is made a heroic ideal while the latter becomes a repository for rejected Shadow material, as discussed in Chapter 4. When this happens, we remain perpetually caught between the opposites, unable to attain the spiritual ideal and at the same time unable to escape the pull of unwanted, unacceptable impulses. The more desperately we seek out such an ideal, the more it alludes us. And the more frustrated and ashamed we become. This is like the problem of the Chinese finger puzzle, where we have two fingers in the opposite ends of the puzzle: and the tighter we pull on one end, the tighter the other end becomes.

The solution is to drop the idea that the opposites are irreconcilable and embrace the idea that they're actually more alike than we suppose. Once we do this, we begin to realize both that our ideals are less noble than we thought and that our ignoble impulses are less terrible. The more we begin to let go of a sharply-polarized view of life, the more the two opposing poles begin to converge. The tension between them begins to dissipate. At some point, we realize we're no longer in the grip of the Chinese finger puzzle; both fingers are free to move.

If we as spiritual seekers are bound and determined to avoid embracing an integrative approach, the only way to get free of the trap is to chop off one end of the finger puzzle (and hope that we miss the finger!). But this "chopping off" approach has certain disadvantages, because it makes us choose between spirit and matter: we can have one or the other, but not both. If we forsake spirit for matter, we become materialists or atheists. If we forsake matter for spirit, we become either ascetics or undiscriminating followers. In either case, we're in danger of losing touch with common sense and consensus reality. In the latter case, we can end up making great sacrifices for spiritual causes that may or may not have merit.*

This kind of problem was common during the 1970s, when many spiritual idealists became filled with the desire to create groups that would serve as models for a new, more enlightened society. This seems to have been a goal of Arica Institute as described by Lilly and Hart's 1975 article. The authors note that "the group is all-important in the Arica system" and that it's best suited for people who "are happiest in a group with a mission." They also mention that Arican assumption that "enlightenment comes most quickly through the group" and note that individualists will probably have "great difficulty...accepting without question the decisions and statements of the group." Elsewhere, they speak of the ideal of creating a world which would function as a family, where "each would give according to his ability and receive according to his need."† (Shades of world socialism! The last quote is straight from a Marxist political pamphlet published in 1875.)

---

* See Michael Downing's *Shoes Outside the Door: Desire, Devotion, and Excess at San Francisco Zen Center* (2001) for an in-depth exploration of what can happen when spiritual devotees are overly accepting of their spiritual leader's questionable acts and policies.

† All quotes are from pp. 345 – 351.

¤ ¤ ¤

WHATEVER THE ORIGINAL ARICAN VISION of the enneagram, few people who study the enneagram today see themselves as the forerunners of a new world order. Most of us are just ordinary people who would like to live more satisfying lives: to know ourselves, have loving relationships, and find absorbing work. Whatever model of the enneagram we develop in the future, it needs to respect these goals and help people achieve them. And it needs to respect the idea that *personality is an asset*, not a liability.

Archetypal psychologists see personality as something tremendously valuable. For Hillman, personality is "the persona through which *soul* speaks." (p. 51). For Jung, personality development is a great achievement; he says we must educate the personality so that it can become "a well-rounded psychic whole that is capable of resistance and abounding in energy."* Robert Johnson speaks of personality development as the basis for individuation, "the process of becoming the complete human beings that we were born to be."† According to Johnson, this process entails three things: (a) becoming complete (whole) (b) appreciating our individuality, and (c) actualizing our life's blueprint (a process we can easily map onto the enneagram; see Fig. 6-3).

But becoming a complete human being is a pretty tall order. Although we often think that the hard part of living is coming to terms with our limitations, we may actually find it a bigger challenge to come to terms with our *potential*—our potential to fully embody who we are as a soul. Venturing forth into the world of *soul* is a big step, one that Jungian author James Hollis says we often try to avoid. We gives ourselves all sorts of reasons why it's not possible, and fear of ego is one of them.

But Hollis says that this is really an excuse; the biggest problem for most of us, he says, is not too much ego but too little boldness. He calls this a failure of nerve, reminding us of Jung's observation that "most of us walk in shoes that are too small [for us]." What gets in our way is not fear of ego inflation but fear of *soul* and its greatness.

---

* *The Development of Personality* (1981), p. 169.

† *Inner Work* (1986), p. 11.

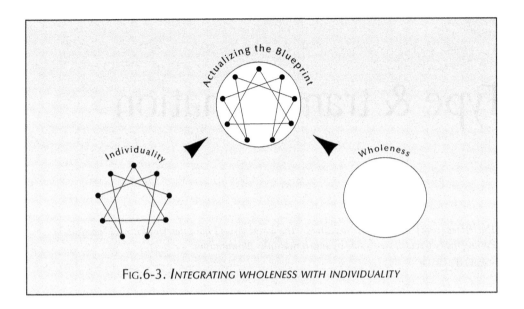

FIG.6-3. *INTEGRATING WHOLENESS WITH INDIVIDUALITY*

However, Hollis tells us that we can overcome these obstacles if we really want to:

> *Choosing to risk one's own authority—to step into the fearful place, to realize through experience that...[we] will be supported by something deep within each of us—is what brings us home to ourselves.* *

That's what real transformation is about: each of us coming home to ourselves. In Chapter 7, we'll see how the enneagram can help us do that.

---

* *What Matters Most: Living a More Considered Life* (2008), p. 78. Note: I substituted dashes for commas in the interests of clarity.

Type & transformation

The [enneagram] fixations are "negatives." The world views I have described are all "positive."
Putting the two sets of terms side by side is mutually illuminating.
– A. G. E. Blake

THE HERO'S JOURNEY is the epic adventure in which a stalwart soul sets forth into the Great Unknown, experiences new things (both wonders and terrors), and returns home a changed person. Most mythologized accounts of the Hero's Journey involve archetypes like the Brave Young Hero, Noble Steed, Damsel in Distress, and Fire-breathing Dragon (for females, we might substitute the Innocent Maiden, Jealous Witch, Fairy Godmother, and Handsome Prince). Whatever the particular archetypes involved, the journey is clearly the stuff of myths and legends. It's part of what most of us call "the world of make-believe."

But as we've already seen, the world of myths and legends isn't necessarily as make-believe as we may have been raised to think. If we start seriously poking and prodding at this thing we call "reality," we're usually surprised to find that it's a little different than we ever believed—less concrete and more fantastic. The enneagram can help us discover new worlds to explore, especially if we work with it from a transformational perspective, the perspective introduced by G. I. Gurdjieff.

Gurdjieff's enneagram gives us a map of the transformational journey, the journey we make as we move through life. It shows us the beginning, the middle, and the end of the journey—and the nine points that mark our progress along the way. At each of the nine waypoints in the journey, we have an opportunity to see life from a new angle (and to see ourselves from a new angle, as well).

While I'm talking here about Gurdjieff's process enneagram (where each point represents a transformational potential), I'm also talking about the personality enneagram (where each point represents a temperament type). As I said in Chapter 6, there are not really two enneagrams, just one:

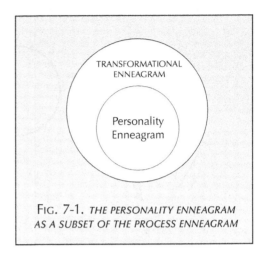

FIG. 7-1. *THE PERSONALITY ENNEAGRAM AS A SUBSET OF THE PROCESS ENNEAGRAM*

the transformational enneagram taught by Gurdjieff. The personality enneagram is a derivation, which is why it makes sense to think of the nine enneagram types as *transformation types* (not fixation types) (Fig. 7-1).

If we limit ourselves to seeing the nine types as fixations, we have to account for the fact that there's an awful lot of energy flowing between these "fixations"—along the figures of the hexad, the triangle, and the outer circle. Energy flows along the *hexad* in this sequence: 1 > 4 > 2 > 8 > 5 > 7 (which happens to be the same pattern as the repeating decimal .142857 that we get when we divide 1 by 7).* Energy flows along the *triangle* in a 3 > 9 > 6 sequence.† And energy flows along the *outer circle* starting at Point 0/9 and returning to the same place after a complete circuit (Fig. 7-2).‡

(If you want to get a sense of the enneagram's dynamism, try envisioning the enneagram with all three energy flows happening at once. I find it helps me remember just how dynamic the system really is.)

---

* In the process enneagram, the flow of energy along the hexad reflects the flow of thought as we anticipate future decisions.

† We'll return to this sequence in Chapter 8 because it's relevant to our discussion of the connecting points.

‡ People who study the personality enneagram don't usually pay a lot of attention to this flow, except perhaps when looking at the wing points (the points on either side of each point). Sandra Maitri has mentioned that each point is considered to be a combination of the two adjoining points. So whether or not we study the outer flow, it's obviously relevant to our understanding of each point of view.

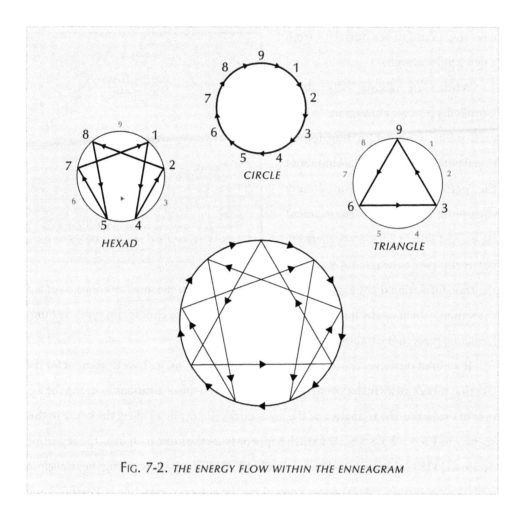

FIG. 7-2. *THE ENERGY FLOW WITHIN THE ENNEAGRAM*

In the transformational enneagram, the circular flow is particularly important, because, as I mentioned above, the purpose of the process enneagram is to depict the sequence of events in a creative process, story, or transformation. While the personality enneagram shows us nine points in *space* (nine points representing locations, like nine people sitting in a circle), the process enneagram shows us nine points in *time* (nine steps or stages). The two are linked in ways that will soon become evident; Fig. 7-3 shows how we can juxtapose the nine points and the nine types.

It's actually quite remarkable that we can see a correspondence between the two—that we can link time and space using the enneagram. But it is indeed possible,

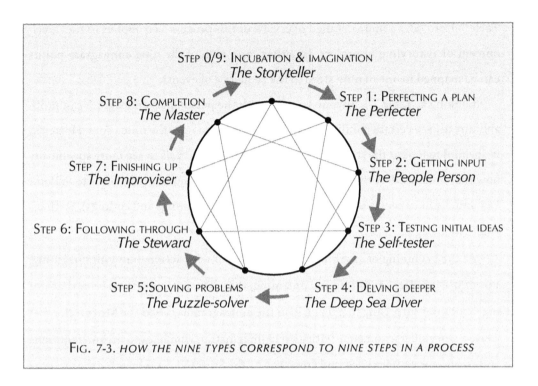

STEP 0/9: INCUBATION & IMAGINATION
The Storyteller

STEP 8: COMPLETION
The Master

STEP 1: PERFECTING A PLAN
The Perfecter

STEP 7: FINISHING UP
The Improviser

STEP 2: GETTING INPUT
The People Person

STEP 6: FOLLOWING THROUGH
The Steward

STEP 3: TESTING INITIAL IDEAS
The Self-tester

STEP 5: SOLVING PROBLEMS
The Puzzle-solver

STEP 4: DELVING DEEPER
The Deep Sea Diver

FIG. 7-3. *HOW THE NINE TYPES CORRESPOND TO NINE STEPS IN A PROCESS*

and it means that for any given point on the enneagram, we can identify both a stage in transformation and a personality type which is attuned to that transformational stage. Simply put, there's a distinct correspondence between Point 1 and Type 1, Point 2 and Type 2, etc., all the way around the enneagram circle. We'll take a look at these one-to-one correspondences in a moment, but first let's look at the process as a whole. We can break it into three phases that remain the same, whether we're talking about a story, natural process, or transformational project:

- ▶ BEGINNING (part I – *Points 1, 2, 3*):
  the initial phase, when something new begins to happen

- ▶ MIDDLE (part II – *Points 4, 5, 6*):
  the "trouble" phase, when complications ensue

- ▶ END (part III – *Points 7, 8, 9*):
  the "resolution" phase, when difficulties are resolved

Table 7-1 provides a more detailed overview of this process as it applies to the development of a storyline or project. In either case, each of the nine enneagram points can be mapped to one of nine steps in the sequence of events.

Looking at Table 7-1, anyone familiar with the personality enneagram can probably already see certain parallels between the nine steps and the nine types. However, it's helpful to look at the steps/types on a point-by-point basis to see more specifically how they are linked. Although the types (and steps) are numbered from 1 to 9, Point 9 is actually like Point 0/9 (because it's the place of beginnings and endings). So that's where we'll begin.

At the beginning of anything new, we start not with action, but with imagining. POINT 0/9 is a place of wishing and dreaming; there's more emphasis on *being* than doing. So it's not surprising that TYPE 9 on the enneagram is called the **Storyteller**, because a storyteller is someone with a vivid imagination who likes to dream, fantasize, and create stories, fairy tales, and fantasies. As the Storyteller, we imagine the world as we would like it to be, and through our imaginings, set the stage for action.

POINT 1 is the place where our dreams and imaginings are first transformed into something definitive—an inspiration, ideal, or initial plan. There's a need to move away from a dreamy perspective, to carve out a concrete point of view—and a need for literalness, black-and-white thinking, and the setting of agreed-upon standards that ensure the translation of vague dreams into attainable goals. Ethics matter, because ethical action is necessary to keep a plan on track. So it's not surprising that as TYPE 1 **Perfecters**, we take a pointed interest in translating vague hopes into perfectible goals that are in accordance with our high ethical values.

POINT 2 is where high ideals become softened and humanized—where the ideal is translated into a form agreeable to real people (so that whatever we are planning can meet the needs of our not-quite-perfected fellow humans). It's the place where justice becomes tempered with mercy. So as TYPE 2 **People Persons**, we enjoy helping

TABLE 7-1.

MAPPING A PROCESS ONTO THE ENNEAGRAM

AT THE **BEGINNING**, things are just getting started:

In a story, we get the basic setup (Pt 1), get introduced to the characters (Pt 2), and see the flow of everyday life (Pt 3)

In a transformational project, we envision our goals (Pt 1), enlist support for them (Pt 2), and organize our efforts (Pt 3)

IN THE **MIDDLE**, things start getting complicated:

In a story, a dramatic event occurs that changes everything: people must reach inside themselves (Pt 4), solve new problems (Pt 5), and confront their ultimate fears (Pt 6)

In a transformational project, we move into a time of difficulty that requires us to get emotionally committed (Pt 4), solve new problems (Pt 5), and accept the transformations that are happening to us as we transform something else (Pt 6)

AT THE **END**, things get resolved:

In a story, there's a breakthrough: we feel elation and a sense of joy (Pt 7), achieve our goals (Pt 8), and learn a lesson from our experiences (Pt 9)

In a transformational project, there's a breakthrough: we experience a sense of effortlessness (Pt 7), achieve mastery (Pt 8), and return to our everyday life enriched from our experiences (Pt 9) people, being with people, and enabling them to fulfill their potential. We see everything in life from a relational perspective and want to make sure to bring our own personal touch to whatever we're doing. We also enjoy galvanizing social support for causes we consider worthwhile.

POINT 3 is the point where planning and organizing flips into high gear, because this is what is needed after we've imagined a creative possibility (Point 9), developed a detailed plan (Point 1), and gained social support (Point 2). Now we can begin the process of developing and testing prototypes (either literally or in the sense of getting into nitty-gritty planning). This is our last chance to test things out before we begin to move into a phase where it's no longer easy to back out. So as TYPE 3 **Self-testers**, we enjoy subjecting new ideas to "reality testing," in an effort to distinguish what works from what doesn't. Any idea that lacks real-world practicality is going to fail the test. We gain particular satisfaction by testing ourselves in the process, always trying to exceed our personal best.

So at Points 1, 2, and 3, we feel energized, action-oriented, and focused on outer accomplishment. We're full of ideas about things to do and ways to do them. Our enthusiasm is natural, because we're not yet at a point in the process where we hit the kind of snags that tend to bog people down.

As we move into the next phase (Points 4-5-6), things start to get more complicated. This is the part that I earlier characterized as "trouble." It's not that the types are trouble, but that the challenges they encounter involve more complications, often of a subtle nature. In the Hero's Journey, this is the point where the hero begins to lose his way (and his overconfidence); in a transformational process, it's where problems tend to multiply too fast for us to keep up with them. This is Keats' "vale of soulmaking."

At POINT 4, we begin our descent into the Deep: we encounter our first really big obstacles, the kind that make us seriously consider whether or not we can continue. We realize that the only way we might possibly succeed is by passionately committing ourselves to the task at hand, putting it ahead of everything else. This degree of commitment demands a lot, but can create great transformative change. So as TYPE 4 **Deep Sea Divers,** we need to marshall our passion to become intensely committed to the tasks that we decide to take on (and conversely, to take on only those tasks in which we can feel 100% invested).

By POINT 5, we're in a very deep, "inward" place, far removed from the outer world, which is why we can become so deeply absorbed in exploring the basic nature of things. This is where impossible problems finally get solved, where they get "reverse-engineered" in a way that creates completely innovative solutions. So as TYPE 5 **Puzzle-solvers**, we take on the role of wisdom-seekers, shamans, and philosophers who see life from a deeply thoughtful perspective, acquiring the knack for converting problems into puzzles and solving them in ingenious ways.

At POINT 6, we're beginning to emerge from the Deep, but we're not out of the woods yet—because this is the place where we face our biggest obstacle yet: ourselves. While it's no easy task to make a total commitment to the work (Point 4) or to tackle impossible problems (Point 5), it's even harder to allow ourselves to be transformed by the very forces we've been using to transform something else. This is the point where the Hero who thinks he's on a quest for the Holy Grail begins to realize that *he* is the Grail, and the journey is about his own transformation. Such a realization comes as a shock; it requires an unprecedented amount of courage for him to continue onward. This is why, as TYPE 6 **Stewards,** we're so aware of fear: because we know we can only go forward in life if we're willing to face our greatest fears, especially the fear of losing our sense of self. So it's important for us to find ways of developing faith, trust, and courage, so we can move towards our fears instead of away from them. If we can manage this difficult feat, our fear becomes transformed into the energy that allows us to serve as true stewards in life.

As we cross from Point 6 to Point 7, we're moving from the middle phase into the last and final phase of the transformational journey (Points 7-8-9). At POINT 7, having faced our fears at Point 6, we experience a sudden sense of elation, the feeling that life is rushing to greet us with open arms. It's easy to forget that we have not yet arrived at the finish line, but still have work to do. As TYPE 7 **Improvisers**, we can't help but feel like upbeat optimists with innovative ideas, but who tend to find it easier to start projects than to finish them. It's hard to buckle down and sit still when there are so many interesting diversions to enjoy!

Finally, we arrive at POINT 8: the pinnacle of our journey. This is the place we have been moving towards, the place of completion, the top of the mountain. But it's also a place of great responsibility, where the need for judgment and self-control is paramount. As Type 8 **Masters**, we learn what it's like to fully embody the truth of our own being but also the importance of managing our energy, so that the power we wield is directed towards a worthwhile end.

However, the true end of the journey is not actually at Point 8, but POINT 9: the place we arrive once we descend from the pinnacle of power and achievement, taking with us all the experiences accumulated on our journey. Point 9 is where we assimilate these experiences: the successes and failures, the pleasures and pains, the joys and the sorrows. It's the place where we either integrate our experiences into the larger landscape of our lives or try to forget them, if integration seems impossible to manage.

Now the circle is complete. When we began, we made up stories that anticipated the journey ahead—these were the stories of the young. Now we tell the tales garnered from actual experience—these are the stories of the old. It's easy to overlook this storytelling process as something trivial and unimportant. But the telling of stories allows both incubation and assimilation, which are two of the most mysterious yet significant processes in transformation. The first involves the preparation of new life that has yet to emerge into the world; the second involves the digestion of raw experience, so that it can be converted into a form that makes it truly universal. (See Table 7-2 for a summary of this transformative cycle.)

¤ ¤ ¤

TABLE 7-2. LINKING PERSONALITY TO PROCESS

PT	PROCESS	PERSONALITY TYPE
9	INCUBATION	**The Storyteller** likes to dream, to imagine things & to listen to inspiring tales. He's able to enjoy companionship and usually accepts others as he finds them. Seems calm & peaceful and is valued for his ability to mediate disputes but may have difficulty with time management or making personal decisions.
1	DEFINING	**The Perfecter** brings great focus to a task, an ideal, or a set of ethical standards. She's precise, even picky, but good with details. Can be self-critical if she thinks she's not meeting her own high standards for conduct. Tends to rely on "black & white thinking" & can have difficulty unbending enough to enjoy intimate relationships.
2	HUMANIZING	**The People Person** is a warm & sympathetic individual who particularly enjoys personal interactions. He's always ready to assist others who need his help. Brings a humanizing touch to cold ideals but can become overinvested in the lives of others and in need of greater emotional independence.
3	ORGANIZATION	**The Self-tester** is a capable multi-tasker with good time management skills & a "can-do" attitude towards life. Although extremely hard-working, she can easily overwork or neglect personal relationships for the sake of getting things done & winning personal recognition for her outward achievements.
4	EMOTIONAL COMMITMENT	**The Deep Sea Diver** delves beneath the surface level of life to find out what's really there. Passionate, moody & sensitive, he often channels his energy into creative projects: drama, writing, high fashion, or art. Can get preoccupied with himself & his moods but is superb as a listener to people who have genuine troubles to share.
5	PROBLEM-SOLVING	**The Puzzle-solver** is fascinated by games, puzzles & creative problem-solving. She's good at reverse-engineering unique solutions to unusual problems. Detached, curious, & thoughtful, she's also shy & unusually sensitive to energy of all kinds. Can find it hard to reach out to others but still appreciates companionship.
6	FOLLOWING THROUGH	**The Steward** serves, preserves & stays the course. He reacts to anxiety by getting deeply-rooted in family and/or community, but sometimes faces his fears head-on by becoming a daredevil, hero, or a feisty scrapper who defends the underdog. Can be overly skeptical of new ideas or overly idealizing of life partners.
7	OPENING UP	**The Improviser** has an inventive mind and restless disposition. She loves life, fun & variety and has a special knack for making something out of nothing. Enjoys the good life, futuristic ideas & travel to exotic locales but can feel hemmed in when life seems uninspiring. Can benefit by getting focused & developing gratitude for small gifts.
8	COMPLETION	**The Master** projects a lot of presence, whether he's physically big or small. Strong, brave, and bold, he's a natural leader who leads by example, upholds fairness and protects the weak & innocent. Acts tough but is tender inside; can have a short fuse that needs controlling. Needs to master his "big" energy to effectively exercise his leadership skills.
9	ASSIMILATION	**The Storyteller** welcomes back the traveler, receives the weary, listens to the stories, absorbs the experiences & shares them with the collective.

OUR BRIEF TRIP AROUND THE ENNEAGRAM demonstrates how it's possible to see the nine personality types as nine stages in a transformative process. Although personality is shaped by many factors, it's my sense that when we're born, we each have within us the blueprint for one of the nine enneagram types, a blueprint which becomes gradually fleshed out over time. This blueprint allows us to "specialize" in a certain kind of transformational work, to take on a certain kind of transformational challenge and see what can be learned from it.*

Although we all like to achieve our goals in life, the point isn't just to reach the goal—whether it's making a million bucks, raising a child, or achieving world peace. It's learning how to appreciate the journey and what it can teach us. At each point on the enneagram journey, we learn something of value:

- *When we're at One*, we learn what it's like to seek out a higher set of principles by which to live and to create a set of standards reflecting those principles

- *When we're at Two*, we learn what it's like to put people first, build relationships, and enjoy our friends

- *When we're at Three*, we learn what it's like to work hard, achieve results, and taste success

- *When we're at Four*, we learn what it's like to value authenticity, appreciate aesthetics, and remain true to our inner vision

- *When we're at Five*, we learn what it's like to be curious, quirky, and playfully inquisitive—to love knowledge more than social conventions

- *When we're at Six*, we learn what it's like to face our fears, value our family, and preserve our most cherished traditions

- *When we're at Seven*, we learn what it's like to wander freely on the earth, seeking out new experiences that produce joy and delight

- *When we're at Eight*, we learn what it's like to feel really big—and how to use our bigness in a magnanimous and chivalrous fashion

- *When we're at Nine*, we learn to appreciate peace and harmony, to be receptive to life's small pleasures, and to enjoy the role of participant

---

* It bears mentioning that I first realized the potential for linking the process and personality enneagrams after reading pp. 325-333 of Bernier's *The Enneagram: Symbol of All and Everything* (2003), in which the author writes of the challenges that we encounter at each point of the transformational process.

Although each of us have one dominant type, we experience life from all nine positions on the enneagram, because we play many roles in life. That's why we can relate to all of the nine positions. The personality enneagram emphasizes the role of our dominant type in governing the way we see the world while the process enneagram emphasizes the way that we respond to changing circumstances in life. When we combine the two, we have a tool that enables us to explore the link between fixed factors (like temperament) and dynamic factors (like changing conditions).

¤ ¤ ¤

You may wonder, "But what about the challenges of each type?"

Well, of course the types *do* have challenges; challenges are a part of life. In the history of the personality enneagram, these challenges have been very well documented: we have enneagrams designed to inform us of our blind spots, false beliefs, defense mechanisms, traps, avoidances, anti-self actions, and more!

These challenge-oriented enneagrams can be quite useful. They alert us to the potential weaknesses of each type, providing us with information that can be invaluable in helping us to sidestep problems before they arise and to repair the damage should we make a mistake. But saying the types have weaknesses is not same as saying that they *are* weaknesses. Saying "I made a mistake" is quite different than saying "I *am* a mistake."

I once devised an Enneagram of Worst Possible Tendencies in order to see just how bad things could get. (And it turns out that they can get pretty bad!) So I realize that the enneagram can be used to look at the Shadow side of human nature. It's just that I see the shadowy aspects of the psyche as just one dimension of something that is infinitely larger (and infinity more intriguing). I also think we learn the most when we study human nature from the perspective of non-judgmental awareness.

There's a traditional Sufi story that speaks to the value of deeply engaging with life but without judging our experiences:

There was an old farmer who lived with his son. In the land where he lived, wealth was measured by the number of horses a family had.

One day, a horse escaped from his pen and ran away.

A neighbor, hearing of the news, said to the farmer, "Oh, that's bad."

The farmer smiled and said, "Maybe yes, maybe no."

Three days later, the farmer's horse returned with 15 wild horses that he led into the pen. Then the farmer closed the gate.

The farmer's neighbor was amazed. He said, "Look, now you have 16 horses. How great!"

To this, the farmer replied, "Maybe yes, maybe no."

The farmer's son went to train the wild horses. But he was young and inexperienced. So he fell off and broke his leg.

Hearing of this, the neighbor said to the farmer, "What a shame."

The farmer replied, "Maybe yes, maybe no."

The next day some soldiers came by, enlisting men for the army.

Seeing the farmer, the commander exclaimed, "You're too old!" Seeing the son, he exclaimed, "And you're injured!" And so the soldiers rode off.

When the neighbor heard this, he said, "You're so lucky."

The farmer responded, "Maybe yes, maybe no."

The point of the story is obvious: we may think we know what's good or bad about a situation, but we really don't. We only know what we perceive.

Even when we speak of transformation, we don't necessarily know what kind of transformation would be best in a given situation—or for a given individual. We often assume transformation is always good, because we think of it in a spiritualized context. But transformation just means change; it doesn't necessarily mean positive change. Or spiritual change. If we idealize transformation (only accepting the kind of transformation that meets our expectations), we limit life's possibilities.

Like the farmer, we never really know what changes are good or bad. Neither do we know how to fix things so that problems never arise. And few of us have the ability to consistently rise above misfortune. Even enlightened people have problems.

But that does not make us hapless victims in a chaotic world. Notice how the farmer in our story isn't very worried about what is happening, good or bad. He seems content.

Also notice that—despite all appearances to the contrary—things basically work out for him and his family. We might ask ourselves: *What does he know that we don't know?*

Whatever it is, it's obviously something worth knowing. And it's something that enables a person to live in a way that takes him beyond the "good versus bad" way of experiencing life.

Until now, the good versus bad paradigm has been the main one in use for working with the personality enneagram. In this chapter, I've been trying to loosen the grip of this paradigm by introducing the novel possibility that what we usually regard as ego types are actually transformation types: that our personality (and individuality) is rooted in an inborn desire to transform ourselves and in turn be transformed by our experiences.

But just what will this transformation look like? That's something we'd all like to know. While it won't look exactly the same for any two people, it will be affected by our enneagram type—specifically, *by the position of our type on the enneagram circle.*

I've already talked about what happens as we move through each transformational point on the enneagram. But I haven't talked about the precise nature of the transformations that take place at each point. If we look at the cycle as a whole, it involves transforming something raw into something more refined. But if we look at each step, it involves something more specialized that may or may not resemble the "raw-to-finished" model. There are points on the enneagram that involve building up, but there are other points that involve *breaking down*—points that involve climbing and others that involve *descent.* Each point plays a unique role that involves a unique kind of transformation.

So if we want to work with the energy of each type in an optimal fashion, it's a good idea to see what kind of transformation occurs there, so that we're not trying to move up when we should be moving down, or right when we should be moving left. We want to pay particular attention to the stereotype of transformation as something that inevitably involves moving from a lower state to a higher state (or put more poetically, transforming the dross of the material world into the gold of spirit). This is indeed one kind of transformation. But it's not the only kind.

Transformation is simply the conversion of energy from one state into another (e.g., the transformation of water into steam by boiling or into ice by freezing). So we can convert spirit to matter (which is the process of *involution*) or matter to spirit (which is the process of *evolution*). Both processes are part of a larger process, which Ken Wilber—following the work of Arthur Lovejoy—calls the Great Chain of Being.

Wilber discusses this cycle at great length in Chapter 9 of *Sex, Ecology, Spirituality* (2000), and less technically in Chapter 17 of *Up From Eden* (1981/1996). His main operating assumption is that life involves both the descent into matter and the ascent back to spirit; a further assumption on my part is that both processes are intended to enhance life in some way and are thus equal partners. Wilber makes it clear that the "fall" into matter is not a fall from grace, or really, any sort of fall. Rather, it is the playful move of spirit into matter, a move intended to discover just how far into the depths it can penetrate: "This is the great game of hide-and-seek, with Spirit being It" (*Up from Eden*, p. 317).

Wilber observes that few people see the whole cycle; they either focus on the process of ascent or descent. The Ascenders are those who fear desire and seek to escape from the world of matter; he describes their state of mind as "Eros full of Phobos." In the following passage, he describes how people in this state have an overwhelming urge to ascend, leaving behind the temptations of Earth:

> In their frantic wish for an "other world," their ascending Eros strivings (otherwise so appropriate) are shot through and through with Phobos, with ascetic repression, with a denial and a fear and a hatred of anything "this-worldly," a denial of vital life, of sexuality, of sensuality, of nature, of body (and always of women) (p. 350).

Wilber later has equally harsh words for pure Descenders: people who lack appreciation for spiritual reality and thus focus only on the material world. He tells us that either position without the other brings imbalance. The solution, he thinks, is for us to make room for both—and to find a way to reconcile their differences in viewpoint.

On p. 319, Wilber includes a diagram to illustrate the involutionary/evolutionary cycle (which we could just call the life cycle); I've simplified the figure to create Fig. 7-4, depicting Wilber's version of the journey from spirit to physicality to unconsciousness

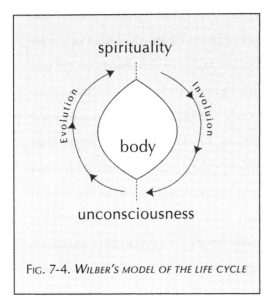

FIG. 7-4. *WILBER'S MODEL OF THE LIFE CYCLE*

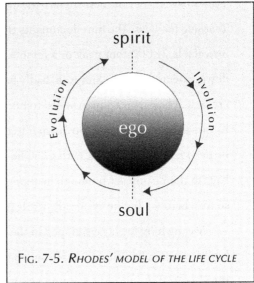

FIG. 7-5. *RHODES' MODEL OF THE LIFE CYCLE*

(involution) and the return journey from unconsciousness to physicality to spirit (evolution).* It's not much of a leap from Wilber's model of the life cycle to one where we conceptualize the move downward as a move not simply from spirit to matter, but from spirit to matter to *soul* (see Fig. 7-5, a version of Wilber's approach using the language of my spirit-ego-*soul* model).

Seeing the descent into matter from this perspective confers upon it the kind of meaning and dignity that is worthy of the Hero's Journey; it also reminds us that the Descent into the Deep is an important part of that journey. Some would even say that it's the most important part, because it's where spirit descends to a place in which we find it very difficult to maintain consciousness, because of the density and darkness. While the descent into darkness is seldom easy, it represents a rare opportunity for an individual to fully experience the Hero's Journey. The person who manages to bring some kind of illumination to the darkness, against all odds, is the one who begins to appreciate the mystery of *soul*.

¤ ¤ ¤

---

* I excluded all the intermediate stages and just kept the process and its three main domains: the spiritual, physical, and unconscious. According to Wilber, we become unconscious at the point of greatest physical density..

THINKING ABOUT the descent into the darkness brings to mind a film I saw not long ago, *Touching the Void*. The film documents the story of two climbers who scaled an almost unscalable 21,000-foot peak in a remote part of the Andes. Unfortunately, on the way down, one of them, Joe Simpson, badly broke his leg. Soon afterward, he fell into a deep crevasse. His partner Simon yelled to him but heard nothing in return; the distance was too great. He could not climb down into the crevasse. Besides, he was sure that Joe must be dead from the fall. Sick with grief, he cut the rope that linked them and tried to get back to their camp, even though he thought he would also die (because the descent was so treacherous). But he eventually made it back.

Meanwhile, Joe lay enveloped in the darkness of a glacial crevasse. He wasn't dead, but he was in a bad situation. He yelled for help and nobody answered. He could hear the groans of the glacial ice moving around him in the pitch black. It sent shivers down his spine. He thought he would soon die, but realized after a while that although he was in pain, he wasn't dying. Not yet.

Joe felt utterly alone. He became more and more angry and frustrated. Soon he was screaming out his rage about being buried alive. He screamed and screamed until he was completely hoarse. Once his anger was exhausted, it gave way to an overwhelming sense of helplessness and misery. And he began to weep.

After a long time, something happened—something shifted inside him. He didn't think he would live, but he became filled with a profound desire not to die alone. So his goal was to try against all odds to make it back to his base camp. He couldn't go up so instead he went down, lowering himself deeper and deeper into the crevasse, hoping to find a way out before he ran out of rope.

Miraculously, he did it. He found a ledge, saw a shaft of sunshine off to the side, and managed to pull himself up to where it came from (not easy with a broken leg). Then he managed to heave himself over the edge and rouse himself sufficiently to continue down the snow slope, across a dangerous glacier, and into a dry area of large boulders. By that time, he was consumed with thirst. Eventually, he found a tiny rivulet that saved his life.

He'd now been traveling for several days and nights. His strength was waning. As darkness fell, things became very fuzzy. He didn't remember what happened over the next few hours. But at some point he realized that he had no more strength left. This is the place he would die.

But Joe was roused from these thoughts by a terrible smell (he said later that it acted like smelling salts, awakening him out of his stupor). He realized with a shock he was in the latrine area for his camp. He couldn't believe it and wasn't quite sure how he got there, but he was suddenly filled with a wild surge of hope. He corralled the last bit of his strength and yelled out for Simon.

He heard only silence in reply. His heart broke for the last time as he lost hope.

But Joe didn't die. Simon was still there. He heard Joe's cries and ran to help him; he hadn't responded right away because he was so shocked to realize that Joe was actually alive. Since arriving back at camp, Simon had been distraught with grief. He refused to leave for days, despite severe frostbite. He'd finally been persuaded by a third companion to go. Joe arrived just a few hours before their scheduled departure.

Touching the Void is the kind of story that illustrates what the descent into *soul* is all about: looking death in the face and realizing the only power we really have to is keep moving towards life, however slowly or painfully. In Joe's case, this entailed going even deeper into the darkness (as it often does). At the lowest point in such a journey, the darkness can seem overwhelming (which is probably why Wilber calls it "unconsciousness"). But even in the darkest point of the descent, we don't necessarily go unconscious. There is always a chance to choose life, even when death surrounds us.

Fortunately, few of us will ever find ourselves inside a crevasse (at least in the literal sense!). But almost all of us will have experiences in life that will take us into the darkness in some way, where we'll have to rouse ourselves to keep moving, even when we're not sure where we're headed. As long as we stay engaged with what's happening, we lose only what's non-essential. That's the lesson of the journey into the valley of *soul*.

¤ ¤ ¤

SO HAVING EXPLORED THE TRANSFORMATIONAL PROCESS, we're now ready to pick up the thread from Chapter 4, where we considered the advantages of seeing the psyche from three perspectives: spirit, ego and *soul*. We've already mapped these three domains onto the life cycle. And since the process enneagram describes the life cycle, we can now take the next step of seeing the circle in Fig. 7-5 as an enneagram circle, which in turn enables us to conceive of Fig. 7-6 and Table 7-3.

On p. 313 of *The Intelligent Enneagram*, A. G. E. Blake has actually depicted the process enneagram in a way very similar to the way the life cycle is depicted by Wilber. Blake equates the top of this enneagram with *Unity* and the bottom with *Chaos*; the right side is labeled *Increasing complexity;* the left side is labeled *Increasing unity.* So the only thing that's missing are the labels *Involution* (for the right) and *Evolution* (for the left).*

I would modify Blake's model in only one way: by introducing the idea that the same enneagram used to describe process can also be used to describe personality, as long as we consider personality to be a vehicle for transformation as opposed to a form of fixated functioning. With this understanding, we now have a model which enables us to see something very useful: how each type can transform itself, where *the nature of the transformation depends on where the type is located on the enneagram circle.*†

This means that we'd expect to find that types which are part of the involutionary cycle (Types 1 – 4) would not transform themselves the exact same way as types that are part of the evolutionary cycle (Types 5 – 8). Type 9, which plays a role in both cycles, would have a unique role that incorporates aspects of both cycles.

So let's take a closer look at how this might work. We'll start with a quick summary of the overall cycle. During *involution*, spirit becomes manifest in matter: it is born into the world. Ethereal energies become images that must be nurtured, promoted, and

---

* However, his discussion about involution/evolution on p. 51 supports the idea that he views the right side of the enneagram as involutionary and the left side as evolutionary.

† I'm aware that transformation isn't necessarily something we control (at least not entirely), but something that we also allow. Either way, the position of our type on the circle means that we find some transformational processes more relevant, useful, or compelling than others.

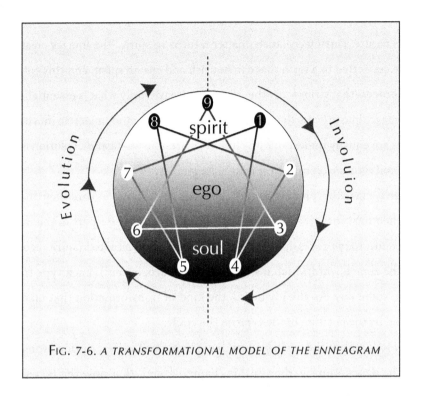

FIG. 7-6. *A TRANSFORMATIONAL MODEL OF THE ENNEAGRAM*

TABLE 7-3. THE LIFE CYCLE MAPPED ONTO THE ENNEAGRAM

INVOLUTION: *CREATING IMAGES (ART)*

Point 9 > 1   moving out of pure spirit (being > stirring > dreaming > imagining)

Point 1 > 2   moving towards ego (anticipating > idealizing > inspiring > humanizing)

Point 3 > 4   moving towards soul (individualizing > authenticating > delving > individuating)

Point 4 > 5   moving towards dissolution (deepening > surrendering > sacrificing > dissolving)

EVOLUTION: *EVALUATING IMAGES (SCIENCE)*

Point 5 > 6   moving away from dissolution (observing > collecting > assembling > systematizing)

Point 6 > 7   ascending towards ego (understanding > teaching > serving > community-building)

Point 7 > 8   moving towards spirit (sharing > celebrating > unifying > consolidating)

Point 8 > 9   moving to pure spirit (absorbing > digesting > assimilating > being) celebrated. So involution is a feminine process that is imaginative, nurturing, and subjective in nature. During *evolution*, matter returns to spirit. The images created in the world are converted to a form that can nourish and enrich spirit, and this entails a distillation process that strips away the "dross" and leaves only what is essential. So evolution is a masculine process that is simplifying, scientific, and objective in nature. Both processes are equally important: involution creates the world and evolution refines the creation and returns its fruits to spirit.

When we map this process onto the enneagram, it shows us three key things about each of the nine types: (a) the nature of the type (whether it's part of the involutionary or evolutionary process), (b) the "zone" in which it's situated (spirit, ego, or *soul*), and (c) the zone toward which it's headed (spirit, ego, or *soul*). Each type transforms energy in some way. As already noted, the kind of transformation that takes place is influenced by the position of the type on the circle.

Now let's look at the cycle broken down by type. The descriptions somewhat resemble the descriptions earlier in this chapter, except that now the focus is on the combined influence of the dominant process (involution or evolution) and zone (spirit, ego, or *soul*).

The *involutionary process* starts at Point 9 (acting initially as "Point 0") where we begin bringing images into the world by dreaming, imagining, and fantasizing about them. So at Point 9, the energy field is pure spirit; we have not really begun to move toward the world of people and things. With this understanding, it's not hard to see why Nines tend to be indefinite and ungrounded—but also dreamy and imaginative.

At Point 1, we're emerging from the world of spirit and embarking on our journey into the world of matter. To take the next step, we need to know the difference between the two, which is why there's so much focus on black-and-white thinking. There's also the sense that it's important to invest the world we create with eternal values, so that the created world can reflect the world of spirit.

At Point 2, we're definitively in the world of ego (everyday life), learning how to express emotions, develop relationships, and nurture new life. This generative, nurturing role comes right after the Point 1 place of values creation because it's only when we learn to love our images of the eternal that they can be born into the created world.

At Point 3, we're at the pinnacle of the ego world, the world of image creation. We create, promote, and project images forcefully into the world, where they take on a life of their own. There's the sense at this point that life exists only if we create it, which is why it's hard to stop working. But because Three is on the Cusp of Four (where we encounter *soul*), there can be the sense that there's more to life than the images we create and the stirrings of dissatisfaction with the purely material aspects of creation.

At Point 4, we're entering the domain of *soul*. Because we're still part of the involuntary cycle, the creative impulse is still active, but we're now looking to create something of greater significance, something eternal (connection to One) but also primordial (drawing from the primordial energy at the bottom of the enneagram).

Crossing to the other side, we begin the *evolutionary process*, which requires a shift from image-creation to image-evaluation (a move from *art* to *science*). At Point 5, we collect, examine, and systematize the images of creation, checking for logical inconsistencies and other fundamental problems. The Five has a certain degree of emotional detachment because this is the quality needed for the new evolutionary task of creating order from chaos.

At Point 6, we're emerging from the world of *soul* into the social world once again, but the focus now is not so much on the individual as on the community—on how to make the reality we've created more functional from a social point of view. Because Point 6 is where we're climbing out of the depths, we're beginning to emotionally react to our experiences there (as we gain some perspective on what has happened). At the same time, we have to deal with any leftover resistance before we can move on. This scenario can create a great deal of agitation and feelings of instability until we become less reactive, so that fear can give way to faith and service.

At Point 7, we're beginning to feel the pull of spirit, which lightens up the atmosphere and speeds up our energy field. We're also beginning to integrate the world of images into the world of spirit, and we start to feel the playfulness of spirit in our lives.

It inspires us and enhances our ability to inject a visionary energy into everything we do. There can be a manic quality here, because we have the sense that it's our last chance to experience the world and understand its patterns before pulling everything together as we move towards unity consciousness.

At Point 8, we unify the images that have survived the "culling" process by fully embodying them. Our feet are on the earth but our awareness is expanding to encompass the world of spirit. Because we've experienced all the steps in the cycle of life, we bear the responsibility to support others in their journey and to bring unity to human endeavors through responsible leadership.

As we move towards Point 9, we approach the zone of pure spirit, where all that has been manifest in the previous cycle of creation is mysteriously assimilated in a way that enhances all life.

If we now shift our attention to the three "zones" of spirit, ego, and *soul*, we notice that the types at the top of the enneagram (8, 9, 1) are in the zone of *spirit*; the types in the middle of the enneagram (2, 3, 6, 7) are in the zone of *ego* (the material world); and the types in the bottom of the enneagram (4 and 5) are in the zone of *soul*. This might tell us why:

> ▸ **top-of-the-enneagram "spirit types"** tend to be irritable, instinctual, and resolute (they gain balance by translating spiritual fire into physical action)

> ▸ **middle-of-the-enneagram "ego types"** tend to be congenial, outgoing, and interactive (they gain balance by getting involved in the world around them)

> ▸ **bottom-of-the-enneagram "soul types"** tend to be solitary, socially-withdrawn, and sensitive (they gain balance by attuning to the depths of life)

Most of us aren't used to looking at the enneagram from this horizontal perspective. But when we do, we can see some interesting patterns. It gives us yet another way to understand the types and their relationship with one another, especially when we combine that knowledge with an understanding of whether they are moving "down" (towards *soul*) or "up" (towards spirit).

¤ ¤ ¤

MOST OF US are used to thinking of transformation as a purely evolutionary process—a process by which matter is raised up or transformed to spirit. But that's only one side of the coin. If we focus only on the evolutionary part of the process, we deny value to the birthing of spirit into matter—to the feminine, generative part of the process.

Each of us is an energy transformer; the type of energy we transform and how we transform it depends on our inner nature, which in turn depends on our enneagram type (because it's associated with our core motivation). When we know the location of the our type on the transformational enneagram, we can discern how our inner nature affects the way we transform energy. We can also understand why no two types experience transformation in exactly the same way: because they're all at a different place on the circle. It's for this reason that the role, path, or theme that's right for one type of person may be dead wrong for another.

Seeing the types as part of a transformative cycle helps bring home the truth that transformation occurs *within the context of the type*, not outside of it. Trying to transcend, deny, or ignore the type will not bring the kind of change that we seek. Permanent change comes as the result of working with the gifts and challenges that arise out of our inner nature, allowing them to show us what we have learned and what we have yet to master. That's how we individuate, refining the substance of our uniqueness.

But individuation doesn't occur in a vacuum. That's why it's helpful to understand not only the nature of the individual types (especially our own), but the various ways in which the types interact. That's what we'll look at next.

8

Enneagram connections

You have to learn to adapt to the quirks that you have in your personality. You have to work to your strengths.
– Trauma surgeon

ONE THING THAT MAKES the enneagram unique among systems for looking at personality is its focus on connections. We've seen in the last chapter that the nine enneagram points can be seen not just as nine categories of personality but as nine steps in transformation. Thus, in the transformational enneagram, there's an obvious emphasis on interaction: each step in the process depends on the steps before and after it.

The theme of connection and interaction pops up again and again in enneagram teachings. Every time we "connect the dots," it's a reminder of the fact that we do not really live in isolation, but in connection. The multiplicity of connections that we can see when studying the enneagram reflects the multiplicity of ways that we can connect with one another.

In this chapter, we'll look at three key ways we can connect the nine points. But these are only a handful of the many possibilities. Once we know the basics of the system, we can study the geometry to see what other meaningful patterns are there, just waiting to be noticed. Each new pattern that we detect provides us with a new way of thinking about the nine types .

In the previous chapter, we saw how to group the enneagram points vertically (as left side versus right side = involution versus evolution), horizontally (by three

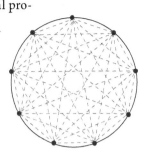

zones: spirit, ego, *soul*), and as three stages of a transformational process (beginning, middle, ending). These are innovative groupings, which is why I spent so much time explaining them. Don Riso and Russ Hudson have also unearthed new patterns such as the Hornevian triads (3-7-8, 1-2-6, 4-5-9) and Harmonic triads (1-3-5, 7-9-2, 4-6-8), which are discussed in their popular book, *Wisdom of the Enneagram* (1999).

There are many more patterns waiting to be discovered. The unlabeled figure on this page shows all the possible connections between the types, so you can see how many possibilities remain.

We'll talk in this chapter about three of the most well-known ways to group the types: by *wing point, connecting point,* and *energy center.* The *wings* of a point are the adjacent points on either side; the *connecting points* are the two points it connects via the inner lines; and the *energy centers* are three groups of adjacent types categorized by the energy they exhibit. (Fig. 8-1 shows these groupings using Type 8 as an example.)

When studying the wing points and connecting points, it's helpful to realize (if it's not yet obvious) that in addition to representing personality types or transformational stages, the nine points can also represent *nine aspects of the individual psyche* while the circle represents the psyche as a whole. So when we're talking about connecting the points, we're talking about looking at the connections between *different impulses within*

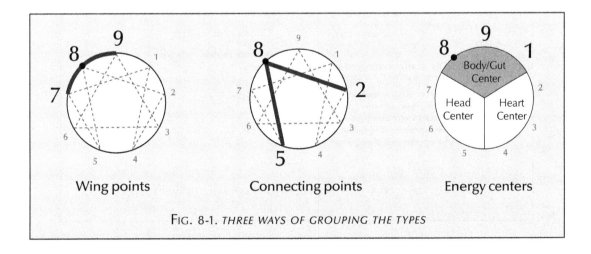

Wing points   Connecting points   Energy centers

FIG. 8-1. *THREE WAYS OF GROUPING THE TYPES*

our own psyche. We each have all nine types within us; so becoming aware of the patterns of connectedness helps us recognize our inner personas and how they interact.

¤ ¤ ¤

THE TYPES ON EITHER SIDE of our enneagram type are called **wing points** (or wing types). They're like neighbors next to our house. As with real neighbors, we often prefer one to the other. In the example above, a person who's an Eight can feel an affinity with either Seven or Nine. If he leans towards Nine, he takes on some of the characteristics of Nine and is called an 8w9 (Eight with a Nine wing); if he leans towards Seven,

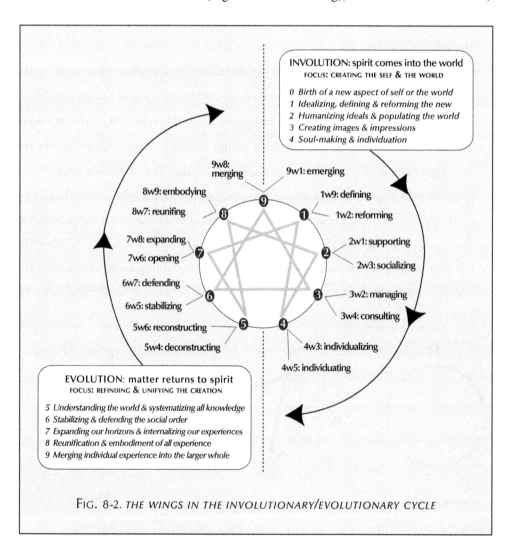

FIG. 8-2. *THE WINGS IN THE INVOLUTIONARY/EVOLUTIONARY CYCLE*

he takes on some of the characteristics of Seven and is called an 8w7 (Eight with a Seven wing). If he has no preference, he's bi-winged.

The wings give us additional resources from which to draw when the energy of our type isn't sufficient for some reason (e.g., when we need to take on a task that's unfamiliar or play a role that isn't entirely natural for our type). Because the wings are so close to the type, they're the first place we go to seek extra support.

Looking at the wings of each type is not so different from looking at the enneagram from a transformational perspective (Chapter 7), because it gives us 18 wings points instead of nine enneagram types. Fig. 8-2 depicts the way that wings transition from one to the next; Fig. 8-3 depicts the names of each type along with its two wing types. And Table 8-1 list key adjectives associated with each wing type. They're also discussed briefly by type in Chapter 11 – 19.

(Incidentally, Riso & Hudson call wing types *subtypes*; they call what most people call subtypes *instinctual variants*.)

The idea that the wings have influence is not without controversy. I remember overhearing a conversation where one participant at an enneagram event was asked about his wing type, and he airily replied, "I do not subscribe to the wing type hypothesis." To me, it's more than a hypothesis, because it's so easy to demonstrate the reality of wing-related differences. All I have to do is divide a type panel by wing and ask some questions for those differences to emerge.

¤ ¤ ¤

IF THE WINGS are the first backup resource for each type, the **connecting points** are a secondary resource. But there's a difference between the two. With the wings, it's possible to lean towards a wing in such a way that it becomes a permanent (or at least highly stable) way of being in the world. When we access the energy of our connecting points, it's usually more of a leap—so the effects are usually more temporary.

TABLE 8-1. WING POINT DESCRIPTIONS

9w1: **ANTICIPATOR** (*moving from inert receptivity towards dreamy imagining*): dreamy, hopeful, receptive, imaginative, anticipatory, participatory. Example: Audrey Hepburn.

1w9: **DEFINER** (*moving from dreamy imagining to definitive planning*): discriminating, detail-oriented, contained, specific, tense, observant, reserved. Example: Harrison Ford.

1w2: **REFORMER** (*moving from definitive planning to social reform*): earnest, involved, resolute, forward-moving, action-oriented. Example: Billy Graham.

2w1: **SOCIAL WORKER** (*moving from social reform to humane support*): helpful, supportive, devotional, caring, sharing. Example: Mother Teresa.

2w3: **SOCIALIZER** (*moving from humane support to gracious socializing*): warm, friendly, sociable, affectionate, outgoing, gracious, diplomatic. Example: Joan Rivers.

3w2: **MANAGER** (*moving from gracious socializing to team management*): adaptable, energetic, enthusiastic, practical, confident, can-do. Example: Oprah.

3w4: **PROFESSIONAL** (*moving from team management to independent consulting*): focused, politic, ambitious, hard-working, practiced, self-motivated. Example: Will Smith.

4w3: **SPECIALIST** (*moving from independent consulting to artistic professionalism*): independent, individualistic, headstrong competitive, stylish. Example: Kate Winslet.

4w5: **ARTISTE** (*moving from an artistic professionalism to art for art's sake*): intense, inward, deep, moody, sensitive, hidden. Example: Bob Dylan.

5w4: **ICONOCLAST** (*moving from art for art's sake to deep curiosity*): curious, arcane, unusual, quirky, offbeat, original. Example: Anthony Hopkins.

5w6: **THINKER** (*moving from deep curiosity to detached contemplation*): shy, objective, intellectual, detached, observant, philosophical. Example: Isaac Asimov.

6w5: **SERVER** (*moving from detached contemplation to shy/dutiful service*): quiet, reserved, analytical, systematic, dutiful, supportive, family-oriented. Example: Ed Harris.

6w7: **WIT** (*moving from shy/dutiful service to hopeful self-expression*): jittery, mentally quick, edgy, off-balance, witty. Example: Woody Allen.

7w6: **COMEDIAN** (*moving from hopeful self-expression to optimistic performance*): wacky, upbeat, fun-seeking, charming, entertaining, quick-witted. Example: Robin Williams.

7w8: **ADVENTURER** (*moving from optimistic performance to adventure-seeking*): adventurous, risk-taking, entrepreneurial, realistic, daring, experience-hungry. Example: Robin Hood.

8w7: **POWER BROKER** (*moving from adventure-seeking to empire building*): bold, unapologetic, impatient, straight-shooting, charismatic, decisive. Example: Donald Trump.

8w9: **POWERHOUSE** (*moving from empire building to empire consolidation*): strong, silent, powerful, unchallenged, deliberate, inexorable. Example: John Wayne.

9w8: **MOUNTAIN** (*moving from empire consolidation to inert receptivity*): calm, slow-to-act, laconic, nature-oriented, impassive, unsentimental. Example: Clint Eastwood.

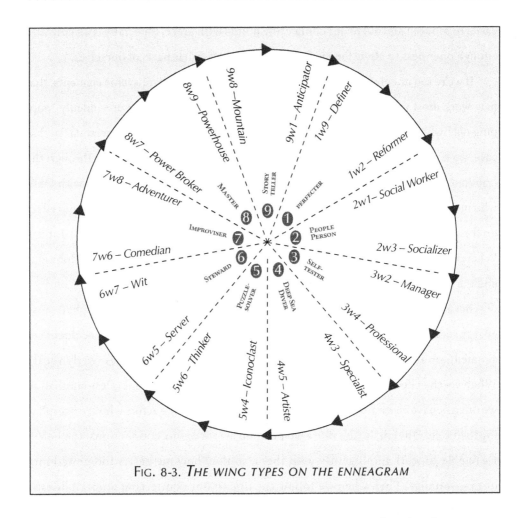

FIG. 8-3. *THE WING TYPES ON THE ENNEAGRAM*

Why do we make this leap? In order to access resources not found within our own type. In that sense, our connecting points are like the wing points. But unlike the wings, they're not directly adjacent, so the energy is literally more removed and thus more dissimilar to that of our type. It's harder to access and takes more effort to integrate.

So it often takes a shock (or at least a significant shift of circumstances) to catapult us "out" of our type and "into" our connecting point. Of course, we don't totally move out of our type, but we do change enough for other people to notice that we're not quite ourselves. This is especially true when we're young and have had few opportunities to integrate all the different aspects of the psyche. When we try out a new role, it's often awkward; we're like actors with a new script. As we mature, it can become easier to move in and out of our connecting points with grace, especially if we cultivate enough openness to allow for the integration of unfamiliar parts of ourselves.

If we're too uncomfortable and try to wall off our unfamiliar psychic elements, that may work most of the time—but these unwanted parts have a way of suddenly "popping out" when circumstances in life compel us to abandon our usual persona. In that case, we have a "trapdoor" scenario in which we appear to suddenly drop through the trapdoor into an alternative persona. This phenomenon is usually associated with Ones who move to Seven, because this move can sometimes have a wildly exhilarating effect on them (perhaps aided and abetted by the effects of alcohol, drugs, or a trip to Tahiti). Whatever the cause for the shift, the result is the abandonment of One-like inhibitions and the access to Seven-like feelings of uninhibited freedom.

But any type can have a "trapdoor" experience: a quiet Five moving to Eight (whose energy suddenly explodes into anger), a placid Nine moving to Six (who becomes very agitated), or an inwardly-oriented Four moving to Two (who becomes overly vocal). Whatever the effects of the move, the energy of the connecting point is less familiar, so we often behave awkwardly when making the connection, like actors who are overplaying their role. Obviously, the more we become aware of our connections, the better we're able to work intelligently with them, so they become better integrated into our personality. Then when we follow the line to our connecting point, it doesn't feel so much like a Jekyll/Hyde scenario. We extend ourselves while simultaneously remaining who we are (that is, retaining our own point of view).

We locate the connecting points by looking at the inner lines on the enneagram (Table 8-2 and Fig. 8-4). Because the inner lines are associated with a directional energy flow (note the arrows), the direction of those arrows is often said to be significant for determining the effect of the connecting points. When we go "against the arrows," we are said to be going in the *direction of integration* to our security point; when we go "with the arrows," we are said to be going the in the *direction of disintegration* to our stress point.

But not everybody embraces this view. Just as the idea of wing types is not accepted by everyone, neither is the idea that the arrows are significant. For one thing, the originator of this directional hypothesis (Claudio Naranjo) characterizes it as a product of his own exploration that was not part of the enneagram teachings he originally received. For another, this way of interpreting the inner lines seems to work better for some people than for others. For a third, the language of integration and disintegration turns some people off.

The idea that the arrows are meaningful makes sense to me, although with modifications. I'm inclined to think that the arrows have meaning because they're part of the geometry of the enneagram, and everything about the geometry is meaningful in some way. Also, my own experience supports the idea that the arrows are meaningful. So the question is, what do they signify?

In my own experience, I draw upon the resources of my stress point of Two (moving towards "disintegration") when I feel a little insecure, awkward, or emotionally vulnerable while I draw upon the resources of my security point of One (moving towards "integration") when I feel more relaxed and able to take in new information. But the language seems unfortunate, since it makes one direction sound better than the other. And that bothers me, because disintegration is akin to a descent into the valley of *soul*, so it's actually associated with transformation. Integration actually depends upon disintegration, because without the willingness to get in touch with all aspects of the psyche—especially the non-aligned parts—no real integration is possible.

That's why we might want to consider revising the way we speak about the connecting points (and probably the way we think about them, too). One possibility is to use the framework of ego, spirit, and *soul* as the basis for calling the point of disintegration the *soul point* and the point of integration the *spirit point*, which is what I do in Fig. 8-4. We can think of our type as our "ego point," where this simply means it's our normal base of operations. We can think of our soul point as the place we go when we fall into familiar patterns that are often unconscious in nature. So this connection can often help us retrench before moving forward in some way; it's like picking up a dropped

TABLE 8-2. DESCRIPTION OF CONNECTING POINTS

*Connecting to the **soul point** (stress point/point of "disintegration") deepens, thickens, or provides some kind of grounding experience that allows us to ground or consolidate our understanding in preparation for future expansion. Connecting to the **spirit point** (security point/point of "integration") allows us to acquire fresh insights, move into new areas, and generally expand our awareness and lighten our spirit.*

ONE (soul point = 4, spirit point = 7). *1 > 4 brings access to deep emotions that help us unstiffen & feel greater empathy; 1 > 7 brings lightness, joy, & the ability to relax and have fun*

TWO (soul point = 8, spirit point = 4). *2 > 8 brings assertiveness, focus & the ability to protect; 2 > 4 brings greater depth and the ability to introspect and discover the inner self*

THREE (soul point = 9, spirit point = 6). *3 > 9 brings rest, relaxation & the chance to "just be"; 3 > 6 brings care, caution & a greater focus on community service & family values*

FOUR (soul point = 2, spirit point = 1). *4 > 2 brings the ability to socialize more freely and give of ourselves to others; 4 > 1 brings the ability to be self-starting, disciplined & focused*

FIVE (soul point = 7, spirit point = 8). *5 > 7 brings playfulness, curiosity & child-like joy; 5 > 8 brings groundedness, assertiveness & the ability to lead*

SIX (soul point = 3, spirit point = 9). *6 > 3 brings the ability to excel & speak up for our ideas or reservations; 6 > 9 brings a lessening of anxiety & feelings of calmness & acceptance of things as they are*

SEVEN (soul point = 1, spirit point = 5). *7 > 1 brings critical focus & practicality (good for completing innovative projects); 7 > 5 brings greater interiority & the ability to think more deeply and systematically*

EIGHT (soul point = 5, spirit point = 2). *8 > 5 brings sensitivity & an understanding of what it's like to feel vulnerable; 8 > 2 brings empathy to enrich leadership skills*

NINE (soul point = 6, spirit point = 3). *9 > 6 brings greater alertness & ability to respond to the needs of others; 9 > 3 brings the desire to excel & work until the job is done*

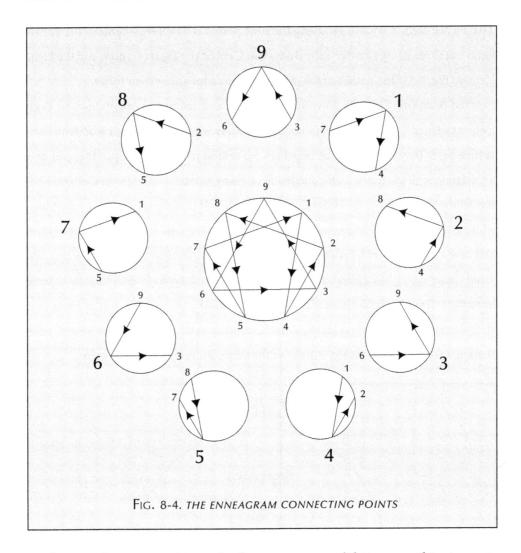

FIG. 8-4. *THE ENNEAGRAM CONNECTING POINTS*

stitch, remembering something we've forgotten, or consolidating something to create a firmer foundation. We typically move to our spirit point when circumstances allow us to venture forth from the familiar into uncharted territory; more composure is required to take advantage of the energy of the spirit point.

Using the language of *soul point* and *spirit point* reminds us that the connecting points are complements, not opposites. I don't know whether this new terminology will stick, but we can try it out for size and see whether it appeals to people who see the types from a transformative perspective.

¤ ¤ ¤

THE THIRD MAJOR WAY of grouping the nine points is by **energy center.** The enneagram has three energy centers: the Body/Gut Center, the Heart Center, and the Head Center (Fig. 8-5). The names of the centers tells us a lot about their focus.

The *Body/Gut Center* is down-to-earth, fiery, and sensate in orientation. So Body Center types (8-9-1) tend to be no-nonsense people who require physical activity to be at their best. They also tend to be impatient (or at least irritable) in disposition and have a hard time with too much intellectualizing or gushy emotions. The *Heart Center* is flowing, feminine, and warm. So Heart Center types (2-3-4) tend to be expressive individuals who particularly value their relationships. They're sensitive to how others react to them and have a hard time with people who seem either overly critical or overly detached. The *Head Center* is airy, masculine, and cool. So Head Center types (5-6-7) tend to be intellectually-oriented people whose relationships are based more on common interests than shared emotions. They enjoy playing with ideas and don't think much of pumped-up emotions or unreasoned action. Fig. 8-5 shows the three centers on the enneagram.

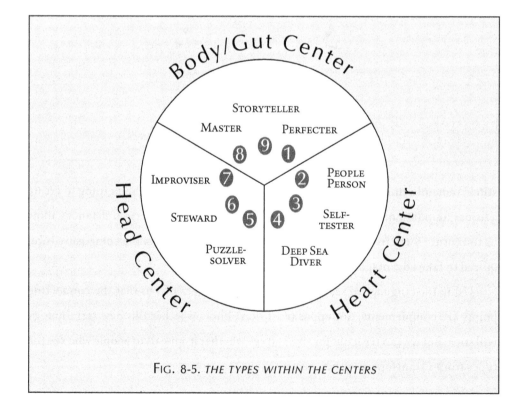

FIG. 8-5. *THE TYPES WITHIN THE CENTERS*

From the perspective of the energy centers, the *inner triangle types* (3-6-9) look somewhat different from the *hexad types* (1-4-2-8-5-7). The descriptions of each center seem to apply somewhat less to the 3-6-9 types that are at the middle of each center (or at least to apply to them in a different way). While the hexad types display the energy of the centers more overtly, the triangle types display it in a much more subtle or inward fashion (or can even seem not to display it at all). So the fiery energy of the Gut Center is on the surface at Points 8 and 1, but the fire seems to be banked at Point 9. The emotional energy of the Heart Center is hard to miss at Points 2 and 4, but is channeled more into action than emotion at Point 3. And the cool detachment we associate with the Head Center is more evident at Points 5 and 7 than at Point 6.

If we take a closer look, we'll also notice subtle differences between the hexad types in each center. The 2-5-8 hexad types most overtly display the characteristics of the center; the 1-4-7 hexad types display these characteristics, but not as blatantly; they're generally more complex as energy types. In *The Positive Enneagram*, I explained all of these differences by juxtaposing the centers on the transformational enneagram. Once we do this, we see that as we proceed around the circle in a clockwise direction, the first types we encounter as we enter each center are 2-5-8; the next types are 3-6-9; and the last types are 1-4-7 (Fig. 8-6).

The types in the first position (2-5-8) can be likened to immigrants entering a new culture for the first time: to survive, they have to adapt to the new conditions, which usually means embracing them as wholeheartedly as possible. So they display the energy of the center in a very unsubtle way: Twos are "super-feelers," Fives are "super-thinkers" and Eights are "super-gut types."

Staying with the same analogy, once the immigrant is better established, he doesn't need to push so hard. In fact, he needs to do just the opposite: to internalize the energy, so it becomes part of who he is inwardly. This is like learning to dream in a new language or to think like a local. It's the kind of process that doesn't show up outwardly but is an important part of the assimilation process, nonetheless. So the types in the second or middle position (3-6-9) don't use the energy of the center to "do" anything outwardly;

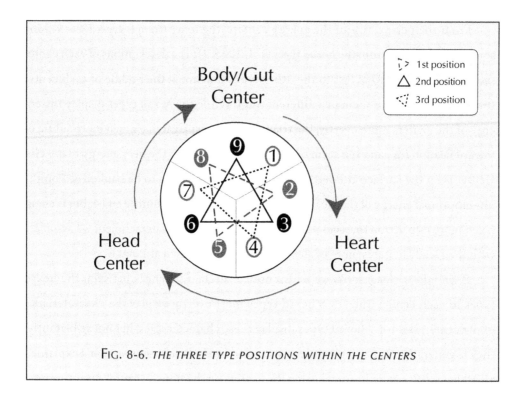

FIG. 8-6. *THE THREE TYPE POSITIONS WITHIN THE CENTERS*

instead, they introvert it, allowing it to change the way they respond to their environment. Threes become receptive to social signals; Sixes become receptive to mental signals; and Nines become receptive to somatic (body-based) signals.

When the assimilation process is complete, we're ready for the third step: synthesis. Over time, an immigrant is no longer an immigrant: he becomes integrated both inwardly and outwardly into his new culture. Just so, the enneagram types in the third position (1-4-7) become integrated into the center, having synthesized its energy in a way that makes them more complex exemplars who display the traits associated with the center in a way that synthesizes what has been learned in the first two positions. They're also more restless and anticipatory in temperament because they're beginning to feel the pull of the next center, so they tend to have a visionary streak or interest in new ways of doing things. Ones synthesize the energy of the gut center by creating complex and elegant ethical systems; Fours synthesize the emotions of the heart center by creating synesthetic (integrative) forms of art; and Sevens synthesize the intellectual energy of the head center by thinking up eclectic innovations and devising futuristic schemes.

Using this approach to explain the behavior of the types within the centers gives us an alternative to the fixation-oriented approach, which relies on the idea that initial-position types (2-5-8) are *overexpressing* the energy of the center, center-position types (3-6-9) are *denying* or *repressing* it, and last-position types are *underexpressing* it. Language like this makes it hard to see the types in a positive light.

Another way to account for differences in the middle-position types (3-6-9) is by thinking of them from an energetic point of view as "black holes" at the midpoint of a miniature universe. The midpoints would be the "anti-matter" that holds the matter around it in place. This view accords with the Gurdjieffian idea that the inner triangle is the force that stabilizes the dynamic activity of the hexad.

One last way to look at the centers is in terms of the role they play in the involutionary/evolutionary cycle discussed in Chapter 7. We saw that involution occurs on the right hand side of the enneagram and evolution on the left. Now if we look at the location of the energy centers, we can see that the Heart Center is on the side of the enneagram, which is feminine/involutionary. This makes sense, since it's the feminine impulse that brings forth new life, nurtures it, and animates the material world. The Head Center is on the side of the enneagram that is masculine/evolutionary. This also makes sense, since it's the masculine impulse that implements objective standards, evaluates acts according to those standards, and rejects anything that doesn't make the grade. The Body/Gut Center straddles both sides, bringing them together by focusing our attention on the ethics that govern our acts—Ones by trying to establish standards that promote ethical behavior, Eights by acting in accordance with their personal code of honor, and Nines by acting in ways that promote group harmony. So from this point of view, the three energy centers symbolize the balancing of two great forces within creation (masculine and feminine) via ethical action.

However we view them, the energy centers play a major role in enneagram theory because they're like three "mega-types" out of which the nine individual types emerge. If we think of the enneagram *circle* as "the one , we can think of the *centers* as "the three" and the *types* as "the nine." This basic configuration of circle-center-type is central to our understanding of the enneagram as a system.

¤ ¤ ¤

Now that we've looked at the enneagram, the types, and the type connections, we're ready to zero in on the enneagram subtypes. Most of what has been published on the subtypes is mainly descriptive and therefore limited in scope. To really understand the subtypes, we need to delve deeper—to understand how the subtype teachings have been formulated and why the current formulations aren't really compatible with a depathologized perspective. That's the focus of the first half of Chapter 9. The second half of the chapter describes an alternative framework for working with the enneagram, the types, and the subtypes—an approach that allows us to focus more on potentials than problems.

Introducing the subtypes

In the end, the only thing you'll really own is your story. I just try to live a good one.
— An Aussie drover from the film *Australia*, 2008

As I WAS SITTING DOWN to write this chapter, a friend came by my house. She said, "I found a book I think you might like." She handed me *Listening is an Act of Love,** by Dave Isey. Even before opening it, I wanted to read it. "What a wonderful title!," I thought.

The book is about StoryCorps, a project started a few years ago by author Dave Isey. As the book jacket tells us, StoryCorps began with a simple idea: that "everyone has an important story to tell." Isey thinks we spend too much time focusing on the stories of celebrities and not enough looking at the stories of the ordinary, everyday people. To remedy this omission, he began traveling around in a mobile recording studio and collecting stories from anybody who would talk to him. In this way, he's managed to amass a database of thousands of stories from people all over the country.

Isey says he expected the stories to be interesting. What he didn't expect was that the stories would be so unique. He thought that after a while, they might all start to sound the same. But they never did. No two stories were alike. What they share in common is their ability to move us, motivate us, and open our hearts.

---

* The full title is *Listening is an Act of Love: A Celebration of Life from the StoryCorps Foundation* (2007).

Studs Terkel said of the book that "this is the kind of book that makes people feel like they count." Harvard professor Robert Coles tells us that it's "the presentation of a people's mind, heart, and soul." One Amazon reviewer notes that "Storycorps is preserving our oral history."

Such a simple idea: collecting people's stories—but something overlooked until now, except perhaps by anthropologists or psychoanalysts. But the stories collected by scholars are seldom valued for themselves, but only for what they reveal. For the anthropologist, stories record the traditions of a culture, so they provide the means by which its customs can be studied. For the psychoanalyst, stories reveal the inner workings of the analysand's psyche. In neither case do the stories themselves actually matter.

But in real life, stories *do* matter. If we don't tell our stories, we lose an opportunity to enrich other people. If we don't listen to the stories of others, we lose an opportunity to enrich ourselves. Either way, there's a loss—a loss of *soul*.

But before we can tell our story, we have to *live* our story. We have to create our story out of the substance of who we are. One way or another, we'll all live *some* kind of story. But if we don't know ourselves very well (either by chance or choice), we may have a hard time living out the kind of story that's really worth telling.

One of the main reasons I study the enneagram is to better understand the stories that people live. Of course, I'm interested in my own personal story, but I'm also interested in the stories of other people—and in the stories we create together in our families, communities, and world. My interest in the enneagram subtypes arises out of my love of story and my interest in working with the enneagram from a more "storied" perspective.

But the 27 subtypes, like the types, are seldom taught from a storied perspective. The ego-versus-essence idea is always lurking in the background, interfering with our ability to envision the subtypes as sources of insight. Chapter 9 shows us why—and what we can do to approach the subtypes in a way that allows them to help us find our myths and tell our stories.

¤ ¤ ¤

ALTHOUGH BRIEF DESCRIPTIONS of the subtypes can be found in a number of books,* longer descriptions are hard to come by. Most of what exists is in one of two semi-published works: Katherine Chernick-Fauvre's *Instinctual Subtypes* and Peter O'Hanrahan's *Enneagram Work*. I call them semi-publications because they're essentially a collection of observations on the subtypes that would require upgrading to be put out as full-fledged publications. Both works are nevertheless interesting as they stand, especially as historical archives that tell us the origins of subtype theory. Chernick-Fauvre has also collected descriptive data based on comments from people about their subtype; O'Hanrahan has focused on the link between somatic factors and the types/subtypes. The *Enneagram Monthly* is another source of material on the subtypes, although not all the published articles cover new ground. However, one article of special note is Gloria Davenport's three-part historical survey of subtype teachings (*Enneagram Monthly*, May – July/Aug. 2001); we'll take a further look at it shortly.

It's my guess that there have been no published books that delve deeply into the subtypes because the theory upon which they're based is so confusing. The ideas seem to make sense if we don't look very deeply at the material. But if we poke and prod, we discover problems that are hard to resolve.

Three things seem clear: (a) the subtypes are part of the original body of Ichazo-Naranjo teachings; (b) the subtypes can tell us something about how the types function in three spheres of life (personal, creative, and social); and (c) we each have a dominant subtype, which is why we can call ourselves a "Social Two" or "Self-preservation Five."

Beyond that, the water gets murky. If we ask someone in the enneagram community about the subtypes, we'll probably be informed that the subtypes are instinctual drives and that the drive that is most dominant for a given individual is the one that's most out of balance. We might hear that the pure energy of the drive becomes distorted as the result of being mixed with the passionate energy of our enneagram type, the result being a compulsive sense of craving or desire that can never really be satisfied.

---

* Examples include Riso & Hudson's *Wisdom of the Enneagram* (1999), Maitri's *Spiritual Dimensions of the Enneagram* (2001), Palmer's *Enneagram in Love & Work* (1995), and Condon's *Enneagram Movie & Video Guide* (1999).

Using this logic, the very fact that we have a dominant subtype is a problem—an indication that our behavior is driven by some sort of deficiency motivation. There's really no way to avoid the conclusion that the 27 subtype profiles represent 27 forms of inadequate functioning (whether we call them energy imbalances, psychological neuroses, character disorders, or spiritual delusions).

That's subtype theory in a nutshell. If you find this conclusion hard to accept (or the logic hard to follow), you're not alone. These negative assumptions about the subtypes are based on a theory of human motivation that is not only negative but convoluted, as we will see. That's why most people who teach the subtypes don't get into the theory very deeply. Subtype teachers simply give it a brief nod before providing the material that people find useful: the 27 subtype descriptions. For most of us, the value of the subtypes lies in these subtype descriptions, because they're so much more specific than the type descriptions.

But without a well-constructed, internally-consistent theory on which to base our study of the subtypes, we have no way to move beyond a one-dimensional understanding. And no way to depathologize them, either. So I'm going to spend a few pages describing the theory, such as it is, starting with a look at the thinking that underlies it. That's the first things that Robert Cloninger did when he went to write a book about positive psychology: to examine the philosophical underpinnings that influence our current ideas about human nature.

Author of *Feeling Good: The Science of Well-Being*, (2004). Cloninger is one of a new breed of positive psychologists that includes Martin Seligman (*Authentic Happiness,* 2002), Mihaly Czikszentmihalyi (*Flow: The Psychology of Optimal Experience*, 1990), and Robert Holden (*Happiness Now!*, 2004). Such investigators have done a number of experiments which show that "thinking positive" brings people greater happiness than "thinking negative."

In Chapter 1, Cloninger contrasted the ideas of very positive and very negative philosophers to see how they differ. He found that positive philosophers such as Plato,

Al-Ghazali, Abelard, and Gandhi share the conviction that human behavior arises out of motives that are essentially growth-oriented in nature. Even when we make evil choices, positive philosophers say it's out of ignorance, not because we have evil within us (p. 10). Conversely, negative philosophers such as Protagorus, Machiavelli, and Hume embrace the dualistic idea that there is no underlying unity to life and that human action arises out of motives that are purely selfish in nature.

Cloninger cites Sigmund Freud as a prime example of a negative philosopher who has had a big impact on modern life. He notes that Freudian psychology is based on "a mechanical, dualistic, and rationalistic view of the world" (p. 26) and reminds us that Freud believed that it was impossible for human beings either to love their neighbor as themselves or to be permanently happy (p. 27).

Anyone who studies Freud knows that he was an atheist who sought to explain human behavior solely by reference to instinctual drives (most notably, sexual libido), which is why there's no way to reconcile his ideas with any sort of spiritual philosophy. In addition, Freud's intolerance for dissenting views made it impossible to dialog with him; he considered his ideas to be akin to dogma and would punish analysts who departed from them with total ostracism. That's what happened to Carl Jung after he dared to imply that sexual libido might not the sole source of unconscious motivation.

Unfortunately, the ideas of Freud have had a big impact on the personality enneagram, which is one reason the types are usually presented in such a negative light. Negative philosophy totally permeates the ego-versus-essence paradigm upon which enneagram teachings are based. There are four separate but related streams of thought that inform our ideas about the types and subtypes:

- Freudian theory (*which is biologically-deterministic and focused on deficiency motivation*)
- Object Relations theory (*based on neo-Freudian theories of personality development that have been empirically discredited*)
- Cartesian dualism (*which directly pits non-spiritual impulses against spiritual impulses, giving rise to an ego-versus-essence approach*)
- Marxism (*which tells us that we can't trust our judgment as individuals*)

Below I explain how this works, but before doing so, I want to make the point that none of these ideas are either empirical facts nor the products of divine revelation. They are philosophies developed by fallible human beings based on their subjective views of life and human nature. This may seem obvious, but it's my experience that philosophical ideas can become entrenched in a way that makes them hard to recognize as subjective. In the case of the enneagram, they've become so much a part of the fabric of our thought that we now find it hard to separate fact from opinion. So it's useful to take a look at subtype theory as it has been presented in the past, with the goal of understanding both its key tenets and the subjective influences that have colored its interpretation.

¤ ¤ ¤

IT SEEMS CLEAR that the subtypes were first taught at Ichazo's original Arica Retreat in 1970. Although early literature on the enneagram is sparse (and mentions of the subtypes even sparser), there *is* a brief description of them in Lilly & Hart's article, "The Arica Training."* In this article, they describe what we would now call subtypes as "ego games" that arise out of the need to satisfy three kinds of instinctual desires: *conservation* (the desire to satisfy our bodily, emotional, and intellectual appetites), *syntony* (the desire to satisfy our sexual appetites), and *social interaction* (the desire to satisfy our need to feel like members of a larger group).

According to the Arica teachings, these ego games must be replaced by alternative modes of behavior:

▸ Conservation (*aka* the distorted self-preservation instinct) must give way to "simple living...where each would give according to his ability and receive according to his needs."

▸ Syntony (*aka* the distorted sexual instinct)† must give way to "freedom for everyone with regard to sexual needs."

▸ The distorted social instinct must give way to "a happy, easy family, completely open to one another, essence open to essence."

---

* Published in Charles Tart's *Transpersonal Psychologies* (1975).

† My dictionary defines syntony as "a condition in which two oscillating circuits have the same resonance." So it's not hard to see why it might be a synonym for sexuality.

These statements seem vague, even substanceless. As described, "simple living" sounds like Marxist living; sexual freedom sounds like a hippie ideal; and the idea of living in a "happy, easy family" (which will happen by way of "the communes that have been started")* sounds like a pipe dream. What could this possibly mean? What would an "essence to essence" relationship actually look like?

Such formulations can't withstand any serious scrutiny. But 40 years ago, they didn't have to. People were seeking a new way of life, and ego was seen as the chief barrier blocking the way. However, from this point of view, it isn't just ego but *ego informed by distorted instinct* that deprives us of the ability to experience essence (or to have "essence-to-essence" relationships with others). In a 1973 interview, Oscar Ichazo tell us how he thinks that exposing ego games will transform our lives :

> When the ego is broken essence quite naturally takes over. The collapse comes at the moment when the ego games are completely exposed and understood: illusion is shattered; subjectivity is destroyed; karma is burned.†

Elsewhere in the same interview, Ichazo says that ego is made up of three connecting parts (intellectual, emotional, and movement). Therefore, any effort to "break the ego" must address the influence of ego in all three areas.‡

It's interesting that Ichazo never used the word *subtype* in this interview; nor did he publish anything about the subtypes in any known source. The teachings we inherited came to us indirectly, through those who attended the Arica workshop. It's not until 23 years later that we have a published record of Ichazo's comments on the topic, in a 1996 interview with *Enneagram Monthly* (*EM*) editors Jack Labanauskas and Andrea Isaacs.§

---

* p. 349. Elsewhere, the authors note that Arica seems to discourage "exclusive unions and the family scene," and to regard the raising of children as the responsibility of the group, not the responsibility of parents (p. 350). These are controversial ideas that few people in mainstream society would be likely to embrace, which is probably one reason that Arica is said to have to have objected to Harper & Row's publication of the Lilly & Hart article in 1986 (see p. 510 in "Owning Enlightenment," *Buffalo Law Review*, by Walter Efross, 51-3, 2003).

† "Breaking the Tyranny of the Ego," in *Interviews with Oscar Ichazo* (1982), p. 20.

‡ The alert reader will notice that he's talking about the three Energy Centers (Head, Heart, and Body/Gut) discussed in Chapter 8.

§ November 1996.

Unfortunately, his comments—like much of his writing—seem so cryptically abstruse that it's difficult to follow his line of thought.* However, the fact that Ichazo speaks of two opposing drives—sexual and spiritual—reveals his continuing tendency to think of motivation in dualistic, oppositional terms.†

As Ichazo's student, Claudio Naranjo takes a similar tack. But he fortunately provides us with more information to work with. In *Character and Neurosis*, he tells us that there are two kinds of motivation—instinctual and spiritual—and that instinctual desire can be expressed in three ways:

> *The theory presented here acknowledges three basic instincts and goals behind the multiplicity of human behavior (purely spiritual motivation excluded): survival, pleasure, and relationship* (p. 9).

These three instinctual desires correspond to the subtype arenas (survival = self-preservation subtype, pleasure = sexual subtype, relationship= social subtype). On the same page, Naranjo mentions Karl Marx as emphasizing the first desire, Sigmund Freud the second, and Object Relations (neo-Freudian) theorists the third, noting that no one until now has "embraced a view that explicitly integrates these three fundamental drives"—no one, that is, until Naranjo. He's the one who would obviously like to develop such a model. His favorable references to Marx, Freud, and Neo-Freudian thinkers such as Melanie Klein, Alfred Adler, and Karen Horney (p. 8) suggests that these are the thinkers with whom he resonates (none of whom would likely wind up on Cloninger's list of positively-oriented philosophers).

---

* What is especially confusing is that, at some point in the 26 years that elapsed between the time that the original subtype teachings were given and the *EM* interview, Ichazo appears to have altered his approach to the subtypes, such that by 1996, he posits the existence of three instincts—self-preservation, relational, and adaptational—and two opposing drives/poles: the sexual and spiritual. But his discussion on them does little to clarify what he is talking about (e.g., to clarify the difference between an instinct and a drive or to explain the relationship between his original and revised theories). This is probably why I have yet to encounter an enneagram teacher who modified his approach to subtype theory based on these remarks.

† I should add that I have no problem with dualism as long as it's seen as something natural that exists within a larger whole (as we see with the yin-yang symbol). My objection is to divisive dualism, which splits the world into good vs bad categories, and then seeks to eradicate what is bad.

Fig. 9-1 depicts Naranjo's view of the self (adapted from a graphic on p. 8 in *Character and Neurosis*). It shows us a psyche divided up into two realms—a lower "personality" realm and a higher "essence" realm. As depicted here, personality is inferior to essence and can never be reconciled with it. In fact, the two actively oppose one another. If there were any doubt of this, they are completely erased by Naranjo's reference to a "Holy War" between our lower (personality) nature and higher (essential) nature (p. 9).

From such statements, we might have the impression that Naranjo sees personality as the product of debased instincts; if so, his position would be similar to the religious ascetics who saw the desire for bodily pleasure as the source of all our spiritual problems. But he seems reluctant to point the finger at instinctual desires as the reason for our woes. Why is this? I suspect it's because Naranjo's point of view is heavily informed by 1960s values, and the free-love ethos of 1960s favored bodily pleasures. So he has to look elsewhere to explain why our "lower" self is neurotically debased. And where does he look? To the debased passions said to arise from the ego, which is equated with our enneagram type.

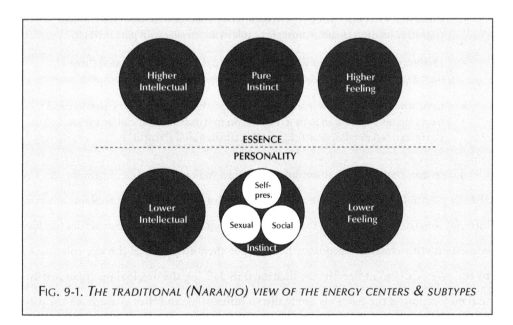

FIG. 9-1. *THE TRADITIONAL (NARANJO) VIEW OF THE ENERGY CENTERS & SUBTYPES*

So for Naranjo, it's not really instinct which is the true enemy in the Holy War against the false or lower self—it's the deficiency motivation created by "the 'passionate' drives [of the lower emotional center] that contaminate, repress, and stand in the place of instinct." To pinpoint the precise nature of our "passionate drives," we need to know our character (enneagram) type. According to Naranjo, here's how type interacts with subtype:

> There are nine basic character types...Each of these exists, in turn, in three varieties according to the dominant intensity of the self-preservation, sexual, or social drives (and the presence of specific traits that are a consequence of a "passional" distortion of the corresponding instinct which is "channeled" and "bound" under the influence of the individual's dominant passion). There are of course nine possible dominant passions and each is associated to [sic] a characteristic cognitive distortion [fixation] (p. 12-13).

Here's how I would summarize Naranjo's ideas, along with what we could logically conclude if we accept his premises:

- *Premise 1:* Motivation can be either instinctual or spiritual, but most motivation is instinctual

- *Premise 2:* Instinctual motivation is almost invariably distorted (due to the influence of the type-related passion)

- *Premise 3:* For each ennea-type, a distorted passion is also associated with a cognitive fixation (so both must play a role in interfering with pure instinct)

- *Premise 4:* We express our distorted instinctual motivation through three drives (self-preservation, sexual, and social), especially our dominant drive

- *Conclusion:* Because few if any people escape the influence of the passion and fixation, most of human action is based on motivations that can be variously characterized as false, neurotic, or ethically debased ("sinful")

There are a number of observations we can make about this argument. As I've already pointed out, it's negative and dualistic. But it has a bigger problem: a lack of internal consistency. It rests on the proposition that motivation is instinctual (an idea consistent with classical Freudian theory), but then emphasizes the key role played by the passions (and indirectly, the fixations) in defiling the original purity of instinctual motivation. If the passions are really so influential, and they come from the nine enneagram types, then how is it possible to make the claim that motivation is actually instinctual? It doesn't make sense to say that motivation is fundamentally instinctual if it is so heavily and consistently influenced by non-instinctual factors.

This is the kind of reasoning that makes Naranjo's argument hard to follow.

Then there's the question of what role, if any, is played by the cognitive fixations in distorting either the passions or the instincts. To say the fixations and passions are "associated" with one another tells us little about how they interact or which one is the primary motivator—and that is a critical omission. Another omission is any explanation as to why one of the three instinctual drives is dominant (i.e., why someone is an SP One rather than a SX One or SOC One).* Being told that the dominant drive is the one "in which the influence of the passion is strongest" tells us nothing about *why* the passion influences one drive more than the other two. Last, when it comes to the subtypes, there's so little written down about them (other than descriptions) that it's difficult to further evaluate the theory that produces the descriptions. Ichazo has published virtually nothing on the subtypes and Naranjo, only a few passages, half of which have already been quoted; the rest are in *Character and Neurosis*, pp. 105 and 160, and in *The Enneagram of Society*, 2004, pp. 108–109 (and none of them covers new ground).

Even if we plug up these holes, nothing will change the fact that the ideas arise out of a negative, dualistic philosophy of life. However much we de-emphasize the negativity—by creating less negative type/subtype descriptions, focusing on ways to dis-identify with type, or joking together about our type-related shortcomings—we're never going to be able to see the types from a transformational perspective until we seriously question the premises that give rise to this negative view, especially the premise that there are parts of ourselves that ought to be eradicated (rather than understood and integrated). The desire to make ego the fall guy for our failures in life isn't going to rid us of our imperfections, it's only going to drive them further into the Shadow. We move towards wholeness only when we see our imperfections as the *prima materia* that

---

* I'm using short-hand designations here for the subtypes: SP One = Self-preservation One, SX One = Sexual One, and SOC One = Social One.

helps us literally "re-form" ourselves. This is why Gurdjieff says we need our chief fault [feature] in order to do transformational work*—and it's why Jung tells us that "we cannot slay our incapacity and rise above it," further admonishing us that "no one should deny it, find fault with it, or shout it down."†

Be that as it may, the Ichazo-Naranjo approach remains the guiding paradigm for the enneagram community, so we need to understand how it affects the way that people teach the subtypes. If we look back to the 1970s, we find the subtype teachings being imparted, along with other enneagram teachings, to a select group in Berkeley by Naranjo and his student, Kathleen Speeth. As far as I can determine, the subtype teachings imparted at that time are essentially the same subtype teachings presented today.

These teachings reflect the view expressed above that our dominant subtype is the one where the passion of our type is most pronounced; see, e.g., the subtype descriptions of first-generation enneagram teachers such as Sandra Maitri (*Spiritual Dimensions of the Enneagram*, 2000, p. 264); Helen Palmer (*The Enneagram*, 1988, pp. 49–51); and Don Riso and Russ Hudson (*The Wisdom of the Enneagram*, 1999, pp. 70–71) .

During the 1990s, a second generation of subtype teachers began to emerge, most notably Katherine Chernick-Fauvre, Tom Condon, and Mario Sikora. Although the actual theory remained the same, there's a noticeable softening of tone among second-generation teachers, who tend to focus on what Condon calls the "high side" of the subtypes in his interview with the *Enneagram Monthly* in June 1999. Chernick-Fauvre and her husband David Fauvre also tend in workshops to focus on what makes the subtypes distinct (rather than emphasizing the idea that they are ego distortions). Mario Sikora uses subtype descriptions to help business professionals type themselves and gain insight into potentially problematic patterns of behavior.

Sikora's work is interesting in that it departs somewhat from the original model by implying that it's natural for subtype motivation to be instinctual (biologically-based), a position based on Richard Dawkins' "selfish gene" idea. In this way, he manages to

---

* *In Search of the Miraculous* (2001), p. 226.

† *The Red Book* (2009), p. 240.

sidestep the whole issue of distorted passions and cognitive fixations. By using a bio-logical model, Sikora can just assume that our actions arise out of the need to prop-agate the species. The only question is that, How does type come into the picture? Sikora says it's a cognitive strategy for dealing with the world, but that doesn't tell us how type motivation differs from instinctual motivation or precisely how the two interact. Most pointedly, it doesn't tell us which one is most basic. Do our instincts determine our cognitive strategies, or vice-versa? And why do we have one dominant strategy (type) or dominant instinct (subtype)? Questions like these have got to be addressed to have a fully-specified theory of motivation.

Admittedly, these are tough questions to answer. It's difficult to critique a theory that is both vague and abstruse, especially if we wish to avoid challenging the basic premise that *enneagram type = ego fixation*. Even if we're willing to drop this premise (or at least leave it open to question), the moment that we attempt to take a really close look at subtype theory, we encounter the theoretical quagmire I've been de-scribing here. Maybe that's why many people simply accept certain propositions as givens and focus mainly on describing subtype differences.

Nevertheless, questions remain. In May 2001, Gloria Davenport wrote an excel-lent three-part article on the subtypes for the *Enneagram Monthly* trying to resolve some of the more troubling questions (or at least to point out that they exist). But she says that although she searched for answers, the search only raised more questions, such as these:

> What is the connection between the ego's passions, fixations, and the subtypes? How does the passion of each type "mess up" the dominant instinct?...And why do we proudly announce to the world our dominant instinct and type [if they are based on fixation]?

I know how she feels, because I had the same questions. My answer is that these questions persist because the existing theory isn't adequate to resolve them. It takes a lot of unraveling before we can understand what's going on.

Although Davenport doesn't answer the questions she raises, she does provide an excellent summary of what we know about the subtypes and how they have been taught, mentioning the views of the major subtype teachers, among them Peter O'Hanrahan. It turns out that he has some interesting and innovative things to say about them.

O'Hanrahan became Kathleen Speeth's student in 1978 and became particularly interested in the instinctual aspect of the subtypes—in their body-based, energetic nature. But he also became interested in the subtypes from an archetypal perspective. I wasn't really aware of his interest in the archetypes before doing research for this book, probably because he speaks of them in print mainly in his unpublished collection of articles, *Enneagram Work* (2003), and then only briefly. Nevertheless, he touches upon an approach that seems quite similar to the one I'm advocating here.

O'Hanrahan begins his discussion on the subtypes by observing that there are several different ways we can view them. One way is as behavioral patterns that are the outcome of mixing the energy of the dominant passion with the instincts. A second way is as the product of early childhood experiences, as described by Object Relations theory. Both of these positions are no doubt derived from his work with Speeth and Naranjo. A third way to view the subtypes, he says, is as the "intersection of archetype and biology," where the enneagram types are seen as archetypes, whose spirit infuses and shapes us in various ways and instincts provide the biological impetus for our acts. In a communication with Gloria Davenport, O'Hanrahan called the archetype a "daimonic spirit (a soul companion or guardian angel) that infuses our life."* This third interpretation represents a significant departure from Naranjo's theory of the subtypes.

O'Hanrahan's third interpretation is so close to my own that it's hard to tell the difference. But O'Hanrahan hedges his bets in his discussion, putting forth this idea as nothing more than a possibility, probably because he's in the difficult spot of trying to reconcile all the opposing positions. (I tried to do the same but ultimately found it an impossible task, because they make radically different assumptions about human nature.)

¤ ¤ ¤

---

* In the original, it reads *demonic*, but I substituted *daimonic* because it better fits the context.

IT'S VERY DIFFICULT to go up against the prevailing enneagram paradigm, both because it's so well-established and because Ichazo and Naranjo are such iconic figures. They are the ones who originally introduced people to the enneagram—and the enneagram is a powerful tool. I think it's because the enneagram is such a powerful tool that we're inclined to accept what its original teachers said about the system as implicitly true, especially if we regard it as "received wisdom." But I would argue that even received wisdom is open to interpretation, because no set of ideas is totally objective; ideas always come through the subjective filter of human consciousness (as the enneagram illustrates). So I would take the position that it's good to raise questions and devise models based upon our own individual understanding.

With that in mind, I'd like to propose a model that is in harmony with a perspective grounded in the ideas of Jung and other individuals discussed throughout this book. Its key premises are summarized below.

1. **Human motivation is wholistic, not dualistic**
   (so it can't be divided into "higher" versus "lower" types of motivation)

2. **All motivation is ultimately spiritual**
   (so there is no motivation originating at the level of either the ego or the instincts)

3. **Motivation becomes individualized at the level of the archetypes**

4. **The nine enneagram types = nine master archetypes**

5. **When we're born, we embody the energy of one master archetype**
   *(which means that our enneagram type is **innate**, not acquired)*

6. **The energy is mediated through three energy centers** *(Body, Heart, Head)*

7. **The energy is channeled into three main stages for activity in life, one of which is most attractive** *(= our dominant subtype arena)*

8. **The enneagram subtypes = 27 individual profiles** *created when the energy of our type is expressed in our dominant subtype arena*

9. **Becoming aware of our subtype helps us be "in sync" with our deepest motivational impulses;** *we're then better able to embody those impulses (to **ensoul** them)*

Now let's imagine how this process might work. We have to start by imagining ourselves as spiritual beings, at the level of what has been called the Higher Self, Divine Monad, or *Atman*. When we seek embodiment as physical beings, we have to make the transition from spirit to matter—to become *ensouled in a physical body.*

Spirit is limitless, but matter is limited. So when we're born, we need some vehicle by which to limit our consciousness, so that it can function in a dense physical body. *That vehicle is our enneagram type.*

The type—which can be envisioned as a master archetype—helps us function in physical life in two ways: by preventing sensory overload and focusing our attention. The narrowing of consciousness supports our ability to be present in the moment and to maintain a stable outlook over time, both of which are necessary for optimal functioning in the physical world. The type also provides us with the foundation we need to further refine our character and deepen our self-understanding, a process that Jung refers to as *individuation.*

The energy of the type is mediated through three bodily energy centers: the instinctual, intellectual, and emotional centers. Everything we do in life requires the energy of one or more of these centers, usually all three. In infancy, the centers are not well-differentiated but become better differentiated as we gain experience in life. By mastering the ability to use these centers, we gain the ability to function as autonomous individuals and to express our individuality in diverse ways.

But our energy centers give us not only the ability to *express* energy but to *receive* it. This is a critical point, because it means that we can potentially develop our expressive abilities without having to be cut off from receptive awareness—basically, to be in a state of "ego" without sacrificing the sense of being in "essence." To accept this idea, we have to realize that both kinds of awareness are actually possible at the same time.

Receptivity gives us the ability to recognize *dharma* (the promises we've made to life); expressivity gives us the ability to inject our actions with an appropriate degree of *drama* (such that they bear the stamp of our individuality). Achieving a balance between *dharma* and drama allows us to serve life in a way that creates a balance between expressing our individuality and surrendering our personal preferences to serve the needs of life. The problem of ego mania does not constantly arise, because our receptive awareness helps us know when we need to curb our desire for self-expression.

The catch—if there is one—is that cultivating receptivity can make us aware of problems and obligations that we'd rather not acknowledge. And that's why individuation is no walk in the park: because it usually kicks us out of our comfort zone, confronting us with familiar illusions and compelling us to see through them. Shadow work takes us into the heart of our inner turmoil, where the opposites within our nature reveal themselves in ways that make them impossible to ignore. The suffering we experience can produce a terrible sense of loss and vulnerability. But it can also break up dysfunctional patterns that create emotional blocks, so it's neither meaningless nor without practical benefit. The eventual result is the ability to accept the limitations we cannot change and to transcend the limitations that are self-imposed.

As for the role of the three subtype arenas, they're a bit like the arenas of a three-ring circus—a circus we call "life"! Having three rings keeps things interesting; there's always a lot going on. We have clowns, jugglers, high wire walkers, and dangerous animals. So while a circus is fun, it's also a place where risky things happen. It demands conscious attention, especially when we're on stage.

Our dominant subtype arena is the one that seems to "pull" us towards it, to attract our interest and energy, for reasons that are mysterious, but have something to do with both our nature and our *dharma*. It's there that we can find the kinds of challenges we need to fulfill our life's purpose.

Becoming acquainted with the 27 subtypes enables us to be more consciously aware of the archetypal roles we play and the dynamics underlying them, so we can sidestep many problems and mitigate others. When really big challenges arise, we can better utilize our resources to overcome them. Most of all, we can feel like our lives really matter, because we have a greater sense of connectedness with life's larger scheme.

So to recap these ideas in brief: Type motivation is the "engine" which drives everything in our lives—that provides our energy, shapes our values, and gives us a characteristic outlook on life. It provides the raw materials that we use to construct a life. The core motivation that is synonymous with our type is essentially spiritual in origin and represents the differentiation of spirit into nine archetypal patterns that can be expressed in three major life arenas: the arena of self, sexuality/creativity, and social life. When we combine the nine types with the three arenas, we can generate 27 subtype categories, three per type. Because these profiles are more specific than type profiles, they give us a deeper insight into our individual nature. The 27 subtype categories can also be used as a jumping-off point for further explorations, because they can be used to generate "families" of both archetypal roles and life themes typical for each subtype.

Fig. 9-2 visually depicts my view of the relationship between the self, the energy centers, and the subtypes. We can compare this model to Naranjo's dualistic model on p. 121 (Fig. 9-1). While Naranjo's diagram divides the self into warring factions, mine depicts the essential unity of the self and its three (undivided) energy centers. While his diagram depicts the subtypes as three emotionally-distorted instinctual drives, mine shows them as three arenas for developing the talents we can use in service to life. All three arenas are present in each of the three centers because there's no way to meaningfully separate them: whatever we do in life, it has a physical, mental, and emotional component. (By the way, the position of the three circles has no special significance; the one on top is not superior to either of the other two.)

¤ ¤ ¤

NOW THAT WE'VE REVIEWED the literature on the subtypes and I've introduced an alternative framework for working with them, we're ready for an overview of the three subtype arenas and the 27 subtypes from a transformational perspective. The three arenas describe three domains of life:

- ▸ the **self-preservation domain** (*independence, individuality, home, family, selfhood*)
- ▸ the **sexual domain** (*intimacy, creativity, spirituality, passion, intensity*)
- ▸ the **social domain** (*social relations, community, politics, prestige, belonging*)

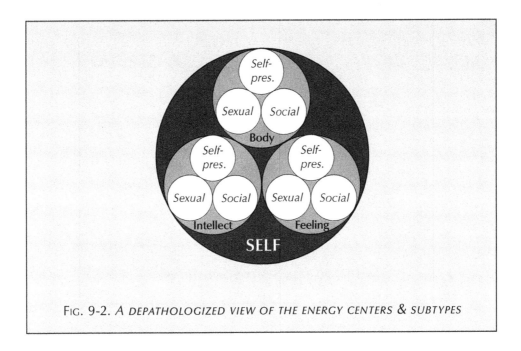

Fig. 9-2. A DEPATHOLOGIZED VIEW OF THE ENERGY CENTERS & SUBTYPES

We participate in all three arenas, but one is more dominant than the other two. Self-preservation (SP) types prefer activities that allow them to express their individuality and maintain their independence; sexual (SX) subtypes prefer intense, creative, and intimate encounters and relationships; and social (SOC) subtypes find fulfillment in group activities and look to the group as a reference point for what they do. Each subtype arena is described at greater length in Table 9-1 on page 134.

Nevertheless, some people seem to be highly dominant in more than one arena. I became aware of this possibility when I noticed that I always scored high on both SP and SX characteristics. So I conceived the idea of creating three additional "combination" subtype profiles: SP-SX, SP-SOC, and SX-SOC (see Fig. 9-3 and Table 9-2). This idea is similar though not identical to Riso and Hudson's notion of a "stacking order," in which there is a dominant, semi-dominant, and least dominant subtype (they would call it a least dominant *instinctual variant*).

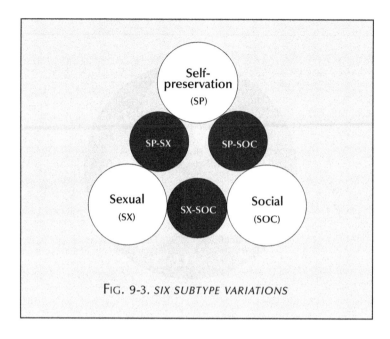

FIG. 9-3. *SIX SUBTYPE VARIATIONS*

There are a few more observations I'd like to make about the subtype arenas, mostly of which relate to the implications of seeing them from a depathologized perspective. The main one is about the terminology that we use to describe them, which doesn't fully capture what they are about. Speaking of independent-minded, self-reliant individuals as "self-preserving" (SP) types makes them sound more self-centered than other people. But in truth, SP subtypes are more focused on the practical realities of life; they're not more narcissistic, selfish, or greedy. In fact, they're usually hardworking and extremely selfless in the way they care for other people. Conversely, just because the SOC subtypes focus more on the group than the individual, that doesn't necessarily mean they are more selfless, humanitarian, etc.—it just means they express their energy in the social arena of life. And just because an individual is a SX subtype doesn't mean they're obsessed with sex—or even with personal relationships. The sexual arena is about *passion,* in the broadest sense of the word—passion expressed through creativity, absorption, the mysteries of *kundalini,* spiritual longing, Shadow work, mystical devotion, and the journey into the depths of our being. It encompasses our highest aspirations, as well as our darkest secrets.

¤ ¤ ¤

PART III EXPLORES the types and subtypes in detail, using examples drawn from life, TV, and film. But it's also helpful to see how the 27 subtypes relate to one another overall. So Table 9-3 lists some of the archetypes and social roles associated with each subtype; Table 9-4 presents brief profiles.

At this point, if you don't yet know your type or subtype, you may want to take a look at the type/subtype test at the end of this book before reading further. Then look at the subtype descriptions in Part III to further explore the key themes and roles for each subtype.

To pinpoint your subtype arena independent of type, you can take the test at the end of *The Positive Enneagram*, now also available online at www.enneagramdimensions.net.

TABLE 9-1. **THREE MAIN SUBTYPE ARENAS**

SP INDIVIDUALS are self-reliant and down-to-earth people who like their own company, take responsibility for themselves, and value their independence. When it comes to their personal security or the safety of their family, they don't take chances. They like to be in control of their lives and their immediate environment. Although they can have a pioneering attitude, they carefully consider their options before moving into unknown territory. If the unforeseen should happen, they usually have a backup plan (perhaps several!) to help things get back on track. They value dependability in others and but have little use for people who are "all show, no substance." In love, they enjoy companionship with someone they like and respect; they are usually more interested in a long-term commitment than casual romance. Because of their independence, they can get a bit lonely at times and need to be careful not to let themselves become socially isolated, especially if they work alone (quite common for this subtype).

◻ ◻ ◻

SX INDIVIDUALS are intense, magnetic, and restless. Their gaze often has a intent, penetrating quality that can makes you feel like they're looking right through you. They're always seeking something that is just out of reach, and usually have a hard time settling down to do one thing at a time or to do anything methodically. They hate to be tied down or stuck with tasks they consider boring, so they need to have work that really engages their interest. They enjoy the romantic chase, but can have difficulty hanging onto one partner for any length of time, either because of fighting, boredom, or the temptation to seek out somebody new. Sometimes they can alternate between being overly-clinging and aloof (which reflects their difficulty in sustaining a steady relationship). Although they can usually pick up a new partner with little difficulty, it can be easy for them to fall into a pattern of serial monogamy. They can have difficulty pursing a moderate course in life, but are inventive, creative individuals that can liven up any social event.

◻ ◻ ◻

SOC INDIVIDUALS are naturally at home in group settings. Although they tend to be cool, somewhat formal, and emotionally restrained, they're very attuned to group dynamics and instinctively know how to work with others. They also know how to make friends with those who share their interests, so they usually have a big network of social contacts. They're often attracted to work that focuses on social or political concerns (as organizers, networkers, or commentators), especially work that makes use of their diplomatic talents. But they don't appreciate people who are blunt, rude, or socially gauche; they see a certain degree of refinement and social restraint as essential for promoting harmony. They don't like conflict and appreciate social structures that help them avoid it. Although they're cordial, they can be hard to get to know really well, because intimacy brings with it the kind of intensity and potential for conflict that's not their cup of tea.

TABLE 9-2. **THREE SUBTYPE COMBINATIONS**

SP-SX INDIVIDUALS have the groundedness and practicality of the SP subtype combined with the restlessness and intensity of the SX subtype. They're often intensely creative individuals who have the self-discipline to getting deeply involved with creative projects for long periods of time, pouring themselves into their work. When they come up for a break, they prefer to be with one or two close companions (rather than a large group). They can find casual social contacts difficult (or tiresome) and will make some excuse to leave if they're forced into social situations they don't like. They're especially keen to avoid highly formal, social occasions like weddings (unless the bride or groom are close friends). When they're down, they'd rather be alone or with one special friend than to seek out the company of people whom they don't know very well. They tend to be somewhat unconventional, although their SP side usually keeps them financially solvent and grounded enough to avoid the extravagances often associated with SX subtypes.

¤ ¤ ¤

SP-SOC INDIVIDUALS are careful, responsible, and dependable individuals who easily adapt to the social rules and conventions of their chosen community. They think of themselves as agreeable people who are friendly but reserved, and they seek out opportunities for social interaction that don't take them too far outside of their comfort zone. So they enjoy congenial gatherings, but nothing too fancy or ostentatious. They would rather be with people they know well than strangers, and they often like to entertain at home, where they feel particularly at ease. They also like to participate in regular social events with established groups. When they approach a new group, they'll often seek out some kind of niche where they can make a special contribution without being the center of attention. They're at their best in familiar or structured surroundings but can feel like a duck out of water in situations that are unstructured, unfamiliar, or unpredictable.

¤ ¤ ¤

SX-SOC INDIVIDUALS are warm, attractive, and socially-aware. They're naturally attuned to current trends and tend to be popular with others, because their personal magnetism is paired with an innate sense of how to make a positive social impact. They know how to entertain people without going over the top—or how to facilitate a group in a way that allows everybody to enjoy the experience. Amiable and charming, they make excellent politicians, diplomats, or PR specialists, especially when times are good. Their weakness lies in their tendency to shy away from tasks that take them away from the center of the action or from relationships that might jeopardize their popularity. And their ability to charm a group can make it easy for them to rely too heavily on their winning ways (and not enough on the actual quality of their work). So they have to be careful to make sure they've got something substantive to back up their believable-sounding claims.

TABLE 9-3. SUBTYPE ARCHETYPES & SOCIAL ROLES

	SELF-PRESERVATION	SEXUAL	SOCIAL
1	Detailer, Craftsman, Pioneer, Settler, Grammarian, Editor, Civilizer, Wilderness Tamer, Budgeter, Auditor, Bookkeeper, Stern School Teacher, Sober Citizen, American Gothic	Crusader, Renunciate, Missionary, Evangelist, Confessor, Picketer, Protester, Reformer, Passionate Lover, Spiritual Counselor, Ascetic, Monk, Nun, Ranter, Demonstrator	Lawmaker, Legislator, Judge, Jurist, Rulemaker, Priest, Chief Examiner, Old Testament Prophet, Miss Manners, Arbiter, Advice Columnist, Impartial Inquisitor, Mother Superior
2	Matriarch, Guardian Angel, Doting Mother, Nurse, Cook, Best Friend, Rescuer, Diva, , Homemaker, Mother Nature, Crone, Matchmaker, Sympathetic Listener, Fairy Godmother	Romantic, Flirt, Femme Fatale, Playboy, Lothario, Madonna, Seducer, Holy Innocent, Pursuer, Stalker, Divine Prostitute, Temple Dancer, Vestal Virgin, Devotee, Saint	Diplomat, Ambassador, Organizer, Neighborhood Networker, Humanitarian, Event Host, Social Smoother, PR Consultant, Stage Mother, Bleeding Heart, Social Climber, Hidden Partner
3	Pragmatist, Achiever, Type A, Hard Worker, Go-Getter, Company Man, Trophy Wife, Hard-driving Manager, Mr. All-Work-No-Play, Comeback Kid, Soccer Mom, Careerist	Superstar, Popular Hero, Cheerleader, Football Star, Media Sensation, Aspiring Star, Venus/Adonis, Fashion Plate, Model, Manicured Professional, Feminine/Masculine Ideal	Politician, Team Leader, Early Adapter, Opinion Leader, Valedictorian, Office Seeker, First Among Equals, Spin Doctor, Master Dealer, Lobbyist, Consultant, Glosser-over
4	Artisan, Bohemian, Individualist, Weaver, Independent Learner, Persevering Seeker, Spiritual Gambler, Depth Seeker, Potter, Wounded Healer , Wordsmith Earthy Creator, Gypsy	Dramatist, Method Actor, Soulmate, Intense Lover, Pained Princess, Anti-hero, Damsel in Distress, Misunderstood Artist, Jealous Competitor, Intense Seeker, Moth to the Flame	Critic, Pundit, Public Artist, Architect, Artistic Director, Refined Elitist, Confronter, Complainer, Informer, Muckraker, Alienated Idealist, Designer, Rebel Without a Cause
5	Archivist, Thinker, Philosopher, Stuff Collecter, Amateur Scholar, Reflector, Observer, Hermit, Nerd, Recluse, Professional Student, Puzzle-solver, Tinkerer, Inventor	Wizard, Sleuth, Detective, Spy, Alchemist, Mad Scientist, Investigator, Internet Wizard, Undercover Operative, Private Tutor, Chat Room Enthusiast, Secret Society Member	Tenured Professor, Scholar, Recognized Expert, Impersonal Guide, Iconoclast, Myth Collecter, Anthropologist, Wise Man/Woman, Tribal Healer, Shaman, Bodhisattva
6	Family Preserver, Loyal Employee, Shy Friend, Concerned Parent, Warm Welcomer, Nervous Nelly, Brave Little Mouse, Obstacle Surmounter, Little Engine That Could	Scrapper, Rebel, Feisty Friend, Underdog, Fierce Warrior, Tender Defender, Defender of the Faith, Beauty Queen, Miss America, Prince Valiant, Idealistic Lover, Braveheart , Skeptic	Social Guardian, Preservationist, Historian, Social Loyalist, Community Builder, Police Officer, Member of the Military, Vigilante, True Believer, Law & Order Upholder
7	Bon Vivant, Magical Child, Fun Parent, Pastry Chef, Gourmand, Home Improver, Family Visionary, Versatile Generalist, "Good Life" Appreciator, Sensualist, Interior Decorator	Trickster, Wanderer, Dance Away Lover, Comic, Mimic, Space Cadet, Artless Charmer, Life of the Party, Rake, Addict, Dreamer, Hippie, Will O' the Wisp, Snake Charmer, Gambler, Adventurer	Visionary, Utopian, Futurist, Social Architect, Armchair Revolutionary, Winged Messenger, Angelic Herald, Courier, Networker, Trendsetter, Jetsetter, One of the Beautiful People
8	Weight Lifter, Father Figure, Protector, Heavyweight, Strong Silent Type, Sampson, Hercules, Atlas, Mountain Mama, Force of Nature, Pillar of Strength, Mother Bear	Knight Errant, God/Goddess, Master, Guru, Rescuer, Gunslinger, Pirate King, Shiva/Kali, Tyrant, Destroyer, Champion, Noble, Honor-bound Avenger, Martial Artist, Samurai	King/Queen, Patriarch, Emperor, Mafia Don, Leader of the Pack, Autocrat, CEO, Boss, Born Leader, Chieftain, Ruler, Tactician, Strategist, One of the Boys, A Real Pal
9	Comfort Seeker, Patient Endurer, Steady Worker, Nature Lover, Putterer, Person of the Land, Peasant, Serf, Herdsman, Crop Picker, Tribe Member, Cowhand, Gardener	Natural Mystic, Personal Retainer, Enjoyer of Pleasure, Merging Lover, Lost Soul, Fairy tale Lover, Receptive Friend, Fantasizer, Tabula Rasa, Tale Spinner, Lover of Love	Cooperator, Mediator, Easygoing Participant, Group Harmonizer, Assuming Facilitator, Coach, Referee, Peacemaker, Go-Between, Blender, Family Counselor, Community Member

Table 9-4. Subtype Profiles

	SELF-PRESERVATION	SEXUAL	SOCIAL
1	**Detailers**: Self-disciplined & independent workers who are seldom careless; find it hard to express emotion or just relax & have fun	**Crusaders**: Fiery, impassioned evangelists with the courage of their convictions; tend to be impulsive & jealous but also brave & determined	**Lawmakers**: The great arbiters of "what is right" & establishers of rules; strict but fair, stern but unyielding in the face of social pressure
2	**Matriarchs**: Loving nurturers who like to care for the young, sick or helpless. Can find it hard to ask for help directly but secretly hope for special treatment	**Romantics**: Attracted to the chase but can find long-term relationships more challenging; have to be careful not to "fall in love with love" or over-adapt to the needs of their partner	**Diplomats**: Social finesse & organizational skills allow them to excel as social smoothers, organizers & emissaries of goodwill
3	**Pragmatists**: Ambitious Type A strivers who make financial security & success a priority; can find it hard to tear themselves away from work	**Superstars**: Dazzle the crowd with their "star" quality but can have difficulty when they step off-stage; need to trade in image to experience intimacy	**Politicians**: Skilled image creators who like the public eye ; excel as "first among equals" but must focus on substance not just style
4	**Artisans**: Independent creators who often work alone to manifest their creative vision; tend to view survival more as metaphorical than literal	**Dramatists**: Intense, self-dramatizing & high-strung individualists with an intensely competitive streak but often considerable artistic talent	**Critics**: Discriminating evaluators of art & ideas who are sensitive to social standards & thus conflicted about expressing their opinions outright
5	**Archivists**: Shy & detached collectors of ideas as well as "stuff"; establish boundaries to protect their space; often open up to small children	**Wizards**: Mysterious & secretive individuals with a few special contacts & unique powers of perception; may be monastic or live alone "in the depths"	**Professors**: Investigators of curiosities & teachers with unusual insights; enjoy social recognition but can use it to ward off intimacy
6	**Family Preservers**: Warm & supportive family protectors who make their homes a haven from the world; see family as their greatest asset	**Scrappers**: Feisty defenders of the weak & lovers of creativity; can over-idealize those they love and be overly skeptical of strangers or new ideas	**Guardians**: Loyal upholders of traditional values & enforcers of community norms; must cultivate independence to avoid true believerism
7	**Bon Vivants**: Joyful celebrators of life & sensual pleasures who often embrace unconventional lifestyles or family styles	**Tricksters**: Appealing wanderers with a charming air & "love 'em & leave 'em" tendencies; wonderfully adaptable but hard to pin down	**Visionaries**: Imaginative planners who can envision a better future & sometimes sacrificially limit themselves to fulfill their plans
8	**Weight Lifters**: Strong independent survivors who "secure the perimeter" to protect loved ones; like to lay in supplies for potential emergencies.	**Knights**: Upholders of honor & protector of the weak, they secretly yearn to experience surrender & experience vulnerability with a trusted partner	**Leaders**: Inspirational figures who lead by example but must exercise self-restraint in order to support rather than oppose authority
9	**Comfort Seekers**: Calm & steady homebodies who love to putter around & do things at home; things can pile up & time management can become a challenge	**Mystics**: Unusual receptivity & a love of nature allow them to feel at one with their surroundings but can make it hard to establish personal ego boundaries	**Cooperators**: Harmonious participators who enjoy blending into the group but can blend in too much (& also use the group to avoid inner work)

Part III

The Subtypes

10

Types, subtypes & archetypes

Our life's a stage, a comedy: either learn to play and take it lightly, or bear its troubles patiently.
– Palladas

TO UNDERSTAND THE SUBTYPES, we need to understand the world of creation. And the world of creation is dramatic—naturally so. It's full of mysterious threads that weave the isolated events of our lives into a purposeful whole. Robert Johnson calls these threads the *slender threads*, and says that they're "the patterns that give meaning to our existence...the mysterious forces that guide us and shape who we are."* These threads can also be seen as archetypes, themes, paths, or roles. Whatever we call them, they're central to life. Without them, we lose our way, our ability to feel like life really matters. We also lose the ability to participate in life's drama with any real sense of conviction.

It's easy to lose conviction in a world devoid of mystery and magic, a world stripped down to its bare scientific essentials, bereft of art, beauty, myth, or drama. So it's not a surprise that drama has lost its meaning—and that it's become common to equate drama with melodrama, that false brand of drama contrived to artificially "pump up" the natural tension in life, often for exploitative purposes, e.g., gaining personal attention, selling products on TV, providing cheap thrills, or hooking us on daytime soap operas.

But melodrama is not drama. Real drama is something natural that arises out of the dynamic play of the opposites, giving our lives definition and tone. It says,

_____
* *Balancing Heaven and Earth* (1998), p. *xi.*

"this is different than that," challenging us to see the unity underlying all apparent differences. Whether these differences may be subtle or stark, they're definitely not artificial. They have a quality of depth and meaning that's missing in melodramatic imitations. (Compare the depressingly obvious dramas in tear-jerking made-for-TV movies and the stories that unfold in great films like *To Kill a Mockingbird*, *The Bridge Over the River Kwai*, or *The Queen*).

Melodrama is to *drama* what *caricature* is to *character*: a parody.

What makes real drama *real* is its organic development, the way it naturally grows out of a real-life situation. Maybe we're caught between two conflicting desires (the desire for two different careers, partners, or places to live); maybe we're faced with a health problem that requires serious attention; maybe we made a mistake that needs correcting; or maybe we're just experiencing a sense of malaise with life. Whatever is happening, it's not something we're able to ignore or rationalize. As the tension builds, the oppositions come more and more sharply into focus—and a real-life drama begins to unfold.

The greatest dramas are those that take us out of the realm of everyday reality (ego consciousness) into the realms of both spirit and *soul*, thereby making life a three-dimensional experience. But this does not happen all that easily, because there are barriers to break through in both directions. These barriers are a good thing, because we need them in order to maintain psychological homeostasis, especially when the ego self is weak or unformed. This is one reason why both young children and mentally disturbed adults need a routine: because they don't have the kind of ego strength and flexibility that permits self-regulation.

But an ego self that's psychologically secure is able to tolerate a certain amount of stress. When individuals with stable egos encounter problems, they don't immediately fall apart, project the problem onto other people, or duck out on the situation. They hold onto the energy of the situation without immediately reacting to it. As the tension builds (and the drama develops), they retain the flexibility they need to adapt to changing conditions. When adaptation is no longer possible (that is, when the situation is at the point of maximum tension), they continue to remain engaged, which allows the tension to build to a point of breakthrough. At that moment, people are suddenly both drawn upwards towards spirit (through intense aspiration) and downwards towards *soul* (through deep surrender). Life becomes something more than it was a moment earlier—and so do they.

Think of a mother caring for a sick child. She prays intently for her child's recovery while caring for him day and night, despite her growing exhaustion. Her intense desire for her children's recovery lifts her upwards into the zone of spiritual aspiration while her physical and emotional exhaustion carry her downwards into the vale of *soulmaking*. If she's not very stable, the experience can be psychologically destabilizing, and she becomes a figure of pathos, because she can't go either very high or low before she begins to unravel. But if she's sufficiently grounded and her love outweighs everything else, she may be carried farther and farther into both the depths and the heights, while at the same time remaining an ordinary human being with whom we can readily identify.

That's the stuff of which great drama is made.*

If we look at the nine types from a dramatic point of view, we'll find a rich array of archetypal conflicts that arise out of type-related differences. Although all the types obviously have different perspectives, some type-related interactions tend to be more oppositional while others tend to be more harmonious. Classic type oppositions are listed below.

- ▸ **Type 1 vs Type 2** – justice vs mercy
  (*following the letter of the law vs making merciful exceptions to the law*)

- ▸ **Type 1 vs Type 3** – effectiveness vs efficiency
  (*getting every detail done right vs getting the job done*)

- ▸ **Type 1 vs Type 5** – ethics vs science
  (*adopting a principled vs scientific perspective*)

- ▸ **Type 1 vs Type 6** – loyalty to the law vs loyalty to the group
  (*adopting a principled vs collective perspective*)

- ▸ **Type 1 vs Type 7** – rules vs fun
  (*basing actions on whether they are correct or enjoyable*)

---

* See also the discussion of high drama versus melodrama in Chapter 14.

▶ **Type 1 vs Type 8** – impersonal vs personal justice
(seeking justice based on codified law vs personal standards of retribution)

▶ **Type 2 vs Type 4** – extroverted warmth vs introverted intensity
(valuing social relationships vs a relationship with the inner self)

▶ **Type 2 vs Type 5** – emotional bonding vs intellectual exchange
(relationship based on emotional mutuality vs intellectual exchange)

▶ **Type 2 vs Type 7** – romance vs fascination
(basing our interests on the potential for sharing vs mental fascination)

▶ **Type 3 vs Type 4** – practicality vs authenticity
(acting out of practical considerations vs the desire for meaning & authenticity)

▶ **Type 3 vs Type 6** – ambition vs caution
(extroverted decisiveness vs introverted thoroughness)

▶ **Type 3 vs Type 7** – work vs play
(channeling energy towards results-oriented vs experientially-stimulating activities)

▶ **Type 3 vs Type 8** – focused effort vs effortless focus (work vs strength)
(achieving results via effortful action vs innate force)

▶ **Type 3 vs Type 9** – scheduled time vs timeless flow
(living according to schedules vs living in the moment)

▶ **Type 4 vs Type 6** – authenticity vs community
(focusing more on one's inner convictions vs the shared beliefs of the community)

▶ **Type 4 vs Type 7** – artistic intensity vs artful dodging
(expressing artistry with emotional intensity vs playful lightness)

▶ **Type 4 vs Type 8** – extreme surrender vs extreme dominance
(feeling that "I am nothing" vs feeling that "I am everything")

▶ **Type 5 vs Type 7** – deep thinking vs quick thinking
(arriving at ideas via pondered rationality vs lightning-fast impressions)

▶ **Type 6 vs Type 7** – duty vs fun
(basing our actions on loyalty to the group vs the desire for interest & innovation)

▶ **Type 6 vs Type 8** – defensive vs assertive adventure-seeking
(engaging in challenging activities to defeat fear vs to channel excess mental energy)

▶ **Type 7 vs Type 9** – congenial fascination vs mystical merging
(basing our actions on the desire for mental pleasure vs the desire for energetic blending)

▶ **Type 8 vs Type 9** – over-dominance vs over-passivity
(acting out of the desire to dominate vs the desire to avoid conflict)

In addition to type-related oppositions, we can identify oppositions related to both energy centers and subtype arenas. Looking at the *energy centers*, we see that Head Center types tends to be mental and detached; they prefer logic to emotion when making decisions and don't like to be emotionally pressured. Heart Center types tend to be more feeling-oriented; they make decisions based on other peoples' responses and how it makes them feel. Body/Gut Center types tend to be practical and action-oriented; they'd rather act than spend time reflecting, and they find messy emotions annoying. So classic centered-related oppositions include scenarios in which we have to decide what standards to use when making a decision (ethical, humane, or scientific); what takes priority in a situation (action, communication, or thought); or what problem-solving approach is best (pragmatic, empathic, or logical). Center-related conflicts include the following:

▶ **Head vs Heart** – *battle of the sexes; logic vs love; science vs art*
▶ **Head vs Gut** – *thinking vs acting, science vs ethics/religion, theory vs practicality*
▶ **Gut vs Heart** – *action vs image; instinct vs emotion; ethics vs empathy*

Looking at the *subtype arenas*, we notice that SP subtypes tend to be practical and down-to-earth; they want to make sure that bills are paid before spending money elsewhere and enjoy the peace of mind they get from knowing their "ducks are in order." SX subtypes, however, find this approach way too constraining. They like to live in the moment and value new, intense, and creative experiences to a stable but dull existence. SOC subtypes are especially interested in the role they play in groups they value. When it comes to relationships, SP subtypes like to spend a lot of time by themselves, SX subtypes seek time with intimate partners, and SOC subtypes enjoy group participation. SP subtypes hate formal gatherings or noisy, chaotic parties; SX subtypes like spontaneous gatherings and opportunities to meet interesting people; and SOC subtypes enjoy carefully-planned social gatherings involving individuals from like-minded groups. Here are some typical subtype arena-related oppositions:

▶ **SP vs SX** – *solitude vs intimacy; responsibility vs freedom; ordinary life vs mysticism*
▶ **SP vs SOC** – *comfort vs consensus; directness vs diplomacy; personal focus vs social focus*
▶ **SX vs SOC** – *informality vs formality; spontaneity vs planning, vivacity vs smoothness*

All three of these factors—type, center, and subtype arena—represent dimensions of opposition that create friction, both between individuals and within an individual (because we have all of these aspects within us).

But there's one additional factor to be aware of: the role of the dominant culture in shaping the way we perceive and treat people of different types/subtypes. It turns out that cultures, like individuals, can be typed—which makes sense, if the nine types are truly archetypal. Here's an example of how some countries have been typed by enneagram teachers: Switzerland (Type 1), Russia (Type 2), U. S. (Type 3), France (Type 4), Great Britain (Type 5), Germany (Type 6), Jamaica (Type 7), Ireland (Type 8), and India (Type 9).

The dominant type of a culture will obviously have a big effect on how each of the nine types and its subtypes are perceived within that culture. I became pointedly aware of this factor when trying to find examples of films featuring the 27 subtypes. It turns out that some subtype themes are easy to find (SX Sevens) while others are not so easy (SP Fours). I also found that some subtypes were treated more even-handedly or realistically than others: it was easy to find films in which SP Threes businessmen were portrayed as greedy crooks, but not so easy to find businessmen portrayals that were genuinely positive. So before plunging into an in-depth look at the subtypes, I'd like to take a quick look at how American culture seems to affect the way that different subtype themes are handled in films and on TV.

It's interesting that although the U. S. is now said to be a Three nation (based on its political and economic system), American pop culture is more Seven-like, which is probably why we see more lightweight, youth-oriented entertainment than serious drama or in-depth intellectual fare. In terms of subtype arenas, the SX arena is heavily dominant (no surprise!). That's why we see plenty of movies that are funny SX Seven), romantic (SX Two), focused on superstars (SX Three), or action-oriented (SX Six, Seven, and Eight). On the shadow side, we see dark or darkly humorous flicks involving horror (SX Five), suspense (SX Six), or Jekyll-Hyde conversions (where SX One falls to the low side of SX Seven). SX themes involving tragic love (SX Four) or mysticism (SX Nine) are less common.

SOC subtype themes are also relatively popular, especially when they combine SX glitz with SOC glamour. Examples include themes involving weddings and other feminine sociable gatherings (SOC Two), high-profile politics (SOC Three), fashion icons (SOC Four), and innovative "happenings" like Woodstock or Burning Man (SOC Seven). Also popular are courtroom dramas (SOC One) and themes involving military conquest and power brokers (SOC Eight). Themes focusing on duty and honor (SOC Six) were unpopular when I was young (because of the Vietnam War), but made a big comeback in the 1990s, after the first Gulf War; and after 911, they become even more accepted. As for SOC Nine themes involving peace and harmony, we seem to like the idea, but we don't create many films with that focus (*Gandhi* being an exception).

SP subtype themes are the least visible (and usually the least popular), because they focus on everyday people living ordinary lives; not much glamour here. But among the more popular themes are those involving the "good life" (SP Seven), stark survival (SP Eight), and slice-of-life themes with a heart-warming element (SP Nine). Among the least popular themes are those involving bohemian individualists (SP Four), ascetic living (SP One), business (SP Three), feminine nurturing (SP Two), social shyness (SP Five), and personal insecurity (SP Six).

There's obviously a lot more that could be said about this topic, way too much to discuss in depth. The point is to show that the images we see of the types and subtypes are culturally-mediated. If we want to know what the subtype is really like, we have to pierce its public image, so we can catch a glimpse of its more subtle qualities.

¤ ¤ ¤

CHAPTERS 11 – 19 describe each type and its subtypes in detail. My goal in these chapters is not only to show what makes each subtype unique, but to convey the idea that the subtypes represent transpersonal archetypes that we are meant to embody, not personality types that we are meant to discard. I believe that the more we become receptive to these archetypes, the more they're able to inform us—to put us in touch with something deep, real, and revivifying. That's why they're worth studying.

I'm indebted to both Tom Condon (author of *The Enneagram Movie & Video Guide*) and Judith Searle (author of *The Literary Enneagram*), whose foundational work on film and literary themes inspired me to use film examples for illustrating subtype differences. Searle's excellent article, "Story Genres and Enneagram Types," was especially enlightening,* which is why I use her thoughtful observations as a touchstone when discussing subtype themes.

When summarizing film plots, I try whenever possible to avoid revealing the end of the film. But in some cases, the ending is part of the example. So I apologize in advance to film buffs for sometimes revealing more than they might like to know.

One last note: Because I can explore only a limited number of film themes in depth, I decided to list more examples in nine summary tables like the one on page 159. In some cases, it's obvious why a particular film exemplifies a particular theme; in other cases, it's not so obvious. If you have questions, check out the PDF film/theme list available on my website.†

---

* Source: www.judithsearle.com/art.html.

† Source: www. enneagramdimensions.net/archetypes_of_the_enneagram.pdf.

Type one – the perfecter

Human nature is what we were put on this earth to rise above.
– Katherine Hepburn, as Rose Sayer in *The African Queen*

IF WE LOOK at the enneagram from a transformational perspective, Ones are the first type we encounter as we start our journey around the enneagram. Since Point 1 is the spot where a new idea gets pinpointed, detailed, and defined, it's not surprising that Ones are the individuals for whom precision and correctness are not just preferences, but necessities.

Ones are like the firstborn in a family: they're extremely independent-minded and responsible. Although they tend to follow whatever rules are in place, these rules must satisfy their high ethical standards. If not, they're more than willing to revise them; Ones take the initiative rather than waiting for direction.

In childhood, Ones tend to be more serious than most children, especially if the adults around them seem at all immature. Ones will readily step in and assume the adult role, if given half a chance. More than most children, they need to be encouraged to play, have fun, and just be a kid. Ones who have grown up too fast may need to go back as adults and re-discover how to live with greater spontaneity and joy.

Despite their seriousness, Ones have an unmistakable idealistic side. It's as if they're caught between heaven and earth, and can't rest until they've established some sort of divine blueprint for human conduct (if not for others, then at least for themselves). Ones who are secular still adhere to some sort of idealized set of rules, drawn from whatever philosophy most appeals to their sense of what is right. They find it difficult to accept human failings, especially their own; thus, they'll do their utmost to avoid making careless mistakes. When they fail to live up to their ideal, they tend to be quite hard on themselves.

The idealism of Ones gives them an aspirational quality that can inspire others, especially if they manage to hold their critical tendencies in check. But that same idealism can make intimate relationships challenging, as the need for closeness collides with the mandate to be true to their ideals. The temptation to make loved ones conform to such ideals is hard to resist, especially since Ones actually demonstrate their love by engaging in just this sort of reform project! They're mystified when partners and other intimates resist being made-over; it's hard for them to realize that there are realms of life where acceptance matters more than perfection.

Ones with a Two wing are more likely to openly voice their objections; those with a Nine wing are more likely to silently disapprove. In either case, this disapproval can pose a big problem for the relationship, especially over the long term, which is one reason why some Ones opt for a relationship with an ideal (God, the law, or some other set of principles) over a relationship with a real and fallible human being.

The wings and connecting points of One can be helpful for putting the One's natural zeal and one-pointedness into perspective. A Nine wing gives them the ability to go into "neutral" (becoming more tolerant), as well as a broader, more universal outlook on life. A 1w9 can look a lot like a Five, because of her natural reserve. But while Fives tend to be analytical in the scientific or technical sense, Ones tend to be more literary, allegorical, or mystical. A Two wing gives Ones warmth and an interest in social activities, especially those intended to improve the world in some way. It's often easiest for a 1w2 to meet people by participating in some sort of formally-organized activity, such as a neighborhood clean-up day, academic classes, or church social functions; activities like these act as ice-breakers that enable Ones to overcome their inhibitions.

Their connecting point of Seven can help Ones to relax and have fun, so they can take life a little less seriously. It also gives them greater mental agility and the kind of flexibility that can temper their tendency to jump to conclusions and hang onto them for dear life! Ones who allow themselves to tap into their Seven connection usually experience a lot of relief from inner tension, especially if they let this happen consciously (without a sense of guilt or self-criticism). Ones who connect with Four potentially gain the ability to experience life from the perspective of *soul,* which gives them the ability to access their deeper, more complex feelings (again, tempering their tendency to rush to judgment). So both connecting points offer solutions to the problem of too much black-and-white thinking: Point 7 provides levity while Point 4 provides emotional depth.

Judith Searle identifies two popular One story genres: the "moral hero" story and a close variant, the lawyer story. In the moral hero genre, the protagonist is frequently a One who's confronted with some sort of moral dilemma that tests her ability to stand up for her principles. In most instances, the One is up to the challenge but may lose a lot in the process: family, friends, or even her life. However, films with this theme usually convey the message that there's some kind of long-term moral victory to be gained.

In the lawyer story, the moral hero is involved with the legal system in some way (e.g., as a lawyer, policeman, or judge). Frequently, there's a conflict between real justice and the justice afforded by the (less-than-perfect) legal system. That puts the law-and-order One in a pickle: she wants to follow the rules but has to choose between unjust rules and an alternative approach that's more just but involves rule-breaking. This is the One's worst nightmare, and there's typically a lot of wailing and gnashing of teeth about what to do.

This dilemma is well illustrated by the Sufi story of Moses and the prophet Khidr (the Green Man). Moses symbolizes the law and Khidr, the divine wisdom behind the law. In the story, Moses wants to follow Khidr. But Khidr tells him that it won't be possible; Moses simply won't be able to do it. But Moses wants to try, so Khidr agrees. What happens afterward is just what Khidr has predicted: when Khidr does things that seem to violate the law, Moses cannot help but question him. After the third time, Khidr

TABLE 11-1.

TYPE ONE: THE PERFECTER

PRECISE, DETAIL-ORIENTED, CONSTRAINED, HIGH-STRUNG, RIGHTEOUS

SEVEN Connection brings spontaneity, joy, fun, lightness, scatteredness
FOUR Connection brings feeling, depth, originality, empathy, moodiness

NINE Wing brings introversion, austerity, reserve, detachment, asceticism
TWO Wing brings extroversion, fervor, commitment, outspokenness, zeal

Other Labels: Perfectionist, Idealist, Initiator, Standard-Setter, Reformer
Challenges: perfectionism, over-zealousness, tension, inflexibility, judgementalism

	SUBTYPES		
	Self-preservation	Sexual	Social
A R C H E T Y P E S	Detailer, Budgeter, Exacting Auditor, Pioneer, Settler, Wilderness Tamer, Dignified Civilizer, Careful Worker, Civic-minded Voter, Sober Citizen, Disciplined Perfectionist, Meticulous Craftsman, American Gothic, Miniature Maker, Frontier Schoolmarm, Picayune Grammarian, Duty-bound Family Supporter, Responsible Person, Honorable Survivor, Copy Editor, Parsimonious Spender, Exacting Bookkeeper, Austere Conserver, Orderly Gardener, Sole Proprietor, Shop or Cafe Owner, Pilgrim, Puritan, Amish	Ordained Priest, Father Confessor, Ascetic, Renunciate, Evangelist, Preacher, Proselytizer, Missionary, Pilgrim, Puritan, Ethical or Spiritual Counselor, Exacting Mentor, Persistent Interrogator, Relentless Investigator, God's Instrument, Fiery Advocate, Angry Demonstrator, "Thorn in the Side," Picketer, Protester, Ranting Crusader, Passionate Advocate, Irritable Intimate, Possessive Friend, Jealous Lover, "Trapdoor" Hedonist, Flaming Idealist, Repressed Hothead	Careful Rulemaker, Righteous Lawgiver, High-minded Legislator, Rulebound Leader, Fair Judge, Impartial Jurist, Inflexible Decision Maker, Champion of Justice, Pope, Spiritual Hierophant, Chief Justice, Religious Educator, Mother Superior, Chief Examiner, Impartial Inquisitor, Parliamentarian, Old Testament Prophet, Law Professor, Instructor, Arbiter, Scribe, Legal Advocate, Tireless Reformer, Miss Manners, Advice Columnist, Etiquette Expert, Refined Literary Critic, Environmentalist
F I L M T H E M E S	**Clean & sober living** is how we overcome temptation (My Name is Bill W.), settle the wilderness (Westward Ho the Wagons, How the West Was Won) or survive hard times (The Grapes of Wrath, All Mine to Give, Colonial House) **Rule-seeking young person** criticizes adults for their frivolous ways (Hideous Kinky, Uptown Girls, Laurel Canyon) **Crotchety elder** tries everybody's patience (On Golden Pond, Scrooge, Decoration Day, Cocoon) **Pride in workmanship** reminds us of basic values (The Red Violin, Where the Lilies Bloom, Note by Note, Witness) **Strict religious groups** take their teachings seriously (Mayflower: The Pilgrim's Adventure; Amish Grace; The Shakers: Hands to Work, Hearts to God) **Dignified individual remains undiminished** by the vicissitudes of life (Camilla, Driving Miss Daisy, Glory)	**Simmering passion** gets channeled into religious work (Priest, Black Narcissus), teaching (The King & I), music (Take the Lead), or elevating a lower-class person (My Fair Lady) **Buttoned-up critic** discovers how to let go (Summertime, Missing, Enchanted April, Kiss of the Spider Woman, The African Queen) **Disciplined creator** finds an outlet for artistic expression (Babette's Feast, The September Issue) or finally loses his ability to maintain discipline (Dr. Jekyll & Mr. Hyde) **Rules are broken** to have some fun (Footloose, Dirty Dancing, The Sound of Music) **Religious zeal** overfloweth (The Bible, Aimee Semple McPherson, John Brown's Holy War, The Nun's Story) **Penalties accrue** after the leaking out of repressed passion (The Piano, Priest, The Salem Witch Trials) or destructive jealousy (Atonement)	**Righteous reformers** lobby for social change (Reds, The Way We Were, Amazing Grace, An Unreasonable Man) **High-minded arbiters** set standards for the rest of us (Judge Judy, The Paper Chase, My Fair Lady, Dragnet, American/Australian Princess, The Ten Commandments) **Person of principle** upholds those principles with varying results (Doubt, A Man for All Seasons, 12 Angry Men, Serpico, To Kill a Mockingbird, The Verdict, Chariots of Fire, Butterfly, Unrepentant: Kevin Annett and Canada's Genocide, Molokai: Father Damien, The Fountainhead, Philadelphia) **Unjust policies** are circumvented (Rabbit-Proof Fence, Australia, Swing Kids, Glory, The Handmaid's Tale) **Officer of the Court** is determined to catch/convict his man (Les Miserables, The Fugitive, Capture of the Green River Killer, Judgment at Nuremberg)

rebukes Moses, reminding him of his prediction. The story illustrates the idea that he who adheres too rigidly to the rules will probably have a hard time understanding the principles that give rise to rules.

The move from laws to principles is not an easy one. Although One-like values have historically been influential in American life, starting with the Pilgrim Fathers, their influence has often taken the form of moral absolutes. They worked because they were the product of shared moral convictions. But as American culture became more diverse, it became more difficult to find a set of rules that worked equally well for all of us. So the challenge on a cultural level has been to find a way to move beyond the rules while still retaining a principled approach to living. This challenge is especially critical for Ones, because of their particular concern with ethical issues.

In addition to the moral hero and lawyer story genres identified by Judith Searle, we can identify a variety of additional One-related themes: themes about the pioneering spirit and how to foster it; about the value of creating artistic works reflecting an exquisite attention to detail; about the nature of limitations and how to live within them; about the challenge of balancing passion with ethics; about the need to channel passion into creative pursuits (rather than just letting it smolder); and about the importance of taking etiquette seriously. We'll explore these themes in greater depth in the following sections.

¤ ¤ ¤

SELF-PRESERVATION ONES THEMES. The themes at SP One involve the kind of modest, no-nonsense individuals that we traditionally associate with independent-minded settlers and pioneers, as well as Pilgrims, Puritans, Shakers, and Amish communities (as well as other conservative religious groups who strictly adhere to the precepts of their belief system). Sober, thrifty, and responsible, SP Ones are willing to work to realize their vision of the American dream. They usually succeed in attaining their goals because they're good at deferring short-term rewards in order to bring about long-term gains.

SP Ones like work that's concrete, specific, and detail-oriented, so they make excellent bookkeepers, copy editors, woodworkers, or jewelers. They have real pride of ownership and will often save up for their own shop, farm, booth, etc., rather than work for somebody else. They seldom get into debt and don't understand people who do. Although SP Ones are willing to take control as managers (at least for a business that has a manageable number of employees), those who work for them don't always find them fun bosses, because they set high standards and don't tolerate shoddy work. They work hard not so much to get ahead (as SP Threes might), but to perfect their skills and produce a product they can be proud of. The paintings *American Gothic* and *Whistler's Mother* capture the extreme austerity of this subtype, which is especially apparent in Ones with a Nine wing. SP Ones with the opposite wing are somewhat warmer and more engaging, but also bossier and more inclined to voice their disapproval.

SP One life themes often involve clean living, conservative values, and a morally-oriented view of life. Nineteenth-century stories were full of such themes, although they became less popular by the mid-twentieth century. They can still be found in films that celebrate the arrival of the Pilgrims (*Mayflower: The Pilgrim's Adventure),* the settling of the American West (*How the West Was Won*), the virtues of clean and sober living (*My Name is Bill W.*), or the joys of fine craftsmanship (*The Red Violin, Note by Note: The Making of Steinway L1037*).

In *How the West Was Won*, God-fearing father Zebulon Prescott (Karl Malden) is leading his family into the wilderness of Indiana in the 1830s. He's every inch the SP One settler-patriarch. Like many pioneer families, his family has sold everything and is moving west to find a plot of land to clear and farm. When trapper Linus Rawlings (Jimmy Stewart) shows up at their camp and one of his daughters takes an interest in him, the father is suspicious—especially after the couple stays up late one night after everybody else has gone to bed. The next morning, Zebulon looks at her sternly, saying, "Daughter, I'm only gonna ask you this once: Is there anything for me to be worried about?" When she says no, he asks no more questions; it's obvious that this is a family where truth is the norm, not the exception.

All Mine to Give is a film about a pioneering family that's based on a true story. Made in the 1950s, it's about a family who move from Scotland to Wisconsin in the 1850s. Twelve-year-old Robbie is the oldest son in a family of six children. When illness strikes, it claims both parents, leaving the six children orphaned as a result. When the mother realizes she's dying, she instructs Robbie to find loving families for the younger children; at the ripe old age of 12, he's presumed to be old enough to take on this adult responsibility. Robbie faithfully follows her instructions, matching each child to the family he thinks will suit it. (The children must of necessity be split up, since no one family would have the resources to provide for them all.) After he's found a family for the last of his siblings, he calmly walks off across the hill to the local mill, where he'll get a man's job.

What's remarkable about this film is both its pathos and starkness. One online reviewer said she started watching it on TV when working out in the gym, and couldn't stop watching it to the very end (resulting in very sore legs the next day!). Another was amazed by the toughness of people in that era, how they just accepted what life brought and did the best they could in bad situations.

In the PBS series, *Colonial House*, we get to see what it's like for modern folks to go back in time, living like colonists in a Plymouth-colony-like community for six months. The goal was to see whether the modern-day colonists could establish a settlement that could maintain self-sufficiency and set up a profitable trade with local native tribes. Because the colony in question is designed to simulate a colony of the 1600s, it was run as a theocracy, not a democracy; the governor has complete say over all matters, both secular and religious. This role was assumed by real-life Texas Baptist minister Jeff Wyers, an individual with distinctly SP One-like values.

Interestingly, unlike the stereotype we might have of such individuals (as overly rigid and old-fashioned), Wyers turned out to be a good leader who earned the respect of other participants because of his leadership and fairness. It's interesting that he and his family adapted noticeably better to the situation than other participants, most of whom suffered a lot from culture shock. (One couple even rebelled to the extent of skinny-dipping on Sundays instead of attending church—something a real Pilgrim would be quite unlikely to do!)

The reason that the Wyers family may have had an easier time adapting may be because their real-life values are pretty similar to those of the colonists they're emulating. Here's how Wyers' daughter Bethany spoke of her experience:

> I expected life to be more simple in the Colony, but instead it was grueling and tough. The day's work was very challenging, but at night I would have a real sense of satisfaction at all we had accomplished. I was very proud that we were able to come up with such a variety of meals considering the very limited ingredients we had. I'm still shocked that I didn't really mind wearing the same clothes day after day, not taking baths, and going to the bathroom in the woods. I left there with a real sense of appreciation for what the original colonists must have felt as they left all that was familiar to them to search for a better life for themselves and others who followed.

SP One themes focus less on violence and more on constructive activities and values, although SP One characters frequently show up in old westerns featuring conflicts between settler farmers who want to fence the land and cattle barons who want to keep it open (a classic Type 1 versus Type 7 conflict); the same conflict shows up for females in stories about conflicts between prim-and-proper Victorian ladies and saloon gals or other independent-minded women who fled West in an effort to escape the stifling propriety of East Coast society.

SP One themes are similar to SP Six themes in their focus on tradition and family values, but SP One themes place more stress on the value of independence and the pioneering ethic. There's a special fierceness reflected in the desire of Ones for independence and their wish to carve out a little piece of the universe for their very own.

Another SP One theme involves pride in ownership or workmanship; SP Ones care about the work they do. They like to create something unique, something on which they can leave their mark. In fact, the idea of literally "making one's mark in life" is a very SP One sort of notion. We see this theme in the film *The Red Violin*, where in 1681, a violin maker creates a violin which he intends to be his masterpiece. Just before he varnishes the violin, he receives word that his beloved wife, who is in labor with their child, has died (along with the child). Distraught, he puts some of her blood in the varnish—giving it a deep red color—and donates it to an orphanage, where it is played by a succession of young violinists for the next century or so. From there, the violin passes into other hands, including the gypsies—and eventually to a Chinese servant who transports it to Shanghai. It's here that the violin is almost destroyed during China's Cultural Revolution. Fortunately, someone hides it; and the violin remains hidden until 1997, when its keeper dies and it's rediscovered and put up for auction. Various people bid for it. But through a bit of trickery, it's switched for a copy. The real violin becomes a present for a little girl, thereby allowing it to remain in use, instead of winding up on display in a museum.

There are several interesting things about this film. One is that its protagonist is not a person, but a violin, an instrument that is brought to life by virtue of the devoted craftsmanship that goes into its making (reflecting the SP One's ability to express his love by creating exquisitely-made objects). Another is the fact that its value increases over time (symbolizing the One-like wish to imbue tangible objects with eternal value). A third is that the violin is obviously not meant to be merely a collectible object, but something that is actually played—and that provides its owners with delight (One's connection to Seven). A fourth is that the final touch in its making (the red varnish) gets is color from the life blood of the woman who inspired its maker (One's connection to Four).

An SP One theme that shows up in some TV sitcoms and films involves the image of crotchety elders who are easily irritated by other people (e.g., Henry Fonda in *On Golden Pond*, James Garner in *Decoration Day,* Hume Cronin in *Age Old Friends* or Jessica Tandy in *Camilla*). Such characters are almost inevitably portrayed in a comic light, which is something of a mixed blessing. While it's true that elderly people can sometimes get irritated or be irritating to others, it's a little troubling to see images of the irritable elderly so much more common than images of, say, the venerated elderly. It makes you wonder whether the real reason that many of these elders seem so irritated is that they live during a time that sweeps old age and life experience under the rug in favor of youth and good looks.

SP Ones are truly the "salt of the earth." They say what they mean and mean what they say, and this straightforward dependability makes them good friends and staunch allies. They can particularly benefit by working a little less, taking time for themselves and their families, and cultivating hobbies that allow them to develop their hidden artistic side (connection to Four).

¤ ¤ ¤

Sexual one themes. SX Ones are particularly intense, even when compared with other SX subtypes. Their intensity is probably the result of the clash between the type (which is highly contained) with the SX subtype arena (which is highly expressive). Here we have a fallible human being trying to fulfill the inner mandate of the One ("Be correct, be perfect, fulfill the ideal!") while trying to contain and channel a very hot inner fire. The result is someone who can feel like she's on the verge of exploding, especially when she lacks an appropriate outlet for her creative impulses. So the SX One is among the steamiest of the sexual subtypes: the combination of intense passion and intense restraint creates a pressure cooker scenario in which a lasting balance can be hard to achieve.

In both art and in life, SX One themes are almost always about this tension, focusing on either (a) how it might be constructively channeled or (b) the dire consequences of repressing its healthy expression. In stories about how a One learns to channel her energy, the story begins with introducing an impassioned but overly-constrained protagonist (either a One or someone whose position is One-like, e.g., a disciplined dance instructor, spiritual leader, or respected teacher). She typically leads a highly regimented, exemplary life but secretly (and usually unconsciously) seeks to break out of this regime, to indulge more fully in life's pleasures. In enneagrammatic terms, this is the One wishing to go to her Seven connecting point, where she can let loose of her sense of duty-bound work ethic and have a little fun.

Katharine Hepburn in *Summertime* (1955) is a good example of such a character: a repressed spinster type vacationing in Venice all by herself—at least until she meets charmer Rossano Brazzi and discovers the joys of shared pleasures. Another example is Baron Von Trapp (Christopher Plummer), in *The Sound of Music*, who runs his house like a military barracks until the arrival of the youthful acolyte Maria, who acts as governess to his six children—and whose Sevenish joy gradually wins over the children and their father. In films like *Dirty Dancing* and *Footloose*, we see the same theme played out in stories of freedom-seeking youth seeking liberation from uptight social policies imposed by unenlightened adults.

In these stories, the tension is resolved because of outside intervention (typically, from a Seven). But what happens if there's no one to help the ability to rein in that passion, despite great efforts to contain, repress, or transcend it? That's when we get a "trapdoor" scenario, where the One—having maintained strict discipline for a long time—finally goes off the deep end (often under the influence of drugs, alcohol, a magic potion, love, or some other powerfully evocative stimulus), becoming manic, crazy, or otherwise irresponsible. When the One comes to her senses, she is of course horrified and repentant (which sends her, as Tom Condon notes, to the "low" side of Four). If the cycle isn't broken, this move from One to Four sends the protagonist into another round of repression (back to One) followed by a moral lapse in judgment (move to Seven) and thence to guilt and self-condemnation (move to Four). The resolution involves breaking out of the cycle of repression by acknowledging one's passion, finding outlets for its expression, and accepting one's failings as part of the human condition.

The most famous trapdoor story is *Dr. Jekyll and Mr. Hyde*, in which the constrained and correct One-like scientist (Jekyll) is transformed into the wildly demented Seven (Hyde). The moral of the story is that casting the traits we don't like into our unconscious just makes them more charged with energy. If we keep refusing to acknowledge those Shadow aspects, we eventually wind up unconsciously embodying them.

Black Narcissus explores the same theme, showing us what happens when we bring together three incompatible worlds: the Type 1 world of an Anglican sisterhood, the sensuous and exciting world of the adventurer (Type 7), and the ineffable world of the mystic (Type 9). At the film's start, we're introduced to a group of nuns who are going to establish a new school and clinic in a remote location in the Himalayas. Their leader, the prim but repressed Sister Clodagh (Deborah Kerr), is using the sisterhood as an escape from the heartbreak of a failed romance, so we realize right away that she may not be the best candidate to head up the project.

The nun's destination is a converted seraglio (a place traditionally housing the wives or concubines of a ruler). It's located in a hauntingly beautiful location: high mountains surround the place, which is on top of a dramatic cliff. Not far down the path sits an Indian Holy Man who never moves; the image evokes the mysterious, shadowy world of Type 9 mysticism. To make matters worse, shortly after their arrival, the Sisters encounter Dean, the local British agent, whose smooth good looks and careless Type 7 charm soon create tension among the sisters. The stage is set for trouble.

First, a nun with a mystical nature (perhaps a Nine?) becomes enraptured and can barely function. Then the heir to the local throne falls victim to the atmosphere of the locale, becoming infatuated with a low-caste but highly-alluring dancing girl (Jean Simmons). Both Sisters Clodagh and Ruth are attracted to Dean, but Clodagh thoroughly suppresses her feelings while Ruth becomes obsessed with him—and filled with hatred for Clodagh, her perceived rival. (The mischievous Dean doesn't help matters by wearing short-shorts in most of the scenes, despite the chilly Himalayan climate! He must have some idea of how this affects the nuns, but probably enjoys the attention.)

But Dean is playing with fire. Eventually, Sister Ruth becomes so crazed to the point that she actually tries to kill Clodagh as the latter is ringing the bell on the cliff's edge. In the process, Ruth loses her balance and tumbles dramatically over the cliff. At that point, it's clear that the mission has failed. The nuns return to the lowlands, where the atmosphere is presumably less stimulating.

Made in 1947, *Black Narcissus* is an unusual film for its time; we'd expect religious movies more along the lines of *Going My Way* or *The Bells of St. Mary,* which offered more traditional and comforting images of religious life. Or perhaps epic films like *The Ten Commandments* or *The Bible. Black Narcissus* is different, because it looks at the psychological side of religion, especially at the shadow side of zeal, showing us what happens when it becomes undermined by sexual or mystical passion.

The 1994 film *Priest* focuses on a One's passion as reflected in the actions of a first-time parish priest who is as judgmental as he is high-minded—that is, until he falls in love. And not with a woman, but a man. He tries—ultimately in vain—to suppress both his passion and desire for companionship. When his congregation finds out he's had a homosexual affair, they become outraged, and he's publicly humiliated. Despite the heartache involved, this humbling experience ultimately makes him a better, less judgmental human being (and arguably, a more compassionate spiritual guide).

In another recent film, *The Piano*, Victorian passion boils over into an adulterous love affair between mute pianist (Demi Moore) and her offbeat piano student (Harvey Keitel). Just as in *Black Narcissus*, an exotic locale seems to encourage departures from social decorum (in this case, the action takes place in the steamy jungles of New Zealand). Sam Neill plays the stern husband who unsympathetically exacts revenge (or justice, if you prefer), showing us a One who, like Sister Clodagh, persists in maintaining a rigid stance, no matter what.

In both *Priest* and *The Piano*, the main protagonists achieve some sort of resolution because of their willingness to admit their true feelings, even when it conflicts with their avowed personal standards or the standards of society. The stiffly-correct head butler in *The Remains of the Day* (Anthony Hopkins) isn't so lucky; by the time he's willing to admit to himself that he's fallen in love with the head housekeeper (Emma Thompson), it's too late. For years, she waited for him to realize they should marry. When he didn't, she finally married somebody else.

On the lighter side, we have stories in which Ones *do* successfully break through their natural reserve to share their feelings of love (Henry Higgins in *My Fair Lady* and the school marm Anna in *The King & I*). We also have films celebrating the accomplishments that are possible when highly-refined SX Ones use their disciplined artistry in creative ways, e.g., to create a magnificent French meal (*Babette's Feast*), new fashion trends (*The September Issue*), or dance programs aimed at uplifting wayward youth (*Take the Lead*).

Take the Lead shows us a "redemption through dance" theme in which SX One strengths are employed to help young people gain discipline and self-esteem. Pierre Delaine (Antonio Banderas) teaches ballroom dance to kids in detention so they can learn to channel their passion in a constructive way. His efforts are opposed by a nerdy Five-like opponent who looks like he's never been out on a date. (So here we have the classic archetypal conflict between Art and Science, each representing a completely different view of the world and different set of priorities.) When the dance teacher is dragged before a parents' meeting to defend himself, he has to answer the question: Why teach dance instead of academics? He doesn't talk, he *demonstrates*. He shows his audience that it's in the *doing* that we learn something new. Then he makes a short but dignified speech: "Ladies and gentlemen, this is what I do at this school. I teach dance—and with it, a set of rules that will teach your kids more respect, teamwork, and dignity." Needless to say, he wins over his audience.

The film *Music of the Heart* is similar in theme, except that here we have exacting violin teacher Roberta Guaspari (Meryl Streep) in the role of youth mentor and disciplinarian. Both films are based on true stories: Dulaine established the Dancing Classrooms program in the early 1980s and Guaspari has been running the East Harlem Violin Program since the mid-1990s.

In most of these films, it's when Ones get in touch with their inner feelings (connection to Four) and their whimsical, humorous side (connection to Seven) that they learn how to enjoy their passionate nature, instead of viewing it with disapproval. Then they're less likely to get involved in "trapdoor" scenarios and find appropriate channels for their passion.

¤ ¤ ¤

Social one themes. It's at SOC One that we see many of the greatest dramas in life unfold, dramas involving ethical philosophy, the development of rule-based political systems, and the legally-sanctioned arbitration of disputes. While the theory can seem rather dry, it comes alive when it affects the lives of real people. And so the themes we see in films and literature are usually about an individual who becomes personally involved in the legal system in some way, either by choice or by chance.

One popular SOC One theme involves a law enforcement agent who—having committed his life to the law and all it represents—makes a personal vow that a certain crime will not go unsolved or that a certain criminal will not get away with a crime. Sometimes the reason has to do with some sort of deeply repressed emotion in the pursuer—emotion that gets channeled into his single-minded pursuit (examples include Police Inspector Javert in *Les Miserables*, Lieutenant Gerard in the movie/TV series *The Fugitive*, and Lieutenant Clarke in the Australian TV miniseries *The Incredible Journey of Mary Bryant*). At other times, the ardent desire for justice seems to arise out of a high-minded but abstract regard for the law and what it represents (*Justice at Nuremberg, 12 Angry Men,* or *The Capture of the Green River Killer.*)

In *The Capture of the Green River Killer,* the protagonist's protracted desire for justice arises out of both a respect for the law and compassion for the victims of the Green River killer, despite the fact that they're all prostitutes and therefore devalued by society. Despite the One-ish genre, it's likely that the protagonist, Detective Dave Reichert, is not a One; he seems more like a counterphobic Six.* How do we know? Because in the opening scene, we see him being chastised for trying to "play hero" in a dangerous domestic situation. He gets wounded and ends up answering the phone—which is how he comes to have responsibility for the Green River case. Part of his incentive for finding the killer probably comes from the SX Six passion for defending the underdog.

Nonetheless, the film is still an example of a theme that focuses on the pursuit of justice. So one thing it demonstrates is how it's possible for a film to have a SOC One theme, even without a SOC One protagonist. This is true for all film genres; we can have romantic comedies (a Two genre) without any Twos, stories about leadership

---

* Counterphobia is associated with the Sexual subtype of Six. A Six who is counterphobic tends to deal with fear by overcompensating (acting impulsively overaggressive or reckless at time); see Chapter 16 for a discussion.

without Eights; or stories involving social outcasts without Fours. In the case of *The Capture of the Green River Killer,* if our Sixish protagonist sincerely wants to catch his man, he has to curb his impulsiveness and cultivate One-like qualities such as discipline and self-control.

Justice at Nuremberg is a another kind of legal story: the courtroom drama, which explores the dramatic interactions of lawyers, defendants, judges, and juries in a courtroom setting. In this case, the theme centers around the actions of judges charged with upholding the law in an immoral system (Nazism). What responsibility do judges have in such a situation? Should they go along with laws that are clearly unjust or refuse to uphold them (which would of course land them in a world of trouble)? According to the American judge in charge of the Nuremberg trials (majestically portrayed by Spencer Tracy), they should resist. Tracy seems a lot like an Old Testament figure when passing judgment on German judges who failed to resist Nazi efforts to use the court system for persecuting their enemies. The film is thus a clear attack of the idea that we can't defend unjust or immoral acts because we are "just following orders."

Justice at Nuremberg was a brilliant film for its time, because it raised the question of how genocide and other crimes against humanity can be perpetrated in a well-educated, highly-cultured society. And it provided an answer: Evil happens not so much because there are evil people, but because good people fail to oppose evil. At the same time, the high-minded premise of the film (that we should resist compromising our principles, no matter what) can seem overly idealistic when viewed decades later. It reflects a black-and-white view of morality with very few shades of gray. From an enneagrammatic point of view, it's a bit like saying, "You know, we'd have a far better world if everybody would just act like Ones."

But would we? Probably not. But this line of reasoning points to a problem that the enneagram can help us understand: the idea that we all tend to think that the world would be a better place if only people cared more about the values that we personally embrace. Depending on our type, we believe the world would be a better place if people were more ethical (One), humane (Two), practical (Three), authentic (Four), rational (Five), loyal (Six), versatile (Seven), strong (Eight), or harmonious (Nine). And we're all right, because all these values are important. But no one type or subtype has a monopoly on good values.*

More recent SOC One films have addressed issues of moral responsibility from a more subtle and complex perspective.† In *Philadelphia*, a cocky, ambitious gay lawyer (a Three) is fired by his law firm after they discover he has AIDS. So he sues—not to get his job back, since he's dying, but to make people aware of the injustice of railroading people with AIDS. In taking his stand, he moves from the SOC Three world of career and advancement into the SOC One realm of social action.

Another relatively recent SOC One legal drama with an interesting twist is *Presumed Innocent*, a film where an innocent lawyer and prosecutor, Rusty Savitch (played by real-life One Harrison Ford) is accused of murder. The murdered woman is a legal colleague with whom he was having an affair. Although Savitch manages via clever maneuvering to eventually get the case dismissed, he later discovers a bloody ax in his own basement that reveals the identity of the real murderer: his wife. When he confronts her, she admits she did it, but her manner lets us know that she's a little mentally unhinged (probably because of the affair).

As the county prosecutor, his duty is clear: he must turn her in. But as a cheating husband, Savitch obviously bears some moral responsibility for creating the situation which led to the crime. In addition, the murdered women is portrayed very unsympathetically (as a cynically ambitious Three), so it's hard to feel bad about seeing her death go unavenged. And then there is the question of his young son who needs a mother.

---

* However, the case can be made that if we take on a SOC One sort of job (i.e., being a judge), then we must seek to embody the values that go with that job, regardless of our type. This is one reason that self-knowledge matters: the better we know ourselves, the more likely we are to find work that's compatible with our nature.

† For an interesting discussion of how our concept of justice is reflected in film themes, see "Changing Images of Justice in American Films," by Ralph Berets (2006), at http://tarlton. law.utexas.edu/lpop/etext/lsf/berets20.htm.

So what does Savitch do? He destroys the evidence. And this is where the film abruptly ends, leaving the audience hanging.

Will he get away with it? Probably. Will he learn to live with it? Probably not. From the SOC One vantage point, ditching one's principles for any reason is unacceptable. While it may be a good thing to appreciate the values of other types (in this case, pragmatism at Three, empathy at Two, family loyalty at Six, and personal justice at Eight), placing those values above those of our own type is going against our own nature. And this is usually a mistake, even if the motive seems positive.

The SOC One always wants to be on the right side of justice, no matter what this requires. In *A Man for All Seasons*, we see the portrayal of a real-life historical drama involving the conflict between King Henry VIII (a SX-SOC Eight) and Sir Thomas More (a SOC One). Henry VIII embodies the archetype of worldly power (and a personal sense of justice); More embodies the archetype of spiritual resolve (and a principled sense of justice). As Chancellor of England, More refuses to validate King Henry's new marriage; King Henry can't abide his all-too-public refusal. But More knows the law, and his refusal is lawful, so he hopes that the law will serve as his refuge. But after perjured testimony from Richie Rich (an unbalanced 3w4) condemns him, More pays for his refusal to budge with his life.

Real-life SOC One themes are not usually so starkly dramatic, although they do often involve social standards, rule-making, etiquette, proper conduct, legislating, and judging. So it's not surprise that SOC Ones are particularly attracted to fields where they can make rules or give advice. They often have refined sensibilities, literary tastes, and an innate sense of what manners are all about.

Nowadays, we often see this variety of SOC Ones portrayed as upper-crust Britishers that seek to enlighten their less-polished charges as to the fine points of socially-acceptable behavior. Professor Henry Higgins (*My Fair Lady*) provides a fictional example; more recently, we've seen reality shows that take a similar tack, especially with young women e.g., *Ladette to Lady* (reform of hard-partying, lower-class "ladettes") or *American Princess* and *Australian Princess* (reform of crass no-class colonials). Although such approaches are usually a bit over-the-top (teaching girls such old-fashioned skills as flower-arranging or the proper way to serve tea), they often have a genuinely transformative effect on the participants, who gradually come to appreciate the benefits of a more mannerly approach to life.

SOC One themes also focus our attention on what can happen when people become so focused on advancing a particular set of principles or beliefs that they lose tolerance for alternative value systems. The archetype is reflected in the figure of the stern taskmaster or stiff-necked reformer.

A good real-life example is the Australian Chief Protector of Aborigines, A.O. Neville, who presided over the controversial 1930s practice of rounding up aborigine children and training them to serve as domestics to white people. He's one of the principal characters in the film *Rabbit-proof Fence*—based on the true story of three children who managed to escape from custody; similar policies in the U.S. and Canada were aimed at "integrating" Native children into American and Canadian culture by sending them to religiously-affiliated schools that were so abusive that it's still not possible to publicly speak out about those abuses.

The film *Unrepentant: Kevin Annett and Canada's Genocide* documents Annett's efforts to expose the truth, which resulted in his defrocking as a United Council of Churches minister. Here we see the juxtaposition of socially-abusive SOC One-type policies (the forced subjugation and conversion of Native children) with the socially-principled acts of a SOC One-type individual who refuses to be intimidated into silence. Reaching back further in history, we have other historical examples, such as the efforts of the Spanish Inquisition to force the "one true religion" on the population (documented in films like *Goya's Ghost* and *Inquisition*), being undermined (at least temporarily) by principled groups such as the Cathars and individuals such as Giordano Bruno and Galileo.

Conflicts such as these remind us of both the pros and cons of the SOC One desire to promote a particular social or religious agenda. The same impetus that produces inspired leaders and principled social reform can also produce terrible persecution in the hands of individuals who lack the discernment to know the difference. (The One-ish concern with perfection is perhaps best employed in the service of developing this kind of discernment.)

One of the challenges for SOC Ones in the modern world is how to live in a world that tends to embrace the activities at Point 7 (fun and spontaneity) and Point 3 (material success and a good image) over old-fashioned principle. Most Ones find it hard to swallow such developments, and so do people in search of certainty in an uncertain world (like Sixes). That may be why we see a backlash against relativism in the form of social movements that are absolutist and fundamentalist in nature.

If you think it can't happen here, take a look at the recent film *The Handmaid's Tale*, based on the premise that ultra-conservative American reformers take over the government, subsequently enacting laws based on Old Testament values that mandate harsh punishments or even death for those who violate the law. Or consider the modern face of mid-Eastern Islam, where early 20th-century gains in social and political parity for women have suffered devastating setbacks in the last three decades.

Although it's easy to find fault with religious fundamentalists or others who take their values seriously enough to go to the wall for them, it's harder to come up with a solution that addresses the valid concerns of such people about slipping moral standards and the loss of values they consider important. As the world gets smaller and smaller, we need to find ways to preserve key values while retaining the ability to be flexible (rather than rigid) and magnanimous (rather than harsh).

Type two – the people person

What are we if we do nothing to help others? We're nothing—nothing at all.
– Henry Marsh (from *The English Surgeon*)

POINT 2 is the place where we learn about relationships. The focus is on creating emotional bonds with other people, so that we can experience love and intimacy. It's also on nurturing the young, caring for the sick, and establishing social networks that offer emotional support.

So the transition from Point 1 to Point 2 represents a significant shift: it's the move from justice to mercy, from the rule of law to the rule of the heart, from the straight and narrow to the soft and curved. There's a warmheartedness at Point 2 that tempts us to think of it as "nicer" than Point 1. But like all the points on the enneagram, Point 2 offers both gifts and challenges. The upwelling of emotion produces a restlessness of spirit, a desire to seek out an object of affection and make it part of ourselves, so that we don't feel alone. This gives Twos the tendency to become over-invested in relationships, which can lead to self-neglect, emotional dependency, or burnout. So their initial challenge is learning how to love others in a way that imposes no obligations. An even greater challenge is learning how to love themselves in a way that is completely self-sustaining.

What makes it hard for Twos to have healthy relationships is their compelling need to define the value of a relationship by the degree to which it makes them feel emotionally bonded. This makes them apt to confuse emotional dependency (or co-dependency) with genuine love. It also makes it hard for them to relate to people who are emotionally reserved, insensitive, or intellectual in outlook; they tend to find people like this unnerving because Twos don't find it easy to relate to someone who doesn't like to share their emotions. Also, because they're an image type, Twos want to feel accepted by others. So they tend to feel rejected (or at least insecure) when they are reaching out emotionally and receive a non-emotional response in return. They can benefit from realizing that such a response is usually not personal; it just reflects a different relational style.

Twos who are secure in their personal identity are able to relate to all sorts of people. They can enjoy their relationships without getting overinvolved or making demands that other people can't meet. They know how to set appropriate emotional boundaries and respect those of others. Most of all, they know how to channel their free-flowing emotions into activities where a personalized, supportive approach is really needed (counseling, catering, Meals on Wheels, animal welfare, childcare, or nursing).

Twos are often appealing children, because they instinctively know how to connect with other people, including parents. Little girls may become "mommy's helper"; little boys often have a sweetness about them that elicits adult approval. Young Twos may become over-compliant once they realize the positive effect on the adults around them. So wise parents would do well to avoid giving Two children affection as a reward for overly helpful behavior; these children need to know that they'll be loved no matter what they do (and also that the adults in their world are impervious to emotional manipulation).

Twos with a One wing tend to be more tense, serious, reserved, and interested in social causes and philanthropy; like Ones, they have a somewhat earnest quality and an abiding concern with social issues, especially those involving people, children, or animals. But they're less utilitarian than Ones and more drawn to professions involving hands-on helping (e.g., social work, counseling, nursing, or elementary education). Twos with a Three wing tend to be more relaxed, casual, and fun-loving. Their interactions with others are less parental and more sociable. They're also more likely to work in the business arena, although their work often has a personal or feminine focus (e.g., personal coaching, family counseling, catering, or wedding planning).

When Twos connect with Eight, they become more grounded, assertive, and dominant. They're able to take charge, assert their needs, and develop personal confidence and leadership skills. But they have to be careful to hang onto their humanity, so they don't become overbearing (especially SP Twos). When Twos connect with Four, they become more introspective and self-aware. They begin to realize how to be themselves without the mirror of another's attention. But the connection to Four also gives them a "double-dose" of emotion, because Two and Four are the most emotional points on the enneagram. So Twos need to learn how to master the emotional intensity of Point 4 in a way that allows them to use it as a resource without getting completely swallowed up by their feelings.

Searle identifies three popular Two story genres: romance, romantic comedies, and the battle of the sexes. While romance is an extremely popular (and lucrative) theme for American film-makers, it's not the only theme associated with the type. We also see themes involving childbirth, parenting, parents and children, the dangers of being a doormat, devouring moms, stalkers, emotionally immature children, emotionally manipulative partners, divas, pampered princesses, long-term friendships and social networks, and movies involving women and women's issues (coming of age, courtship, marriage, and menopause). More recently, we see films about men learning to embrace their feminine side—learning how to emotionally bond, allow themselves to be vulnerable, develop relationships with their children, and take on the role of stay-at-home Dads.

Females of all enneagram types have been traditionally assigned the role of Twos (especially SP Twos), whatever their actual type. And in many traditional societies, they are still assigned this role: the role of the self-sacrificing partner, who willingly sets aside her own life in order to devote herself to her family and community. Although this is an important and dignified role in life—and one that many women are happy to play—non-Two females may find some aspects of this role quite grating. They're much

TABLE 12-1.

TYPE TWO: THE PEOPLE PERSON

WARM, FRIENDLY, EMOTIONAL, OUTGOING, INVOLVED, SUPPORTIVE, AFFIRMING

FOUR Connection brings depth, authenticity, artistry, soulfulness, intensity
EIGHT Connection brings assertiveness, leadership, charisma, bluntness

ONE Wing brings seriousness, responsibility, commitment, focus
THREE Wing brings aspiration, lightheartedness, optimism, liveliness

Other Labels: Networker, Organizer, Caregiver, Socializer, Helper
Challenges: over-involvement, nosiness, demandingness, entitlement, loss of self

SUBTYPES		
Self-preservation	Sexual	Social
ARCHETYPES *Matriarch, Guardian Angel, Mother Nature, Doting Mother, Effusive Caregiver, Homemaker, Cook, Nurse, Midwife, Fairy God-mother, Best Friend, Eager Helper, Sympathetic Listener, Inquisitive Matchmaker, Busybody, Gossip, Dramatizing Martyr, Self-sac-rificer, Would-be Rescuer, Needy Giver, Emotional Blackmailer, Diva, Maestro, Crone, Devouring Mother, Good Samaritan, Best Friend, Softhearted Sentimentalist*	*Soulmate, Twin Flame, Twin Soul, Total Romantic, Devoted Partner, Selfless Lover, Hopeless Flirt, Co-quette, Skilled Courtesan, Geisha, Lothario, Seducer, Siren, Femme Fa-tale, Enchantress, Casanova, Play-boy, Harlot, Divine Prostitute, Ma-donna, Sacrificial Christ, Messiah, Vestal Virgin, Saint Francis, Temple Dancer, Holy Innocent, Anointed Saint, Devotee, Pampered Prince or Princess, Paparazzi, Stalker, Victim, Emotional Vampire*	*Diplomat, Ambassador, Community Builder, Gracious Organizer, Neigh-borhood Networker, Humanitarian, Social Worker, Human Resource Manager, Event Hostess, Social Smoother, Behind-the-scenes Ma-nipulator, Power Behind the Throne, Hidden Partner, Public Relations Consultant, Social Climber, Ambitious Parent, Stage Mother, Bleeding Heart, Do-gooder, Marriage Broker, Intimate Supportive Counselor, Matchmaker, Go-Between, Social Historian, Com-munications Expert*
FILM THEMES **Loving parents protect** their kids (*House of Cards, À La Place du Co-eur, Not Without My Daughter, Mrs. Doubtfire, One Minute to Nine*) **Resourceful parent(s)** keep families together thru thick & thin (*Prize Winner of Defiance, Ohio; I Remember Mama, Alice Doesn't Live Here Anymore, In America*) **Strong-willed parent** hopes to influence kids' lives (*Fiddler on the Roof; October Sky; Real Women Have Curves, Bollywood/Hol-lywood, Father of the Bride*) which sometimes backfires (*Mommy Dearest; East is East*) **Love is shown** by providing food & comfort (*Paula's Home Cook-ing, Yentl*), TLC (*Fly Away Home, Nurse Edith Cavell, Florence Night-ingale*) or unconditional accep-tance (*Darshan: The Embrace*) **Magical mother figure** can make life better (*Wizard of Oz, Touched by an Angel*) or worse (*The Glass Menagerie*)	**"Boy meets girl"** and off we go (*Love Story, When Harry Met Sally, Sleepless in Seattle, Ghost, He's Just Not That Into You*); or parents seek good marriages for their children (*Arranged, East is East, Bollywood/Hollywood*) **Love/Sex** is a modern-day rite of passage (*Summer of '42, The Gradu-ate, Man in the Moon*) **Intimates** are stalked, emotionally manipulated, or worse (*Fatal Attrac-tion, Black Widow, The Blue Angel, All This and Heaven Too*) **Love conquers all** , even across time, space & even death (*Some-where in Time, A.I., Ghost, The Ghost & Mrs. Muir, Bicentennial Man*) **Romantic person** sacrifices too much for love (*Steel Magnolias, Sweet Charity, Of Human Bondage, Look-ing for Mr. Goodbar*) **Self is sacrificed** for a higher con-cept of love (*The Miracle Worker, Jesus of Nazareth, Mother Teresa of Calcutta, City of Joy*)	**Women friends hang together** through thick and thin (*Steel Magno-lias, 9 to 5, Sisterhood of the Traveling Pants, Jane Austen Book Club, Fried Green Tomatoes, The Joy Luck Club, How to Make an American Quilt*) **Gracious living** inspires convivial social relations (*The Martha Stewart Show, Flowers Uncut* & other TV decorating shows; depression era flicks like *Top Hat* & *The Philadel-phia Story*) **Social occasions** make life worthwhile (*Steel Magnolias, Four Weddings & a Funeral, Masters of Reception*) **Social conventions** may promote conviviality (*Protocol*) but also su-perficiality (*The Razor's Edge*) **Humanitarians** make the world a better place (*The Dorothy Day Story, City of Joy, Extreme Makeover: Home Edition, Dogtown, Oprah's Big Give, Richard Simmons' Sweatin' to the Oldies*)

happier when allowed the opportunity to serve their families without giving up the other parts of themselves that cry out for expression. Even Two females need to learn how to play the role of helpmate without becoming over-identified with it.

Type 2 males have the opposite problem (a problem they share with Type 4 males). Males are stereotypically expected to be "manly," and that usually means tough-minded, emotionally contained, and action-oriented. But Type 2 men tend to be tender-hearted, emotionally expressive, and relationally-oriented. They want to be lovers, not fighters. Their desire for love doesn't mean they can't be masculine, but it *does* mean that they've got to be more aware than other males of the difference between stereotypical masculinity and a more compassionate masculinity that allows for the open expression of tenderness and other soft emotions.

While Twos have a genuinely devotional or sacrificial nature, the only way to access the real thing is to get past the desire to be *seen* as sacrificial—and this can be tricky for an image type like a Two!* Real devotion is the kind that's always present, whether seen or not. So the Two who becomes disappointed when his efforts are not really noticed (much less appreciated) would do well to think about his actual motivation for giving. Twos who give only in expectation of attention will never feel really good about their efforts. The only way that Twos can become happy is when they can give to others in a way that brings them inner fulfillment. Then when they get appreciated, it's a delightful surprise (rather than "wages for work done").

Mother Teresa found a way to give from the heart when she founded the Missionaries of Charity in the 1940s. As a young nun, she'd taught school in India for some years. She enjoyed the work but didn't feel it was her true calling. She became filled with the desire to give Christ's love to the poor of Calcutta, especially to the "poorest of the poor." Her conviction gave her the strength to press her superiors for the chance to pursue this dream, despite their repeated refusals to grant her permission. As a Two, she must have been sensitive to their disapproval but she persisted nonetheless, despite the barriers

---

* For more discussion on image types, see Chapter 13.

put in her way. As the result of her persistence, she was eventually allowed to establish her order. And of course, she was quite successful; in the decades that followed, she became world famous as a selfless humanitarian, eventually winning the Nobel Peace Prize for her efforts to help those least able to help themselves.

¤ ¤ ¤

SELF-PRESERVATION TWO THEMES. The archetype of the Mother is always what first comes to mind when I envision this subtype: the Great Nurturer, Earth Mother, and Mother Nature. Even when SP Two themes involve males, the emphasis is on their role of nurturer and personal supporter. It's unfortunately difficult to find examples of SP Two males in films—with the exception of men pretending to be women, e.g., Robin Williams in *Mrs. Doubtfire*—probably because we still haven't figured out as a culture how to portray men as nurturing and manly at the same time. Bill Cosby is an exception (in his role as dad on the *The Bill Cosby Show* and more overtly, in the delightful Jello commercials that he did with kids); see Tom Condon's comments on the dearth of male Two roles in modern films on pp. 39–40 of *The Enneagram Movie & Video Guide.*

We see the SP Two archetype particularly come to life in films focusing on the role of matriarchs in traditional cultures (*My Big Fat Greek Wedding, Yentl,* or *Bollywood/ Hollywood*), where SP Twos are stereotyped as humorous but domineering characters who are totally in control of family affairs.

But sometimes the stereotype isn't so funny. In the epic drama *Sunshine* (which follows the lives of three generations of a Hungarian Jewish family), Miriam Margolyes plays the quintessential family matriarch. After her brother-in-law's death, she's persuaded by her husband to take in the orphaned daughter and raise her as part of her family. It's obvious that she thinks she made a big sacrifice. But it's equally obvious that she didn't love the little girl very much.

When the girl grows up, she and her cousin (Ralph Fiennes) fall in love, and the two become lovers. It's no surprise that a pregnancy eventually ensues, which means that the couple must wed. At the announcement of the betrothal, the mother faints in a highly dramatic fashion and then lies moaning on the floor. Judging by the family's bland reaction ("She's only fainted"), they're used to this kind of behavior—and also to her almost instant recovery. Although she obviously likes to be seen as motherly, she shows her true colors as she recovers sufficiently to subject her husband to a verbal tongue-lashing (in a separate room, but within easy earshot of the entire household):

> *I told you not to take her in! But you insisted! [She mimics his original words.] "My brother's only child is an orphan. This is our responsibility." [She shifts back to her own perspective.] Well, your responsibility is to your real family. So now I'm insisting: Get her out of the house!...I curse her! May her womb dry up! May she never have children!*

At that point, her husband—horrified by his wife's words—asserts himself, shouting, "No!!!," and they battle verbally. In the heat of battle, she inadvertently lets it slip that she knows that his heart still belongs to another woman whom he was not allowed to marry. This revelation shocks him into silence—and allows the audience to understand that she's such a witch because she's trapped in a loveless marriage.

A scene like this illustrates the trap into which SP Twos can fall: trading love for power, intimacy for household influence—not necessarily because it's what they really want, but because it's what they settle for, either because of their nature, their assigned role in life, or both. (For real-life examples of this archetype, look for episodes of *Wife Swap* or *Trading Spouses*; at least a third of the wives seem to be trapped in the role of "resident hausfrau"; there are also a few scary examples of Devouring Mother types who have embraced the role in a way that makes their kids long for the day when they're old enough to leave home.)

Nevertheless, the negative or shadow aspects of the SP Two archetype now exercise less influence than in the past, because modern women in Western culture have more freedom to choose their role in life. So we now see more images of caregivers as people who choose to give, often as paid professionals who don't give away their services for free.

For example, Patsy Lemmers is an African American woman employed by Tori Spelling who physically resembles the housekeeper Beulah from the 1930s. But there the resemblance ends. Patsy is not a cook or housekeeper, but a highly trained baby nurse who's highly respected for her professional talents. She appears on the TV reality show *Tori and Dean: Home Sweet Hollywood*. Although Patsy lived with the family for a while to care for their babies, she was paid well for her efforts and given the respect and appreciation she so richly deserved.

Another example is Southern cook Paula Deen on Network's *Paula's Home Cooking*. Paula's mission in life is to serve up "comfort food," the kind we remember from childhood (especially holidays or birthdays). She got her start setting up a catering business on a shoestring and later started a popular restaurant, A Lady and Sons, in Savannah, Georgia. Her chance to be on TV came after receiving many accolades for both her restaurant and several cookbooks. (When she had a chance to write them, I can't imagine.) Paula's sunny disposition shows us the SP Two at her best: warm, cheery, accepting, and encouraging. Her pragmatism, enterprising nature, and love of entertaining suggest a Three wing.

Michele Duggar (of *19 Kids and Counting*) is an SP Two who fulfills the traditional role of wife and mother. She wasn't forced into the role but embraced it because she wanted to. She's a natural nurturer who really loves her kids; they in turn support her efforts to keep the household in one piece. Because she belongs to a Christian group that respects the role of motherhood, she doesn't feel diminished by being a stay-at-home mom. Yet she doesn't come off as a super-matriarch, either.

The emerging model for SP Two parenting encourages us to love without smothering and protect without trying to overcontrol. Still, there are times when parents must go to extraordinary lengths to protect the ones they love. *Not Without My Daughter*, *House of Cards*, and *A la Place du Coeur* show us parents whose fierce love for their children allows them to overcome insurmountable odds.

In *Not Without my Daughter*, based on a real story, an American woman marries an Iranian man and they all live happily in the United States until the daughter is around school age. At that point, they go back for a visit to Iran, at which point the husband announces that they will not be returning to the United States. Stuck in an Islamic state where women have few rights, both mother and daughter are miserable, especially when the husband becomes increasingly abusive. It's obvious that the mother could leave if she so desires, but not with her daughter, who under Iranian law is considered to belong to her father. But she refuses to abandon her daughter to the life she would have to live in post-Khomeni Iran—hence, the title of the film. Against all odds, mother and daughter finally manage to make a difficult cross-country escape to Turkey.

In *House of Cards*, an archeologist and his family are living on-site in Central America when a tragic fall takes his life. His small daughter Sally becomes withdrawn and begins to exhibit autistic symptoms although her grieving mother (Kathleen Turner) barely notices, because she's so distracted by grief and preoccupied with bringing her family back to the States. By the time Mom *does* notice, Sally's developed the unfortunate habit of climbing to high places, although nobody knows why. Eventually, her behavior attracts the interest of child protective services, whose officials insist that she be treated by an expert in autism, Dr. Jake Beerlander (Tommy Lee Jones).

At this point, Mom's protective instincts go into high gear. Now that she's aware of the problem, she's determined to re-establish emotional contact with Sally. And she's convinced that Sally's seemingly meaningless behavior is actually meaningful, so she wants to decipher her silent signals. Dr. Beerlander, by contrast, just wants to treat the symptoms using behavior modification.

The drama centers around the conflict between these two positions. Ultimately, the mother's faith is vindicated; we discover that Sally actually witnessed her father's death and that what seems like bizarre behavior is a symbolic response to trauma. Mom's protective instincts eventually allow her to find an imaginative solution that leads to the healing of the entire family.

In *A La Place du Coeur*, Bebe is a young black man betrothed to Clim, a young white woman. They're childhood friends who have fallen deeply in love. But then Clim is accused of rape by a racist policeman, based on the testimony of a young Bosnian woman who has conveniently returned to Bosnia. The couple are at a loss about what to do; they have little money and public opinion is against them. In an interesting twist, it's the young woman's mother, Marianne, who believes in Bebe's innocence and is therefore determined to travel to Bosnia and find the missing witness—and get her to recant her testimony. Despite many difficulties, Marianne's persistence eventually uncovers evidence that clears Bebe's name.

Many films focus on the role of mothers in creating a home that meets the emotional needs of their kids, despite health problems (*Dawn Anna*), the loneliness of divorce (*Alice Doesn't Live Here Anymore*), financial hardship (*The Prize Winner of Defiance, Ohio; In America*), or sudden traumas (*Dawn Anna, House of Cards*). What makes SP Two themes different than SP Six themes (which also center around the family) is the focus on love as the force that binds people together and makes it possible to overcome seemingly hopeless odds.

SP Twos who allow love to inform their actions can give freely without having any sort of agenda in mind. They know how to help in a way that gives people what they really need, but doesn't insist on giving them what they don't! Family members of SP Twos can support them by encouraging them to take a break and giving them positive attention when they do, so they become as good at accepting love as giving it.

¤ ¤ ¤

SEXUAL TWO THEMES. SX Two represents the place of love and romance, so the focus here is on the whole cycle of dating, meeting a potential mate, courtship, and (ideally) bringing that courtship to a successful conclusion. The traditional conclusion has been the wedding, preferable a "fairy tale" wedding. (Interestingly, marriage *after* the wedding is more of a Six theme, because marriage—unlike romance—is a social institution that promotes cultural stability.)

There have been so many things said about romantic love that it's hard to know what more to say here. Of course, the "boy meets girl" theme has a zillion variations which follow the basic pattern of "boy-meets-girl, boy-loses-girl, the two reconcile and live happily every after"—or at least as long as the film credits run! This kind of story is the stuff of many popular romantic comedies (e.g., *Sleepless in Seattle, When Harry Met Sally, Nine Months, Notting Hill*), most of which don't bother to look too deeply into the complex dynamics of real-life intimate relationships. The problems encountered are based on funnily enjoyable misunderstandings that are eventually straightened out, resulting in a happily-ever-after ending.

Although romantic comedies vastly outnumber love stories that lack a Hollywood ending, there are a number of film themes that explore romantic love from a slightly deeper perspective—looking, for example, at the issue of what can happen when one of the partners (often an SX Two) gives up too much to the beloved, who happily allows it until it becomes clear that no gift comes without some sort of price.

In *Steel Magnolias*, the SX Two character Shelby (Julia Roberts) is a brittle diabetic who manages to fall in love with a guy who's pretty clueless about her condition. She's not supposed to have children because it could seriously compromise her health. But she knows her husband wants a child, so she throws caution to the wind and gets pregnant anyway. The baby is fine, but Shelby is not; a few months later, she needs a kidney transplant. Her health continues to deteriorate, with predictably tragic results: one day, she collapses and never regains consciousness. While the movie ultimately ends on a hopeful note, it reminds us of the potentially serious consequences of both giving ourselves away for the sake of love (or conversely, allowing our Two partners to sacrifice themselves to prove their love to us).

Real love seldom demands that kind of sacrifice, because both partners value each other too much to let this happen. But young, inexperienced Twos can be so eager to show their love that they jump into the relationship with both feet, giving a lot to their partners but sometimes wanting commitment before the partner is ready to give it. In *He's Just Not That Into You*, Beth (Jennifer Aniston) has been living with her boyfriend Neil (Ben Affleck) for several years, hoping she'll get what she most wants in life: a proposal of marriage. She's more intent on getting engaged than enjoying the relationship as it is. One day, tired of waiting, she asks Neil his intentions. When he hesitates, she feels betrayed and walks out on the relationship. Time passes, allowing both individuals to think about what they really want in life. When they meet again, they're both more mature. Beth realizes she wants Neil even without a ring; and Neil realizes that he's ready for commitment (so she gets the ring anyway). Not all the other couples in the film fare so well, but as the voice-over at the end suggests, happy endings aren't necessarily about getting the right guy (or gal)— they're about feeling happy with our lives, whatever happens with our romantic relationships. That's a big lesson for SX Twos.

Millionaire Matchmaker's Patti Stanger knows that lesson very well. So does John Gray, author of the popular *Mars and Venus* series. Both of them caution people who date to go slow and allow romance to develop gradually, not to give away the store on the first date or sacrifice our identity to please our partners.

An SX Two theme that comes up a lot in real life is the problem of romantic love versus love for one's children. Single parents can get pretty lonely; it's appealing to seek out a partner. But how do we balance our needs for companionship with our kids' needs for nurturing? That's a tough question for any single parent.

The best scenarios involve partners who love our kids as much as they love us. In *Dawn Anna*, based on a true story, a single mom (Debra Winger) with four kids struggles with health and financial problems. Although she's not looking for a partner, life manages to send somebody her direction—someone who persists in courting her, despite her seeming lack of interest. He eventually wins her over, and then he wins over her kids. His love and support help the family weather an unexpected tragedy that deals the family an added blow.*

Stepmom addresses the related question of how we manage to do what's best for our children when bitter feelings towards an ex-partner and his new wife put the children— who must go back and forth—in a no-win situation. In this case, the situation is brought to a head when the ex-wife (Susan Sarandon) discovers she has terminal cancer. She realizes she has to shift gears and put her children's welfare before her own bitter feelings about the divorce—and above her jealousy of the new stepmom (Julia Roberts).

The Substitute Wife also features a terminally ill woman (Lea Thompson) who is worried about what will happen after her death. So she decides to seek out a new wife

---

* It's hard to find film examples that explore the question of romantic versus parental love in a serious way; I selected *Dawn Anna* because it's one the better examples (probably because it's a true story—and in real life, many parents place their children's needs before their own).

for her husband while she's still alive. She can't wait, because her family are Old West homesteaders living on an isolated farm, and all four children are young. The only possible candidate is a past-her-prime whore (Farrah Fawcett), whose saucy manner doesn't initially sit very well with the hardworking husband. (It's a classic SP vs SX conflict.)

Although the husband is not happy about the whole idea, he reluctantly goes along with it for his wife's sake. Over time, the various relationships get sorted out (and in a way that seems believable); the husband finds he can respond to his wife-to-be without dishonoring his current wife, especially when he realizes that this makes her genuinely happy. The result is a story of sacrificial love at its very best.

Arranged marriages also involve a kind of sacrificial love, because it requires young people to sacrifice their freedom to choose a marriage partner in deference to the family's desire to play a major role in the selection process. Nowadays, arranged marriages usually involve families from traditional cultures who are seeking to preserve the traditions of that culture. The question is: What is actually sacrificed? And does this sacrifice tend to produce happy marriages?

The answer in modern Western films is usually no. Most of us find it hard to imagine marriage without spontaneous romance, and we see this idea reflected in the plots of lighthearted ethnic comedies like *Hollywood/Bollywood*, *Fiddler on the Roof*, and *East is East*, where the parents' choice of partner isn't very appealing. The parents are portrayed as well-meaning but out of touch with modern trends.

The film *Arranged* takes a slightly different approach, exploring the issue of arranged marriages in a more serious way. The story begins with the hiring of two new teachers at a Manhattan school, one Jewish and the other Muslim. Both come from conservative families who hope to find a suitable husband within their respective ethnic and religious communities. Thrown together in one classroom, the two gradually become friends, despite their ethnic differences (and the bumbling interference of the school principal, who wants to "celebrate diversity," but can't help but try to convert both of them to a staunchly feminist outlook on love and marriage). Outside the classroom, both must put up with the inevitable troop of unsuitable suitors; and both of course despair at ever finding a partner who's the right match. Meanwhile, their budding friendship is opposed by their shocked families. So their challenge is to honor their parents' wishes while at the same time asserting themselves as independent young women.

What makes this film unusual is that neither of the protagonists openly rebels against the idea of an arranged marriage. On the contrary, both women like and respect their own ethnic traditions and only make waves to the extent that they feel pushed towards suitors who aren't right for them. After the usual array of difficulties, the right suitors finally turn up (although this admittedly involves a little self-interested intervention). Ultimately, both women are betrothed to men they are happy to marry. The film then fast-forwards a year into the future, where we see them sitting happily together on a bench in the park, each with a babe in arms.

Darker SX Two themes involve the emotional manipulation or stalking of partners and potential partners (*The Blue Angel, Fatal Attraction,* etc). At SX Two, people get into trouble for emotional reasons, often because they're romantically obsessed with the object of their desire (not, for example, for financial gain or some other non-emotional reason). So the crimes we see are crimes of passion, events that occur when intense feelings go spiraling out of control.

But the passion of the SX Two can also show up as intense devotion, whether to a belief, an ideal, or a person (especially in a 2w1). SX Twos are often passionate animal lovers whose love of animals can lead them to get involved with organizations interested in animal welfare (traditionally, the ASPCA, although more strident activists may opt for a more radical alternative, such as PETA). Saint Francis of Assisi provides us with an image of the animal lover who was radically committed to the cause of love; Leo Buscaglia was a modern-day "lover of love," who said he never married because he couldn't do justice to a family while also promoting the cause of love in his public work. And the passion we see in the poems of Rumi ("give me passion, passion, passion") and the works of Kahlil Gibran very much captures the spirit of this subtype.

SX Twos embody a potent archetype: the archetype of Romantic Love. Although love is something we all seek, the experience of falling in love can be like grabbing a tiger by the tail. For SX Twos—who live with this archetype all the time—the desire for romantic love can seem all-consuming. So they need to be careful to avoid getting so intoxicated by the object of their devotion that they lose the ability to enjoy life without a partner. Twos who manage to break free of the desire to make the romantic love their only goal in life actually find that their relationships improve, because they acquire the patience to wait for a partner who's the right match (instead of just an easy catch).

¤ ¤ ¤

SOCIAL TWO THEMES. SOC Two themes involve social work and humanitarian causes (One wing), personal networking, love and friendship (Three wing), power-behind-the-scenes themes, and the kind of social activities in which personal relationships matter (e.g., weddings, funerals, baby showers, diplomatic functions, and class reunions). SOC Twos enjoy creating events that bring people together, especially in a way that promotes real fellowship. So they're attentive hosts/hostesses and take care to ensure that everyone present feels included in the festivities. They're particularly adept at using their personal touch to transform ordinary events into memorable occasions. Their special strength lies in their ability to personalize the impersonal.

I've mentioned *Steel Magnolias* as an example of a film where the protagonist denies her own needs, but it's even more striking as an example of the whole SOC Two approach to life, where life is seen as a series of personally meaningful events that bring people into shared fellowship. The film is appropriately set in the deep South, a place where the social graces still matter; even strangers are welcomed like long-lost relatives when they visit your home. Shortly after the film begins, a disoriented and newly-divorced Annelle Depuy Desoto (Daryll Hannah) arrives in town looking for a job as a hairdresser; she's hired by Truvy Jones (SOC Two Dolly Parton) to work at her hair salon. Since the hair salon is the meeting place for all the local women, Annelle is quickly adopted by the friendly locals who frequent the place.

The salon is also the launchpad for social festivities like weddings, parties, and holiday events. And it's easy to see why: Truvy is pure sunshine as a hairdresser whose mission in life is to make women feel beautiful. And Truvy doesn't just care about women; she cares about everybody, even her moody and withdrawn husband. Her good cheer and patient support eventually pull him out of his inexplicable funk, and he eventually surprises her by setting up a second salon. Upon seeing it, the delighted Truvy happily proclaims, "I can't believe it! I'm a chain!"

Steel Magnolias tells us not only that love triumphs, but that the love of women—and especially women in communion—has a special power to transform. Other examples of women-in-communion films include *9 to 5*, *Sisterhood of the Traveling Pants (I & II)*, *The Color Purple*, *Thelma & Louise*, and *Fried Green Tomatoes*. The shadow side of many of these films lies in their treatment of males, which is generally not all that complimentary. In *Steel Magnolias*, the men behave like large children; in *9 to 5*, they're humorously dumb; in *The Color Purple*, they're exploiters; in *Thelma & Louise*, they're smarmy; in *Fried Green Tomatoes*, they lack power; and *How to Make an American Quilt*, they're insensitive. But considering the long list of films that denigrate female concerns as trivial or silly, the men still get off pretty lightly in these films.

Another major SOC Two theme is the need to make the world a better place through hands-on humanitarian efforts. Most SOC Twos don't confine their concern to human needs, but empathize with the needs of all living creatures. We see this concern expressed in the work of socially-involved Twos such as Mother Teresa, Princess Diana, Florence Nightingale, Albert Schweitzer, Sally Struthers, and Richard Simmons.

For a more light-hearted example of social concern, check out *Quincy*, the 1970s TV series where Jack Klugman plays a pathologist who manages each week to find some way to make a passionate speech about the needs of some neglected group in America, e.g., people who rely on "orphan" drugs that are not made available at affordable prices because they're for disorders that are too rare to make the drugs profitable for drug companies. The Quincy character could be 1w2 or 2w1, but it's his people-oriented focus that makes me suspect the latter. (As an IMDB online reviewer observed, Quincy is fond of meddling and always confronts his chief adversary by screaming, "People's lives are at stake here!!!")

Reality show producers are often attracted to SOC Two humanitarian themes. The popular TV series *Extreme Makeover: Home Edition* is a good example .The object is to build a completely new home for a deserving family in only one week, with help from tons of volunteers and contributions from the show's sponsors. Its host, carpenter Ty Pennington (who seems like a 2w3), is good at providing those "Michael Landon" moments that let the viewers have a good cry while also feeling inspired by the efforts of Ty's team, community volunteers, and the target families (who are usually deeply committed to community service). *Oprah's Big Give* was a one-time competition to see who could do the most to inspire people to donate time and energy to worthwhile community projects. (Oprah's a Three, but leans into both her wings, making her a genuine humanitarian but with a highly practical vision of how to help people.) MTV's *The World's Strictest Parents* offers troubled teens the chance to move in with families whose strict-but-loving ethos inspires them to change their ways, which is pretty amazing, considering they're only there for a week. It's amazing to see how strict limits combined with unconditional love can change a young person's attitude so quickly.

We also see SOC Two themes in documentaries about the efforts of humanitarians to provide hands-on assistance to people involved in accidents and natural disasters (911, Hurricane Katrina, or the 2010 Haitian earthquake); to people in trouble because of violence, abuse, exploitation, or addiction; or to the weak and disenfranchised (children, animals, the elderly, and others who especially need personalized attention). As I mentioned earlier, animal welfare is a particularly popular SOC Two theme that shows up in TV shows and documentaries, such as *Dogtown,* a show documenting the efforts of a real-life animal rescue organization that adopts abused or abandoned animals and restores them to health. Others programs show us how helping animals helps people transform themselves: *Wild Horse Redemption* documents the efforts of prison wardens to rehabilitate inmates by giving them the opportunity to train wild horses; TV's *Dog Whisperer* features an episode showing how inmates are transformed by training service dogs.

Social service and social action are both SOC Two themes, and they can look very similar, but they're not quite the same thing. The difference between the two is illustrated in a recent book, *Hope Endures* (2008), by Colette Livermore. It's about her experiences as a nun in Mother Teresa's Missionaries of Charity. She joined the order when she was only 18, out of her passionate desire to ameliorate the suffering of the poor. She envisioned herself working in rural Africa or some other obscure locale, bringing the help necessary to improve their lot. But she was disappointed with the order's approach, because she felt that it afforded her no way to be an individual or to get real medical training. So she left after 11 years, going on to get the medical degree that allowed her to help the poor on her own terms.

Having read Mother Teresa's letters,* I wasn't surprised at Livermore's disappointment. Mother Teresa had a distinctly devotional streak, so her goal was to express Christ's love by doing simple things to care for the poor and dying. Colette Livermore was focused less on sacrificial service and more on social action. Both are SOC Two paths, but the path of social service is more specifically devotional (focusing on service as a vehicle for the expression of a devotional ideal) while the path of social action is less devotional and more pragmatic (and more potentially political).

These two paths converge in the poignant work of Henry Marsh, whose work is the focus of *The English Surgeon (2007)*. Marsh is an English brain surgeon who became aware of the terrible conditions in Ukrainian hospitals (the combined result of corruption, the legacy of Communism, and an almost complete lack of medical screening equipment). With the help of a Ukrainian colleague, he began making annual trips to Ukraine to donate his services to patients in need of brain surgery.

---

* *Mother Teresa, Come Be My Light: The Private Writings of the "Saint of Calcutta"* (2007), Brian Kolodiejchuk, ed.

Many of the stories in the documentary are sad, focusing on patients whose diagnosis comes too late to save them. But there are success stories, as well; Marsh performs the successful removal of a benign tumor that is still small enough to be operable. The man with the tumor, Marian, is still young; the operation transforms his life.

The English Surgeon celebrates the efforts of one caring individual to compassionately serve the needs of the poor, but it also brings to our attention the need for massive changes in the Ukrainian medical system, changes that seem unlikely to come any time soon. Meanwhile, Dr. Marsh continues his one-man crusade to improve the lives of whomever he can help, even if it's just to show that he cares. In this way, he's like a modern-day Albert Schweitzer, Clara Barton, or Florence Nightingale, putting up with the terrible limitations of the present, in hopes of paving the way for a brighter future.

Type three –
the self-tester

We don't as Americans tend to think we're philosophical.
*We don't think we **have** a philosophy, that we just do what works.*
– Diana Ravitch, author of *Left Back: A Century of Failed School Reforms*

THREES ARE THE GREAT PRAGMATISTS of the enneagram. Hardworking, ener-
getic, and optimistic, they are the people that take pride in their 24/7/365 work ethic.
If Ones focus on principle and Twos on humanity, Threes focus on achievement. It's
not that they lack an interest in principles or in nurturing relationships, simply that
the desire to test themselves and stretch their limits is even more compelling. In their
quest for achievement, Threes are willing to spend a great deal of their time cultivat-
ing the physical, mental, and emotional qualities necessary for meeting—and then
exceeding—their personal best.

From the transformational perspective, Threes are at that point on the enneagram
that represents the heart of life, which is why they're so involved in the affairs of the
world, so immersed in the lively commerce of the marketplace. They test themselves
against life, against others, and against their own past performance, always trying to
achieve something they've never achieved before. Their competitive spirit arises in re-
sponse to the need to get a sense of how they're doing. And the most direct way of real-
izing this goal is to see how well they measure up against others, especially in activities
where success can be objectively assessed (sports, business, and school).

Like Twos and Fours, Threes are *image types*, the types whose focus is on self-identity. So the question, "Who am I?" looms large, although young Threes may not consciously see this as a motivator. It's usually not until they've achieved their material goals (often when they're still young) that they begin to realize that there's still something missing from life, something intangible. This same sense of "something missing" may arise when they encounter relationship problems they can't fix or health problems that force them to stop filling up their days with constant activity. However it happens, when Threes stop their whir of activity and become receptive to their inner signals, they have the chance to get to know themselves in a new way: not just as successful "doers"—whose self-worth depends upon visible tokens of success—but as souls who have intrinsic worth, whether or not they're able to produce the kind of tangible results valued by the collective.

But this is a real challenge for Threes, one that takes them well outside of their comfort zone. The world of reflection is a tough place for Threes to travel, because it robs them of their greatest asset: their ability to grapple with concrete problems requiring practical know-how. When put into a position where there are no outer obstacles to overcome, a Three can become disoriented, even fearful. She needs to understand that when confronting the obstacles of inner life, her success will depend upon the ability to stay present (connection to Nine) and ride the fear (connection to Six). Threes who are able to ride the wave discover that their fear is gradually replaced by a sense of inner presence that supports their outer work. Not only do they feel good about themselves, but their efforts acquire a greater nobility of purpose, now that their work is an expression of who they are inside (instead of a defensive maneuver designed to cover over a sense of inner vacancy).

Another result of being an image type is that Threes—like Twos and Fours—are sensitive to other people's approval. Twos seek approval by trying to anticipate and meet the emotional needs of others; Threes seek approval by excelling in approved-of activities and getting along with people who matter; and Fours seek peoples' recognition of their uniqueness and artistry. Threes are less serious than Ones and less emotionally

	TABLE 13-1. **TYPE THREE: THE SELF-TESTER**		
	HARD-WORKING, DECISIVE, COMPETITIVE, REALISTIC, PENETRATING SIX Connection brings caution, thoroughness, detail-orientation, anxiety NINE Connection brings calmness, neutrality, ability to stop, zoning out TWO Wing brings conviviality, people skills, managerial ability, social outlook FOUR Wing brings independence, focus, intensity, drive, commitment Other Labels: Type A, Competitor, Achiever, Doer, Pragmatist Challenges: over-work, under-play, imperviousness, fear of intimacy		
	SUBTYPES		
	Self-preservation	Sexual	Social
A R C H E T Y P E S	*Determined Achiever, Adaptable Go-Getter, Ambitious Individualist, Hardworking Bootstrapper, Success-oriented Career-seeker, Activity-oriented Parent, Soccer Mom, "Do everything" Mom, Horatio Alger, Organized Pragmatist, CFO, Results-oriented Entrepreneur, Dedicated Apprentice, Ambitious Journeyman, Mr. or Ms. "All- work- no -play," Hard-driving Executive, "Type A" Personality, Comeback Kid, Big Fish in a Small Pond, Company Man/Woman*	*Public Personality, Aspiring Star, Life Coach, Rising Star, Shining Star, Popular Hero/Heroine, Attention-getter, Sex Goddess, Glamour Queen, Fashion Plate, Commercial Model, Manicured Professional, High School Cheerleader or Quarterback, Model of Airbrushed Perfection, Media Sensation, Personal Mentor, Masculine/ Feminine Ideal, Venus, Adonis, Athlete, Exaggerator, Swindler, Master Manipulator, Plagiarist, Grifter, Embezzler*	*Team Leader, Office Seeker, Opinion Leader, Politician, Large-scale Event Organizer, Head of the Class, Valedictorian, First Among Equals, Early Adapter, Effective Presenter, Credentialed Consultant , Lobbyist, Image Consultant, Team-oriented Coach, Organizational Expert, Prestige Elite Member, Public Opinion Expert, Spin Doctor, Glosser-over, Political Smoother, Master Deal-maker*
F I L M T H E M E S	**Personal obstacles are overcome** by those who persist (*In Pursuit of Happyness, The Other Side of the Mountain, My Left Foot, Breaking Away*) **Extreme trials** can bring about the arousal of survival instincts (*Empire of the Sun, Interview with a Vampire, TV's Survivor*) or the surrender of the superficial (*Castaway, Terms of Endearment*) **Materialism** can obliterate ethics (*Wall Street, Risky Business, Maxed Out, Disclosure*), culture (*Radiant City*), common sense (*Czech Dream*), or the willingness to parent (*The Baby Dance*) **Success is easy** if you don't make waves (*How to Succeed in Business Without Really Trying*) or care about others' feelings (*Absence of Malice*) **Energetic immigrants** seek success in the New World (*Hester Street, Far and Away*)	**Pushing hard & dreaming big** can bring stardom (*The Right Stuff, Top Gun, Rocky, Donahue, Oprah, Superman*) **Image-magic** can create new opportunities for success (*Working Girl, Tootsie, Hancock, Mrs. Doubtfire, The Great Imposter*) **Success isn't worth much** without ethics (*Jerry Maguire, The Devil's Advocate*), love (*Shadowlands*), meaning (*Broadcast News*), or authenticity (*The Truman Show*) **Success** is sought at any price (*All About Eve, The Thorn Birds, Dangerous Liaisons, The Deliberate Stranger, The Talented Mr. Ripley, Broken Glass*) **The desire for success** makes relationships difficult (*A Star Is Born, Bed of Roses, Workaholic, Absence of Malice, Kramer vs. Kramer, Bee Season*)	**Superficial conventions** cover over empty lives (*Six Degrees of Separation, Ordinary People*) **Social prestige** gained without ethics yields little of lasting value (*Primary Colors, The Firm, Regarding Henry, The Philadelphia Story*) **Wheeler-dealers** can be lifesavers (*Schindler's List, Wallenburg: a Hero's Story*) but can also fool the uninitiated (*The Spanish Prisoner, Six Degrees of Separation*) **Teamwork** is key to success (*Apollo 13, The Great Escape, Hoosiers, The Amazing Race, The Bad News Bears, SuperNanny, The Great Debaters*) **Fashion** determines both social success & failure (*What Not to Wear, Clueless, America's Next Top Model, The Fashion Police*) **Success** uplifts & inspires others (*Mr. Holland's Opus, SuperNanny, Oprah's Big Give*) perhaps changing society & its conventions (*Bicentennial Man*)

sensitive than either Twos or Fours, so it's easier for them to behave in a way that conforms to social expectations most of the time. They're not selling out; they simply see no reason to diverge from social norms if they have no strong alternative preference.

Threes are the children who become business whizzes before they're even out of high school, especially in businesses where initiative, a winsome manner, and common sense reap rewards. They often have a paper route, start a micro-business, or become deeply involved in family-run businesses. Michael Rubin, founder and CEO of CGI Commerce, says that when he was eight years old, he sold stationery door to door. By the time he was 14, he opened a ski shop. And at 21, he had a business that generated over $100k in revenue. He loves business: "It made me feel good to be a winner. And business made me a winner."

Youthful Threes gain accolades by excelling in well-established arenas; they try to do well in school, although they're usually more attracted to extra-curricular activities like sports and clubs than scholarly pursuits. Threes are often the kids that seem most well-rounded; they're prime candidates for designations like Most Popular or Most Likely to Succeed. Like young Twos, they adapt almost too well to the needs of those around them, especially adults.

Threes draw much of their emotional tone from their wings. Threes with a Two wing tend to be more extroverted, sunny, and even-tempered; they find it natural to be involved in the marketplace of life and particularly avoid work that is solitary in nature. They like to fit seamlessly into their social environment and enjoy making the effort to be a team player. Threes with a Four wing tend to be more contained, independent-minded, and inclined to mood swings. They prefer independent consulting to working for a large organization and are drawn to recognized fields such as management, real estate, marketing, or sales. They tend to be more introspective and curious about the deeper questions in life, especially after they get financially established.

The connecting points of Six and Nine allow Threes to potentially see life from a less deadline-oriented perspective. By connecting to Six, Threes can access the ability to "stop, look, and listen": to exercise greater caution before committing themselves to hastily-conceived plans. So this connection provides Threes with a reality check, re-minding them to look before they leap. By connecting to Nine, Threes get the ability not only to slow down, but to stay in the moment (assuming Threes allow themselves to jump to Nine before they're completely exhausted). There's a tendency to wait too long, so that the move to Nine becomes a move to mindlessness instead of *being*.

Searle identifies two major Three story genres: the success story and the imposter story. The success story draws attention to the Three's ability to work hard and achieve something of note. Traditionally, these were called Horatio Alger tales, based on the popular stories by the author of the same name, who was famous for writing popular 19th century rags-to-riches novels.

The imposter story focuses on a less palatable quality often associated with Type 3: the ability to create a deceptive impression. So this category obviously includes sto-ries about imposters, scam artists, grifters, and cheats. But it also includes (or should include) stories about using "impression management" for wholesome purposes; the most poignant example in a film is probably *Schindler's List*, a film about business-man Oskar Schindler's use of wheeler-dealer tactics to save many Jewish lives during World War II.

So let me momentarily digress to discuss the nature of deception and what it means for Threes. Point 3 seems to be the place on the enneagram most associated with unprincipled, shady, or deceptive practices, the implication being that Threes are less ethical than other types. But all nine types can be guilty of ethical violations; Threes are no more or less ethical than any other type. The reason this concern with ethics comes up at Point 3 is that it's at the heart of the image-creation process—and image creation involves getting people to see reality from a new or different angle. This is something that Threes excel at, although we all do it. Whenever we create a story to tell our kids at bedtime, we're engaged in image creation. When a rock star gets on a stage and weaves a spell around the audience, he's created a world of images (one that most audiences welcome). When we write an effective resumé, we're trying to create an image of ourselves that we hope our potential employers will like.

Image creation isn't something bad. It's a natural part of involution: the process by which spiritual energy creates material reality (see Chapter 7): Point 9 *imaginings* become Point 1 *ideals*, ideals which become clothed in *humanity* at Point 2 and which emerge as fully-fledged *images* at Point 3 (and which begin to disintegrate at Point 4). It's true that some images may be better (more luminous, inspired, or generative) than others; and it's also true that images can be used for cynical or destructive purposes (e.g., to cheat, lie, or steal from people). But it doesn't mean there's anything wrong with the process itself: what matters is the kind of images we create and for what purpose. While negative images can certainly harm people, positive images can help them think positive, overcome obstacles, and refuse to give up during hard times. So while Threes are negatively stereotyped in films with images like the greedy businessman, cynical manipulator, or corrupt politician, these negative stereotypes should be taken with a grain of salt. (The same of course can be said of all type-related stereotypes.)

Before moving on to the subtype arenas, there's one more Three theme that re-quires mention: the perennial conflict between love and work. Balancing the two can be a major challenge, because the mandate to achieve is very strong for Threes, espe-cially during early adulthood. But this is precisely the same time when people seek a partner, date, marry, and begin a family. So how can we fully commit ourselves to both at the same time? We can't, at least not easily. But because Threes are so achievement-oriented, the need to achieve can engulf everything else. When this happens, Threes find themselves either alone or with a partner who's not very happy. Being aware of this dynamic potentially allows Threes to be proactive in finding solutions before the problem gets out of hand.

¤ ¤ ¤

SELF-PRESERVATION THREE THEMES. The SP Three subtype embodies the American Dream at its best: the dream of starting small, working hard, and achiev-ing a secure foothold in life. This kind of Horatio Alger theme is popular in American culture, so there are quite a few films depicting determined protagonists overcom-ing all kinds of adversity to achieve their goals, whether it's to become an artist in the absence of functioning hands (*My Left Foot*), a female writer in post-Victorian Australia (*My Brilliant Career*), a financial broker despite homelessness (*In Pursuit of Happyness*), or a functioning human being despite quadriplegia (*The Other Side of the Mountain*). The emphasis at SP Three is on achieving a personal goal against great odds, especially a physical goal. For many Threes, there seems to be a pivotal moment in life when the Three—having lost everything or reached the end of her patience—vows "Never again!," like Scarlett O'Hara in *Gone with the Wind*. Never again will the Three put up with physical or financial insecurity. From that point on, she will devote all her time and energy to creating a secure foundation in life.

Some people think this makes Threes materialistic, but materialism only becomes a problem when it's taken to extremes. To accuse Threes of materialism misses the point, because it implies that there's something wrong with the desire to imagine a new idea and translate it into a physical reality. If nobody wanted to do this, just think of the things we'd miss out on: new technology, medications, emergency treatments, modes of transport, and other advances that make life less painful and more interesting. As long as we live in a material world, we need people who focus on material manifestation.

Of course, it's possible to go overboard in that department, getting so caught up in the desire to accumulate wealth that it becomes an end in itself. When that happens, we can start losing track of our original goals. We might even end up like the two protagonists in *Wall Street*, which depicts a naive young broker (Charlie Sheen) getting seduced into insider trading by a corrupt and cynical older broker (Michael Douglas). As *Videohound's Golden Retriever* notes, Douglas is "greed personified," but he's also persuasive, which is why he's able to gull his younger counterpart into sacrificing his ethics for gain.

But it's not just greedy businessmen (or Threes) that are attracted by the prospect of easy money; it's all of us. It's one of the challenges we encounter as we traverse this point on the process enneagram. In *Czech Dream*, two Czech student film-makers wanted to document the emergence of consumerism in the post-Communist Czech Republic, as reflected by the public interest in the new "superstores" opening all over the country.

So they pretended to plan a new superstore and hired publicists to create a big public stir. They even had a "grand opening" for the store, complete with ribbon-cutting ceremony and the promise of a surprise (the surprise being that the store didn't really exist!). Their efforts worked; about 3000 eager shoppers lined up as much as three hours in advance to take advantage of the opening day deals. When the ribbon was cut, customers surged towards the new store only to discover it was a giant façade! (The film-makers were smart enough to give out a small memento to each of the disappointed shoppers, so they wouldn't get lynched!)

The same eagerness to snag a bargain can make people vulnerable to the credit card industry, with its "buy now, pay later" ethos. The documentary *Maxed Out* tells us how the credit card industry tries to keep us all in debt, but not quite so indebted that we can't keep buying. While the film concentrates on the deceptive practices of credit card companies, the film also makes clear that no matter how much we might like to blame them for our financial woes, they don't actually force us to buy anything; they only make it easier to make a bad decision.

And what about the real estate bubble during the early 2000s? Around 2004, everybody seemed to get the idea that they could get rich quick on real estate. TV shows like *Flip This House* and *Flip That House* showed eager investors all the possibilities! (Maybe we should have been watching *The Property Ladder* instead, which featured amateur house flippers making a mess instead of a profit.) By 2008-09, the house-flipping shows had virtually disappeared, replaced by shows like *Real Estate Intervention*, in which an empathic but realistic real estate agent (Mike Aubrey) explained the new housing economy to shocked homeowners who couldn't believe it's actually possible to lose money on real estate.

The desire for bigger and better homes isn't something that just appeals to house flippers, but to ordinary families seeking more space on a budget. *Radiant City* is an understated morality tale that shows us what can happen to people in communities in which material comfort takes priority over everything else. It's filmed in one of those huge mega-tract housing developments that's miles and miles away from the big city. Because of the distance, the homes are big, the neighborhoods are safe, and the price is low: an ideal combination. There's only one problem: the community is totally manufactured, so it lacks organic vitality.

At first, *Radiant City* seems like a documentary, featuring ordinary people talking about the pros and cons of living in this kind of community. It also features commentaries by architects who have designed alternative communities which avoid the vacuousness of the mega-tracts. It's not hard to see that something is missing in these communities, something important, which is why one husband practically begs his wife to move back into the city, even if it means a smaller house. She's not interested, of course, having become so accustomed to the amenities of the new home that she barely notices the soullessness of her surroundings. It's not until the final shocking scene that we see just how unpleasant such a Pleasantville can become—and realize that the film is actually a drama, not a documentary.

A related theme concerns the need to balance outer life with inner life. This is difficult for all Threes, because they typically find it hard to introspect. It's especially difficult for SP Threes, because of their material orientation. The combination of the Three's pragmatism and the SP's concern with security make it natural for them to take time and money seriously. When they acquire things, they feel fulfilled, even in a spiritual sense. But there usually comes a point in the life of an SP Three when (due to failure, illness, or other life circumstances), she has the opportunity to undertake a different kind of challenge, one that requires her to step outside the arena of material acquisition and into the arena of inner exploration.

The film *Castaway* shows us the inner odyssey of an extreme workaholic who unexpectedly finds himself stranded on a desert island. The castaway is Chuck Noland (Tom Hanks), the very image of a "go, go, go" FedEx manager who's the only survivor when a FedEx cargo plane crashes in the South Pacific. Although Chuck manages to inflate a life raft and make his way to a nearby island (with only a few water-logged packages for company), he must learn to survive using his wits, all the while hoping for rescue.

Initially, he's clueless; he can't figure out how to make a fire or build a functional shelter. Slowly, he acquires the skills necessary for physical survival. But after the days stretch into weeks, and the weeks stretch into months, Chuck finds himself facing psychological and spiritual crises that turn out to be even more challenging. Finding a Wilson volleyball among the packages, he turns "Wilson" into a companion, so he doesn't feel so alone.

The film fast-forwards four years into the future, and we see how island life has affected Chuck in the long run. No longer the flabby executive, he's thin but fit. He can fish, make tools, and find shelter from the elements. Although a bit crusty, he's in touch with his instincts and the natural world—and deeply bonded with Wilson, whom he treats as a friend, confidante, and religious figure, all rolled into one.

But Chuck hasn't yet given up on the chance to find his way back to civilization, so he builds a raft and courageously sets forth on the open sea, an effort which turns into the psychological equivalent of the Hero's Journey. First he has to make it through the crashing surf and then through endless days of sun beating down on the raft. After awhile, he begins to go in and out of consciousness, so he doesn't notice when the cords around Wilson begin to loosen. When he awakens, he sees that the ball has slipped off the raft and is now floating off into the distance. Distraught, he screams out, "I'm sorry, Wilson!!!" His last vestiges of emotional control are stripped away, and he sobs uncontrollably.

Resigned to die, he's miraculously rescued by a passing ship, returning home against great odds. Not surprisingly, he finds that he no longer fits into his old life. His former fiancée is married and his friends live the kind of life that no longer makes sense to him. He's changed too much, and so have his values. At the end of the film, we see him standing in the middle of a rural crossroads, wondering what to do next.*

---

* It's to Hanks' credit as an actor that he was able to so eloquently convey the inner sufferings of his character when all he had to talk to was a volleyball! Near the end of the film, we discover that his character Chuck almost didn't survive the psychological ordeal; at one point, overcome with despondency, he tried to take his own life. Although this failed, the experience produced a spiritual opening which allowed him to persevere, despite great odds. So the story is not just about outer perseverance, but the inner journey of the soul.

Hanks apparently underwent his own personal odyssey in making the film, losing 55 pounds in just four months and exercising two hours every day so he could look the part of the fit and lean survivor. He also became a true survivor, after an infection in his knee caused a serious case of blood poisoning. It's ironic that to play the part, he exhibited the same kind of intense commitment that his character exhibited in the film (but not surprising, since Hanks is a Three in real life).

Like all SP subtypes, SP Threes can benefit from lightening up and learning to take life a little less seriously, especially after they've got a little material security. Although they provide others with inspiring examples of what is possible with hard work and effort, they can also go overboard in that department, forgetting how to stop and smell the roses. They especially benefit from allowing themselves to step back from time to time, in order to take stock of where they've been and where they're going.

¤ ¤ ¤

Sexual three themes. It's at SX Three that we find the individuals with "star" quality: the ability to catch and hold the attention of the crowd. They can make mesmerizing performers or captivating mentors, but often find it challenging to reconcile their public image with their private lives. The contrast between the two is just too great to make for easy transitions. While all Threes can find it challenging to balance work with intimacy, it's particularly tough for Sexual Threes, because they tend to get so caught up in image creation—and are so good at it—that it's hard to let go of the image once they step off the stage (either figuratively or literally).

There are many films whose theme revolve around the transformation of people living ordinary lives into individuals who represent a cultural ideal (e.g., *Rocky, The Right Stuff, Superman*). So the same Horatio Alger themes that we see at SP Three come up at SX Three, but in a slightly different way. While we see SP Threes overcoming hardship to establish some kind of tangible foothold on life, the urge to overcome at SX Three is about rising above the ordinary to become something (or create something) extraordinary. So SX Threes tend to excel in a way that sends them skyrocketing to the top of their field (often the entertainment field or into some sort of role that allows them to take advantage of their intense focus and personal magnetism).

SX Threes are able to project an image of the cultural ideal, especially a gender ideal; figures like Oprah or Miley Cyrus show us a feminine ideal towards which to strive while Tom Cruise or Arnold Schwarzenegger provide a masculine ideal. Individuals like these are able to capture the imagination of the public, which is why they so often succeed in fields when personal image matters—and so often attract a following, whether as an intensely driven individual mentor or a megastar entertainer.

However, when it comes to intimacy, there's often a stark contrast between the on-stage image-creator and their off-stage counterpart that can make relationships a challenge. Sometimes, the problem is the result of the SX Three's inability to step away from her image; sometimes, it's that her partner won't allow her to step away because he likes the image better than the real person. Another problem is that competitive people are often attracted to other competitive people. When they get together, they sometimes find themselves competing with one another, especially if they work in the same field. When partners begin to seriously vie for the spotlight, they lose the ability to see one another; this ever-popular theme shows in films like *A Star is Born*, where a male superstar is eclipsed by an up-and-coming female newcomer with whom he falls in love. (The fact that this film keeps getting remade suggests that most couples still find it difficult to find marital bliss when the wife's career clearly supersedes the husband's.)

The climb to stardom holds many ethical challenges, because there are so many junctures where we have to choose between ethics and quick advancement. If success is the only thing we value, we risk exchanging long-term happiness for short-term satisfaction. Tom Cruise often explores this theme in his films. Cruise is an SX Three in real life and usually plays them in films (e.g., *Top Gun, Magnolia, Rain Man, Far and Away,* and *Jerry Maguire*).

In *Rain Man,* Cruise plays self-centered hustler Charlie Babbitt, who's always just one step ahead of the bill collectors. When his father dies, Charlie hopes the inheritance will bail him out. But most of the money has been left to provide for the care of someone whose existence comes as a surprise: his brother Raymond. Raymond is a Fivish autistic savant who's been living at an institution for most of his life. Angry about losing the cash, Charlie basically kidnaps Raymond from his institutional home, hoping to bribe the institution to give him some of what he feels he's owed. But Charlie doesn't realize what it takes to care for someone with his brother's needs and sensitivities. Needless to say, he's not very happy once he finds out! But Charley's cynicism is eventually dissolved by Raymond's helpless vulnerability, and he slowly rediscovers his humanity and ability to love.

Jerry Maguire is another Cruise film with a similar theme. Cruise plays a sports agent who suffers a nervous breakdown because of his guilt over the unethical work he's done as a sports promoter. Maguire decides to change his ways. But he also decides to speak out against the shady practices of the trade in his office, which gets him fired. He starts his own firm, but loses most of his former clients. The rest of the film focuses on the barriers he encounters, both personal and professional, as he tries to rise above his habit of manipulating people to get his way.

Unethical manipulation is always a temptation at Point 3, because it seems so easy to pull off and potentially brings such big rewards. In *Absence of Malice*, Sally Field plays a Threeish journalist looking for her "big break." In her quest for personal recognition, she doesn't quite notice the devastating effect that her probing inquiries are having on one of her interviewees, who commits suicide shortly after the interview. When told what happened, she has the decency to feel shocked and dismayed that her insensitive questioning caused such a terrible outcome.

Broken Glass is a story of journalistic ambition with a less morally-evolved protagonist. It's about real-life journalist Stephen Glass, a rising young writer with *The New Republic*, who was so intent on making a name for himself that he simply concocted whole stories and passed them off as investigative reports. Unlike the journalist played by Field, Glass seems to have no trace of a conscience; when his web of deceit is unveiled, he never expresses any sort of regret for what he did (although he's probably deeply sorry that he got caught.) It's guys like this that gives Threes a bad name!

All About Eve also involves a protagonist whose narcissism and preoccupation with stardom causes her to calmly manipulate a famous actress and ultimately trample her into the dust, so she can take her place. *The Talented Mr. Ripley* shows us a more complex character who will lie, cheat, and even murder in pursuit of his goals—but is still able to feel some sort of sorrow about what he feels he's been "forced" to do.

The Devil's Advocate explores what happens when hungry, ambitious types are recognized as such by master manipulators who know how to turn another's desire for gain to their own advantage. In this case, the master manipulator turns out to be the Devil, played quite convincingly by Al Pacino. The ambitious person is Keanu Reeves, playing Kevin Lomax, a brilliant young defense attorney in Gainesville, Florida, who's just successfully defended a man whom he knows to be a child molester. Lomax is courted by big city lawyer John Milton (Pacino), who wants Lomax to join his firm. The salary and perks are too amazing to turn down, so he accepts and begins his long journey down the road to perdition. By the time he sees the light, he has to take drastic action to escape Pacino's clutches. Then he suddenly wakes up to find that the whole awful experience was only a dream. We see him back in the courtroom in Gainesville, where he makes the decision (previously rejected) to step down from defending the child molester in the middle of the trial—a stand that will not only lose him his case, but probably get him disbarred. Afterwards, he's approached by an admiring reporter who says he's "a star," and wants to create a media frenzy so Lomax won't be disbarred. After a little urging from his wife, Lomax agrees to an interview. As the couple is walking away, we see the reporter morphing into Al Pacino, who begins laughing darkly while exclaiming, "Vanity—definitely my *favorite* sin!"

The Truman Show shows us the other end of the stick: what can happen to truly innocent people who get deceived or manipulated without their knowledge. Truman (Jim Carrey) is born as an unwanted baby who's adopted by a TV corporation so he can star in *The Truman Show*, a real-time soap opera where everybody is an actor except Truman. The show's creator, Christof (Ed Harris, playing a Three with a Four wing), broadcasts the show 24/7 around the globe. This gives viewers the chance to live vicariously through Truman, and the show becomes a raging success.

As the film opens, we discover that Truman is a 30-year-old insurance salesmen who seems to be living a happy but predictable life in a nice little seaside community with his overly agreeable wife. The only problem is his growing yen to travel and experience new things. (Truman, like Carrey, is a restless 7w6, so Carrey is convincing as a wannabe traveler). But since the community is just a gigantic movie set, Truman can't actually travel anywhere (much like the characters in Britain's *The Prisoner*). A lot of the film's humor revolves around the innumerable obstacles that magically arise whenever Truman tries to escape. (Of course, they're not really magical but the result of Christof's clever manipulations.)

Finally, Truman becomes deadly serious about getting away—serious enough to risk his life for the chance to be free. He braves his fear of water to sail into the bay, where he spots an Exit door on the edge of the set. At this point, Christof decides to talk to him directly, his voice seeming to come from the sky, like God's.

After Christof has explained the situation, Truman asks him, "Was nothing real?" Christof replies softly, "*You* were real. That's what made the show so good to watch." He then attempts to persuade Truman not to leave: "There's no more truth out there than in the world I created for you. The same lies, the same deceit. But in *my* world, you have nothing to fear."

What's interesting here is Cristof's sincerity. He's not being cynical here; he really believes what he's saying—and provides us with an example of a Three explaining why it's okay to create a special world made of images: because it's no better or worse than any other—and it has the advantage of being safe (so we never have to retreat to Point 6!). But this argument carries little weight with Truman; he's a Seven, not a Three. His greatest fear is being hemmed in, not lack of physical security. Now that he's aware of a wider world, he's ready to experience it. He smiles at the camera, bows deeply to the unseen audience, and walks grandly through the Exit door.

While the SX subtype arena typically focuses on romance, romance can be a difficult area for SX Threes, as mentioned earlier. Real romance requires intimacy, and intimacy requires both vulnerability and lots of time spent with a prospective mate (time that the Three could be working). Threes find both vulnerability and time away from work unappealing, especially young, ambitious Threes like real estate mogul Chad Rogers, featured on TV's real estate reality show *Million Dollar Listing*.

Chad is unintentionally amusing as an emotionally immature (although real estate-saavy) hustler who's so wrapped up in his own image that he has no clue just how stuffily narcissistic he really is. (If we saw him playing himself in a sitcom, we might think he was over-acting. But he's not acting, he's just being himself!) Chad gets away with his hubris because he's good at what he does: selling million-dollar homes. We know he's a SX-SOC Three because, as he notes, "It's not about the money, it's about becoming a brand." He's full of social affectations and wants to promote his public image more than anything else.

But Chad is lost as soon as he steps out of his role as real estate agent extraordinaire and into his role as partner to Victoria, his long-suffering Niney girlfriend. While he tells her she's special and arranges for luxurious dates, their time together is never really their own, because Chad never turns his cell phone off. When the inevitable happens and he has to leave, he always tells her he'll make it up to her later. It's only a matter of time before Victoria figures out that she's never going to take priority over Chad's career. He'll probably have a number of Victorias in his life before he realizes that success without intimacy is a pretty empty proposition.

While Chad's intimate ineptitude is extreme, it demonstrates the Three's tendency to put clients ahead of partners. While it's easy to write this tendency off as the product of narcissistic self-preoccupation, the real truth is a little more complex. For Threes, intimacy is difficult while working with clients is easy, because Threes can meet the needs of clients without ever having to become emotionally vulnerable. Also, work keeps their minds occupied, so they can screen out messy feelings.

But intimate relationships are different. Intimate partners don't care about what we *do* as much as who we *are*—especially who we are with *them*. They specifically want to share feelings, both the happy and the sad. In *What Dreams May Come*, we see what happens when a Three and Four fall in love and get married and try to make a life together. The Three is physician Chris (Robin Williams); the Four is artist Annie (Annabella Sciorra). One day, when the children are mostly grown, a fateful car accident takes their lives, sending Annie into a state of clinical depression that requires hospitalization. In typical Three fashion, Chris is sad but able to cope. He waits for what he thinks is a decent interval for Annie to get better, but she's too devastated to rally.

One day, she looks at him hard and asks, "Why aren't *you* in here? Why didn't *you* go crazy when the children died?" He says that he thought he was supposed to be strong. After a pause, he says, "I loved them, Annie, but they're gone." Then his expression hardens a bit, and he says, "Now you've got a choice. Life either goes on— or not." In that moment, she's got her answer: he's able to cope because he'll always choose survival over love. She gives him a look of love mixed with pity, and says softly, "Sometimes when you win, you lose." But she also decides to try to overcome her grief, and slowly regains some semblance of composure.

She comes home and more or less resumes her life, but one year later, there's another loss—and this time, it's her beloved husband Chris who dies. After death, Chris finds himself in a wonderfully vivid landscape reminiscent of the place where he originally met Annie, but even more exotic. He's amazed and delighted (as was I, watching the marvelous special effects). Various guides appear to help him acclimate to his new environment. But then he receives some stunning news: Annie's become so depressed that she's killed herself. At first, Chris is glad, thinking they'll soon be reunited. But he's informed that suicides don't come to this wonderful place (which he is told he's actually creating himself); they go to a self-created hell of darkness and confusion. That's where Annie will remain for eternity.

He refuses to accept this idea and insists on trying to save her (which is one way Threes show their love—by trying to effect a rescue). With the help of a guide, he descends into Hell, a place full of horrifying images of lost souls, fire, and darkness. These images gradually erode his confidence and he begins to be afraid. But he still wants to save his wife, so he doesn't give up. He eventually locates her, but she's too deeply confused to recognize him. When his cleverest efforts to rouse her end in failure, he has to decide what to do next. So now comes the real test: Will he stay in Hell with her or abandon her to her fate? When the children died, he chose emotional survival over love. Will it happen again?

No—this time, love wins out. He decides to stay. With that, he reminds her of her own words: "Sometimes when you win, you lose." And he sits down, resigned to enter her world of darkness and confusion.

With that decision, something begins to shift. In some small corner of her consciousness, she understands what is happening and struggles to wake up. As she emerges from the fog, she recognizes Chris just as he is losing consciousness. And she screams out, "No, no, *no*!!! Don't give up!" And with that final scream, the hellish scene is suddenly transformed into the beautiful landscape where Chris originally found himself: horror gives way to wonder, leaving the couple breathless but happy. So the circle is now complete. After a pause, Annie turns to Chris and smiles. Then she says, "Sometimes when you lose, you win."

It's never an easy lesson to win by losing, but it's an especially tough lesson for the ultra-competitive SX Three. It may be trite to say that "love conquers all," but sometimes love is the only thing that provides the incentive to learn the art of surrender.

¤ ¤ ¤

SOCIAL THREE THEMES. Like SP Threes, SOC Threes are energetic workers. And like SX Threes, they're intuitively aware of how to create a public image that can attract positive public attention. But their particular talent lies in creating the impression that we're all in this together—that we're all on the same team. As a result, they can make other people feel appreciated for their ability to contribute to a larger effort.

SOC Threes are good at bringing diverse individuals together under a common banner, because they are socially adaptable and willing to give way to the will of the group enough to create a cohesive unit. The combination of drive, adaptability, and optimism often brings them success as public figures, team leaders, high-profile organizers, executives, successful managers, political lobbyists, advertising executives, or public relations specialists. But they're so good at creating a favorable impression that they have to be careful not to promise more than they can actually deliver. It's easy for them to get carried away by their own rhetoric and sometimes forget that the promises they make have to be backed up by deeds.

It's no surprise that SOC Three themes in films often involve power and its potential abuse, usually when it's motivated by the desire for public acclaim; themes involving political candidates are especially popular (e.g., *The Candidate* and *Primary Colors*). *The Candidate* focuses on the corrupting influence of the political process, showing us an apolitical liberal (Robert Redford) convinced by others that he should run for office, mainly because he's attractive and the son of a former governor. They tell him he can say what he likes (because he's not expected to win, anyway), so he takes the opportunity to speak out on the issues that matter to him (environmentalism, abortion rights, and other liberal causes). But he soon finds himself actively campaigning—and also straying from his original message in order to gain broader support. Against all odds, he wins the election. In the last scene, we see him looking completely bewildered as he whispers to his political handler, "Marvin...What do we do now?"

Primary Colors is another film that focuses on a candidate running for office. It was apparently inspired by Bill Clinton's first run for President, and features Jack Stanton, a likable Southern governor (real-life Three John Travolta), campaigning for the highest office in the land. The theme here is the discrepancy between the appealing public image that the candidate projects and the scummy stuff that goes on behind the scenes. The TCM online web page summarizes what goes on as involving, among other things, "an attempt to blackmail the candidate with doctored audiotapes detailing a past sexual encounter; an alleged bastard child of Stanton's from a black teenager; a possibly illegal real estate deal known as Tidewater Estates; the uncovering of a candidate's past as a cocaine-addicted homosexual by Stanton's campaign; and the suicide of one of Stanton's longtime friends [and aides]." (The suicide is connected to the aide's unwillingness to use smear tactics on Stanton's opponent.)

Both films present us with a decidedly troubled vision of how political campaigns are run, and especially the role of image-making (and image-breaking) in the process. *The Candidate* suggests that it's the political process itself that corrupts us while *Primary Colors* places more responsibility for shady tactics on the individual who employs them. So the latter film is actually more optimistic, because it suggests that corruption is not an inevitable fact of political life but a choice that can be changed.

Schindler's List and *Wallenberg: a Hero's Story* show what is possible when pragmatic means are employed to bring about humanitarian ends. Both involve individuals with a social focus who were involved in business ventures in central Europe during WWII. Although their initial motivations were profit-oriented, both individuals were eventually drawn into using their profit-oriented activities as a cover for helping Jews avoid the gas chamber.

Oskar Schindler was a flamboyant big-spender who wanted to establish a successful manufacturing business; Raoul Wallenberg was from a leading Swedish family whose connections helped him obtain a position in an import/export company. But the priorities of both businessmen gradually changed as they became aware of the mass Jewish genocide in progress: Schindler started using his business as a front to save Polish Jews and Wallenberg used his connections to issue Swedish passports and set up safe houses for Jews in Hungary. Both sacrificed everything to help other people: Schindler lost all his money in the process and was never again a successful businessman; Wallenberg was arrested by the Soviets and disappeared into the Gulag Archipelago, never to be heard from again. Both are examples of men who used their political clout for a truly noble purpose. Films like these (and *people* like these) show us that the same methods used to further one's political or social position can be used for altruistic purposes—if only we're able to see beyond our limited vision of what constitutes "success."

In *Mr. Holland's Opus*, we see a fictional example of this kind of transformation. Mr. Holland (Richard Dreyfuss) is a frustrated musician whose fondest desire is to write a great symphony. Stuck in a job as a high school music teacher, he eventually finds a way to channel his creativity into his work, creating a remarkable music program that transforms his students' lives. But he still feels a sense of gnawing dissatisfaction, because he feels he's never fulfilled his big dream in life. In a surprise tribute to him, attended by hundreds of students and former students, one of the former students—who's now the state governor—tries to make him understand the nature of his real work in life: "*We* are your symphony, Mr. Holland. We are the melody and the notes of your opus. And we are the music of your life."

Because SOC Threes are great team players, they're often good at helping others develop teamwork. For example, SOC Three Jo Frost (TV's *SuperNanny*) is great at mobilizing families to work together. She has a knack for finding fun and practical ways to discourage poor parenting practices and to break down barriers to communication. And all without making any one person the "bad guy," an approach that helps the families to heal. She introduces new activities that make family time more fun, giving people hope for the future

In *Apollo 13*, we see the same "can do" spirit employed to motivate teams working on a moon launch. When things go badly wrong, the same approach enables the team of astronauts—aided by diehard teams on the ground—to overcome nearly insurmountable obstacles to getting everybody safely back to earth. And in TV's *Oprah's Big Give*, SOC Three skills are employed to raise money for worthy causes; the idea is genius: each competitor starts out with a little capital and/or in-kind support and competes with other people to see who can gather the most support, put on the best event, or raise the most money for some worthy cause. Team-building skills figure prominently in many tasks; those who can get the most people on board are generally the most successful.

Stories like these demonstrate how the SOC Three culture of the United States can support not just business and political interests, but other worthwhile enterprises, especially those that benefit from efficiency, teamwork, and organization.

Team skills also figure prominently on TV's *The Amazing Race*, in which two-person teams compete in challenges that take them around the globe. Pairs of Threes are very common, and they usually do very well at "cooperating to compete." While other teams get distracted by nerves, emotions, or exhaustion, the Three teams are like the Energizer Bunny: they just go and go. They seldom argue, and when they do, it's not for long, because most Threes are too goal-oriented to get caught up in interpersonal melodramas (especially when there's a competition in progress). I noticed that Three teams tend to get most rattled in challenges involving animals or small children, because that's when their extreme goal-orientation can make them too pushy to get good results. The same problem comes up when they get too competitive and start stepping on the toes of other teams, who sometimes join forces to defeat them. The Three teams that do the best are the ones who have the patience to slow down when necessary, to maintain good relations with other teams, and to avoid cutthroat tactics.

SOC Threes are usually attuned to changing social trends, so we see plenty of SOC Three themes in films and on TV that involve makeovers of our features, clothes, and homes. The theme here is that changing our outer appearance is the first step in changing our lives. So someone with a "loser" image (bad hair, bad wardrobe, bad makeup, or bad-looking real estate) can become a winner on TV shows like *Ten Years Younger*, *What Not to Wear*, or *Designed to Sell* and in films like *Clueless* or *Pretty Woman*).

SOC Threes like to do the makeovers; other types are on the receiving end. Although it's easy to write off this approach to transformation as superficial, most of the people receiving makeovers seem happy afterwards—and better able to participate in the social world.

Type four –
the deep sea diver

They didn't get it. I thought the point was to do something different. I don't want to make
a cake just to please the judges, because then it's not me. Even if I win, I've sold out.
– Type 4 competitor on the Food Network Challenge

FOURS FIND authenticity compelling. They want to understand who they are and why they are in the world. And they want to know how they can fit into this world in a way that allows them to remain true to themselves. So Fours are indeed the deep sea divers of the enneagram—and especially the deep sea divers of the emotions. They pick up on emotional nuances the way that Sixes pick up on danger or Eights pick up on power dynamics. So they can spot insincerity a mile away and can have a hard time adjusting to a world in which surface appearances count for so much.

More than others, Fours are aware of discrepancies between how people feel versus how they *say* they feel. When the two aren't the same, Fours feel uncomfortable. Upon which information should they rely, what they're picking up from their intuitions or what people are saying to them? What they really want to do is to point out the discrepancy, so that the conflict can be resolved. But Fours discover early in life that this kind of information usually isn't welcome. They learn to ignore it (sort of), but they never manage to ignore it completely. The awareness stays with them, accounting for a lot of the moodiness associated with this type.

Four and Five are both bottom-of-the-enneagram types: the two types that flank the lowermost point on the circle, where involution mysteriously turns into evolution. The transition zone between the two is chaotic in nature, and the chaos is felt mostly strongly by Fours with a Five wing and Fives with a Four wing, because they're right next to the bottom of the circle. Judith Searle has written about this bottom-on-the-enneagram energy for the *Enneagram Monthly** and A. G. E. Blake says that the 4 – 5 region is "associated with turbulence, fire, and chaos."† As a 4w5, I've always been aware of this chaotic energy and the need to find a constructive way to work with it.

At Point 4, the turbulence evokes deep emotion while at Point 5, it evokes deep mental absorption. In both cases, it brings forth originality, although at a price—because it separates these bottom-of-the-enneagram types from the surface-level world of casual social interaction. This means that both types can find it challenging to establish lasting ties with other people or to adjust their behavior to the demands of society. Fours seek to overcome the social barrier by expressing themselves in some artistic fashion while Fives use their intellectual expertise to bridge the social gap.

Fours are the last point in the involutionary cycle, so they're still involved in the business of image creation; that's why they tend to be more artistic than scientific. But since they're at the end of the cycle, they're beginning to see through the image-creation process and to make some sort of effort to disengage from it. This is one reason why they're so sensitive to inauthenticity—because they're in the process of discovering that there's more to life than what we create, especially what we create in a material (matter-is-real) sense. So they strive to see beyond material reality—to penetrate the images; that's why they keep poking and prodding at them, looking for what they symbolically represent.

As children, Fours are usually pretty serious, just like Ones. But Ones tend to be a little more outgoing than Fours, who can easily feel overwhelmed by the insensitivity of other children. Fours are also sensitive to environmental aesthetics, which as children they can't control. If the aesthetics aren't quite right (which is likely), they look for some place they can make their own, like a bedroom, and that's where they usually spend a lot

---

* "The Gap at the Bottom of the Enneagram," Sept. 1997.

† *The Intelligent Enneagram* (1996), p. 342.

TABLE 14-1.
TYPE FOUR: THE DEEP SEA DIVER

INTENSE, ORIGINAL, MOODY, DEEP, INDIVIDUALISTIC, CONCERNED WITH AUTHENTICITY

ONE Connection brings discipline, principles, manners, grounding, irritation
TWO Connection brings consideration, kindness, friendliness, dependency

THREE Wing brings pragmaticism, groundedness, competitive spirit, social outlook
FIVE Wing brings inwardness, shyness, intellectualism, complexity, transpersonal outlook

Other Labels: Intensifier, Dramatist, Originator, Individualist, Tragedian
Challenges: sadness, moodiness, longing, inability to fit in, narcissism, hypocrisy

	SUBTYPES		
	Self-preservation	Sexual	Social
A R C H E T Y P E S	*Earthy Bohemian, Absorbed Artisan, Original Craftsman, Imaginative Creator, Teller of Life Stories, Originator of New Forms, Subtle Weaver, Colorful Gypsy, Patient Wordsmith, Deep-level Editor, Independent Learner, Garden Artist, Interested Teacher, Individualist, Persevering Seeker, Wounded Healer, Explorer of the Deep Psyche, Spiritual Gambler, Edge-Walker, Velveteen Rabbit*	*Great Dramatist, Uncompromising Artist, Depth Poet, Method Actor, Talented Writer, Russian Novelist, Restless Soul Mate, Unfulfilled Lover, Depth or Archetypal Psychologist, Moth to the Flame, Total Submissive, Divine Lover, Vengeful Suitor, Fierce Competitor, Romantic Rival, Intense Seeker, Passionate Embracer, Misunderstood Artist, Unappreciated Creator, Damsel in Distress, Drama Queen/King, Self-fascinated Intimate*	*Pointed Pundit, Social Critic, Insightful Commentator, Social Synthesizer, Distinctive Fashion Designer, Artistic Trendsetter, Personally-committed Architect, Tasteful Artistic Director, Creator of Public Art, Original Stylista, Feng Shui Consultant, Self-conscious Goth, Maker of Fashion Statements, Refined Elitist, Social Muckraker, Alienated Idealist, Ugly Duckling, Status Quo Challenger, Uncompromising Authenticator, Unpopular Confronter, Ambivalent Truth-teller, Pained Isolate, Rebel Without A Cause*
F I L M T H E M E S	**Persisting in one's creative vision** can bring fulfillment (*My Left Foot; Maya Lin: a Clear, Strong Vision; My Brilliant Career; Joan Baez: How Sweet the Sound*) but also conflict with others (*Vincent & Theo; Pollock; Alice Neel, The Girl with the Pearl Earring*) and even persecution (*Artemesia*) **Ordinary moments** can have extraordinary depth & sweetness (*Lost in Translation, Girl with the Pearl Earring, The Family Man*) **Life after loss is possible** with a little toughness, humor & wisdom (*Moonlight Mile, A Rumor of Angels, Out of Africa*) **We survive psychologically** only when we find purpose & meaning in life (*Magnolia, Safe, The Hours, Lost in Translation, The Miracle Worker, Being John Malkovich*)	**Star-crossed love** is either doomed (*Romeo & Juliet, West Side Story, Dr. Zhivago, The New World*) or associated with pain that has the potential to transform (*The Piano, City of Angels, House of the Spirits*) **"Moth to the flame" type** finds ordinary life trying (*Dancer in the Dark, The Hours, French Lieutenant's Woman, The Wizard of Oz, House of the Spirits, Girl: Interrupted, Revolutionary Road*) **Spiritual seekers** search for the meaning of life (*Hideous Kinky, Holy Smoke, Into the Wild, The Razor's Edge*) **Ambitious artistic types** fiercely compete for artistic predominance (*The Turning Point, Amadeus, Project Runway*) **Personal renewal is possible** when love penetrates deep wounds (*What Dreams May Come, In America, Magnolia*)	**Failure to fit in** brings social isolation (*The Glass Menagerie, Anastasia*), ostracism (*Scarlet Letter*) or institutionalization (*Manic; Girl, Interrupted; Tom & Viv*) **People on the fringe** eventually find their place in life (*Ugly Betty, Dumbo, The Ugly Duckling, The Elephant Man, White Oleander, Georgy Girl*) **Moody teens** find it hard to accept the conventions of society (*Rebel Without a Cause; Manic; Girl, Interrupted; World's Strictest Parents*) **Art or fashion mavens** dictate trends (*The September Issue, The Devil Wears Prada, Flowers Uncut*) and give refined critiques (*America's Next Top Model, Project Runway, Top Chef*) **Public recognition** eventually comes to artistic pioneers (*Isadora, Vincent & Theo, Coco Chanel*)

of their time. Parents may be at a loss to understand why their child sometimes withdraws into his own world. If the parents get frustrated or annoyed, the sensitive Four will readily pick up on those feelings and internalize them, starting a cycle of rejection and shame that can persist into adulthood. But young Fours don't have to grow up feeling alienated. Even parents who don't entirely understand their sensitive child can still help him bloom by providing love, acceptance, and opportunities for self-expression. Once they know it's normal for their child to seek their own way of doing things (and his own space to do them in), they're more likely to offer support instead of criticism.

Fours with a Three wing tend to be independent-minded, creative, and ambitious. They're ambivalent about their interactions with people (being somewhere between extroverts and introverts), but they usually retain the ability to adapt to other people's requirements and fit into the larger social order. Fours with a Five wing are just as independent-minded and creative, but are guided more by their inner muse than the dictates of society. They often exhibit strikingly original artistic talents that take them far afield from cultural norms.

The connection to Two gives Fours the ability to form emotional bonds with other people, enabling them to "come up for air." They can potentially relax, socialize, and make friends. But it can be a challenge for the depth-oriented Four to open up to this connection, because it requires him to place more attention on social interaction than on personal expression. It also requires him to move into that part of himself which is secretly concerned with image, which is precisely the part that feels least authentic. To access the energy of Two in a healthy way, Fours need to make peace with their discomfort, so they don't have to go overboard in the authenticity department (and lose the opportunity to connect with people in socially conventional situations).

The connection to One potentially gives Fours discipline, focus, and good manners. This enhances their ability to produce artistic works that are not only inspired, but exquisitely crafted. It also gives them a critical eye, and the ability to give artistic critique. The combination of discernment and criticality can be potent; so Fours need to exercise caution in how they express their understanding to others, so they don't give the impression of being elitist or dismissive of others' opinions.

Judith Searle describes four Type 4 genres: melodrama, love and loss, doomed love, and artists who sacrifice for art. Alas, alas—there doesn't seem to be much hope for Fours here! All these categories sound pretty negative. But this is not Searle's fault; it's reflects the way that many people view the energy at Point 4: as melodramatic, doomed, and sacrificial. And there's actually some truth to this portrayal, especially if we focus on the key role of sacrifice. Sacrifice and surrender are a part of the Four dynamic, because—remember—we're at the end of a cycle. So before something new can begin, something old must be sacrificed. We must clear the decks, empty the vessel.

From a transformational perspective, all the emphasis on death and loss makes sense. We're at a place in the cycle that is akin to the alchemical process of *nigredo*, the stage of putrefaction in alchemy in which the soul is decomposed into its primal elements. So the preoccupation with death at Four is much like the preoccupation with death in the 12th house in astrology or the Death card in the Tarot. It's not innately morbid or indicative of mental abnormality. But we live in a culture which is so death-phobic that we're not comfortable with individuals who are preoccupied with this phase of life. There's no role for them in modern American culture. Unlike Indian mystics, people in our culture don't meditate on the dead. Unlike the ancient Egyptians, we don't spend our lives preparing for the afterlife. And unlike shamanic cultures, we don't send emissaries in to the land of the dead to gain wisdom for the living. As a result, the death processes associated with Point 4 may indeed seem unnatural and morbid. And this may be one reason why so many Fours have a sense of not belonging: because their concerns seem weird or strange to others.

Fours have sometimes been labeled Tragic Romantics. While I agree that Fours are drawn to tragedy, it's not tragedy in the unhealthy, morbid sense. It's tragedy in the sense that the word is used by Arthur Koestler, to describe the plane of existence concerned with depth, mystery, death, and meaning (and perhaps most of all with *soul*).* And while I'd agree that some Fours can be melodramatic (especially SX Fours), I actually think that it's a little more common at Point 2, if we think of melodrama as drama that's emotionally overinflated. (Recall the scene from Chapter 12 involving the mother from *Sunshine* who faints whenever she hears news she doesn't like. That's melodrama, not drama. See Chapter 10 for more discussion on the difference between the two.)†

When we take melodrama to an extreme, we wind up with the old time morality plays involving heroes, villains, and kidnapped heroines tied to the railroad track. There's actually a comedic element here, which has to do with the fact that tragedy taken to absurd extremes turns into comedy or farce. A lot of comedies contain one or more melodramatic characters whose character is actually there to provide comic relief (because the archetype is pushed to such an extreme that we can't take it seriously). For example, the old Shirley Temple movies often featured an especially crotchety millionaire for Shirley to charm; *The Wizard of Oz* featured the nasty neighbor/Wicked Witch as an evil Type 1 who is made into such a caricature that we know deep down that we don't have to fear her.

Point 4 is not about melodrama; it's about *real* drama, the kind I talked about in Chapter 10. There I observed that drama and melodrama aren't the same thing, but it may be useful at this point to distinguish "ordinary" drama from drama that is particularly intense and attenuated (what I would call *high drama*). High drama is the product of archetypal conflicts that seem fateful, painful, or tragic in nature; they're the product of very real archetypal energies, not a scriptwriter's overheated imagination. Examples include Greek tragedy, Shakespearean tragedy, and modern plays like Albee's *The Zoo*

---

* Koestler contrasts the tragic plane with the trivial plane (the plane of everyday life). See pp. 145–146 in *Janus: A Summing Up* (1978) or *The Act of Creation* (pp. 363–365) for a discussion.

† Whether we're talking Type 2 or 4, we need to be careful to avoid focusing too much on over-emotionality as a defining trait of either type, because it is not. Both Twos and Fours have the greatest potential of all the types to develop highly-differentiated emotions, which is an asset, not a liability.

Story. The themes of doomed love, love-and-loss, and sacrifice-for-art are all subsets of this genre. In modern life, such themes tend to become trivialized to the extent that we no longer see fate as having any real power in our lives, which is why the two genres—-melodrama and high drama—can seem like the same thing. But for Fours, maintaining the distinction is especially important, because it gives them a way to distinguish self-indulgent emotional wallowing from genuinely redemptive suffering.

But Type 4 isn't just about darkness and suffering. It's also about seeing through the superficial, discovering the extraordinary within the ordinary, developing our individuality, upholding our artistic integrity, reaping the rewards of inner development, making emotional breakthroughs, and exploring the feminine mysteries of life. Seeing these additional dimensions of Four allows us to gain a more subtle understanding of what the type is all about.

¤ ¤ ¤

Self-preservation four themes. The SP Four subtype is somewhat invisible from an enneagrammatic point of view. While enneagram books often describe Fours as emotional, volatile, and melodramatic, SP Fours tend to be emotionally constrained, especially in public. They're first and foremost survivors, and in order to survive, they tend to hide their emotional sensitivity as much as possible (sometimes even from themselves). They like to work independently, so they're often attracted to work they can do at home or at least on their own, e.g., graphic arts, web design, and earthy sorts of creative work (original pottery, tile work, cake decorating, or landscape design). Although they're more emotionally grounded and patient than other Fours, they're also more prone to depression, because their emotions tend to weigh heavily upon them. SP Fours are not all that visible in films, either; as an SP Four myself, I seldom see my own energy mirrored in films. Public figures who seem like SP Fours to me include Nicholas Cage, Linda Hamilton, Susan Sarandon, and Joan Baez.

I once sat in a group of 14 SP Fours (13 of whom were female) at an enneagram workshop. Most seemed like solid, earthy women with a direct manner who would talk frankly but not in a way that was terribly self-revealing. They had the same tough but tender manner that we sometimes see in SP Eights, as well as a pretty good sense of humor! They gave the impression of being survivors, but survivors with emotional scars. Despite the Eight-like exterior, it's doubtful whether they could have sustained this Eightish persona for long. Fours tend to tire more easily than other types, and SP Fours find casual social encounters wearying. They need time alone for creative work or time with a single close friend who understands them. They especially value their independence, and travel like gypsies, bringing their homes with them to whatever extent possible.

One key SP Four theme involves surviving a great loss by saturating it with love. SP Fours who work through their fears of emotional pain are able to access a deep fount of love and share that love with others. So they're good people to approach when you need someone to listen to your troubles. While Fours have little use for small talk, they're excellent listeners when it comes to emotionally devastating experiences (the kind that most people don't want to hear about). SP Fours are particularly well-suited for this task because they possess the groundedness necessary to simply sit with people in a way that strengthens them emotionally.

One of my favorite movies about emotional survival is the film *Moonlight Mile*, about which I wrote in *The Positive Enneagram*. Susan Sarandon and Dustin Hoffman play a couple who have just lost their only daughter in a car accident; both are devastated by the loss, but cheer each other up with love and humor. Although Sarandon is often typed as an Eight, she sure looks like an SP Four in this film (remembering that SP Fours can look a lot like Eights, because of their plain-spoken manner and directness). Sarandon plays a writer whose tolerance for all the social ceremony surrounding the death is limited. I was fascinated to see just how much like me she seemed in the way she dealt with the constant phone interruptions by well-meaning people sending condolences. She put up with it to a certain point, until she just couldn't stand it anymore. Then she simply yanked the phone out of the wall, something I might do under similar circumstances.

(If you think this sounds more like an Eight than a Four, think again. Fours have access to a lot of emotion. When they finally get fed up, they can blow up in a big way. I once got furious and smashed a hole in my own wall when banging on it to get my neighbor to turn down his unbearably loud stereo.)

In America is another film about emotional survival, in which we see how an Irish-Canadian family devastated by the loss of their little boy uses love and magic to survive the loss. Little Frankie is the one who has died; the remaining family members—Mum, Dad, and their two young girls, Christy and Ariel—pack everything they own into their battered station wagon and head for the Big Apple, where Dad hopes to make it as an actor. Since they've no money, they end up in an abandoned building peopled with strange tenants. Mom finds ways to make their five-storey walkup habitable and gets a waitressing job while Dad seeks acting jobs. It's a tough life, especially since everyone is still grieving the loss of Frankie. But the parents don't forget their remaining kids; they manage to make life something joyful, amid grief and financial hardship.

For example, on one sweltering Manhattan day, we see everybody virtually melting in the heat. Dad decides something must be done, and procures an ancient air-conditioner that looks like it must weigh a couple hundred pounds. He has to cart it home by hand, because he sold the car to get money to live. Lugging it across the streets and up five flights of the stairs is a testament to the love he feels for his wife and children. When it's finally in place and hooked up, everybody cheers. It's a moment of triumph.

Another time, Dad (a Seven deflated by grief) takes the family to a carnival, where Ariel begs for an E. T. doll, which he can't afford. She's too young to understand this and he can't bear to say no, so he asks his wife for the rent money to bet on a ball-throwing game to get the doll. They exchange a look between them, then she hands over the money. Christy understands what's at stake; she prays fervently to her brother Frankie for help. Dad keeps missing his shots, but with the very last one, he wins the doll and gets back the money. That's the way these parents approach all the difficult moments in life: they put their whole heart and soul into whatever their doing, and they do it together, hoping and praying that something will work out. In the end, it does. Not because of luck but because of love.

Another SP Four theme running through the film is the power of magic to light up our lives, even in times of grief and trouble. The soundtrack, which is exotically magical, evokes in us the sense that life—despite its pain—is a place full of unimagined possibilities. (The soundtrack alone makes the film worth seeing.)

Lost in Translation conveys a similar message—that magic can be found in the unlikeliest of places or at the strangest of times. It depicts a brief encounter between two lonely strangers in Tokyo, one a Four and the other a Seven. The Four is Charlotte (Scarlett Johansson), a reflective young newlywed who's tagging along with her celebrity photographer husband; the Seven is Bob (Bill Murray), a famous but jaded actor who has come to Tokyo to makes whiskey ads. The two keep bumping into one another in the hotel lounge, which is how they gradually strike up a friendship. Although it's hard to imagine a less likely setting for real intimacy, that's what develops during their brief time together—not sexual intimacy, but something deeper and more subtle. In the most impersonal of locales, they develop an extraordinarily personal bond, based on a shared desire to make sense of their lives (Charlotte because she's just gotten married and Bob because he's in a mid-life crisis). Each is able to give the other something that is missing from their lives; they both leave the encounter richer for the experience.

The Family Man is a film about learning to value the ordinary things in life, especially family life. The protagonist, Jack Campbell, is a successful but arrogant businessman (probably a Four, played by Nicholas Cage, leaning hard into his Three wing). Although Jack's got everything material in life, he's somehow lost his heart along the way. However, when he intervenes to save a stranger's life, an angel intervenes to change Jack's life for the better. That night, Jack goes to bed in his own apartment but wakes up the next day—which happens to be Christmas—in bed next to the women whom he loved when he was younger.

He now finds that they're married with two children. They live in a dumpy-looking house, and he works in his father-in-law's tire shop. It's a big shock. He's not exactly delighted with his new life—at least not at first. But his little daughter eventually charms him and he starts to fall deeply in love with both his wife and his new family. At the point where he's on the brink of wholeheartedly embracing his new life, he suddenly finds himself suddenly dumped back in the old one. But now that he knows what really matters, he can turn the dream into a reality.

(Wikipedia points out the similarities between *The Family Man* and *It's a Wonderful Life*, in that both begin on Christmas Eve, involve an angel, and teach us to value the ordinary things in life. But while the subtext may be the same, the message is different, in part because the two characters are different enneagram types. Jimmy Stewart, as always, plays his genial Niney self—in this case, a man who's irritated because he never got to go anywhere or do anything. On the other hand, Cage plays a self-important "image" type in the Three to Four range who never learned to appreciate the little things in life. While Stewart's lesson is to appreciate the life he already has, Cage's is to change his life before it's too late.)

One thing I like about the films described above is that they convey the idea that learning to value the ordinary doesn't mean giving up the extraordinary (i.e., settling for a life devoid of richness, passion, or intense emotions). It just means learning how to find the magic within the mundane.

¤ ¤ ¤

SEXUAL FOUR THEMES. This is the subtype that we think of when we think of Fours: artistic, temperamental, and intense. SX Fours can be quite self-obsessed and dramatic (and, yes, even melodramatic at times!) and can also become extremely angry when crossed (connection to One). However, they're also one of the most intriguing of the 27 subtypes because of their creative talent and dramatic flair. Many of the well-known actors in our times are SX Fours, because of their tremendous commitment to their craft and their ability to immerse themselves so completely in the characters they play. Examples include Kate Winslet, Johnny Depp, Winona Ryder,

Nicole Kidman, Anne Bancroft, and Nicholas Cage; examples of superstar non-actor Four entertainers include singers Michael Jackson, David Bowie, and Björk, as well as dancers such as Rudolph Nureyev.

Successful SX Fours usually possess tremendous self-control and discipline (connection to One), at least as applied to their work. SX Fours may express their energies outwardly (via acting, dance, or other dramatic arts) or in a more introverted way (via writing, painting, or art). Their private lives are often tumultuous (even as compared to other SX subtypes) because the combination of intense emotions, sexuality, and originality creates a highly-combustible mix that can be hard to contain.

All SX subtype themes involve love, sexuality, and creativity, but at SX Four, there's an intense demand to pierce the veil, to get to the very core of creation, the bottom of the wellspring of life. So there's an intensity of purpose around whatever they do (and especially around their relationships). SX Fours can be intensely preoccupied with their intimate partners, potentially seeing the relationship from a mystical perspective. Some may be drawn into spiritual paths that take them into the unconscious, into descent, Shadow work, and the depths of *soul*. They can also go to the edge as spiritual seekers, like moths to the flame.

We see this spiritual seeker theme played out in the film *Hideous Kinky*, a memoir based on the real-life upbringing of Sigmund Freud's great-granddaughter, Esther Freud. During the 1960s, a single Bohemian mom Julia (played by real-life Four, Kate Winslet) takes her two girls, the dreamy Lucy (age 5) and practical Bea (age 7), to Morocco to live. Mom Julia is in search of a Sufi sheikh who can give her an experience of *fana* (annihilation of the ego). Bea, who's clearly a One, gets tired of all the traveling, and insists on going to school; so Julia agrees to leave her with friends in the city. Meanwhile, Julia and Lucy spend several days hitchhiking to a Sufi *tekkia* in the middle of nowhere. When she sees the sheikh the next day, he's very kind, but he asks her age, which is just 25. Then he inquires with a smile about her family. Julia looks aghast. She doesn't know what to say, because she's always put her quest ahead of her children. She finds herself crying. Looking at his compassionate face, she realizes the truth, and says slowly, "I'm not ready, am I?" That night, she has a nightmare where her daughter Bea appears in the *tekkia* but is choked by a black hand.

Upon returning to Algiers, she discovers her friends have left town and nobody seems to know what happened to Bea. Frantic, she searches everywhere, finally locating Bea helping out at an orphanage. Bea is not all that happy to be found, since she's now got the kind of disciplined life she always wanted. But Julia asserts herself, (at one point yelling, "I'm your Mummy, not her!"), taking Bea back ; this is the Four connecting with One in order to reclaim what she has lost. Soon after, her other daughter Lucy gets very sick, but Julia is penniless and can't afford the medication her daughter needs. Fortunately, Julia's friend Bilal saves the day by selling his splendid new uniform to buy the needed medicine. It's at this point that Julia realizes just how backwards she's got her priorities. After Lucy recovers, the family returns to England, so the girls can have a more stable life.

So here's an example where a Four has to sacrifice her personal "moth to the flame" spiritual quest, instead finding her meaning in life by sacrificing her own needs in order to satisfy the needs of her children. This can be a tough lesson for the individualistic Four.

In another Kate Winslet film, *Holy Smoke*, Winslet again plays a Fourish spiritual seeker. This time, she's unencumbered by kids. So when she finds an Indian guru and experiences ecstatic states of consciousness, she's drawn to join his group. Her extremely conventional family are highly suspicious of anything outside of the norm, so they hire a deprogrammer (Harvey Keitel) to set her right. Part of the humor in the film comes from the fact that we gradually begin to see how what passes for the "norm" is crazy in its own way (starting with the idea of hiring a deprogrammer). Although Keitel initially wears down some of Winslet's resolve, she soon sees *his* weak spots and how to exploit them, eventually turning the tables on him.

Holy Smoke is an interesting film because it avoids stereotyping the spiritual journey to an exotic locale as something inherently crazy, instead calling into question the craziness of the status quo. If *Hideous Kinky* reminds us that there's a wrong time to embark on a spiritual quest, *Holy Smoke* allows for the possibility that it isn't necessarily crazier than any other path in life.*

Neither is it surprising that Winslet was cast in both films because, as an SX Four, she probably found both themes compelling. Two other "spiritual seeker" films are *The Razor's Edge* and *Into the Wild*, both of which feature Sevenish protagonists who undertake the Hero's Journey into the wilderness. It's interesting that when Sevens get serious about life, they often develop an unexpected ability to "go deep"; we see this with the Seven actors that play zany roles in their youth (e.g., Jerry Lewis, Steve Martin, Bill Murray, and Robin Williams), who go on to play more serious roles later in life. When they mellow a little, they turn out to be compelling dramatic actors whose energy can seem a lot like Fours. (Conversely, Fours who learn how to lighten up and take themselves less seriously can seem a lot like Sevens.)†

Regarding romance, Fours never seem to have an easy time of it, at least not in modern films. SX Fours tend to suffer a lot for love, if they find it at all. In *House of the Spirits*, Meryl Streep plays a Chilean 4w5 mystic who marries a man who turns out to be highly unscrupulous (Jeremy Irons, playing a 3w4). After years of marriage, having realized the depths of his depravity, she ceases to speak to him directly, communicating with him via her grown-up SX Four daughter (Winona Ryder). The daughter, meanwhile, has fallen in love with a revolutionary (Antonio Banderas), a former peasant on her father's estate who's become involved in liberationist politics. After the 1970s military coup, she is arrested and tortured to reveal the whereabouts of her lover, which she doesn't know. While she is lying on a floor in jail, obviously *in*

---

* For an interesting discussion on *Holy Smoke* and Western spirituality, see Kate Pullinger's "Soul Survivor: Women Directors' Special" at http://www.rickross.com/reference/general/general329.html.

† It's useful to note briefly that there's an invisible connection between two pairs of types: Types 4 and 7 and Types 2 and 5. Fours and Sevens share a love of freedom and aesthetics. Mature Fours seem lighter (like Sevens); mature Sevens seem emotionally complex (like Fours). In the case of Twos and Fives, they represent the twin attributes of emotion (Two) and intellect (Five), and are often paired as married couples. Mature Twos become more comfortable with their intellect (like Fives); mature Fives become more comfortable with their ability to socially interact (like Twos).

extremis, she has a vision of her mother, who reassures her that everything will be all right. And so it is—she's eventually reunited with her husband who's been secretly hidden by her father (it seems he's finally managed to do something decent for his family). The couple escapes the junta by flying to Canada.

So we get a happy ending for the daughter, but only after she's completed the entire Hero's Journey, descending into hell and living to tell the tale. And this is usually how things work in romances involving Fours, at least on the screen. More often than not, the romance is either tragic or involves a lot of trials and tribulations.

The most prototypical "difficult romance" theme at SX Four is probably that of doomed or star-crossed love. It's the story of *Romeo and Juliet,* a story we tell in film over and over, devising variants to reflect the special concerns of each passing generation (*West Side Story, Love Story*, and *High School Musical*), never seeming to tire of the message that love conquers all (even death). Disney's *High School Musical* drops the theme of death (no surprise), so it's more like an SX Two romantic comedy than an SX Four tragedy.

In some ways, "doomed love" is a variant on the broader theme of "love and death," which reminds us of the link between the two; it has been pointed out that the French refer to orgasm as *la petit mort* or "little death." It also seems that great love often attracts great trials; so often, the person who perseveres in love is eventually transformed by it. If he's fortunate, he may actually be reunited with the one he loves. But the main focus seems to be on transformation, rather than romance.

In *City of Angels*, Nicholas Cage plays an angel who falls passionately in love with a human (Meg Ryan), so he makes the fateful decision to give up his divinity in order to be with her. As fate would have it, no sooner does this miracle take place than she's in an accident and dies, leaving Cage alone to live as a mortal man.

In *Dr. Zhivago*, based on the Pasternak novel of the same name, we see the lives of two soulmates, Yuri and Lara, who meet after each has already married somebody else. Lara's husband is a hard-faced revolutionary who spends his time hunting down White sympathizers; Yuri's wife is his childhood sweetheart whom he doesn't have the heart to leave. Nevertheless, Yuri and Lara keep crossing paths in the aftermath of the turbulent Bolshevik Revolution. Finally, they lose track of one another for good, due to both the cruelties of fate and the deliberate machinations of a villainous but clever man who is jealous of their love (he's the very epitome of the manipulating-Three-from-hell).

Speaking of doom, no chapter on Fours would be complete without mentioning *The Hours,* a Four-fest that exemplifies the melodrama often associated with the type. (If everybody knew the enneagram, we could just call it *The Fours* instead of *The Hours.*) I don't like the film much, because it presents Fours in such a dismal light, but the acting is excellent, and the film does manage to touch on some of the stereotypes most associated with the type: despair, suicide, oversensitivity, and the difficulty of living an ordinary life.

Most of the principals are Fours (Meryl Streep, Julianne Moore, and Nicole Kidman); Ed Harris (often said to be a Six) is believably cast as a Four. Streep is a SOC Four whose focus is social events; Moore is an emotionally repressed SP-SOC 4w5 (with Harris as her grown-up son dying of AIDS, a probable SX Four); and Kidman is an SX Four (and puts in a brilliant, Oscar-winning performance as a suicidal Virginia Woolf).

The plot is hard to follow, because it's a theme-driven movie that seems to focus on the difficulty in getting through "the hours" (of the day). It involves vignettes from three different time periods: early 1940s Britain (where we see Virginia Woolf coming apart at the seams), post-WWII America (where we find Julianne Moore trying to cope with the horrors of suburban life), and Meryl Streep (where we watch Streep trying to organize a dinner party in honor of her poet friend, played by Harris, who unfortunately kills himself by jumping out of a window before the party takes place). (I thought he could at least have waited until after the party!)

The theme seems to be that it's hard for artistic souls to live in the dreary worka-day world. The film offers us a bleak, existential message that precludes the possibility that life might seem less bleak if only the main characters could allow themselves to be transformed by their suffering, as others have done. The only somewhat heroic character is Julianne Moore, who almost kills herself because she's so undone by her conventional life as a 1950s housewife. Her big personal victory seems to be her decision to settle for the lesser sin of deserting her family. The Ed Harris character who kills himself in the last vignette (because he's slowly dying of AIDS) is her now grown-up son, who bears the scars of his mother's desertion.

The Hours was a hard film to watch, because I kept noticing opportunities for the characters to improve their lot in life (or at least their attitude), opportunities that they all seemed determined to ignore. Their endless self-dramatizing did little but make them miserable. As for their artistic sensitivity, while this can be a challenge for Fours, it's also an asset when constructively channeled (as the successful Fours who play these characters certainly understand).

The discovery of the right artistic channel is a genuinely important theme for many SX Fours, because it can make a big difference in the Four's quality of life. *The Turning Point* invites us to compare the life of a prima ballerina (a Four who opted for art over family) with the life of a married dance teacher (a 7w8 who opted for love over art). Which is better: to pursue your talent, whatever the costs, or to live a less glamorous but family-oriented life with your partner and children? Maybe it depends upon our type: Anne Bancroft, the Four, picks the former; Shirley Maclaine, the Seven, picks the latter. However, each now seems envious of the other's choice. But by the film's end, we get the feeling that they both got what they most valued in life.

Vincent & Theo explores the tension that builds up when an artist (Vincent Van Gogh) creates art that nobody understands and his brother (Theo), an art dealer, can't find buyers for his brother's work. The creative energies of the artist become side-tracked into issues other than his art, creating emotional imbalance and the inability to focus.

Artemesia explores a somewhat different issue for artists: how to be true to our own art when it comes into sharp conflict with the prevailing mores of our culture. The story depicts the plight of a female artist trying to paint the male anatomy during the

Renaissance, which was a time when the Church forbade it. For that reason and others (mainly a love affair with a fellow painter that was reputed to start with a rape), the artist gets into major trouble with the Inquisition, and she's put to the thumbscrews to testify against her lover. (Ouch!) So the story depicts a persecution-for-the-sake-of-art scenario, in which the main character is portrayed as a misunderstood figure whose biggest crime is being born well ahead of her time.

Artistic talent and envy often seem to go together, which is probably why Fours are often said to have problems with envy. There is some truth in this idea, if we see envy as a potential side effect of the ability to make artistic comparisons. All image types make comparisons, but at Point 4, it becomes something of an art form. It's what enables Fours to notice very subtle differences of all sorts, especially differences of an emotional or artistic nature. This ability is a gift, because it allows those who possess it to cultivate an art form to a very high degree (and even to make their lives into a work of art). But it can also be a curse, because it makes it hard to overlook artistic flaws—and to feel genuinely distressed by them. Fours can become envious of those who don't have this challenge (while at the same time looking down on them for their insensitivity!).

The film *Amadeus* explores what happens when a Four allows himself to become completely obsessed with envy, becoming consumed with destructive hatred for a talented rival. In this fictionalized story of the relationship between Wolfgang Amadeus Mozart (a manic Seven) and court composer Antonio Salieri (a brooding Four), Salieri becomes so envious of Mozart that he abandons his own work in order to destroy the life of his rival. Like *The Hours*, it's a little over the top, but does address the Fourish potential to become boorishly fixated on both his envy and his inner angst, instead of channeling the same energy into some sort of constructive activity. Fours who becomes completely self-dramatizing lose the perspective needed to bring about positive change.

My favorite Woody Allen film, *Love and Death*, is a satire of this sort of autistic self-absorption; its title is immediately recognizable as a play on the epic Russian novel *War and Peace*. From an enneagrammatic point of view, it's a send-up of Fours—specifically, of the SX Four tendency to see life as a tragic drama with themselves in the lead role.

There's an especially hilarious scene between Sixes Diane Keaton and Woody Allen, where Keaton gets totally lost in herself as she delivers a very long and self-dramatizing soliloquy to her solemn and attentive companion. (If you're a Four and can't laugh at that scene, you'd better send your sense of humor out for repair!)

SX Fours can benefit from realizing that they tend to have the kind of energy that requires artistic expression, whether or not the products of that expression ever receive the kind of recognition that the Four would like. SX Fours who keep their attention on their creative path and seek support from the people who appreciate their work are much more likely to find what they're seeking than those who allow themselves to get overly concerned with the opinions of the collective (whether positive or negative). The focused creator is the one who's most likely to produce the best work.

¤ ¤ ¤

Social four themes. This subtype tends to be quiet, reserved, and particularly sensitive to the feedback of others, so they usually make a greater-than-average effort to find a group in which they can feel socially accepted while still being themselves. They're particularly drawn to cultural arenas like high fashion, the art or music worlds, literary criticism, or haute cuisine—arenas that are part of mainstream culture but that celebrate artistic diversity. Their work often involves the ability to notice departures from good taste (whether in fashion, food, art, or wine) and to comment on them as writers or judges. Watch any panel of food judges on TV cooking competitions and you will find some SOC Fours, especially when it comes to high-end cuisine. (They are usually aided and abetted by SOC Ones, who never fail to point out a messy station or subtle departures from culinary decorum; the Fours prefer to focus on more arcane issues involving artistic presentation and subtleties of seasoning).

Sometimes SOC Fours are hard to type, because they don't come across as Fours—at least not right away. Their quietness and hesitation to speak might be mistaken for meekness (although they are anything but meek when you enter the realm of their special expertise). Also, they hide away their sensitive side, much like SP Fours. But while SP Fours are generally more direct and forthcoming, SOC Fours tend to be more indirect and conciliatory, except when they decide to take a stand. That's when you find out they're Fours.

SOC Four themes focus a lot on belonging versus not belonging, which is closely related to the theme of authenticity versus conformity, since the price of authenticity is often social ostracism. It's the tension between the desire to be authentic and the desire to belong that's a special challenge for SOC Fours. This is why they are often the ones accused in team competitions of "throwing people under the bus," especially when the competitions involve artistic judgment (e.g., TV's *Project Runway*, *Top Chef*, or *Shear Genius*). In a typical scenario, one of the judges asks, "Who do you think is responsible for xyz problem?" Most people would try to dodge the question (a smart move). But Fours aren't very good at fudging. So they're more likely to speak the truth as they know it, for better or worse, thus getting into trouble with their fellow team-mates, most of whom know when to keep their mouths shut. The Four who blabs isn't usually trying to deliberately throw anybody under the bus; he is just choosing personal authenticity over group loyalty.

Of course, society needs people who won't always go along with the group. But SOC Fours need to be able to discern the difference between speaking out when it's really necessary and doing so simply to release pent-up irritations and frustrations. When they indulge in the latter, it's more like complaining, and that's when it *really* gets them in hot water with other people. It also gets them in trouble with themselves, because deep down, they know what they're doing and they're ashamed of it. That's one reason SOC Four is sometimes called the "shame" subtype.

Sometimes, the shame arises out of a true scapegoating situation, as when an individual is cast out of a family or social group for no good reason. This shames a person, whether or not they are actually guilty of any offense. Because Fours are willing to speak out when others might not, they do sometimes become the victims of scapegoating, which is why we see so many SOC Four films with this theme, e.g., films about rebellious or disenfranchised teens (*The Wild Bunch*, *Rebel Without a Cause*, *Manic*, or *Girl, Interrupted*), people cast out of polite society for some kind of unpardonable social sin (e.g., *The Scarlet Letter, The Four Feathers,* or *Tom & Viv*), or those who suffer ostracism for a long time before finally gaining social acceptance (e.g., *The Devil Wears Prada, Ugly Betty, The Elephant Man, My Fair Lady, Dr. Bahasaheb Ambedkar* or *Oliver Twist*).

In many of these examples, the protagonists didn't do anything wrong; they were simply cast into situations that made it hard to avoid becoming a social untouchable. Although not all of the protagonists in these films are SOC Fours, the theme of ostracism is a SOC Four theme because it looks at how individuals of any type respond to social ostracism. But it's an especially poignant issue for SOC Fours, because they're the ones who are constantly grappling with the issue of how to be themselves and still be acceptable to the group.

Mature SOC Fours can have a significant positive impact on the world, especially the highly refined world of art and fashion. Emotional refinement is one of the gifts at SOC Four, and these Fours know how to show the rest of us *why refinement matters*— how it can bring something subtly exquisite into life. It goes hand in hand with the SOC One idea that manners matter. We see the potential benefits of refinement in TV shows in which young people (usually young ladies) are introduced to a more refined way of life (e.g., *From Ladette to Lady, American Princess,* or *Australian Princess*), often by very well-appointed, middle-aged Brits who are either aristocrats or their high-class servants. I already mentioned the same theme (and the same shows) when discussing SOC Ones, because both subtypes focus on refinement. At SOC One, the emphasis is manners and correctness (refinement via *rules*); at SOC Four, the emphasis is more on grace, artistic , and emotional restraint (refinement via *art*).

But the two themes are clearly intertwined. In *The September Issue*, a documentary about the preparation of the September issue of *Vogue* magazine, the focus is on Diane Wintour, the editor, and Grace Coddington, the creative director. (Wintour is said to be the model for Meryl's Streep's character, fashion editor Miranda Priestley, in *The Devil Wears Prada.*) Judging by her social reserve and exquisite taste, Wintour is probably a SOC One. Although she's often portrayed as an "ice lady," I saw her as a woman of great reserve and shyness. When we put her shyness together with her perfectionism, we get someone who is so identified with an ideal that she seems almost to be living in a different world. But in order for an editor to edit, she has to have something to work with. And it's Grace Coddington, the SX-SOC Four, who gives her that "something."

Coddington is an acknowledged styling genius, whom even Wintour respects and admires. The former has an amazing sense of artistry and an eye for the innovative. Like Wintour, she's totally absorbed in her work. But hers is not an easy talent; Coddington pours herself so completely into what she does that she can't help but be emotionally affected by Wintour's constant editorializing. For example, when she notices that some of her pictures have been cut, she tries to act casual, but it's easy to see the thinly-veiled hurt feelings that she's helpless to prevent.

One reason the two women complement one another is that each is willing to fight hard for her point of view. As a result, each is constantly pushing the other to refine her work; the ultimate result is an exquisitely-wrought final product.

While it's easy to see the fashion world as lacking in depth or social significance, from a SOC Four perspective, it can be appreciated as an art form with genuine transformative power. Art transforms us because it captures the light of the divine in a physical object, enabling us to be aware of what Sufi teacher Llewellyn Vaughn-Lee calls "the light within matter," and what archetypal psychologists call *soul*.

Soul can seem far from spirit; it emerges most visibly at the end of the involutionary cycle, where the material density and darkness compel us to ask, "What's this world all about, anyway?" Art answers that question by providing us with experiences that allow us to *see through* matter, so we no longer feel trapped in its literalness. As the worlds of dreaming, symbolism, metaphor, and archetype come alive in us, they give meaning to the material world—and dignity to life.

Type five –
the puzzle-solver

I thought my presence was making the apes nervous. But it wasn't that. It was the machine, the camera. So I stopped using it. And it was then that I began to see them for the first time.
– Anthony Hopkins as a Fivish scientist-gone-native in the film *Instinct*

THERE'S A POIGNANT QUALITY about Point 5 that's eloquently captured by the above quote. The character who speaks these lines, Dr. Ethan Powell, is a reclusive Type 5 ethologist dedicated to his work with African apes. He studies them as a scientist would study anything: with fascinated detachment. But one day, he decides to lay aside his camera. And that's when he begins to really *see*—to directly experience the nature of their lives. Their experience becomes his experience, and he gradually "goes native," ultimately becoming a virtual member of the group. When poachers come to prey upon them, he kills two of the poachers in their defense. The irony, of course, is that he's managed to overcome the barrier that makes Fives feel isolated, but in a way that brings him into communion with the instinctual—rather than the social— world (connection to Eight).

Incarcerated in a hospital for the criminally insane, Powell has lost any interest in rejoining the human race and does not speak. Cuba Gooding plays the ambitious Three psychiatrist charged with trying to break through his silence. Gooding succeeds, but Powell manages to turn the tables on the young psychiatrist, teaching him a lot more about humanity than he's managed to learn from his academic education.

The real-life story of Temple Grandin is not so very different (documented in the film *Temple Grandin*). Grandin overcame severe autism in part through her innate bond with animals and in part due to her ability to devise unusual and innovative methods for handling her oversensitivity to environmental stimuli. As an adult, she became renowned as an authority on ways to build humane cattle pens and slaughter-houses. How did she do it? Through careful observation of cattle and how they react to their environment, especially man-made structures like gates, pens, and dipping vats. She noticed things that nobody had ever noticed before—like how shiny reflections or slick, steep ramps can spook the cattle. Or how they become calm when held closely by mechanical wings. Many of her suggestions for change were extremely simple and inexpensive to implement, but they created a much more humane experience for the cattle (as well as a less stressful experience for their handlers).

It's the Five's ability to really notice what's going on in his or her environment that accounts for one of the main Five labels: the Observer. I call them the Puzzle-solver, which focuses on the outcome of all those observations. Fives enjoy problem-solving, and they're usually good at it. Shy, sensitive, and intellectually-oriented, they enjoy working with ideas and often do so in unusual ways. It's probably this ability to see life from a unique perspective that accounts for their puzzle-solving genius.

At the same time, Fives can find it hard to access their emotions, at least in the conventional sense, because their emotions come from a deep place which takes time to reach. As a Five once explained to me, "Fives don't understand people whose emotions change like the weather. Emotions matter too much for that." Five creative genius Henry Darger put it another way when, commenting on his reaction to the death of his father, he said that "I did not cry. I had that kind of deep sorrow that, bad as you feel, you cannot...I was in that state for weeks."

Ironically, their emotional and intellectual depth often puts them at a social disadvantage. The social world is the world of interaction, appearances, and changeable emotions. It's a world of witty quips and subtle social rules, rules that separate those "in the know" from others. Fives can't compete in such a world, nor do they want to. It's not that they don't want to connect with other people, but that they need to connect in a way that makes sense to them. It's often easiest for Fives to connect through

TABLE 15-1.
TYPE FIVE: THE PUZZLE-SOLVER

SHY, INTELLECTUAL, CURIOUS, INGENIOUS, QUIRKY, UNCONVENTIONAL

EIGHT Connection: brings grounding, realism, drive, aggressiveness
SEVEN Connection: brings humor, whimsy, optimism, absent-mindedness

FOUR Wing brings moodiness, intensity, inwardness, iconoclasm, depth
SIX Wing brings reserve, detachment, impassivity, kindness, political & social interest

Other Labels: Thinker, Observer, Scientist, Researcher, Investigator
Challenges: isolation, autistic detachment, feeling unneeded, inability to communicate

SUBTYPES		
Self-preservation	Sexual	Social
ARCHETYPES Detached Philosopher, Solitary Puzzle-solver, Silent Pattern Observer, Mental Tinkerer, Shy Philosopher Systems Analyst, Thinker, Theoretical Inventor, Blueprint Creator, Amateur Scholar, Serious Hobbyist, Knowledge Collector, Collector of Oddities, Space Protector, Reflective Thinker, Detail Analyzer, Professional Student, Intellectual Treasure Finder, Solitary Hermit, Sensitive Parent Childlike Hobbyist, Observant Friend, , Armchair Philosopher, Reclusive Intellectual, Gawky Nerd	Amateur Sleuth, Secret Agent, Professional Spy, Double Agent, Fascinated Scientist, Serious Alchemist, Secret Investigator, Private Eye, Undercover Operative, Charlie Chan ("Inscrutable Oriental"), Behind-the-scenes Internet Wizard, Chat Room Enthusiast, Chess Player, Private Tutor, Secret Photographer, Psychoanalyst, Underworld Guide, FBI Profiler, Exchanger of Confidences, Weirdo Voyeur, Secret Society Member, Wizard of Oz, Eccentric Inventor, Mad Scientist	Group Observer, Recognized Expert, Intellectual Authority, Honored Teacher, Tenured Professor, Knowledge Dispenser, Dispassionate Facilitator, Impersonal Guide, Scholarly Historian, Describer of Oddities, Dispassionate Bodhisattva, Occasional Iconoclast, Published Scientist, Etymological Researcher, Myth Collector, Anthropologist, Arcane Expert, Tribal Healer, Tribal Elder, Shaman, Witch Doctor, Exorcist, Esotericist, Sage, Wise Old Man/Woman
FILM THEMES **Shy or isolated persons** are drawn out of their shell by the plight of others (*Turtle Diaries, Awakenings, Shadowlands*), by love (*Son-rise, Fahrenheit 451*), or friendship (*David & Lisa, The Blue Butterfly, The Station Agent*) **"Lost" people** are found but only temporarily or not completely (*Awakenings, Charly, A Beautiful Mind*) **Extreme sensitivity** can bring emotional withdrawal or breakdown (*The Luzhin Defense, The Collector*) but can indicate an inventive mind (*Crumb, Temple Grandin*) **People can become isolated** when exploring new worlds (*2001: A Space Odyssey, The Razor's Edge*) **Intelligent non-human** seeks connection (*Bicentennial Man, Star Trek, E. T., Starman, A. I.*)	**Subterranean sexuality** creates unusual sexual situations (*The Collector; sex, lies, and videotape; Crumb; Kinsey*) **Autism** is no barrier to love (*Rain Man*), is cured by love (*Son-rise*) or is part of a mystical healing crisis (*House of Cards*) **Brilliant thinker** is redeemed by love (*A Beautiful Mind, The Luzhin Defense*) **Creepy but intelligent psychopath shares confidences** with the privileged few (*Silence of the Lambs, Capture of the Green River Killer*) **Dark shadows** fascinate (spy, horror, comedy-horror, sci-fi, mystery flicks, e.g., *Twilight Zone, Invasion of the Body Snatchers, The Outer Limits, The Day the Earth Stood Still, The Adventures of Sherlock Holmes,* later *Harry Potter* films, *Brazil, Fargo, Dr. Who*)	**Astute thinkers serve others** via teaching (*Goodbye Mr. Chips,*) helping fellow prisoners (*Shawshank Redemption*), thinking up ingenious ideas (*Apollo 13, A Beautiful Mind, Awakenings*), solving cases (*The Adventures of Sherlock Holmes, Hercule Poirot* films) or writing a country's constitution (*Dr. Bahasaheb Ambedkar*) **Refusal to acknowledge feelings** eventually creates social disasters (*Tom & Viv, Damage*) **Esoteric, magical, or shamanic knowledge** reveals hidden dimensions of life (*The Da Vinci Code, Meetings with Remarkable Men, The Razor's Edge*) or helps people reap financial rewards (*21*) **The desire to share ideas** inspires intellectual forums (Book TV programs), resistance to anti-intellectual regimes (*Fahrenheit 451, 1984*) or industrial change (*Temple Grandin*)

their writings or teachings. But to find real intimacy, they need time alone with poten-tial friends and lovers. Like Fours, they need the freedom to be themselves without feeling pressured to conform too closely to social norms.

In the enneagram world, Fives are often saddled with the burden of being "stingy"—either with their time, space, or energy—simply because they're more in-terested in using their energy for their own projects than in investing it in social activi-ties. But it's not so much that Fives always find social activities unappealing, simply that they need a good reason to participate and a means of feeling comfortable in the group. When I was doing a lot of Eastern European folk dancing, I ran into a lot of male and female Fives there; I imagine they were attracted by the unusual harmonies and mathematical intricacy of the music and the steps. It probably didn't hurt that a part-ner isn't necessary (most of the dances are line dances) and that it's possible to make friends in a casual, non-dating sort of way.

Like Fours, Fives reside at the bottom of the enneagram, in the realm of *soul*. This gives them unusual depth of understanding but it also gives them depth of feeling, as mentioned above. Although Fives have a reputation for being cerebral, they're capable of tremendously deep devotion to those for whom they care. But they're more likely to show their caring through action than words, and the action is likely to be under-stated; Fives don't shout their devotion from the rooftops (especially male Fives). But they might spend a lot of time making sure the locks work, the bills are paid, and the insurance policy is up to date—or at least provide you with thoughtful advice.

Point Five is the first point we encounter as we pass from the involutionary to the evolutionary side of the enneagram. And so it's somewhat akin to Point 1, the first point on the involutionary side. In both cases, the emphasis is on setting standards. But at Point 1, we set standards for ethical behavior where at Point 5, we set standards for rational understanding. However, both Points 1 and 5 are more analytical than sociable (more masculine than feminine), which is one reason that they're said to be "lookalike types" (types that may be mistaken for one another). However, Fives are much more likely than Ones to use purely intellectual means for tackling problems, even ethical problems. They're also much slower to act, being inclined to think about a problem from every angle imaginable before suggesting a potential solution.

While Fives may be one of the hardest types to understand, they're often one of the easiest types to recognize. They have a distinctive energy that sets them apart from other types; it's hard to miss once you're familiar with it—a kind of impassive mental alertness and clarity. This mental alertness makes Fives interesting companions, if you happen to share the same interests and are willing to draw them out of their shell.

Fives can use their two connecting points to access abilities which can boost their social confidence. From Point 7, they gain a bit of charm and the ability to sense the pulse of a group. Also, the mental agility of the Seven enhances the Fives' problem-solving skills, enabling them both to "switch gears" and think on their feet, coming up with ingenious solutions to unusual problems. From Point 8, they gain authority and groundedness, a real asset for people who tend to be shy. They also get the energy to overcome their natural tendency to procrastinate (while they endlessly mull over the merits of each potential course of action). But Fives that get angry can suddenly jump to Eight in a way that seems completely out of character (and like a trapdoor phenomenon; see my comments in Chapter 11). Unaccustomed to expressing anger, Fives don't always handle it very well. For best results, they need to be aware of the potential for losing control and have a plan for dealing with the sudden influx of emotion.

Young Fives may be at a disadvantage, for several reasons. One is that children are expected to be compliant, and while Fives are quiet, they're not necessarily compliant. When pushed too hard to conform in the family or at school, they tend to withdraw. The second reason is that their shyness and bookishness can be a social liability, so they come in for teasing from other kids (although probably less so today than when I was growing up, because the digital revolution has made nerdiness more socially acceptable). But the biggest difficulty for young Fives is their sensitivity to outer stimuli and consequent need for privacy, which is often ignored by the non-Five adults in their lives. Even if they have their own space (like a bedroom), it's seldom treated with the kind of respect that Fives require to feel comfortable. And of course, once brothers and sisters figure out the Five's vulnerabilities, they may use them to gain a psychological edge, not realizing the potentially negative and long-lasting effects of toying with a Five's sensitivities.

Fives with a Six wing (5w6) are a good fit for the Five stereotype of a heady, detached individual who is seldom perturbed by outer circumstance (except when jumping to Eight in anger, as mentioned above). Their interest in human affairs is often directed into topics like politics, philosophy, or economics, especially for males. This doesn't mean they don't care about people, but that their concern is directed more towards their own friends and family (to whom they are typically loyal) than towards those outside their immediate circle, whom they regard from a more abstract perspective.

Fives with a Four wing (5w4) don't fit the Five stereotype as well, because they usually have a certain amount of emotionality and are subject to the effects of the chaotic area at the bottom of the enneagram (see Chapter 14 for a discussion). They have the unenviable task of trying to integrate their emotions into a mental framework that doesn't quite know how to classify them. People who know the enneagram may wonder whether the 5w4 is really a Five. (I've had the same experience being a 4w5; I've got enough mental energy and interest in science to make people wonder whether I'm really a Four.)

Judith Searle originally spoke of three Five film genres: science fiction, horror, and black comedies; recently, she added a fourth: sleuth stories (like Sherlock Holmes. While I agree that all of these themes are Fivish, all but the last one focus our attention on the darkest aspects of human consciousness. Here again we see the influence of the "bottom" energy: the energy that takes us down to the depths of the human psyche, where we find all the unresolved Shadow material we've managed to ignore by staying either on the surface (in ego consciousness) or by trying to ascend to higher consciousness. If we don't delve deeply enough at Point 4 (thus unearthing our unresolved emotional issues), guess what happens at Point 5? Whatever is left over is projected outward and turns into something alien and horrible! Then it shows up in Hollywood flicks designed to diminish our fears by making light of them (horror-comedy and black comedy having become especially popular genres during the last two decades). The beginning lines to TV's *Outer Limits* (a cult classic series airing 1963 – 65) captures the mood of such genres:

> *There is nothing wrong with your television set. Do not attempt to adjust the picture. We are controlling transmission. We will control the horizontal. We will control the vertical. We can change the focus to a soft blur or sharpen it to crystal clarity. You are about to experience the awe and mystery which reaches from the inner mind to the outer limits.* *

The reference to "awe and mystery" reminds us that the appeal of sci-fi/horror comes in part from the way it introduces us to possibilities that are outside the bounds of our normally-circumscribed expectations. It's not just about monsters from outer space. (Imagine what it would be like for a caveman to find himself suddenly transported to Times Square; it would seem like a horrific experience.) At their best, such genres prepare us for new modes of consciousness and alien encounters that we might otherwise find overwhelming.

But I'd hate to think that Point 5 has nothing more to offer us than horror. When we delve more deeply, we find it has a lot more: stories about shy people coming out of their shells; alienated people (including actual aliens and robots) becoming humanized and/or accepted by humanity; autistic people who rejoin humanity or who manage to humanize the "normal" people around them; brilliant thinkers saved by love; intellectuals who help people solve problems (this would include the sleuth genre); and memorable teachers who inspire their charges. Point 5 themes also direct our attention to everything in life that is obscure or unusual: unsolved mysteries, obscure rites and rituals, shamanic practices, scientific oddities, physical paradoxes, intellectual puzzles, and esoteric knowledge.

¤ ¤ ¤

---

* Despite the creepy introduction, the *Outer Limits* was unusual for a horror show in having many programs with a distinctly poignant feeling, so it has a 5w4 "feel" to it; compare this with the much cooler *Twilight Zone*, which is much more detached and cerebral (5w6).

SELF-PRESERVATION FIVE THEMES. This is the subtype that's often called a "Castle" Five (as in, "My home is my castle"). The idea of a home as a castle captures the extreme reserve and need for privacy, especially private space that is theirs alone. SP subtypes tend to be reserved anyway, and so do Fives: when we put the two together, we get a very private person who does not tolerate incursions on her space.

Not surprisingly, many SP film themes focus on the problem of social isolation and what to do about it. The wings become relevant here, because SP Five films with a 5w4 protagonist often focus on the emotional pain caused by social isolation while those with a 5w6 protagonist focus on the issue of isolation from a more abstract angle (e.g., often through the concerned eyes of a non-Five).

Compare the characters of Spock (*Star Trek*) and Data (*Star Trek: The Next Generation*). Spock is a 5w6 while Data is a 5w4. Although Spock is literally alienated (his father is an alien), he's seemingly unconcerned about his inability to feel, a theme much played up in the original TV series (with lots of jabs from William Shatner's 3w4-like Kirk character and DeForest Kelley's 2w1-like Dr. McCoy).* It's as though Kirk and McCoy are actually using their emotions *on behalf* of Spock, who seems unable to do this for himself. Their pokes and jabs are designed to break through his surface-level impassivity. Of course, every once in a while, we see Spock's more vulnerable side, and discover that underneath his impassive exterior, there's a real person with real (albeit buried) emotions. It's the interplay between outer impassivity and inner emotion that makes the character memorable.

Viewers liked Spock very much, so when *Star Trek* creators devised *Star Trek: the Next Generation*, they created Data, an android. Unlike Spock, Data seems to be capable of accessing some sort of feeling, although in an obtuse, 5w4-like way. He's not technically supposed to have emotion (because he lacks an "emotion chip"), but he has a very Four-like longing to be human—or at least to experience a sense of kinship

---

* The relationship between Dr. McCoy and Spock exemplifies the tie between Types 2 and 5 that I mentioned in the last chapter; they are very different, but each needs the qualities of the other to obtain some sort of psychic balance.

with other humans. The biggest difference between Spock and Data is that the latter seems more vulnerable and thus easier to identify with.

However, one interesting thing about the Spock character is how it has evolved during the last 40 years, in the *Star Trek* films that followed the original TV series. As we get to know Spock better, we gradually realize that his seeming lack of emotion belies a very subtle and sensitive emotionality that's expressed in unusual ways. It's no coincidence that during this same period, American culture has become progressively more open to introverts, nerds, and unconventional techno-thinkers.

The only caveat here is that most enneagram observers type Spock's alter-ego, Leonard Nimoy, as a 1w9 (not a 5w6). This makes sense, given Nimoy's ascetic demeanor and silent intensity (he's probably an SX subtype, as well). So the Fivishness we see in Spock is tinged with a fire we might not see in a true 5w6.

It's actually somewhat rare to see SP Fives as actors; when I was looking for examples to include in this book, I realized that a lot of the actors who play SP Five-style roles (as shy or isolated people) are actually Sevens playing their connecting point of Five (Robin Williams as a shy physician in *Awakenings* and Jeff Bridges as an alien visitor in *Star Man*); Eights playing their Five connecting point (Robert DeNiro as a man awakening from sleeping sickness in *Awakenings)*; or Sixes playing their wing: (Jon Tunturro as a painfully-inhibited chess genius in *The Luzhin Defense).* However, the socially-inhibited butterfly collector in *The Collector* who decides to "collect" a female (by kidnapping her) is played by Terence Stamp, a real-life Five.

Anthony Hopkins is probably the best-known Five actor today. In *Shadowlands*, he plays the writer C. S. Lewis as an SP Five who is a confirmed bachelor living with his brother—until he offers to do an American female friend (Joy Grisham, played by Three Deborah Winger) a favor by marrying her so she can legally remain in Great Britain. They continue to live separately, which seems a suitable arrangement to Lewis, who is oblivious to the fact that his wife is actually in love with him and wishes he would notice. Lewis actually has feelings for her himself, but does not dare acknowledge them (even to himself), because this would disturb his quiet and orderly academic existence.

But when Joy contracts terminal cancer, the whole arrangement blows up; in a moment of weakness, she ends up confessing her love to him. He's initially upset, but soon comes to the painful realization that he also loves her. This realization would be difficult for anyone in such a situation, but for someone as self-contained and sensitive as Lewis, the pain seemed almost beyond words. It's one reason the film is so poignant.

One IMDB reviewer observed that here was someone who lived his life one way—mostly in his mind—who was suddenly confronted with his true feelings. Another mentioned the discrepancy between what Lewis' passionate Christian writings and the boring predictability of his own life (which completely lacked the passion of the writing). Falling in love plunged Lewis into the depths of his own feelings, where he found his heart.

2001: a Space Odyssey (1968) is arguably the best example of a film that offers us a glimpse of the world from an SP Five's point of view. Developed by science fiction writer Arthur C. Clarke and surrealistic film maker Stanley Kubrick (both Fives), it's a work designed as much to create an atmosphere as to explore a theme. And the atmosphere is one of wonderfully detached expansiveness that seems both awe-inspiring and austere—just like space.

Most of the film takes place in space, somewhere near Jupiter, aboard a space station transporting scientists who will study a mysterious black monolith that has been discovered on one of the moons of Jupiter. In the distant past, the monolith had appeared to a group of peaceful but unevolved apes, who then quickly evolved (if you can call it that) to the point where they were able to kill other apes using tools. Now that the monolith has been seen again, we are given to understand that it provides clear evidence for the existence of intelligent extra-terrestrial life. But just what kind of intelligence are we talking about? That's not yet clear.

Aboard the spacecraft are three hibernating scientists, two astronauts (Keir Dullea and Gary Lockwood), and the highly-advanced HAL 9000 computer, which is basically running the ship. The astronauts have the kind of disembodied existence that is not so different from the disembodied existence of HAL, whom we gradually realize has some all-too-human flaws. So it's rather hard to tell the difference among the three of them, which is part of the film's message: that we really don't know what distinguishes the consciousness of apes, humans, machines, and black monoliths. When HAL begins to give the astronauts wrong information, seemingly on purpose, the two astronauts are troubled and decide to disconnect HAL's circuits. But HAL reads their lips and manages to silently terminate the lives of everybody on board except Dave, who eventually disconnects him (a memorable process, as HAL slowly "regresses" to a more primitive and vulnerable childlike state).*

And then something mysterious happens to Dave, something hard to fathom. After disconnecting HAL, he leaves the space station on a shuttle, where he encounters the monolith in space; he then finds himself accelerating through a fantastic corridor of colors in space, arriving at a Louis XIV room where he is completely alone. Evidently, time passes, because we see him growing old; eventually, we see him lying on the bed, on the brink of death, at which point the monolith appears in the room. The next image is of a shimmering cosmic fetus in space. And that's the end. (Or is it the beginning?)

What has died and what is being born? We don't really know. But the image gives the impression of something wonderful yet incomprehensible. The process that started with the discovery of tools for killing seems to be leading towards developments that represent some sort of cosmic leap in evolution.

The amazing thing about *2001* is its continuing ability to evoke awe, even 40 years after it was originally produced. Its timeless quality is very much like the austerely timeless world of the SP Five, who is more focused on the fascinating dimensions of her inner reality than the time- and space-constricted world of social interaction.

Yet we have to wonder whether the interior world of the SP Five is rich enough to sustain her in the absence of human contact. Even when the Five seems to pull back,

---

* We never find out why HAL starts losing his marbles, but can't help but wonder whether it has anything to do with the monolith.

is she pulling back because she wants to be alone, because she's unusually sensitive, or because she's unable to bridge the communication gap? That's the question raised in films about people who are socially isolated, especially those with autism, e.g., *Rain Man*, *House of Cards* (Chapter 12), and *Temple Grandin*.

Rain Man focuses on the difficulties of two brothers getting to know one another when one is an autistic man with many sensitivities (see discussion below); *House of Cards* (discussed in Chapter 12) raises the question of whether trauma can cause autistic symptoms. I've already mentioned Temple Grandin, whose life is documented in the film by the same name. The focus in the film is on Grandin's determination to overcome both her sensitivities and social difficulties from college onward. The film does a wonderful job capturing the experience of what it's like to be so sensitive and how it's possible to nonetheless use those sensitivities to achieve something worthwhile in life.

Son-rise is the purportedly true story of how a family found a way to reverse the effects of infantile autism. When toddler Raun Kaufman is diagnosed as severely autistic, his loving parents Bears and Suzi are determined to re-establish contact with him. Somehow, they have the intuitive sense that what they need to do initially is to go into his world, not demand that he come into theirs. So that's just what they do: all day, every day, one of them sits with Raun, doing whatever he does, allowing him to lead them into his silent, inner world. They have the feeling that this non-threatening, receptive approach will eventually arouse his curiosity. Slowly, Raun begins to respond, gradually becoming more social, until he is a normal little boy who doesn't remember ever having been different than other children. (The Kaufmans take the position that autism can be cured, if it's caught early enough and treated properly, although this claim remains controversial.)

The film *Charly* focuses on the social isolation that comes to people who have a low IQ. Sometimes people of low intelligence seem less human than other people because we have no way to meaningfully connect with them. But what if we had a drug that could raise their IQ? Based on the short story *Flowers for Algernon*, *Charly* (a misspelled version of Charley) shows us the transformation of a dumb but happy bakery worker who's given an experimental drug that makes him brilliant. Always good-natured, Charly becomes a highly thoughtful man who retains his kind nature. He experiences the joys of love but also the pain of realizing how the "funny" pranks played on him at the bakery were more cruel than humorous. At some point, he notices that Algernon, the mouse on which the drug was first tested, is not as bright as he once was. He confronts the sad truth that sooner or later he's going to be "dumb" again.

Awakenings is about yet another kind of social isolation: the isolation associated with the aftermath of sleeping sickness. It's based on experiences of real-life neurologist Oliver Sachs, who worked with victims of a 1920s epidemic of sleeping sickness that left them unable to move or talk for decades, except when prompted by others. After the drug L-dopa was found to help Parkinson's Disease, Sachs wanted to try it for reviving sleeping sickness victims. Its initial effects seemed miraculous; they totally "woke up"—but only temporarily. The dramatic gains they made were gradually lost, and the patients fell back to sleep once again.

Robin Williams plays the Sacks-inspired Dr. Malcolm Sayer, a Five who is extremely introverted. But he's also a kind man, so when it becomes clear to him that the drug L-dopa might revive his patients, Sayer wants to use it on all of them. Because it's expensive, the only way the hospital can afford the treatment is for him to seek the support of wealthy donors. We see Sayer nervously giving a speech to them, trying his best to explain how the drug protocol works. But between his shyness and use of scientific jargon, he's unsuccessful. Desperate to break through the communication barrier, he finally gets rid of his notes and begins to speak from the heart; his audience responds with the needed donations. Although in the end, Dr. Sayer cannot save his patients, the concerted efforts he makes on their behalf allow him to save himself—to gain the courage and confidence he needs to emerge from his social cocoon.

Films like these show us the way that shy or isolated people like SP Fives experience the world. They help us appreciate their sensitivities and talents, and they also give us ideas for ways to get around barriers to communication. While our inclination is to bring SP Fives into the world that we already know, we might also want to consider the possibility that the world of the Five is also worth knowing—and that becoming receptive to that world is another way of bridging the communication gap.

¤ ¤ ¤

SEXUAL FIVE THEMES. Here is where we find most of Searle's film themes: the sci-fi, horror, spy, and mystery flicks that I include in the Dark Shadows category. SX Five is also the place of secrets, taboos, exclusive confidences, unusual or hidden spiritual paths, subterranean love and sexuality, and bizarre or unexpected happenings.

If SP Fives are relatively self-contained and impassive, SX Fives are intensely curious and intellectually restless. They see intimate relationships as part of their quest to go to a deeper level, especially intellectually or esoterically. It's helpful to have an interested confidante who's receptive to their compelling need to discern hidden patterns and explore new arenas of inquiry. Although SX Fives are a bit more people-oriented than SP Fives, they still feel caught between the desire for intimacy and the need for privacy. This can result in a more emotional or "jerky" style of relating that is the result of lurching forward, then (feeling overwhelmed), quickly stepping back. Other people can find this reactivity confusing and don't always know how to respond. By the same token, SX Fives don't always know how to respond to the subtle intricacies that intimate relationships involve. This lack of social finesse can lead to misunderstandings and feelings of frustration for both the Five and her closest friends and confidantes.

SX Fives seek out close friends with whom they can share their ideas. But they often prefer to take the lead in intellectual matters, which is why they enjoy intellectually mentoring other individuals. Generally speaking, they would rather have one dedicated apprentice than a large group of casual pupils who lack intellectual competence or a serious interest in the subject matter.

Sherlock Holmes' relationship with Dr. Watson illustrates the kind of intimacy that is most valued. Holmes likes to be the primary investigator and is fond of engaging in long soliloquies with Watson, his appreciative listener. He likes the fact that Watson, while less keenly observant than Holmes, can still follow Holmes' logic. And he especially appreciates what Watson contributes in the way of medical knowledge.

For SX Fives, personal validation means intellectual validation, which is why they get annoyed with people who nod approvingly when they speak but who obviously don't understand a thing they're saying. They want to speak to an educated listener who can intelligently respond to their comments, and perhaps even enhance their own understanding. That's their idea of a satisfying intellectual exchange.

SX Fives have an aura of quiet intensity and an inquisitive quality that can both attract and repel people. It can attract people because it evokes a sense of unseen realities that aren't bound by the limits of social convention. It can repel people for much the same reason: because it reminds them of parts of reality that are completely different than what they're used to, dimensions of being that are beyond what we know or can control. This is a place where we drop through the Rabbit Hole, go Through the Looking Glass, stumble into the Twilight Zone, or venture beyond the Outer Limits. Once we're there, we meet characters like Rod Serling, Freddy Kruger, the Mad Hatter & Red Queen, the Pod People, the Rain Man, kinky cartoonist Dick Crumb, Hannibal Lecter, Bela Lugosi and his alter-ego Dracula. Such an excursion is as fascinating as it is dreadful.

SX Five is also the place of espionage, counterespionage, secret projects (like WWII's Enigma Project or Manhattan Project), encrypted messages, decoding devices, behind-the-scenes dealings, and ultra high-tech gadgets. Judith Searle assigns the spy genre to Type Six, and as far as spy films go, she may be right—because spy films are designed to create suspense, and suspense is more associated with Point 6 than Point 5. But in real life, the activities that involve secret research or the keeping of secrets are probably more Five-like (and require the Five's secret-keeping abilities).

A blurb for National Geographic's series *Taboo* captures the nature of SX Five territory rather well:

In all societies there are those who find themselves isolated from their fellow humans. In Australia, a man's belief that his right leg is not part of his body has devastating consequences. In Bangladesh an entire community is mistrusted, and cast adrift on the country's waterways. In England, a man rejects his society's food customs by choosing to eat road kill. They all have one thing in common. They are outsiders, misfits, taboo.

What's interesting is how getting acquainted with one of these quirky individuals can change the lives of more conventionally-minded people, helping them to see past their social conditioning and superficial orientation towards life. As discussed in Chapter 13, *Rain Man* is the story about two brothers—one a cynical Three and the other an autistic Five savant. Raised apart, they only get to know one another after their father's death. Tom Cruise plays Charlie Babbitt, the Three; Dustin Hoffman plays his older brother Raymond, who was institutionalized during Charlie's early childhood by their father, who became concerned that the oblivious Raymond might accidently hurt toddler Charlie.

Despite his quirks and sensitivities, Raymond can perform extraordinary memory feats but who suffers from a complete lack of social skills and extreme sensitivity to any change in his routine. Charlie's Three-ish insensitivity and Raymond's Fivish oversensitivity put the two characters on a collision course.

A pivotal change in their relationship happens after Charlie gets totally frustrated with Raymond's behavior and announces to him, "I think this autism is a bunch of garbage. You can't tell me that you're not in there somewhere!" Raymond does not, of course, respond. So Charlie takes him to a small-town doctor who informs him that Raymond is simply wired differently from other people, helping Charlie to better understand what he's dealing with. As Charlie begins accept Raymond's quirks, Raymond becomes more relaxed and less rigid. He nevertheless remains autistic. So the bond that begins to form between the brothers is based mostly on Charlie's willingness to accept Raymond as the individual he is, instead of expecting him to conform to some sort of cultural ideal.

In the documentary *Crumb*, we get an rare peek at the personal life of Robert Crumb, quirky creator of the "Keep on Truckin," "Cheap Thrills," and "Fritz the Cat." Crumb is a great example of an SX Five: a brilliant, quirky cartoonist with strange sexual preoccupations that often show up in his cartoons. He's an obvious iconoclast whose forward-looking leaps into kinky cartoonery has managed to offend a wide range of people over the years. One of his cartoons shows a cramped room resembling a well with its sides completely covered by huge electrical switches and cables; a sign with a skull and crossbones reads *Danger: High Voltage*. (The image brings to mind the ubiquitous duct work in Terry Gilliam's underground classic *Brazil*.) At the bottom of the well/room is a skinny naked figure with huge but obscured genitals cowering in mock terror; the caption reads "The little guy that lives inside my brain."

The first thing Robert says in the film: "If I don't draw for a while, I get really crazy, really depressed and suicidal...but [laughs weakly] then I get suicidal even if I do." This is meant as a quasi-joke, but there's a dark edge to it. Robert has two brothers, Maxon and Charles, that are also talented artists who are even more bizarre in their lifestyles. Maxon has lived in a derelict hotel in San Francisco since 1980 and spent years panhandling while sitting on a bed of nails; Charles lived as a hermit with his mother, in a barren room piled high with books but little else. What is wrong in this family? We get a clue when Charles remarks that their father was a "tyrant"; a online source characterizes their father as a tough Marine who frequently beat the kids. Considering their sensitivity (all three seem like Fives, with Charles a probable SP Five), that kind of treatment would probably be guaranteed to push them over the edge. Robert seems the most well-adjusted of the three brothers. Charles took his own life a year after *Crumb* was made; Maxon continues to live in the hotel but now sells some of his art to support himself.

None of the brothers were popular as teenagers and, in fact, seemed to have been on the receiving end of a lot of teen cruelty. Those were lonely years but for Robert, at least, it was a prelude to better days. He may not have originally been a ladies' man, but—as he says with a wicked smile— "All that changed after I became famous." Even so, Crumb never became mainstream; he passed up offer after offer to appear with groups like the Rolling Stones or on shows like *Saturday Night Live*, even though he needed the money. It just wasn't him.

While *Crumb* is a testament to Robert's professional success and the recognition he's gained in some segments of the art world—he's been called the Bruegel of the last half of the 20th century" and "the Daumier of our times"—it's hard to believe that anyone watching the film would actually want to swap lives with Robert Crumb: his world (and his mind) is just too bizarre for most of us. But *Crumb* sure gives us an idea of what life looks like from an SX Five perspective.

¤ ¤ ¤

SOCIAL FIVE THEMES. The world of the SOC Five is the world of knowledge, learning, and teaching, whether it takes place in the halls of academia or around a ceremonial fire in a traditional tribal setting. As professors, experts, and teachers of advanced, specialized, or esoteric knowledge, SOC Fives are able to participate in society but in a way that allows them to maintain the distance they need to feel comfortable in a social setting.

SOC Fives are more motivated than other Fives to communicate with other people and gain public recognition for their intellectual accomplishments. They enjoy the prestige of being honored as experts in their field. And they enjoy using their expertise as the basis for creating social ties that don't bind too tightly. Where the emphasis at SP Five is on knowledge for its own sake and the emphasis at SX Five is on knowledge used for secret, hidden, or unusual purposes, the emphasis at SOC Five is on imparting knowledge in a way that serves the community in some way (thus providing them with a social role they can live with).

We see this pattern played out in *The Shawshank Redemption,* where introverted banker Andy Dufresne (Tim Robbins) winds up in prison after being convicted of murder based solely on circumstantial evidence. Receiving two life sentences in the maximum-security Shawshank Prison, he has no real hope of ever being free again. Prison life is initially hellish for Andy, who is too bookish to know how to defend himself. But somehow, he manages to survive. His life improves after he's befriended by an older, wiser inmate, Red (Morgan Freeman), who shows him how to avoid trouble and create a social niche for himself.

Because of his education, Andy is soon able to establish and run a prison library, where he finds satisfaction in taking on the SOC Five mentoring role of educating illiterate inmates. His education also allows him to provide financial advice to the prison warden and guards, thus ensuring his ability to continue to develop the library. Unfortunately, the warden is a corrupt and brutal man, and this fact begins to create problems for Andy, who is asked to use his financial expertise to launder the warden's kickbacks. Having little other choice, he complies.

But Andy's seeming compliance masks his secret preoccupation: digging an escape tunnel (here we see the impressive secret-keeping ability that some Fives possess). Although it takes years, the tunnel is eventually his ticket to freedom. Once out of jail, Andy shows up in the warden's bank with meticulously-prepared documents allowing him to withdraw all the laundered money. He subsequently escapes to a small fishing village in Mexico, where he's later joined by Red, after his release on parole.

Tom & Viv show us what can happen when a SOC Five is confronted with a situation which forces him outside of his restricted emotional comfort zone. Fives of this subtype sometimes use their social role as a way of avoiding intimacy (especially Fives with a Six wing). In this film, based on the marriage of T. S. Eliot to his aristocratic English wife, Vivien Haigh-Wood, Eliot (William Dafoe) is initially captivated by the beauty and aliveness of his English rose (Miranda Richardson). Unfortunately, he's even more captivated by her aristocratic heritage; marriage to Vivien will give him entrée into respectable British society.

Eliot's proposal of marriage is regarded with relief by her family, because unbeknownst to him, Vivien is a bit of an embarrassment to them, due to both her unpredictable emotional outbursts and unconventional ways (which are probably the result of hormonal imbalances combined with an SX Four disposition). The family doesn't tell him about the situation in advance, in hopes that marriage will both settle her down and get her out of the household. But disaster strikes almost immediately, when she has heavy bleeding on her wedding night—and an emotional meltdown to match. Unfortunately, Eliot reacts with extreme revulsion (probably covering over his feelings of panic, because both events violate his need to maintain strict control over his emotions). Dafoe is very effective in playing the part; as the *New York Times* book reviewer put it, "In Tom & Viv, Mr. Dafoe captures Eliot's chilling inability to deal with anyone's emotions, especially his own."

Despite ongoing difficulties, Vivien is able to play the role of creative muse to Eliot over the next few years; the film hints that it's her passion for his work that enables him to exercise his creative genius (he having little access to his own passion, because he's so deeply repressed it). Although Vivien can definitely be a handful, she's admirably creative and spunky. As the drama unfolds, we begin to sympathize with her plight as a creative person trapped within the narrow confines of British society. As she becomes increasingly hemmed in, she becomes more and more quirky. Eliot predictably withdraws, increasing her desperation. Finally, Eliot and her family decide that enough is enough—and decide to have Viv clapped away in a mental hospital, although she's clearly not crazy in any conventional sense of the word. She dies some years later without Eliot ever having made the attempt to communicate with her after her incarceration.

In many ways, *Tom & Viv* can be seen as a SOC Five morality tale, where we see what can happen when emotional repression and a disembodied intellect combine to produce a well-reasoned argument for considering unconventional emotionalism as grounds for institutionalization. Underlying this coolly rational argument is a distinctly irrational impulse based on the need to suppress one's emotions at all costs—even if it means destroying the life of another. The better solution, of course, lies in working with one's emotions, so that they seem altogether less disturbing—and less likely to produce feelings of revulsion. (We sometimes see a similar pattern of fending off emotions at SOC One, but the motivation is different. Fives feel paralyzed by emotion and thus unable to think, which can bring on a sense of panic; Ones feel assaulted by emotion and potentially unable to restrain their behavior, which creates shame and feelings of failure.)

A Beautiful Mind shows us the odyssey of a brilliant but arrogant theorist into a man whose heart has grown to match his intellect. It's based on the real-life story of

SOC Five John Nash, the Nobel Laureate inventor of game theory. Nash's youthful aspirations for greatness combine with a constitutional tendency towards mental instability to derail an individual whose native brilliance leads him to overestimate his own worth. It's only after going through a lot of suffering (multiple incarcerations in mental hospitals and repeated shock treatments) that he begins to realize the value of love and human relationships. Although Nash never completely rids himself of his voices (which in the film are accompanied by visual hallucinations), he becomes motivated to keep them at bay, which he finally manages to do. No longer arrogant, he gradually finds his way back into the world of academia. But this time, he welcomes the opportunity to teach ordinary students, something he previously disdained as beneath him. (Nash is sensitively played by Russell Crowe, an Eight accessing his Five connecting point.)

Dan Brown's *The Da Vinci Code* puts the spotlight on yet another SOC Five dimension of experience: the dimension of esoteric knowledge, especially knowledge that has the power to fundamentally alter our lives. By suggesting an alternative interpretation of the life of Jesus (specifically, that the Holy Grail is actually a secret lineage descended from the union of Jesus and Mary Magdalene), it generated a lot of controversy but also opened peoples' minds to new ideas. I don't know Brown's enneagram type, but his father—a math professor—was probably a Five. Both of his parents were interested in codes and ciphers, and they apparently devised elaborate treasure hunts involving esoteric puzzle-solving for their children on birthdays and holidays. Raised in this kind of environment, it's not surprising that Brown grew up to write *The Da Vinci Code* and other novels that tantalize us with the prospect of discovering hidden knowledge.

Fives understand that knowledge is power. And the deeper our understanding, the more power we possess. SOC Fives enjoy unearthing life's secrets and using their understanding to serve the public interest, sometimes by teaching people what they know (as professors and other academics) and sometimes by keeping the knowledge to themselves but using it in service to society (as healers, wise men/women, high priests, or shamans).

The enneagram itself is an esoteric system that has only recently come to public attention. So it's not surprising that two of its most influential teachers—Claudio Naranjo and A. H. Almaas—are Fives, probably SX-SOC Fives. This accounts for the intensely intellectual character of Naranjo's *Character and Neurosis* and Almaas' *The Enneagram of Holy Ideas*—and also the desire of both individuals to act as gatekeepers of enneagrammatic knowledge.

Type six –
the steward

Present fears are less than horrible imaginings.
– William Shakespeare

SIXES ARE TRADITIONALISTS who understand the power of cultural customs to fos-ter, support, and sustain human society. They're the kind of folks that we like to have around when we need to get something done and aren't sure upon whom we can rely. Sixes like to help other people, which is why they make loyal friends, devoted part-ners, and dependable employees. But unlike Twos, they usually don't mind accepting help when they need it. In fact, they enjoy the reciprocity of helping and being helped, because it allows them to feel that they're a part of something larger than themselves. Most Sixes find the sense of belonging reassuring.

Type Six has probably had more labels than any other type: the Trooper, Loyalist, Devil's Advocate, Guardian, Skeptic, Loyal Skeptic, Questioner, and my own, the Steward. They all emphasize very real aspects of the type. The Loyalist, Trooper, and Steward focus our attention on steadfastness of the type. The Loyal Skeptic, Skeptic, Devil's Advocate and Questioner address the "show me" attitude that we see in scien-tific Sixes. And both the Guardian and Steward emphasize their service orientation.

But none of these labels (including mine) points directly at what is probably the biggest challenge for this type: overcoming fear. It doesn't take long to discover this omission, because anyone who studies the Ichazo teachings will soon encounter the original names for the passion (fear) and the fixation (cowardice).

While I don't consider fear to be a vice, sin, or passion, I do see how it can be a challenge—and not just for Type 6, but for any of us. I once had an experience of feeling like I fell down a psychological well and became overwhelmed with feelings of fear for three days. I knew perfectly well there was nothing to be afraid of (at least, nothing rational). But I still couldn't shake off the feeling of paranoia. After three days, it began to slowly fade, although for months I still had bouts of fear that would suddenly arise out of nowhere. After that experience, I realized that fear is an energy field that can exist independently of anything happening in the outer environment. It helped me understand what it must be like to be a Six: someone who is extra-sensitive to that field all the time.

All of the type labels that we use to describe Type 6 are relevant to the issue of fear in one way or another, because they all speak to ways in which people respond to fear: with hesitation, skepticism, protectiveness, or faith. Many of them (like the Loyalist) remind us that life often seems less fearful when we ally ourselves with some established group, cultural tradition, or protective organization (like the police or military).

If we shift to thinking about Point 6 on the process enneagram, we discover that it's associated with our greatest fears and vulnerabilities. But what exactly makes it so fearful? According to Nathan Bernier, Point 6 represents the point in self-development where we see ourselves as we truly are. Bernier notes that occult schools call this point the "Threshold." To pass through Point 6 correctly, he says, we must harmonize the light and dark sides of our nature. So it's little wonder that we become afraid when confronted with this daunting task. Bernier goes on to make the interesting observation that "some people 'declare' their own victory or defeat early: they crystallize a positive or negative self-image and spend the rest of their lives trying to confirm it" (p. 330, *The Enneagram: Symbol of All and Everything*).

So Point 6 becomes the place where there's a natural temptation to become stuck in a rigid approach to life. But Bernier notes that there's a "negative shock" here that's designed to keep us from falling victim to such a fate. He sees this shock as something

TABLE 16-1.
TYPE SIX: THE STEWARD

CAUTIOUS, CAREFUL, ALERT, WATCHFUL, SKEPTICAL, SERVICE-ORIENTED

NINE Connection brings calmness, grounding, slowing down, apathy
THREE Connection brings confidence, decisiveness, moving out, overcompensation

FIVE Wing brings shyness, modesty, service-orientation, analytical ability, detail-orientation
SEVEN Wing brings wit, humor, nerves, restlessness, mental quickness

Other Labels: Protector, Server, Loyal Guardian, Overcomer, Skeptic
Challenges: fearfulness, paranoia, counterphobia, over-deference, conformity

SUBTYPES

	Self-preservation	Sexual	Social
ARCHETYPES	Shy Loyalist, Gentle Friend, Family Preserver, Quiet Doer, Faithful Companion, Concerned Parent, Responsible Parent, Protective Guardian, Loyal Employee, Tentative Friend, Persistent Worrier, Nervous Nelly, Warm Welcomer, Gracious Host or Hostess, Dedicated Homemaker, Anxious Home Protector, Brave Little Mouse, Little Engine That Could, Obstacle Surmounter	Fiery Rebel, Feisty Friend, Debater, Underdog Fighter, Scrapper, Runt of the Litter, Fierce Warrior, Tender Defender, Defender of the Faith, Emergency Medical Technician, Battlefield Medic, Cowardly Lion, Beauty Queen, Miss America, Boy or Girl Next Door, Prince Valiant, Braveheart, Dauntless Explorer, Sensitive Creator, Aesthetic Appreciator, Idealistic Lover, Shy Sensualist	Conserver of the Social Order, Accurate Historian, Loyalist, Careful Recorder, Community Builder/Volunteer, Dutiful Committee Worker, Dedicated Prosecutor, Staunch Traditionalist, Community Protector, Police Officer, Firefighter, Member of the Military, Socially-sanctioned Hero, Pillar of the Community, Boy/Girl Scout, Upholder of Law & Order, Reluctant Whistleblower, True Believer, Vigilante
FILM THEMES	**Traditional families** support us through thick & thin (*Sarah: Plain & Tall; Little Women; Old Yeller; Our Town; Cheaper by the Dozen, The Winslow Boy*) **Tradition offers a framework** for living (*Steel Magnolias*); failure to observe it can bring misfortune (*Himalaya, Groundhog Day*) **Safe havens** aren't so safe after all (*Sorry, Wrong Number; Patriot Games; Wait Until Dark; Hostage; Gaslight*) **Anxiety is better** than pomposity (*What About Bob?*, Woody Allen flicks, Billy Crystal flicks) **Unfamiliar situations** create anxiety (*The Out-of-Towners, National Lampoon's Vacation, About Schmidt*) **Loyalty & friendship** make life worth living (*The Killing Fields, The Big Picture, Saving Private Ryan*)	**Phobic** individuals face their fears (*The Red Badge of Courage, The Four Feathers, Superman, Bambi, Resurrection, David & Goliath, Marathon Man*) **Fear or concern spark a counterphobic response**: aggression (*24, Ransom*), dangerous distractions (*Fearless, The Year of Living Dangerously*), bold bluffing (*Julia*), brash confidence (*Pretty Women*), pro-active parental concern (*Safe Passage*) or southern charm (*The Prince of Tides*) **Skeptics** are confronted with evidence of non-logical realities (*Contact, The X-Files, The Outer Limits*) **Grateful partners** place their loves on too high a pedestal (*Chilly Scenes of Winter, Vertigo, Tori & Dean: Home Sweet Hollywood*) **Feisty folks** defy authority (*Cool Hand Luke, One Flew Over the Cuckoo's Nest*) **Sudden danger** requires a decisive response (*88 Minutes, The Fugitive, United 93*)	**Superhero hides his real identity** behind a socially-conventional persona (*The Scarlet Pimpernel, Superman, Spiderman*) **Faithful service** ultimately brings a well-earned thanks (*Scrooge, Mrs. Brown, Goodbye Mr. Chips*) **Stalwart souls** respond when duty calls (*Why We Fight, Boys Town, Scouts to the Rescue, Dragnet, Rescue 911*) **The greater good** can require great personal risk or sacrifice (*The Right Stuff, Grace is Gone, United 93, Ladder 49, 911, The 300 Spartans*) **Pressure to conform** causes a loss of individuality (*Butterfly, Das Experiment*) or sparks courageous resistance (*The Insider, Das Experiment*) **Ordinary people band together** to oppose a fearful enemy (*Norma Rae, Erin Brockovich, Fight in the Fields, Red Dawn, A Paralyzing Fear: The Story of Polio in America*)

beneficial, because it prevents us from getting stuck in stagnation, because we must "react to it in one way or another: either you fight or you die." He also observes that "we should be thankful for difficulties, since only with them can we become strong and grow" (pp. 330–331).

From the personality perspective, the negative shock at Six is not so much an event as an ongoing state of consciousness—a state that predisposes us to be hypersensitive to the hazards in our environment, so that we can't become complacent. One way for Sixes to become more comfortable with the fear they feel is to realize that their sensitivity to danger actually serves a useful purpose; it doesn't come out of nowhere for no reason. It's designed to be a spur, to provide an incentive to stay alert, engaged, and ready to act.

As the second point on the evolutionary cycle, Point 6 represents the transition from the depths back to the world of ordinary life. It corresponds to Point 2 on the involutionary side of the enneagram. Both points are about learning how to participate in the social world. At Point 2, we learn how to relate to people as individuals; at Point 6, we learn how to relate to people in groups (in families, at church, or in community organizations). In both cases, making a connection with others enables us to translate something abstract into a form that's more personal and pragmatic. At Point 2, it's the abstract ideals of the One; at Point 6, it's the abstract ideas of the Five.

As children, Sixes particularly benefit from structure and order. Some are shy and timid; others are feisty and full of bluster. Their behavior depends a lot on what it takes for them to feel secure. Young Sixes have a tendency to feel like a small person in a big world, especially if that world is unpredictable or chaotic. They tend to feel happier and more secure when they know what's expected of them. So they particularly benefit from participating in structured activities where they can get a sense of belonging (e.g. Scouts, Boys and Girls Clubs, or church youth groups). Like all children, as Sixes mature, they tend to gain confidence, especially if they have confidence-building life experiences. Sixes who may have been terrified to open their mouths in fourth grade may become accomplished speakers, performers, or leaders as adults.

Sixes with a Five wing tend to be shyer, more studious, and more service-oriented than Sixes with a Seven wing. They can make extremely dedicated researchers, scholars, or tutors. But they can have a harder time letting go of old habits and inflexible attitudes. I had a friend in graduate school with this wing and she was extremely capable when it came to scholarly work that requires great attention to detail (like generating accurate conversational transcripts). But she found it hard to be spontaneous, even about little things; she needed routines to feel comfortable in life.

Sixes with a Seven wing are notable for their sense of humor, which they use to take the edge off their fears. They have lively minds and enjoy mental humor, especially word play. The line between 6w7 and 7w6 can seem blurred at times, because both types use humor to cover over nerves and have a quick intellect. But the 6w7 tends to be more self-conscious and hesitant to jump into unfamiliar situations than the unconventional Seven; the 6w7 is also more naturally focused and persistent.

Sixes connect with Points 3 and 9. Sixes connecting with Nine can gain a sense of peace that enables them to slow down, think logically, and make more grounded decisions. The calm Nine energy can allow them to be less reactive and jumpy, especially in situations that are anxiety-provoking. A Six connecting with Three can better channel his energy into constructive activities that make a positive impact on the world, which in turn helps him gain a sense of progress and accomplishment. My father, a Six, was shyly proud of the speeches he wrote for the CEO of his company. In somebody else, that pride might have been hubris; but for him—an accountant— writing speeches seemed like a special accomplishment.

One other thing to mention is that there are two types of Sixes: phobic and counterphobic. Basically, these categories describe two different ways of dealing with fear, either by retreating in the face of it or moving forward to oppose it. I already touched on this distinction when talking about children, noting that they tend to be either timid or blustery. Generally speaking, phobic behavior is more associated with the SP and SOC Sixes, especially those with a Five wing. In SP Sixes, it can show up as an anxious desire to please; in SOC Sixes it can show up as the dutiful desire to support whatever social order the Six favors. Counterphobic behavior is usually associated with SX Sixes, who often adopt the strategy of "going where angels fear to tread," psychologically and/or physically. They can be defensively aggressive (adopting an in-your-face attitude) or seductive (not so much sexually, but more in a way that's designed to disarm you with warmth and kindness). Some counterphobic Sixes can't resist thrill-seeking, getting involved in high-risk sports like car racing, mountain climbing, or skydiving.

Searle describes four Six genres: the spy story, thriller, fear comedy, and labor drama. All but the last genre involve fear and trust issues; the labor drama involves the coming together of individuals with a common mission, so it's a SOC Six genre. I would include only those spy stories that are highly suspenseful (specifically designed to provoke fear); spy stories that are more focused on high-tech gadgets, code-making/breaking, and other arcane arts are more associated with Point 5.

But Point 6 themes aren't just about people overwhelmed by a threatening world. They're also about the celebration of cultural traditions; the value of family life; people banding together to defeat a common enemy (of which the labor drama is one example); ordinary people overcoming their fears or courageously venturing forth into unfamiliar territory; heroes, both fictional and nonfictional; superheroes who have two personas (one meek and the other brave); stories about science versus faith or fear versus faith; and stories about the overidealizing of partners or close friends (because of the need to feel that it's safe to let down their guard in intimate situations).

¤ ¤ ¤

SELF-PRESERVATION SIX THEMES. This is the subtype most associated with personal safety and integrity, a sense of home, safe havens, family preservation, conservative values, and cultural traditions. We see a prime example of this subtype in the culture of the TLC show *19 Kids and Counting*, a reality show about the religiously conservative Duggar family. For the Duggars, family is everything. They do just about everything as a family, and that's the way they like it.

Both their conservatism and large family might predispose some people to dislike them, but the Duggars are hard to dislike; they're a pretty well-balanced family that manages to make family life look fun and stimulating. They demonstrate the possibility of living a family-oriented lifestyle, even in the midst of a youth-obsessed, go-getter culture. They're fond of practical jokes and like to spring surprises on one another. And they don't seem to take themselves very seriously.

Dad Jim-Bob (yes, that's his real name) sets the tone for the group. As a 6w7, he has a sense of fun and a willingness to try new things, despite a certain timidity that he obviously strives to overcome. On one episode, he took his family to give blood, although he himself is quite squeamish (he did manage to give blood, though). On another, he took the oldest children skydiving. On one hot summer day, he and his sons created a giant waterslide on a hill at his farm; everybody had a great time sliding into the temporary pond at the bottom. We see his sense of humor on an episode in which he was delivering books written by his wife Michelle to a class where he and Michelle were speaking. A student noticed the books and said to Jim-Bob that he was sure glad he didn't have to take a class where they were studying the Duggars! Jim-Bob related the story to the class with a big grin on his face.

On yet another episode, we see the Duggars visiting a large Amish family; some of the Duggar kids were impressed with the obedience and courtesy of the Amish children. Jim-Bob asked an Amish elder the secret of a successful marriage. The reply? "'I'm sorry' and 'Forgive me.'" His wife, Michelle, laughed and exclaimed, "There you have it! [Marriage] counseling in a matter of ten seconds!"

Stories like this can sound hokey to modern ears. But the Duggars look and sound genuinely happy. We don't see too many TV families that look like the Duggars these days, either in fiction or on reality TV; gone is the era of *Ozzie and Harriet* or *The Waltons*.

These days, we're more likely to see SP Six characters showing up in "fear comedies" like the films made by Woody Allen or in thrillers featuring timid baby sitters or other vulnerable people. In Woody Allen flicks, Allen always plays some version of himself: a nervous, witty 6w7 who possesses a lot of hope but a sense of personal insecurity that's hard to shake.

We see the same nervous energy in the character of Bob (Bill Murray), in *What About Bob?*. Bob is a clingy, nervous client of psychiatrist Dr. Leo Marvin (Richard Dreyfuss), whose Threeish snobbery is no barrier to the puppyish Bob, who has a way of making his desire to follow Dr. Marvin everywhere seem endearing rather than annoying—at least it's endearing to the audience and Dr. Marvin's family. It's not so endearing to Dr. Marvin, the Three, probably because Bob's insecurity arouses his own latent nervousness (one of Three's connecting point is Six). So the more Bob is around, the more nervous Marvin becomes, to the point that they pretty much switch roles by the end of the movie.

My favorite comedic treatment of the SP Six's uncomfortability with new situations is *The Out-of-Towners* (the Jack Lemmon 1970 version). Lemmon is hilarious as a nervous first-time visitor to NYC who has planned a romantic night with his wife before meeting with a company executive the next day. He's got everything all set: an elegant dinner, after-dinner entertainment, and a luxury hotel room. But soon before the plane lands, things start to go wrong: the plane gets diverted to Boston, the couple wind up on an overcrowded train to NYC (with no food available), and their room reservation gets misplaced (and the hotel is full because of a transit strike). Our intrepid couple has more challenges ahead of them: getting robbed, sleeping in Central Park, losing their only food (Crackerjacks) to a dog, being attacked by demonstrators, and being chased by a cop on horseback. (Anyone who's ever travelled anywhere new can sympathize with their plight, not just Sixes.) George starts out optimistic, but eventually "goes counterphobic," becoming more and more defensively hostile as the movie progresses. Of course, he does it in a way that seems more funny than nasty. He and his wife both breathe a huge sigh of relief as they finally board their plane back to the Midwest. (They don't yet know that the plane is about to be hijacked!).

The *Out-of-Towners* reminds me of the extreme care my Six father used to take when planning family vacations. He would check and recheck everything, making sure he had multiple backup options, just in case. Like George, Dad would become very irritable when things didn't go right, his irritation thinly veiling his agitation.

One of the ways that he tried to keep uncertainty to a minimum was by opting for the tried and true over the novel. On road trips, this invariably meant motel stays at Howard Johnson or Holiday Inn—places he knew and trusted. Same thing when we went out for family dinners: we went to nice restaurants, but the food was seldom anything unexpected.

Just as with SP One film themes, it can be hard to find examples of SP Six film themes that actually take the type seriously: with SP Ones, there's a tendency to poke fun at their seriousness while with SP Sixes, there's a tendency to poke fun at their fearfulness. There's also a tendency to blow off the importance of family values (and the role that families play in ensuring the stability of a culture). It's easiest to find films that celebrate the family by looking back half a century (especially if we're looking for intact families that aren't divorced, separated, blended, or atypical in some other way). There we find old Disney films like *Old Yeller* or its sequel, *Savage Sam*, along with films like *Our Town*, *Cheaper by the Dozen*, or *Little Women*. It's possible to find more recent films (e.g., the newer versions of *Little Women* or *Anne of Green Gables*), but there's a difference in orientation. The older films clearly celebrate family values and are made for an audience that includes adults; the newer films are framed more as coming-of-age stories suitable for an audience of pre-teens. One possible exception is the recent Jane Austen revival, in which family values are shown in a positive light (although the emphasis is mainly on the developing relationships among the young adults of courtship age).

One film that portrays an SP Six in a realistic (and positive) manner is *Steel Magnolias*, which I've already mentioned when discussing the SOC Two women-as-friends theme and SX Two sacrifice-for-love theme in Chapter 12. But we can also look at the relationship between mother M'Lynn (Sally Field) and her brittle diabetic daughter, Shelby (Julia Roberts). At first, the exact nature of their relationship is a little hard to discern, because we always see M'Lynn in her role of gracious hostess and patient mom. But there's some tension there, which we come to realize is rooted in her understandable anxiety over Shelby's health, which is much worse than anybody realizes. M'Lynn is powerless to prevent her daughter from repeatedly throwing caution to the wind; we get the impression (subtly conveyed) that's she's tried and failed to get Shelby to exercise caution. Now all she can do is watch and wait, hoping for the best—and stepping in to help when help is needed (for instance, when Shelby needs a new kidney after she had a baby against medical advice).

It's only towards the very end of the film that we fully comprehend just how much it took for M'Lynn to stand back and allow Shelby to make her own decisions, all the time knowing the probable consequences. Ultimately, M'Lynn emerges as a quietly heroic figure who fully embodies the principle of "grace under pressure."

Another film that takes a sympathetic view of SP Six concerns about safety is *The Capture of the Green River Killer*, featuring Dave Reichert as the dedicated Six assigned to the case. One of the most poignant scenes takes place between him and his teenage daughter. She returns late from a date to find Dad waiting for her on the front porch, looking serious. She thinks his concern is because of his work on the Green River Killer case and that's why he worries about her. She reasons, "Well, it's not like something bad ever happened to *you*." It's then that he tells her the truth: that he himself was attacked by somebody down by the Green River when he was a kid, but was lucky enough to get away. She becomes very quiet, trying to digest this new piece of information. Finally, she looks at him very seriously and says slowly, "Thank you for keeping me safe, Daddy."

There are a lot of moments like this in the film, which is less about law enforcement than about love, caring, and family support. I've watched it many times, not quite understanding why I could find a film about a serial murder investigation inspiring. I finally realized that it was Reichert's caring and quiet determination that inspired me—and the way his family stuck with him during the 20 years that it took to solve this series of terrible murders.

Another concern at SP Six is the need to uphold tradition—and the problems that can ensue when we allow modern cynicism to override our respect for tradition. That's the theme explored in *Groundhog Day*, a cult favorite for Bill Murray fans. Murray is known for making films that are very entertaining but have a serious point. In this fantasy, he plays a bored and cynical TV weatherman, Phil Conners, assigned the task of covering *Groundhog Day* celebrations in the tiny burg of Punxsutawney, Pennsylvania, along with a news crew that includes his producer Rita (Andie Macdowell). Rita is as likable and friendly as Phil is obnoxiously cynical. After the report is done, Murray can't wait to get out of town, but a snowstorm (which he erroneously predicted would bypass the area) makes them turn back to Punxsutawney, where they stay the night. When Phil wakes up the next morning, he finds that it is once again Groundhog Day. The same thing happens over and over again, forcing him into an endless loop of repeating the same day, ad infinitum. The rest of the story revolves around Phil's gradual loss of cynicism and growing ability to appreciate small town values (an appreciation which comes only after he gets to know and genuinely care for the people of the town).

Himalaya is another film that reminds us of the importance of tradition. It's the story of a Himalayan village whose members make an annual journey across the mountains to exchange salt for grain. Traditionally, the date of the journey is decided by the wise elders based on the counsel of the lamas, so that the timing is auspicious. But a ambitious young tribesman with modern ideas decides this tradition is hopelessly old-fashioned. He sets off early, but his experiences soon show him the importance of honoring the counsel of the elders.

Watching *Himalaya*, it's easy to take the perspective of the Himalayan traditionalists, because they clearly seem wiser than the ambitious young leader. But how do we respond to the traditions of our own family, community, and culture? Do we really know how to tell the difference between those that have the power to enrich our lives from those that are empty conventions? That's the question we're invited to consider at SP Six.

¤ ¤ ¤

Sexual six themes. There's certainly no shortage of movies with themes involving this subtype! Fear is a powerful emotion. And when we combine it with the passion of the sexual subtype arena, we have a potent recipe for drama. It's at SX Six that we find all the films in which suspense is a major ingredient: films like *The Manchurian Candidate, Fail-Safe, Marathon Man, Mission: Impossible,* and virtually all Mel Gibson and Alfred Hitchcock films.* TV's fantastically frightening series *24* is a virtual Six-fest of paranoia, torture, and terrifying counterphobic projections. And then there's the perennial BBC favorite, *The Prisoner* (both the old and new versions), which tells us we can never trust what we see—anything that seems too pleasant probably isn't. As one character from the series observes, "Everything is suspicious if you look at it properly. Everyone has secrets."

That really sums up the SX Six view of life, which is why there's so much questioning, suspicion, and skepticism associated with this subtype. Hollywood has exploited it to the max, making literally thousands of films designed to amp up our fear and diminish our sense of faith in life, in other people, or in ourselves. However, such films don't necessarily tell us that much about the dramas encountered by ordinary SX Sixes (the ones that don't happen to be employed as government agents, undercover cops, or forensic investigators).

Julia, a film reputedly based on the memoirs of Lillian Hellman, gives us an opportunity to explore fear in a way that ordinary people can relate to. It involves two main characters, Julia (Vanessa Redgrave) and Lillian (Jane Fonda), who have known each other since childhood. But Julia (probably a 7w8) seems to have nerves of steel while Lillian is more of a nervous Nelly. When the girls grow up, Lillian becomes a famous playwright while Julia gets involved in social activism in pre-WWII Europe. After Germany invades Austria, Julia gets involved in a Nazi resistance group. Money is urgently needed for the cause; Julia sends a message: Is it possible for Lillian to smuggle the money into Berlin on her way to a Moscow writers conference?

The messenger conveys a special message from Julia: "I must remind you for her that you are afraid of being afraid. So you will [tend to] do what you cannot do. And

---

* Gibson's action-oriented films are more Seven-winged while Hitchcock's more introspective style (which often brings in an element of horror) are more Five-winged.

that would be dangerous for you—and for us." (The warning relates to the counter-phobic Six's tendency to take on tasks that are too risky, because they become fixated on the idea that they must overcome their fears.)

Lillian thinks back to an incident in childhood where she and Julia are hiking. when they come upon a fast-moving brook. Julia crosses easily by scampering across a narrow log perched high above the water. Lillian is petrified, but attempts to cross by the same route. But halfway across, she freezes and almost falls; Julia has to help her across. Lillian is disappointed with herself; but Julia just smiles and says, "Don't worry; you'll do it the next time."

Lillian apparently decides that the time for redemption has arrived. So she agrees to deliver the cash. But she's so terrified that she makes several potentially disastrous mistakes. It's only with the help of Julia's colleagues that Lillian survives the interminably long, tense train trip from Paris to Berlin.

Julia's impact as a film is due in part to the way this whole episode is handled—not by glossing over Lillian's fear but by allowing us to experience it right along with her. Whether we're Sixes or some other type, we're all asked to face our fears at some point in our lives. That's why we can relate to Lillian's distress.

When we have no way to work on fear, our fear can begin to work on us, creating problems and eroding the very foundation on which we stand. In a recent episode of TV's *Dog Whisperer*, dog behaviorist Cesar Millan observed that "fear brings aggression," whether in animals or in people. In many episodes involving aggressive dogs, we discover that the dog's aggression is triggered by their owner's anxiety: when the human being gets nervous, the dog automatically assumes a defensive (counterphobic) stance. Once the owner becomes more confident (usually with Cesar's help), their dog's behavior changes—often instantaneously—showing us how merely stepping out of a cycle of fear can quickly change a negative energy dynamic into something more positive. With dogs that are fearfully aggressive because of past abuse, it takes more time, but the same principles apply. Cesar does not react to the aggression but uses his own calm, assertive energy to help the animal settle down, while at the same time correcting inappropriate behavior and providing opportunities for the dog to become more balanced. While it's interesting to watch the dog change, it's even more interesting to watch the response of Cesar's pack: as soon as the behavior of the new dog changes from fearful to calm, the newcomer gets a friendly reception from all the other dogs. (It's humbling to watch; I always find myself wondering whether I as a human being could ever be as instantly accepting in a similar situation.)

When left unchecked, fear can become so ramped up that it can create the complete inability to trust, which can in turn make a Six's behavior unpredictably scary. In *The Year of Living Dangerously*, one of Mel Gibson's more thoughtful films, we see how quickly fear and distrust can lead to the loss of civilization. We also see the consequences of betraying the trust of others (whether because of ambition, lust, or reckless disregard).

The action takes place in 1965 Jakarta, Indonesia. President Sukarno's autocratic regime is threatened by Communist insurgents. Australian Guy Hamilton (Gibson) is one of a large number of reporters competing for a story in increasingly chaotic conditions. Although he arrives in the country with no contacts, he has the good fortune to meet up with the enigmatic Billy Swan, a warm-hearted Type 2 cameraman (Linda Hunt) with good contacts. He takes pity on Hamilton, sharing his own contacts. Unlike most Westerners, Swan is neither frightened nor caught up in the desire for a story; he maintains an almost Zen-like calm in the midst of chaos. Swan has become a patron of the poor and visits them frequently, handing out care packages to ease their woes.

Swan also introduces Guy to another one of his protegés, Jill Bryant (Sigourney Weaver), a British attaché. The two become wildly intoxicated with one another (the craziness of the situation adding to their intoxication). Caught up in the frenzy of the times, Guy becomes obsessed with getting a big story, taking chances that cross the line. Jill shares a piece of "hot" British intelligence with him about an incoming shipment of arms to the Communists, which will probably create even more chaos in the capital; she tells him in confidence, trying to save his life (warning him so he can leave the country before things turn ugly).

But Guy can't help but see it as an opportunity to make a name for himself (connection to Three). However, if he breaks the story, it will jeopardize the lives of all the Westerners still in the country, including Jill. Aware of Guy's increasingly frenzied behavior, Billy writes the following entry in his personal journal:

> *You have changed. You are capable of betrayal. Is it possible I was wrong about you?*
> *You abuse your position as journalist and grow addicted to risk...Why can't you give*
> *of yourself? Why can't you learn to love?*

The enneagrammatic answer is that Guy is a young counterphobic Six (moving unhealthily to Three) while Billy is a Two with loads of principle (big One wing). But Billy is pointing out something very important: that real trust is always rooted in love. The idea of "growing addicted to risk" speaks to the dilemma encountered by SX Sixes who seek to conquer fear but end up becoming addicted to its adrenaline rush. The antidote to fear is faith and trust, which (as Billy reminds us) is rooted in love—that's why the word *courage* comes from the French word *coeur* (heart). Courage comes to us once we have the ability to love; without love, there's no basis for trust.

SX Sixes who learn to love, learn to express their faith and hope in creative ways. They often have a creative streak, and they enjoy making things—especially traditional Americana handicrafts like rugs and quilts that enhance their homes. More technically-oriented SX Sixes can make inquisitive scientists who know how to strike a balance between curiosity and skepticism; they also tend to be more practical in orientation than Fives and have the ability to communicate technical ideas in a non-technical fashion. It's not unusual for them to have a feistiness that shows up as a tendency to buck authority figures who are too overbearing or controlling.

As far as romance goes, SX Sixes are probably as romantic as SX Twos, and even more sentimental. But they have a shyer more tentative style that can be very appealing in a partner. They also tend to idealize their partners or other people they admire;

I saw this tendency in my father, who adored my mother and literally treated her like a queen. The only potential problem with this rosy scenario is that it's sometimes possible for people to fall off the pedestal—and when they do, they sometimes fall a long way! It happened to me once with an SX Six friend, and I never did figure out how; one day he was eager for companionship and the next he seemed to question everything I said. So SX Sixes have to watch out for their tendency to "blow hot and cold" based on changing mental projections of the other person. If they can keep their projections in check and allow their emotions to be grounded in their heart, SX Sixes can be devoted partners and friends.

¤ ¤ ¤

SOCIAL SIX THEMES. During the early part of the last century, social Sixes were probably one of the most respected types on the enneagram. Organizations like the Boy and Girl Scouts were started in the early 1900s to promote social Six values such as duty, honor, and tradition. I'm old enough to remember a time when all the kids in my neighborhood were Scouts and hoped to go to scout camp during the summer. I was in Girl Scouts for ten years and still remember the pledge: *On my honor I will try to do my duty to God and my country, to help other people at all times, especially those at home.* (Later they changed the last part to "and obey the Girl Scout law," but I always liked the original version better.)

I wasn't exactly the perfect Girl Scout; I could never get my yellow scarf neatly tied and often forgot parts of my uniform. But I enjoyed the group activities and was proud of the badges I earned. (There was even one for sock-darning—it was a long time ago!)

When the youth culture of the 1960s caught on, it was not kind to SOC Six ideas and organizations like the Scouts; the military became unpopular and returning Vietnam Vets found themselves isolated and shunned from mainstream society. Ideas like tradition, duty, and patriotism became unfashionable. It wasn't until the time of the Gulf War that the anti-tradition sentiments of the Sixties generation began to give way to a more military-tolerant cultural ethos. At the same time, new TV reality programs like *Rescue 911* began to appear, where unseen interviewers asked rescuers, "Do you think you're a hero?" (The answer was always no; everyone questioned said they were just doing what any decent person would do under the circumstances.)

But it was probably 9/11 that caused a dramatic resurgence of appreciation for SOC Six values; suddenly, there were American flags everywhere and a military career seemed like an honorable choice. Everyone was acutely aware of the heroic role played by firefighters during the collapse of the twin towers in New York; the entire country suddenly woke up to the true meaning of duty. There was a profound shift in the way people viewed the police force, military, and firefighters.

The recent film *Grace is Gone* addressed some of the questions that have arisen since 9/11, focusing especially on what happens to families when women are killed on the front lines. SOC Six Stan Phillips (John Cusack) is a husband and father of two girls, Dawn (age 8) and Heidi (age 12). Stan was originally in the military, which is where he met his wife, Grace. She continued to make the military her career, eventually becoming deployed to Iraq. Meanwhile, Stan became the manager at the local Home Depot so he could take care of his two girls.

The film starts out with Stan rallying his "troops" at the beginning of the day's work. His management style is clearly military in nature: hearty but a little stiff. The stiffness isn't a problem at work, where he has mostly male employees. But when it comes to fathering two little girls, Phillips is obviously clueless. He does his dutiful best but doesn't seem to know how to show affection in a way that really creates a father-daughter bond.

One day, he is awakened by a knock on the door. Upon opening it, he sees two military men there. They soberly inform him that his wife has been killed in the line of duty. He just stares at them, unable to take in the news. His predicable world has been forever shattered.

His girls are still asleep. How can he tell them that their mother is dead?

Well, he can't. He can barely take in the news himself. So that morning, he abruptly changes course and instead asks them where they'd like to travel. His oldest daughter Heidi realizes how bizarre this request is; both kids are both in school and Dad isn't the type to take off on a whim. But little Dawn is thrilled and says she wants to go to a Disney-type theme park in Florida. So they all set forth on a road trip. At one point, when Dawn falls asleep, Heidi takes the opportunity to ask her Dad a serious question.

> H: *Dad, do you ever think that Mom should have stayed home?*
>
> D: *All the time.*
>
> H: *Why did she have to go?*
>
> D: *She was doing her duty. You know that.*
>
> H: *But what exactly does that mean?*
>
> D: *We've talked about this. We have people all over the world, looking out for our safety. When we discover a threat, we have to act on it. That's the way the world is.*
>
> H. *But on the news they're saying that we went to war with the wrong people.*
>
> D: *(Slowly and deliberately, and with unusual feeling). You can't always believe everything you hear on TV, can you? Sometimes you just gotta trust that you're doing the right thing. You gotta believe.*
>
> H: *(After a long pause.) Well, what if you can't?*
>
> D: *Then we're all lost.*

This is the first time that we begin to see Dad begin to get in touch with his feelings (and also to emotionally connect with his daughter). The last line eloquently expresses the SOC Six view of the world: that sometimes we "just gotta trust that you're doing the right thing." (Of course, that's an idea that cuts both ways: we can all think of times when faith is needed and other times when faith is too blind to be a good thing.) For Stan, learning to trust in his own parenting abilities enables him to get to know his daughters for the first time. By the time he finally breaks the news about Grace, the three of them are able to grieve as a family.

On a lighter note is *An American Carol,* a politically-incorrect satire based on *A Christmas Carol* which features a Michael Moore look-alike taken to task by three angels for trying to abolish the Fourth of July holiday. The angels—representing General

George Patton (Kelsey Grammar), George Washington (Jon Voight), and the Angel of Death (Trace Atkins)—try to convince "Michael" of the error of his ways. Whether you like this flick or hate it, it has many SOC Six themes (patriotism, American values, a pro-tradition stance) that are actually presented from a SOC Six perspective (something rare in Hollywood).

Another key SOC Six value—loyalty—is the main focus of *Mrs. Brown,* a film exploring the relationship between Queen Victoria (Judy Dench) and her loyal retainer, Mr. Brown (Billy Connelly). The film's title refers to fact that they became unusually close after the death of her husband, the king—so close, in fact, that court insiders started calling her "Mrs. Brown" behind her back.

The relationship between the queen and Mr. Brown begins when Mr. Brown is summoned by the queen's advisors. He was a favorite of the late king's, and the advisors hope he can rouse the queen from her grief. While she remains sad, Brown's steadfast devotion moves her, and she slowly begins to come around, allowing him to take her for a daily ride on horseback. As she heals, their friendship grows. But soon her family and the court become jealous, forcing her for the sake of propriety to cut off their innocent relationship. She becomes rigidly polite; and he becomes the butt of court jokes but nevertheless remains in faithful service to her for many years, despite the loneliness and ostracism. At the end of the film, when he is dying, we see her at his bedside, tenderly ministering to his needs: his faithful servanthood acknowledged, he can die in peace.

Another SOC Six issue is the relationship between the individual and the group, particularly the conflict between individual values and group loyalty. While SOC Fours have the tendency to speak out too loudly or too quickly, SOC Sixes sometimes do the opposite: to try to blend in, out of fear. The Spanish film *Butterfly* explores this issue through the eyes of Moncho, a shy, asthmatic young boy living in a small village in Spain at the outset of the Spanish Civil War. Although Moncho's father is sympathetic to the Republican government that is now in power (and opposed to the

Fascists), his main focus is on his family, not politics. So far, the war hasn't touched the village, so most villagers are thinking about things closer to home.

Moncho is about to go to school for the first time and is afraid the teacher will be mean. On the first day, he's terrified when the teacher asks his name; when called to the front, he wets his pants. As his classmates roar with laughter, he runs in shame from the room and into the forest, too mortified to go home. He is found there by a search party and returned home. The teacher Don Gregorio—who turns out to be a very kind man—comes to apologize for upsetting him. The next day, he takes Moncho under his wing, so he's no longer frightened. As the film unfolds, Don Gregario is shown to be a fine teacher, much beloved by his pupils. However, he's also an extreme free-thinker who abhors authoritarianism.

Under his teacher's care, Moncho learns new things and begins to acquire greater self-confidence. At one point, Don Gregorio gives Moncho a net and takes him on a hunt for butterflies; hence, the film's title. Over the course of the film we see Moncho getting into various kinds of innocent mischief and also becoming acquainted with his family and other people in the village; the ways events unfold, we are encouraged to think of the village as a charming spot and a wonderful place to raise a child.

But this is no slice-of-life film. Eventually, the war begins to catch up with the villagers and people are forced to choose sides. We realize that Don Gregorio is strongly committed to his free-thinking views and will probably go to the wall for them; Moncho's father is too fearful to do the same. When push comes to shove, he forgets his Republican loyalties.

In the last scene, disloyal subjects who have been rounded up by the opposition are loaded onto an open truck as the villagers look on. All the people we see are familiar faces we have seen before in the marketplace or at village events. They're everybody's friends and neighbors. At first, the villagers are frozen in silence. But then they become afraid. Some people begin to shout epithets at the departing prisoners, so no one will think they're Republican sympathizers. Soon, everybody is yelling. Moncho's family does it, too.

The last person led out of the jail is Moncho's beloved teacher, Don Gregorio. Moncho's mother tells Moncho that he must participate. Moncho hesitates, but then an expression of hatred gradually comes over his face, and he begins to chime in with the crowd, "Atheist! Red! Son of a bitch!" He even works himself up enough to run after the departing truck with the rest of the boys, throwing stones and yelling epithets. The film ends with a close-up of his frowning face staring at the truck as it rumbles off into the distance. We can only wonder how he'll feel when he's older and better able to understand what happened.

The film *The Insider* offers us a modern variation on this theme. It's a fact-based story about whistle-blowing, group loyalty, and caving in to political pressure based on the experiences of scientist Jeffrey Wigand, who blew the whistle on the tobacco industry by divulging that tobacco executives knew tobacco was harmful at a time when they claimed to Congress that they had no such knowledge. One of the things that makes the story interesting is that Wigand was a very reluctant whistle-blower who had a lot to lose (like medical benefits for an asthmatic daughter and severance pay for his family). He had signed a non-disclosure agreement, by which he felt both ethically and legally bound—at least until his former employer began to threaten him in ways that made him realize the management's complete lack of ethics. That's when he decided to pull the plug.

He was shocked to discover that *60 Minutes*, which had been eager to run the Big Tobacco story, was suddenly reluctant to air their interview with Wigand; it seems that this had something to do with economic and political pressures from CBS and its parent company, Westinghouse (top management was apparently afraid of certain conflicts of interest that might adversely affect a forthcoming merger). Although the interview was finally telecast, the whole sordid story (including the part about *60 Minutes*) didn't come out until *Vanity Fair* published "The Man Who Knew Too Much," the article that became the basis for *The Insider*.

Both *Butterfly* and *The Insider* feature probable Six protagonists who are bound by social custom to conform to the expectations of the group. But in the former case, the protagonist is too young and too scared to resist, so he succumbs to his family's pressure to conform. In the latter case, the protagonist is a scientist whose ethics are mocked, thus giving him the incentive to go against his former bosses. He also has support (or at least the illusion of support) from powerful media figures and governmental agencies to bolster his resolve.

As both *Butterfly* and *The Insider* make clear, there are no easy answers when it comes to questions of duty and loyalty. When ordinary humans get caught up in larger-than-life conflicts that inspire great fear, it's hard to know how to avoid being overwhelmed by the situation. But the qualities we cultivate at Point 6—qualities like loyalty, trust, and the willingness to serve—are designed to give us the kind of courage we need to avoid that sense of overwhelm, so we can act out of conscience rather than compulsion.

Type seven – the improviser

It is absurd to divide people into good or bad. People are either charming or tedious.
– Oscar Wilde

SEVENS ARE mentally quick, full of ideas, and up for a good time. They're naturally enthusiastic about life and adaptable to changing circumstances. These traits make them popular not only as friends, but highly effective as salespeople: Sevens are the kind of people who can sell snow to an Eskimo—and leave him feeling good about the transaction! They don't have to push for a sale; they just have to be themselves. They even seem inexplicably luckier than other people; doors open for them and they happily walk through them. So they start out with a lot going for them in life, both personally and professionally.

Ironically, one of the biggest challenges for Sevens is figuring out how to live with all that luck and talent. Sevens can seem a little *too* lucky and talented for their own good—a little too able to adapt, improvise, and get by. The result is that they're often able to glide through life by slipping around potential challenges, never developing the kind of character that exercises their moral muscles. Then when they encounter a really big obstacle—the kind they can't slip around—they can find themselves stuck in a funk because they lack the maturity to deal with such situations in a principled way (either by accepting the inevitable or by working patiently to change the situation). So one of their challenges is develop themselves in a way that allows them to gain real substance (discipline, character, and focus) without sacrificing the childlike joy that keeps their spirits up.

Because of their innate playfulness, young Sevens are not always taken as seriously as they might like to be. Because they make us laugh, it's easy to write them off as mere entertainers. But the smart Seven is able to turn this perception to his advantage, even purposely playing the fool in order to do things and say things that others couldn't get away with. She may also be able to acquire information that's not available to others, using it to accomplish her ends in ways that are unusual or unexpected.

It's a little more difficult for Sevens in modern Western culture to willingly play the fool, because seriousness is something we value (especially when it comes to our public image or career). But in many cultures—aboriginal cultures and others that see life from a non-linear, non-literal perspective—people don't worship seriousness the way we do. So traditionally, we have figures like Wily Coyote from Native American lore, Reynard the Fox from pre-medieval Europe, and Br'er Rabbit, from Native American/ African culture. Sufis have always embraced the Fool, the Joker, the Crazy Person, and the Trickster. Even Western Civilization has fairy tales like *The Emperor's New Clothes*, which remind us how pomposity can get in the way of seeing what's really there.

Trickster figures exist to lighten us up and help us let go of our over-seriousness and fixation on end products instead of process. Often, the only person who can pierce the armor of self-importance around a powerful individual is either a child or a funny guy, who can get away with comments that would be a hanging offense for anybody else. Witness all the trickster figures in Shakespeare who whisper in the ear of the King, thus changing the course of political affairs. There have surely been more than a few tricksters who have produced the same effect in real life. From a Jungian perspective, "jokesters and tricksters play an important role in society...they bring in the opposite and break the stalemate."*

---

* Robert Johnson, in *Balancing Heaven and Earth* (1998), p. 39.

Table 17-1.
Type Seven: The Improviser

High-spirited, optimistic, entertaining, funny, fun seeking

FIVE Connection brings inwardness, depth, analysis, sobriety, slowing down
ONE Connection brings ideals, detail orientation, grounding, primness

SIX Wing brings playfulness, happy-go-lucky outlook, comic ability, flexibility
EIGHT Wing brings groundedness, focus, charisma, follow-through, hard-edged realism

Other Labels: Optimist, Enthusiast, High Flier, Entertainer
Challenges: scatteredness, irresponsibility, sense of entitlement, selfishness

	SUBTYPES		
	Self-preservation	Sexual	Social
A R C H E T Y P E S	Bon Vivant, Salon Designer, Renaissance Man or Woman, Family Visionary, Magical Child, Fun Parent, Pastry Chef, Gourmet Chef, Gourmand, "Good Life" Aficionado, Communard, Family Entertainer, Visionary Entrepreneur, Interior Designer, Home Improver, Versatile Generalist, Idea Glutton, Self-improvement Junkie, Intellectual Spinner, Self-fascinated Narcissist	Artless Charmer, Dance-away Lover, Shameless Hedonist, Space Cadet, Comic, Class Clown, Mimic, Hippie, Manic Escapist, Rake, Alcoholic, Addict, Minstrel, Dreamer, Artist, Trickster, Vagabond, Aimless Wanderer, Juggler, Innocent Fool, Jack, Panhandler, Self Actualizer, Wily Coyote, Gambler, Jack of All Trades, Snake Charmer, Clothes Designer, Raconteur, Troubadour, Angel of Mercy, Charming Con Artist, Pickpocket, Artful Dodger, Wilderness Explorer	Social Planner, Political Visionary, Innovative Architect, Sacrificial Idealist, High-Flying Utopian, Optimistic Futurist, Armchair Revolutionary, Intellectual Anarchist, Winged Messenger, Angelic Herald, Swift Courier, Idea Networker, Aquarian Thinker, Innovative Communicator, Human Potential Activist, Fun Designer, Fashionista, Trendsetter, Popular Jetsetter, One of the Beautiful People
F I L M T H E M E S	**Life is a joyful, full-bodied experience** (*The Station Agent, Uptown Girls, Footloose, Chocolat, Lifestyles of the Rich and Famous*) **Gourmet food** makes life worth living (*Take Home Chef, Guy's Big Bite, Julie & Julia*) but can be sacrificed for healthier alternatives (*Graham Kerr's Galloping Gourmet* becomes *Take Kerr*) **Unconventional lifestyles** can offend the conventional (*A Thousand Clowns, Three's Company, Pregnant Man*) but can open us to alternative lifestyles (*Mask, Ellen [DeGeneres], Off the Grid: Life on the Mesa, Garbage Warrior*) **Self-indulgent "slob"** lacks sensitivity but flourishes nonetheless (*Animal House, Father Goose, Alfie, The Blues Brothers, Cheech & Chong's Up in Smoke, Educating Rita*)	**Romantic outlaws** have multiple adventures (*The Adventures of Robin Hood, Butch Cassidy & the Sundance Kid, Captain Blood*) **Tricksters** rule (*Beetlejuice, The Wizard of Oz, Good Morning Vietnam, Mork & Mindy, Cabaret, The Sting, Paper Moon*) or get tricked (*What Dreams May Come, The List of Adrian Messenger, Amadeus,* Monty Python flicks) **Travel's great** (*Michael Palin's Pole to Pole*) but even better with a friend (*Bill & Ted's Excellent Adventure, The Endless Summer, Around the World in 80 Days, The Adventures of Huck Finn*) **Adventurers** are out for fun, gain & excitement (*Star Wars, Indiana Jones & The Temple of Doom, Back to the Future,* Warren Miller skiing flicks, *Into the Wild, The Sound Barrier*) **"Superficialists"** go deeper (*The Razor's Edge, Touching the Void, Lonely are the Brave, The Man Who Would Be King*) **Commitment phobes** move towards commitment (*About A Boy, Something's Gotta Give*)	**Visionary Sevens** advance innovative ideas (*TED: The Future We Will Create, Tucker: a Man & His Dream, Garbage Warrior, Flash of Genius, The World of Buckminster Fuller, Philip Johnson: Diary of An Eccentric Architect*) but sometimes go over the edge (*The Mosquito Coast, Fitzcarraldo/Burden of Dreams, Man of La Mancha, Into the Wild, Lost in La Mancha*) **Seven sacrifices himself** by serving others (*Hideous Kinky, Cider House Rules, Lilies of the Field, A Tale of Two Cities*) **Unconventional teachers** make class a blast (*The Dead Poets Society, Renaissance Man, To Sir With Love, Harry Potter* films) **Flamboyant youth** seek sex, drugs, & possibly a new vision of society (*Hair, Woodstock, Dust & Illusions*) **Jetsetters** lead the pack (*Born Rich, Lifestyles of the Rich & Famous, House Hunters International*)

The playfulness of the Seven arises out of a natural lightness of being that contrasts dramatically with the creative tension we see at Point 6. From a transformational perspective, Point 7 is the place we land after facing our fears at Point 6. So it's not surprising that the first sensation is one of giddy relief (7w6) which gradually morphs into a keen interest in new experiences, products, and lifestyles (7w8).

As the third step in the evolutionary process, Point 7 is akin to Point 3 on the other side of the circle: right in the thick of the action. This may be why both Threes and Sevens are high-energy individuals, thoroughly immersed in the extroverted world of outer activity. But while Threes are adaptable "image creators" (and serious about their work), Sevens are imaginative "image synthesizers" whose work inevitably turns into play. Why the difference? I suspect it's because image creation requires us to think up new images and make them as "real" as possible (by taking them seriously and trying to embody them as individuals) while image synthesis is more about seeing what we can do with existing images to create innovative new patterns (with the goal of transforming our world).

Transformation requires freedom, which is why Sevens tend to have a naturally libertarian perspective on life. They don't much care for authority and seldom have much serious interest in exerting authority over others. However, this love of freedom can create problems for young Sevens, especially in school.

As children, Sevens are fun-loving and mischievous, usually in a harmless sort of way. They tend to seek out sports or other physical activities that help them channel their high spirits; otherwise, they get restless and bored. Although they like learning new things, they have a hard time sitting still in school. And that's why they often get labeled as hyperactive. A story is told about Gillian Lynne, the English ballerina, who was almost diagnosed as learning-disabled. But the psychologist watched her dancing to the radio and told her mom, "Mrs. Lynne, Gillian isn't sick; she's a dancer." When her mother enrolled her in a dance class, Gillian was excited: "The room was full of people like me—*people who had to move to think.*"

Of course, most schools aren't set up for children who have to move in order to think. But parents of Seven children might take heart at realizing that their children's restlessness might be more easily addressed with dancing, tumbling, or circus class than with drugs.*

While Sevens like variety, they can become scattered when they have too many things going on at once. On the other hand, if they have to do the same thing over and over again in exactly the same way, that doesn't work, either. When stuck with tasks they don't like, they tend to feel trapped, and this can make them anxious and unable to finish. Sevens who fail at school, at work, etc., can become hypercritical of themselves and despondent (connection to One).

That's why, although *sobriety* is said to be desirable for Sevens, I can't help but wonder if sobriety is an appropriate goal for individuals whose nature is to be so light and free. When I meet up with Sevens that I'd really call sober, they usually seem a bit flat to me, as though somebody has let all the air out of their balloon. It's as though they've jumped to their connecting point of One and decided to stay there permanently.

Point 1 is a good touchstone for Sevens, because it can help them get grounded, so they make their plans actually happen instead of just talking about them. But it's a poor long-term destination because it imposes too many restrictions: what seems like order to a One can easily become a prison for a Seven, especially when it's self-imposed (because it can create an individual who's not just sober but solemn).

Sevens usually do better when they allow a little disorder into their lives, just not so much that they lose track of themselves or their goals in life. Sometimes they can gain focus by figuring out lots of different ways to do the same thing (or conversely, pursuing the kind of career that provides them with lots of variety). That way, they use their imagination to avoid boredom.

Sevens can also gain focus from their other connecting point (Five), because the energy at Point 5 gives them the ability to find order from within (and the kind of grounding that comes from the depths—from connecting with the mental dimension

---

* Gillian Lynne story related by Ken Robinson in *The Future We Will Create* (2007).

of *soul*). While it's not the easiest connection to make (especially for young Sevens), it can really help them slow down and be still. Even when Sevens are older, the challenge of meshing the light, quick energy of Seven with the slow, methodical energy of Five is more work than play. But they can use a combination of ingenuity and life experience to figure out some solution that will work for them.

Sevens with a Six wing tend to be the ones most "up in the air," because they combine the highly intuitive sensibilities of the Six with the mental quickness of the Seven, making for a very airy (but potentially spacy) persona. This is the fidgety kid who can never sit still in school because her mind is racing at 100 miles per hour or the manic comedian (like Robin Williams) whose wit is so quick that his speech can hardly keep up with his thoughts. It's also someone who's full of fun (and more than a little bit of mischief). Sevens with an Eight wing are less likely to be speedy and more grounded. They tend to be physically adventurous and usually enjoy travel. When they settle down, they're often attracted to innovative lines of work or entrepreneurial schemes. But they can have anger problems and a tendency to become hard-edged or even morose when things don't go their way. Some Sevens with this wing don't think they're Sevens because they feel kind of dense or heavy (especially SP Sevens). Physical activity and interesting projects can help them get their energy moving again, so they can shake off the blues.

It's easy for other types to envy Sevens, because they seem so charming, multi-talented, and entertaining. The shadow side to all this fun is their need to stay "up," which can sometimes seem like an addiction, leading to drug or alcohol problems or a Peter Pan (irresponsible) lifestyle. It's a tricky situation, because Sevens really do have a genuine need to maintain a sense of buoyancy. So they have to use their inventive minds to figure out a way to juggle their need for fun and artistic stimulation with the need to be responsible.

Judith Searle mentions three Seven film genres: adventure, sci-fi adventure, and travel; these are the themes we see over and over again in Hollywood films. But there are a few other Seven themes that focus on other dimensions of the type—those involving gourmet cooking, fantasy homes, alternative family structures, tricksters, addiction, charismatic drifters and romantic outlaws, going "deeper," eternal youth, screwball comedic situations, teen fun and hijinks, social visions and visionaries, futuristic cities and architecture, and lifestyles of the rich and famous.

¤ ¤ ¤

SELF-PRESERVATION SEVEN THEMES. This subtype is often called the Gourmand, and it's easy to see why. When we combine the Type 7 flair for creativity with the SP love of home and hearth, and we get somebody with a fondness for good living, especially gourmet food. My own term, the Bon Vivant, represents an effort to expand on this idea a little, but they are both similar in focus.

The "gourmand" aspect of SP Seven points at the theme of refined and elegant living, as exemplified by Orson Welles in his famous commercial for Paul Masson wines. Beethoven is playing in the background as a casually-elegant Welles intones Monsieur Masson's message that "we will sell no wine before its time."

Chef James Beard is another SP Seven who thoroughly embodies this archetype. Beard was interested in food from an early age but started out pursuing a career in theatre. When he couldn't get work, he and a friend started a catering company to take advantage of the new American entertainment, the cocktail party; his first book, *Hors D'Oeuvre and Canapés*, was published in 1940. Although WWII food shortages brought an end to his business, after the war Beard started the first TV cooking show, bringing French food to middle class Americans during the 1950s and establishing the James Beard Cooking School in 1955. He taught French cooking to his students for the next 30 years.

But not all SP Sevens are gourmands, at least not in the classic sense. There's an SP Seven archetype that we might call a "slob Seven" that applies more to Sevens with an Eight wing who can seem either grouchy (like aging bachelor Cary Grant in *Father Goose*) or raucous (like the guys in *Animal House*) or both. They like food, but favor beer over wine and burgers over chateaubriand. Modern Food Network celebrity Guy Fieri embodies a combination of both the "slob" and the "elegant" styles. He looks really hip, but he likes classy "dives," and even has a show called *Diners, Drive-ins and Dives.* Here's the promo:

> *Join me as I tour the country's classic "greasy spoon" restaurants and local hot spots. I get to drive a classic car, sample the most unusual culinary creations you can imagine and talk with all the folks that make it happen. What more could a guy like me ask for?!*

What more, indeed! But Guy *does* have more, including another show called Tailgate Warriors, where he tries to find the best tailgating parties at major NFL games across the country. Not to mention two restaurants (Johnny Garlic's—a "dynamic California pasta grill"—and Tex Wasabi's, featuring rock-n-roll, BBQ, and sushi).

Along with The Good Life, SP Sevens have a penchant for seeing family from a distinctively unconventional perspective. "Family" seldom includes just blood relatives; it usually includes a whole assortment of other people—people who become like family by virtue of some kind of link that's meaningful to the Seven (like some shared set of ideals). So it's here that we find alternative living situations, unusual homes, and non-traditional households, often in non-traditional settings (like intentional communities, ashrams, artist communities, or off-the-grid locales). Places like Findhorn in Scotland, Alpha Farm in Oregon, Slab City in the California desert, and Stephen Gaskin's The Farm in rural Tennessee and publications like *Communities Magazine* (focusing on intentional communities around the world) embody the Seven-like ethos of creating a family based on some sort of shared vision. Films like *Off the Grid: Life on the Mesa* or *Garbage Warrior* are about maverick communities that are "off the grid"— that is, not connected to municipal water, electric, and other systems that create dependency on the government or anybody else. So most have a distinctively freedom-loving ethos, although some are more cohesive and intentional (Reynold's Greater World Community) while others are more loose-knit and accidental (e.g., Slab City, which became a community after an army base closed after WWII and Snowbirds started moving in each winter). Most such alternative communities are not entirely utilitarian; they tend to make art, music, and beauty a priority (reflecting the Seven appreciation of aesthetics).

Even Sevens who don't live in alternative communities often make their homes and gardens unusual in some way; an extreme example is Necker Island, a private Caribbean getaway for Seven entrepreneur Richard Branson that was recently No. 1 on a list of the top ten luxury homes in the world. It features a hilltop view, beautifully appointed open-air rooms, a private lagoon/pool, a gorgeous white sand beach, and even a floating trampoline. (If this sounds good, you can hire Necker Island for just $36,000 a night!)

Sevens who lack the means to buy an island still like to create an environment that stimulates the imagination. If they lack a big budget, they improvise with whatever they've got. On the reality TV series, *Little People, Big World*, Matt Roloff and his wife Amy live with their four kids on an Oregon farm. Matt, Amy, and one of the kids are dwarfs; the other three kids are average-sized. Matt, the Seven, spent years of his childhood in hospitals, dreaming of the day when he would have a family and his own place. When Matt married Amy, he bought a farm with a small rundown house and a few out buildings. Over the years, the imaginative Matt built an incredible assortment of fantasy structures: a Western town, pirate ship, super tree house, princess castle, covered bridge, zip line, and pumpkin-throwing trebuchet. He also expanded the house twice, put in little-people-sized counters, and a swimming pool. Matt even installed an innovative thermal heating system that draws heat from the earth.

With all the kid-friendly amenities, it's no surprise that their household is a hangout for all the neighborhood kids; adult family friends also abound. Matt sometimes rents the land out for corporate events and gives tours of the place during pumpkin season. For a while, Matt even moved his business into his home (complete with employees). So although the family is traditional in some ways (e.g., they send their kids to a Christian school and Matt's parents live right down the road), their family lacks any sort of rigid boundaries—at least, that's the way it looks from a viewer's perspective.

Amy Roloff is a Two mom, very interested in her kids and ruler of her household. While friendly, she doesn't like renting out the property to strangers and would like to plan more family-focused activities. Recently, she and her husband have had some marital conflicts, ostensibly because he's not family-oriented enough. Like most Sevens, Matt tends to be restless and can't sit still for long unless he's busy with a new project. So he dislikes attending the kind of events that take him away from his projects. While he enjoys doing things with his kids, they have to be things he really likes—stuff like camping, inventing new gadgets, and building innovative structures.

When the kids were younger, Matt's projects probably made more sense to Amy, because she saw them as something for the kids. But now that the kids are growing up, she doesn't understand why Matt is never satisfied and wants to keep building. She gets frustrated with his constant need to invent something new:

> I think sometimes it gets outta control because there's only so many projects you can do... [when] you're constantly thinking and doing and thinking about those things...I think you really forget about the simple things in life...if you're always trying to find the adrenalin in projects, the simple things in life seem quite boring and don't quite satisfy you.

It's not hard to see why Amy doesn't understand Matt's motivation: to a Two, people clearly matter more than projects. But to Matt, life without projects is like a day without sunshine; he gets irritated and a little martyr-like when obliged to participate in activities that don't interest him (temporarily turning into a "sacrifice Seven").

The Roloffs' difficulties illustrate the kind of misunderstandings that can crop up when two people with different enneagram types (and core motivations) who happened to have been running along a parallel course begin to grow apart because a change of outer circumstances makes them see that what looked like a common interest (raising a family) was actually two different paths that happened to be compatible—at least for a time. In situations like these, it's hard to predict what will happen. But understanding the dynamics of the situation may help people avoid needless feelings of hurt and betrayal. It's comforting to realize that our beloved partner hasn't changed, he's just doing what comes naturally (and what he's actually been doing all along).

One final note about SP Sevens: the security-oriented energy of the SP doesn't always combine well with the light, fast energy of the Seven, leaving the SP Seven with the task of figuring out how to integrate them. I once knew an SP Seven mom who seemed like a typical Seven—light-hearted and open-minded—when interacting with adults, but who played the role of martinet with her seven-year-old daughter. She seemed almost like two different people. It was hard to watch her talked animatedly with adults and then turn to her daughter (probably a Four) with a look of pained disapproval (connection to One).

And one of the most boring talks I've ever attended was by an SP Seven who was bound and determined to avoid any appearance of frivolousness. He spoke for an hour in a monotone and never cracked a smile. (A Sufi teacher once observed that the kite flies the highest for the person whose feet are firmly planted on the ground—but we can't forget to fly the kite!)

¤ ¤ ¤

SEXUAL SEVEN THEMES. Of all the 27 subtypes, this is one with the most film and TV examples. High-spirited, exuberant, and eager for adventure, SX Sevens get a lot of media attention. They do fun things in fun ways, and they make the people around them feel glad to be alive. The three themes Searle mentions for Type 7—adventure, sci-fi adventure, and travel—are all SX Seven genres. Like most people, I enjoy these genres, but the films I like best are the ones that focus as much on character as on plot.

One of my favorite adventure films is *The Man Who Would be King,* based on a Rudyard Kipling story. The two protagonists, Peachy and Daniel, are 19th century adventurers who are hoping to make their fortune by finding some small kingdom to rule in the nether regions of the Himalayas. Peachy (Michael Caine) is a more happy-go-lucky sort while Daniel (Sean Connery) is more intent on his goals. They succeed in crossing the mountains into unexplored territory and gaining favor with the locals by supplying them with guns, which enables them to defeat their enemies. But their biggest stroke of fortune comes after the locals come to believe that Daniel is a God-King. They shower Daniel with riches and other perks to which he soon grows accustomed;

he also begins to believe his own myth, a development that seems worrisome to his more realistic companion, Peachy. In the end, the locals realize they've been wrong in their judgment; they see the interlopers as the scam artists that they actually are. Daniel is executed and Peachy is badly maimed but survives the ordeal; it's he who returns to tell the tale.*

Both characters are adventurous SX subtypes, but Daniel is more like an 8w7 while Peachy is more like a 7w8 (ditto for the actors in real life). While both characters are willing to take chances, Peachy is much quicker to back off when things start going south. Without Daniel, it's likely that Peachy would have escaped before disaster struck. However, because Sevens are restless, they tend to take chances over and over again, which ups the chances that they'll finally encounter the kind of challenge that can't be overcome by either tricks or retreat. Sometimes they get lucky (like the two Sevenish adventurers from *Touching the Void*; see Chapter 7); sometimes they don't (like Peachy).

An SX 7w8 can look a lot like an SX 6w7. Why? Because they both have an adventurous nature and tend to seek out risky activities, especially those involving physical danger. At first glance, it can be hard to tell the difference between them. But their motivation is slightly different. Although both enjoy the "rush" they get from high-risk activities, SX Sixes experience this rush in response to conquering their fears while SX Sevens enjoy the feeling of freedom and "no limits." Sixes also seem a little more anxiety-driven than Sevens (and benefit most from remembering to temper risk with Six-wing caution) while Sevens are more pleasure-seeking than Sixes (and benefit most from remembering to temper optimism with Eight-wing realism).

Traveler Christopher McCandless could probably have used a little of the latter. *Into the Wild* is the story of his treks around the country and into the wilderness. He begins as a young adventurer who rejects city life and sets forth into the world, with the ultimate goal of spending the winter in the Alaskan wild. He visits a lot of different

---

* Michael Caine has said that this is the film he would most like to be remembered for, observing that "no one makes pictures like this any more."

places, but still wants to go to Alaska, despite the warnings he gets along the way. Undeterred, he gradually makes his way north, ultimately settling into an old school bus for the winter. When spring floods cut him off from civilization, he returns to the bus, where he gets sick and (apparently) starves. People who watch the film seem to be evenly divided between those who admire his adventurous spirit and those who deplore his foolhardy idealism.

It's because SX Sevens are such a restless lot that we see so many travel themes with an SX Seven flavor: *Around the World in Eighty Days, Bill and Ted's Excellent Adventure,* and *Two for the Road*; we also see a lot of roaming outlaws, e.g., *Butch Cassidy and the Sundance Kid, Captain Blood,* and *The Getaway.* These outlaws embody the Trickster archetype in a big way. Charming outlaws like Seven Errol Flynn's Robin Hood and Captain Blood barely seemed like criminals; their illegal acts somehow don't seem like real crimes (either because they steal from bad people, give to the poor, or got a raw deal from society). In both *Butch Cassidy and the Sundance Kid* and *The Sting*, Robert Redford and Paul Newman make an entertaining team whose actions we enjoy, whether it's bank robbing (*Butch Cassidy*) or getting even with nasty thugs *(The Sting)*. Traditional English ballads about highwaymen took a similar approach: these outlaws were invariably portrayed as charmingly daring, rather than criminally dangerous.

Mork of TV's *Mork & Mindy* was a popular trickster figure from the 1970s whose manic antics made the show a big hit (and made Mork's alter ego, Robin Williams, an instant star). Tricksters are quick wits, and their mental moves both delight and surprise us, which is why they can say things that are outlandish, controversial, or even crazy—and get away with acts that would land the rest of us in big trouble.

You might wonder how the Seven-like Trickster archetype differs from the Three-like Deceiver archetype, since the actions of both involve deception. The Trickster is deceptive but playful (much like Sevens) while the Deceiver is more intent and serious (much like Threes). That's why Trickster figures tend to seem more benevolent.

When people who fit the Trickster archetype get carried away, they tend to find themselves on the receiving end of the trick. That's why there's a danger in the Seven's tendency to feel like "the rules don't apply to me." This lack of concern is ironically the product of too much ease: because Sevens have so much luck and charm, they can easily begin to get the sense that there's no sticky situation they can't manage to wiggle out of. Sometimes they push the river, just to see what will happen. They're always surprised when their luck runs out.

TV's *Locked Up Abroad* features a whole array of young travelers with this breezy view of life. The show's title tells us what it's about: winding up in jail in a third-world country. Most of the shows feature young protagonists who are broke, bored, and yearning for a little adventure. Somebody offers them a few thousand dollars to carry just one small package of drugs (often something they see as innocuous, like marijuana). They think to themselves, "Sure, why not? It's just once." The destination country is usually someplace warm and exotic, so they spend a week or two enjoying the beach and other amenities before being contacted by local drug dealers. That's when things start to turn sour. The unfortunate "mules" are inevitably asked to carry far more drugs than they were told in the beginning (or drugs that are more hard-core). But since the people they're dealing with seem really scary, they can't back out. Even before getting to the airport, they sense impending doom. Security is always much tighter than they imagined—way too tight for them to easily slip through. When they're caught, they're shocked to find themselves summarily deposited in the local jail. After questioning, they usually go straight to prison, where they are eventually informed of their sentence. Nobody gets off with less than four to seven years.

As they relate their pathetic stories, we don't know whether they're still in jail or not. What we *do* discover is that the experience has changed them in a big way; virtually without exception, they have a completely changed attitude towards life. The boring lives that they once disdained start to look pretty attractive after years in a third-world prison in Bangladesh, Colombia, or Turkey (see *The Midnight Express* for a true story about the grim world of a Turkish prison). It's not that the speakers have become "clean and sober" in the moralistic sense but that they've become reconciled to limitation in a manner that enables them to better appreciate small joys in a new way. They no long require mind-blowing experiences to satisfy their need for variety.

So it's at SX Seven that Peter Pan can be potentially transformed from the *puer aeternus* (eternal child) to an independent individual who retains her love of life without the need to flee her adult responsibilities (due to a panicky fear of becoming trapped). We see this growth curve in the TV and film roles of Sevens like Robin Williams, Steve Martin, and Bill Murray, all of whom started out playing crazy characters on film or TV shows (*Mork & Mindy* for Williams, *The Jerk* for Martin, and *Saturday Night Live* for Murray), but who gradually grew into roles requiring greater depth, feeling, and vulnerability.

SX Sevens seem (like good wine) to acquire greater "bottom" as they age. They do, however, take longer to settle down than just about any other subtype, because of their over-abundant energy and hunger for new experiences. That's why they can be such heartbreakers as partners: not because they don't care about their lovers but because they feel so compelled to keep moving. The idea of settling down doesn't usually work until they've gotten some of the wanderlust out of their systems. That's when they can actually begin to internalize their external experiences in a way that allows them to gain depth and poise.

¤ ¤ ¤

Social seven themes. Here's where we find the individual who enjoys changing the world—and doing it in a way that's visionary, artistic, and unconventional. SOC Sevens like being in the vanguard, seeing ahead into the future; they're the ones that best fit the Planner label that's often applied to Sevens. They love to try out new ideas in whatever they do, and can make great inventors (especially if they have a little SP practicality). But they have to be especially careful to trim their projects to match their budgets and timelines (just ask SOC Seven Terry Gilliam, whose ill-fated, over-budget attempt to make a phantasmagorical version of the Don Quixote story is documented in *Lost in La Mancha*).

My parents once got a great deal on a house that was built by a visionary guy who used top-quality materials to create a beautiful home with the perfect view of the

Tetons. He actually built it for himself, but by the time he'd completed it, he was dead broke. If he'd had just a little more judgment, he probably could have had his dream home, instead of having to immediately turn around and sell it at a loss.

But it can be hard for SOC Sevens to reign in their vision. They tend to go for the stars and hope for the best—and sometimes they succeed. When they lose, they seldom whine about it, because they figure that if one idea bombs, another will take its place. And they're usually right.

In the epic film *How the West Was Won*, one of the plot lines involves Lilith, a feisty Burlesque entertainer moving West (Debbie Reynolds), and Cleve, a riverboat gambler (Gregory Peck), who becomes interested in Reynolds after overhearing that she's inherited a California gold mine. In the course of their journey West, the two develop a great fondness for one another—which is pretty good, considering they're both adventure-seeking Sevens. However, once Cleve discovers the mine is played out, he vanishes. Although Reynolds loves him, she says she doesn't blame him: she understands his nature (because they're the same type, although she's a feisty SX Seven and he's more of a smooth-talking SOC Seven). But one day not too long after-wards, he hears a familiar voice singing in the ballroom on a Sacramento riverboat and realizes it's Lilith. Cashing in his winning hand, he leaves the game and sponta-neously proposes to her. She accepts and the happy couple go off to invest his win-nings in a business ferrying people across San Francisco Bay.

Fast forward 40 years: Cleve has just died and Lilith is selling the belongings of their Nob Hill mansion at auction to pay off their debts. She says that they made and lost three fortunes together. But she's obviously lived a happy life and doesn't regret a thing. Lilith's attitude shows us why Sevens are willing to take chances: it's just more fun. They'd rather take a chance on winning big than staying safe. Win or lose, they get a lot of freedom and the ability to experience something new—and that's their true measure of wealth!

The SOC Seven desire for freedom was one of the main inspirations behind the American Revolution. Even the original Pilgrims and Puritans brought with them this love of freedom; their culture may be classically One in orientation, but there's a connection to Seven that supports the pioneering spirit. After the colonies became well-established, the New World attracted plenty of explorers, inventors, and other freedom-loving individuals. When the British tried to reign in the colonies in the late 18th century, the freedom-lovers cried foul. They tried unconventional protests (like the Boston Tea Party) that were more whimsical than radical in orientation. Even their increasing radicality was expressed more in writing (in pamphlets like Tom Paine's *Common Sense*) than in radical acts. It was only the refusal of the British government to budge even an inch that finally broke the camel's back, resulting in the Declaration of Independence (a document full of SOC Seven ideas that were visionary for their time).

As I mentioned earlier, SOC Sevens are often called "sacrifice" Sevens. This is because, although they may be willing to dedicate themselves to carry out their plans, they tend to think of making commitments as a form of martyrdom. And they aren't shy about letting other people know it! To other types, it seems strange; most of us find this attitude puzzling. But for the freedom-loving Seven, settling down is a serious business.

But SOC Sevens are also capable of making a really big gesture in service to their ideals, often in a dramatic fashion—like Nathan Hale saying, "I regret that I have but one life to give for my country." A fictional example is the dissolute character of Sidney Carton in *A Tale of Two Cities*, who allows himself to become a stand-in for Charles Darnay, a man condemned to die by a citizen's tribunal during the French Revolution. He does it so that Darnay can escape with his wife Lucy, whom Carton loves. Like Hale, his parting words have the eloquence we would expect of a Seven-like protagonist: " 'Tis a far, far better thing I do than I have ever done: 'tis is a far, far better rest that I go to than I have ever known."

When the SOC Seven lacks balance, we see a different sort of sacrifice—the kind that has a fanatical edge. In *Mosquito Coast*, when brilliant-but-erratic inventor Alli Fox (Harrison Ford) feels unappreciated at work, he abruptly packs off his family to the Mosquito Coast of Nicaragua, where he plans to establish a new society. He buys a plot of land deep in the interior and proceeds to enlist his family's aid in building a village in the jungle. Things go well until the arrival of a God-fearing missionary whose vision of the ideal society is quite different from Fox's: we have a classic One versus Seven conflict in the making. The missionary's arrival infuriates Fox, who responds by pouring all his energy into an impressive new invention: a gigantic ice machine that can also create air conditioning (which he's sure will impress the natives more than a disembodied God). He succeeds in building the machine, but becomes more and more mentally unhinged, making increasingly unwise decisions which eventually result in the destruction of everything he has created.

The Mosquito Coast presents us with conflicting visions of what constitutes "civilization." Is it the air-conditioned paradise presented by Fox or the God-fearing society promoted by the missionary? Both positions represent two extremes that cannot be reconciled (because neither protagonist is willing to give an inch).

A similar conflict is handled quite differently in *Garbage Warrior*, a documentary about maverick architect, Michael Reynolds, who has been building eco-friendly structures out of old tires, pop bottles, and adobe for forty years. Like Alli Fox, Reynolds has radical views: he sees humankind on a collision course with nature unless humankind develops fundamentally new ways of living. But unlike Fox, Reynolds is willing to bend a little to make his vision a reality. That's what makes him persistent instead of fanatical.

All of Reynolds' houses are built from recycled materials. After he started building in 1969, his unusual and innovative designs soon caught the interest of celebrities like Dennis Weaver and Keith Carradine, each of whom asked Reynolds to build an "earthship" house for him. Other wealthy patrons commissioned houses, but were disappointed when some of the experimental designs didn't quite work (resulting in leaky roofs and other problems), leading to lawsuits in the 1980s, despite the fact that Reynolds sold his homes "as is," explaining upfront that they were experimental in nature. (In some ways, it's hard to blame the disappointed patrons; in one instance, the sun came in through the windows in such a way that it was able to melt a typewriter! Reynolds remarks that he was immensely thankful that it was a typewriter on the table, and not a baby.)

Reynolds admits he made many mistakes, but says he's learned from them, building progressively better and more innovative structures. However, by the 1990s, his earlier mistakes began to catch up with him, eventually coming to the attention of local zoning officials. The officials pressured him so much that he finally voluntarily give up his New Mexico architecture and building licenses in 2000.

At that point, he fell into a deep depression; this was his personal Dark Night of the Soul. But after a year, he decided to bite the bullet and began to build houses that complied with local zoning regulations (what he calls "cookie-cutter" houses," each exactly like the one next door). They still incorporated Green building techniques, but did not appeal to his adventurous side. It was a bitter pill to swallow; he chafed under the new building restrictions but managed to get all his permits in order to construct a legal subdivision in the northern New Mexico desert near Taos.

But Reynolds hadn't yet given up on the idea of finding a way to build truly experimental houses. So he read the law, bought a suit and tie, and went off to the state legislature to lobby for legislation making it possible to construct experimental buildings. It was a gutsy move for a guy with virtually no political connections. In the film, we see him trudging from office to office, trying to gain support for his "crazy idea." The only problem is that, because of his manner and the language of the bill, it really *did* sound crazy to most legislators. After a lot of effort, he finally got the interest of a sympathetic legislator who helped him to re-work the bill (mostly by getting rid of all the messianic, end-of-the-world rhetoric), so he could build his houses. Meanwhile, Reynolds and his team journeyed to the Andaman Islands after the 2004 tidal wave and to Mexico after Hurricane Rita to help rebuild, using the experimental techniques he'd refined after 35 years of building.

As a result of these humanitarian efforts, things finally began to turn around for him. Reynolds' work was finally recognized by the American Institute of Architects and his license (which had been revoked) was restored; he was even asked to give a lecture at their headquarters in Colorado. And in 2007, New Mexico House Bill 269 (the Sustainable Development Testing Site Act) was passed into law, paving the way for the legal sanctioning of experimental house designs that do not comply with existing building standards.

So Michael Reynolds' willingness to make genuine sacrifices in order to implement his vision paid off in the end. When confronted with opposition, instead of either giving up or railing about the rules, Reynolds decided to pull back, retrench, and work through the system (instead of flailing against it). He did what was necessary to demonstrate that his work was the product of a real visionary, not just the crazy whim of a rebel against society.

Type eight –
the master

He who has never learned to obey cannot be a good commander.
– Aristotle

WHEN I THINK of Eights, the phrase to come to mind is *Heaven on Earth*. Eights are the most expansive type on the enneagram; they evoke both the grandeur of heaven and the groundedness of earth. Even quiet Eights tend to radiate a tangible aura of power and strength. Where many people need to muster up the energy to get something done, this is seldom a problem for Eights, who have energy to spare. Their challenge is finding ways to channel all that energy and maintaining patience with people who don't quite match their energy level.

On the transformational enneagram, Point 8 is the place of completeness. It symbolically represents the pinnacle of achievement, because it's at the end of the evolutionary cycle that began at Point 5.* So just as Fours represent an extreme (as the last point in involution), so do Eights (as the last point in evolution). If Fours are in the place of greatest depth, "thickness," and darkness, Eights are in the place of greatest elevation, aspiration, and expansion. Both points are on what has sometimes been called the "power axis": the axis that involves the greatest intensification of energy on the enneagram circle. It's this energy that gives Fours their emotional intensity and Eights their charismatic ability to lead. Both types have the similar

---

* Point 8 is also at the pinnacle of the entire involutionary/evolutionary cycle.

challenge of acquiring the kind of self-control that allows them to channel their energy in an appropriate way.

Because Eights have vulnerable hearts, they sometimes try to protect themselves emotionally by cutting off their feelings. Though this may help them temporarily, it also curtails them, by circumscribing their ability to move into arenas that require greater psychological integration. To entirely fulfill their potential, they must be brave enough to get in touch with lost and denied feelings. This will allow them to move out of the "big fish in a small pond" frame of mind (because they no longer need to keep their world artificially small so that they can feel bigger than they really are).

Eights can also feel intellectually vulnerable; they tend to secretly consider their direct style inferior to the more subtle, intellectual approach of head types. While they have an intuitive understanding of how to take on a leadership role and connect with an audience, they can find the nuances of communication (especially written communication) challenging. Courage for an Eight consists in venturing forth into those areas of life in which they are not naturally dominant (like writing, diplomacy, or nurturing), in the interest of continued growth.

When I was first introduced to Eights, I heard a lot about the connection between this enneagram type and revenge: about how an Eight who feels wronged will seek to avenge that wrong, pursuing justice even to the ends of the earth. While I could see this tendency, I felt that it would be useful to understand where it comes from, instead of simply assuming that Eights seek vengeance because they are in the grip of ego, have anger issues, or lack self-control. I got a clue what was going on when studying Ken Wilber's "Big Three" domains of life (Ethics, Art, and Science). I realized that the Gut/Body Center is also the Ethics Center (while the Heart Center is the Art Center and the Head Center is the Science Center).

In enneagram circles, we often speak about ethics in connection with Type 1, but actually ethics are of special interest to all three Gut types. And what is of special interest to Eights is the domain of *personal* ethics: the domain of honor and chivalry.

TABLE 18-1.
Type Eight: The Master

CHARISMATIC, DOMINANT, POWER-SEEKING, RESPONSIBLE, HONOR-ORIENTED

TWO Connection brings softness, tenderness, compassion, vulnerability
FIVE Connection brings shyness, reticence, reflectiveness, depth, inhibition

SEVEN Wing brings assertiveness, creativity, brashness, quickness, mental facility
NINE Wing brings calmness, deliberation, patience, ability to observe & be patient

Other Labels: Leader, Boss, Monarch, Protector, Mover & Shaker, Consolidator
Challenges: toughness, lack of empathy, ingratitude, vengefulness, misuse of power

SUBTYPES		
Self-preservation	Sexual	Social
ARCHETYPES Father Figure, Silent Protector, Guardian, Powerful Presence, Heavyweight, Giant, Strong Silent Type, Sampson, Hercules, Atlas, Mountain Man, Mountain Mama, Force of Nature, Wilderness Survivor, Prepared Survivalist, Mother Bear, Grounded Warrior, Weight Lifter, Pillar of Strength, Unsung Hero, Little Orphan Annie, Silent Power	God or Goddess, God's Instrument, Big Brother, Master Craftsman, Reliable Rescuer, The King's Champion, Old-West Gunslinger, Knight Errant, Charismatic Hero/Heroine, Honor-Bound Avenger, Personal Intimidator, Pirate King, Buccaneer, Martial Artist, Avenging Angel, Angel of Death, Shiva/Kali, Destroyer, Ruthless Tyrannizer, Powerful Lord or Lady, Hunter or Huntress, Samurai Warrior	Unchallenged Patriarch, Sun King, Reigning Queen, Emperor/Empress, Court-holder, Ruler, Autocrat, Chairman of the Board, Big Boss, Born Leader, Leader of the Pack, Mafia Don, Military General, Commander-in-Chief, Respected Chieftain, Benevolent Dictator, Gifted Tactician, Top-level Strategist, Commander in Chief, Social Controller, Tough-love Parent, Dominant Friend, One of the Boys, A Real Pal
FILM THEMES **Honest effort** creates the foundation for right livelihood (*A Home of Our Own, The Stand, Holmes on Homes*) **Silent resolve** inspires others in a dire situation (*Invincible, Shackleton's Antarctic Adventure, The Hanoi Hilton, The Unsinkable Molly Brown, The Longest Day*) **Purity of heart** brings special strength (*Invincible, Sampson & Delilah, The Green Mile*) **How to live big** (*The Rosie O'Donnell Show, Donald Trump's The Apprentice*) or cook big (*Emeril, Throwdown with Bobby Flay, Iron Chef, Iron Chef America, Dinner: Impossible*) **Big guys** throw their weight around (*The Babe Ruth Story, Cobb, Raging Bull*)	**Sparks fly** when Eights mate (*Gone with the Wind, The Quiet Man, Cleopatra, The King & I*) **Tough guy** shows his vulnerable side (*The King & I, Good Will Hunting, Magnolia, The Shootist, The Mission*) **Retribution is sought** for unacceptable acts (*The Searchers, The Godfather, High Noon, Skins, The Outlaw Josie Wales, The Sons of Katie Elder, Taras Bulba, Righteous Kill, Gladiator*) **Chivalrous knights** uplift the weak (*The Magnificent Seven/The Seven Samurai, Gladiator, Spartacus*), restore the kingdom (*Excalibur*), or otherwise uphold the code of chivalry (*Sir Gawain & the Green Knight, Ghost Dog: Way of the Samurai*) **Powerful females** use beauty to rule (*The Tyra Banks Show, Dangerous Beauty, Xena: Princess Warrior, Cleopatra*)	**"Tough Love" types** help people change their errant ways (*The Dog Whisperer, The Chef Jeff Project, The World's Strictest Parents, An Officer & a Gentleman, Twelve O'clock High*) **Dominant buddy/boss** sets the tone & calls the shots (*Good Will Hunting, Cake Boss, American Chopper, The Deer Hunter, Tough as Nails*) **Titans clash** and ordinary people quake (*Heat, Stalin, The Godfather, The Last King of Scotland*) **Even mobsters** need emotional support these days (*Analyze This, Analyze That, The Sopranos*) **Inspirational leaders** change the world (*Patton, MacArthur, Elizabeth, Stand and Deliver, Dr. Bahasaheb Ambedkar*) **Mass events** create major shifts in the world (*The Day the Earth Stood Still, Krakatoa, War of the Worlds, Independence Day, Armageddon*, historical epics & other epics depicting massive change)

One of the dilemmas for modern Eights is that they live in a world that has mostly forgotten this domain. Eights with integrity can't help but live according to an honor-based creed. So they never quite understand Three-like values that place pragmatic considerations or legal contracts above an individual's word of honor. Such a reordering of values is inconceivable to an Eight, especially in personal relationships. We see the conflict come up in TV competitions like *Survivor*, when Eight contestants like Rupert Boneham become angry when lied to by other people, even when they've watched the show and ought to know how it works (i.e., that duplicity is part of the game).

To an Eight who trusts someone, no interaction between individuals is ever really a game. The key word here is "game"; Eights who have framed *Survivor* as a game (e.g., "Boston Rob" Mariano or Russell Hantz) won't have the same problem as Rupert, because they don't think that they have to be honorable in a game whose rules specifically permit deception.

As children, Eights are big people in a small body. My favorite anecdote about young Eights comes from my little Eight friend Hanna, who at the age of three, was fond of frequently announcing "I know *everything*!" She was quite adamant—adamant enough to make the adults around her fall on the floor laughing at her innocent hubris. I was a little worried that she'd have problems when she started school, but by that time, she had more self-control and got along fine.

Knowing Hanna's type helped me both to understand her and to understand Eights, especially the connecting points. I noticed that whenever she was disciplined, she would go off in the hallway and curl up on the floor, even after she was no longer in timeout. I realized after awhile that she was going to her connecting point of Five, because she needed time to recover from the blow to her pride. She also retreated to Five in unfamiliar situations.

After her little brother was born, she often accessed her other connecting point of Two: she loved being a big sister playing the role of Mom (her biggest problem being a little too much exuberance in her mothering!). While Eights can find their heart at Two, they have to be careful to pull in their energy a little so that they don't come off like "super Twos," overbearing or hyper-controlling.

Although the energy at Eight is always big, the wings determine whether that energy is expressed in a more extroverted, physically-assertive fashion (8w7) or a more introverted, internalized fashion (8w9). With an 8w7, "what you see is what you get": they tend to be brash, in-your-face, and bold in demeanor. And that's the way they like it. Like 7w8s, they enjoy exploring the nature of power and playfully testing the limits of their influence. An 8w9 is more interested in what they can accomplish by exerting power, and also how they can obtain maximal results with minimal efforts. They're doing post-grad work in the "art of the deal," which is why they value elegance and restraint more than obvious power plays.

Before I studied the enneagram, I was pretty intimidated by Eights—by their big energy, bluster, and executive ability. But I came to realize that they have vulnerabilities like everybody else. Understanding Eights allows me to see them as real people (instead of symbols of power). As a result, I'm less intimidated by their bluntness or bluster.

Searle identifies three Eight genres: war, action-adventure, and Mafia stories. I see "war" as part of a larger category that includes apocalyptic scenarios and other themes involving mass shifts (mass redemption or destruction), whether from natural or man-made causes. The Mafia category I see as part of a larger Power Broker category that includes power, cartels, and authoritarian/totalitarian themes. I would also add genres such as stories about people who set an example by standing tall or refusing to budge; Tough Love parents; stories about knighthood, chivalry, valor, especially living up to chivalric or Samurai codes; stories about retribution and revenge; stories about hands-on leadership; and themes involving buddies and comradeship.

¤ ¤ ¤

Self-preservation Eight themes. In a certain sense, SP Eight is the most self-preserving of the self-preserving subtypes. The archetypal image is of a big, strong, solid individual who "stands his ground." While most SP Eights are diligent, there's an effortlessness about their way of working that reflects the tremendous strength that goes with this subtype, which is well-represented by archetypes like Atlas, Hercules, or Sampson. Although these archetypes conjure up the image of physical strength, the subtype is also associated with a tremendous strength of *will*, the kind of will that most people would find hard to fathom.

A good example is Mike Holmes of TV's *Holmes on Homes*. Mike is a big guy with a big heart who takes on home remodeling messes that other contractors have created and failed to correct. He comes in, rips out all the bad work, and "makes things right." No matter how tough the problem, Mike is willing to take it on. When things go wrong, he just keeps plugging away. It's not an act for the cameras; it's how he really is.

TV's *Extreme Makeover: Home Edition* also features a lot of guys like Mike—big-hearted SP Eight contractors, donating their time and energy to build a home for a deserving family, probably because there's nothing an Eight likes better than to do hands-on work for a noble cause. It offers them a way to connect with their emotions (connection to Two) without making them uncomfortably shy (connection to Five).

Perhaps the will we see in SP Eights comes in part from their connectedness with nature, and especially with the earth—a connectedness that often translates into a desire to do things that are highly practical and physically challenging. It also creates the conviction that physical survival is paramount, which is probably why this subtype is so associated with a survivalist ethos, the creating of family compounds, the securing of perimeters, and the stockpiling of supplies. SP Eights see self-reliance as essential and are even less likely than other Eights to ask for help when they need it; they have to learn to admit their vulnerabilities and seek assistance when necessary.

One of the SP Eight's many strengths is his ability to inspire other people in survival situations (think of John Wayne in war movies). But military organizations also try to instill a personal code of honor that will serve a similar purpose during extreme survival situations. *The Hanoi Hilton* portrays a survival situation where all of the American POWs housed in the infamous Hoa Lo Prison during the Vietnam

War were tortured to break their spirit and to procure anti-American statements to be used as propaganda. The torture was so prolonged and extreme that the prisoners soon realized that each had a limit as to how much he could take, no matter how tough he was. So instead of defining courage by the ability to withstand torture unto death or insanity, the POWs adopted a new ethos: "Take physical torture until you are right at the edge of losing your ability to be rational. At that point, lie, do, or say whatever you must do to survive. But you first must take physical torture." Adopting that sort of creed allowed them to preserve their sense of honor and dignity, even in defeat.

Virtues like honor, dignity, and purity of heart are an intrinsic part of the SP Eight way of life because they ennoble the Eight's survival efforts, so that life is more than just a dog-eat-dog struggle to live. In films like *Invincible*, we see these values brought to the forefront and shown to be a force for good. *Invincible* is the story of a Jewish blacksmith, Zishe Breitbart, from a small *shetl* in the early 1930s. Zishe is recruited to perform as a strong man in Berlin's "Circus of the Occult." Initially billed as a Teutonic hero in order to appeal to Nazi sympathies, he later reveals his true identity as a Jew, becoming an inspiration to local Jews but a pariah to the rising Nazi party.

Another source of inspiration to Zishe is his corrupt boss' pianist, the beautiful and talented Marta (played by real-life pianist Anna Gourari). She's a Fourish figure who loves beauty but is being blackmailed into working for the man running the Circus, because she's a stateless person. Much admired by Zishe (though not in a prurient way), she takes him into a room with a tank full of exquisite jellyfish and tells him of her dreams:

> I have a vision...Now look at these beings [the jellyfish]. For me, they have the purest of souls. I have never seen anything more beautiful or delicate. I want to play music to match this vision. It's deep inside me.

So we have two figures of great purity in the midst of a hotbed of corruption. What will happen? Ultimately, Zishe publicly exposes Hanussen to be a fake psychic. As a result, Hanussen is arrested and Marta is freed. As the result of his experiences,

Zishe becomes deeply religious and is gifted with the vision to discern the coming Holocaust. He implores the people of his village to become strong, like Sampson. But they don't really understand what he's saying. Fatefully, Zishe gets a small cut on his knee, which becomes infected; the leg must be amputated. After several more operations, he eventually succumbs to the infection, but comes to serve as an inspiration to later generations of Jews. At the end, the film says that "the Invincible lives on in the tales and ballads of the Jewish people."*

Invincible was never distributed much beyond film festivals, so it gained very little public exposure. But it's a good film for illustrating why *innocence* is such an asset in Eights: because it enables them to transcend their boundaries in a way that uplifts and inspires.

The Green Mile, based on a Stephen King story, is a strange but inspiring fantasy about a Gentle Giant that winds up on Death Row in the early part of the last century. He has been convicted of the murder of two little girls. Huge, black, and bereft of education, he looks like a big, dumb guy that somehow got himself into trouble. Initially, he's a nondescript figure. But one day, he heals the head guard (Tom Hanks) of a debilitating urinary tract condition in a way that seems miraculous; later, he brings a mouse back to life and heals a woman with brain cancer. By then, all the guards on Death Row realize he's someone very special and cannot possibly be guilty of murder. How can he be content to die?, they wonder. He says that he's ready to go, because the world is just too full of pain, and he can feel it all. So like Zishe, he lives a short but exemplary life, even if only he and a handful of prison guards are aware of it. Both characters are men who help through their actions, not their words.

Another one of my favorite SP Eight films is *A Home of Our Own*, featuring Kathy Bates (an SP Two) playing her connecting point of Eight. She's Frances Lacey, a tough, survivor-oriented single mom raising six kids in the 1960s. When she loses her dead-end

---

* The character is based upon a real-life Jewish strong man of the same name who was an inspiration to the Jewish people, especially during the Holocaust, but it takes certain liberties with the truth for purposes of dramatic license; the real Zishe Breitbart died in 1925, seven years earlier than the time when *Invincible* takes place.

job in L.A., she packs her kids off in their old car and heads for Montana to make a new start for her family. Allowed to move into a partially-finished house by a kindly Japanese man, she and the kids set about transforming it into a real home. There are only two problems: they have no money and Frances won't accept help ("charity") from anybody, not even Christmas presents for her kids. That makes for tough times, both financially and emotionally. Nevertheless, she and the kids manage to hobble along until one of them accidently sets fire to their half-built house, burning it to the ground. It's only then that Frances realizes that (a) her kids are still too little to take on adult responsibilities and (b) life works better when you let other people help you every once in a while. She softens up enough to allow the community to pitch in and rebuild her house.

A Home of Our Own is an inspiring film but instructive, too, since it shows us both an SP Eight's strong points and weaknesses. Frances is so grimly self-reliant that she insists on tit-for-tat at all times; on the other hand, underneath her gruff exterior, she's actually a good person who really loves her kids. In the end, she allows their innocence to help her regain some of her own.

Another interesting SP Eight character is *Dinner Impossible's* Robert Irvine, who's asked each week to fix an unusual meal for a group in a very short amount of time. Robert is a big, muscular guy with obvious military training. Whether he's tasked with creating main course dishes with impossible ingredients (like candy or ice cream), combining cuisines that don't go together (like Chinese and Irish), or making entrées on Barbie-sized plates for Barbie's 50th anniversary, his mission is clear: to create really great food out of really strange ingredients or under bizarre conditions. Although he pushes his crew pretty hard, he's got a great sense of humor and a tender side that is quite endearing. Robert shows us the ability of a big guy to use his considerable energy in service to something greater than himself.

I've already mentioned Rupert Boneham from *Survivor:* he's an SP Eight whose skills at underwater spear fishing enabled him to play the valuable role of food-provider in *Survivor: Pearl Islands*. Rupert saw his role as so important to the group's survival that he couldn't believe they would ever vote him off. But after a few weeks on low rations, he sort of "went native," became increasingly menacing as his Eightish survival instincts began to kick in. His tribe mates found his manner unnerving, so despite his fishing skills, they ganged up to vote him off (which is often the only way to defeat a big, tough Eight—by using a "safety in numbers" approach). In the 2010 Heroes vs Villains edition of *Survivor*, Rupert returned as a key member of the Heroes tribe. But Rupert became very invested in trying to retain his identity as a hero, which hampered his ability to maneuver (the show, after all, is not called *Heroic Action*!). At the end, Rupert wasn't sorry about the way he played, saying that he felt very good about it, especially "the way I showed that I deserved the label of *hero*."

¤ ¤ ¤

SEXUAL EIGHT THEMES. SX Eights are probably the most charismatic of the 27 subtypes. The combination of SX charisma with Type 8 largesse produces an individual who is tremendously influential by virtue of sheer presence. SX Eights are the individuals who can walk into the room and immediately catch our attention; we sense their presence in a visceral way. They don't need a big name or image to impress us; all they need is themselves.

SX Eights are usually pretty fiery in temperament, especially if they have a Seven wing. They are the ones with the biggest tempers and the shortest fuses: watching Donald Trump on TV's *The Apprentice* provides us with a view of this subtype, up-close-and-personal. SX Eights also tend to have big appetites (for food, alcohol, or whatever else gives them pleasure), so they really have to be careful about how they satisfy those appetites or they can easily create chaos for themselves and other people.

This is why they particularly benefit from adopting a personal code of conduct based on some kind of chivalric ethic: because it gives SX Eights a genuinely worthwhile reason to curb their appetites and cultivate self-control. Chivalry is about making sacrifices (whether literally or figuratively) on behalf of a higher cause. Its origins in Europe lie in mid-Eastern Sufi teachings, where chivalry was associated with personal sacrifice in response to a transcendent need. When it came to Europe during the Crusades, it gave rise to the ideal of courtly love, which is basically lust elevated to a level where it becomes expressed as devotion—not only to the lady of one's choice but to a noble cause or ideal. In this way, the basest of cravings is transformed into the noblest of desires.

It's easy to see why the chivalric archetype is so powerful and how it came to inspire medieval culture: the courtly ideal, the quest for the Grail, the Knights of the Round Table, and the soaring architecture of the great cathedrals. It's harder to find modern-day examples because chivalry is a heroic ideal and we do not live in heroic times—in times when people see the world from a larger-than-life perspective. (In Arthur Koestler's terms, modern people live more in the "trivial" than the "tragic" plane.) Even our concept of heroism is different in modern times, in that it focuses more on what we do for other individuals or society than on what we do to satisfy a transcendent ideal.

But the original chivalric ideal is clearly based upon the premise that there's a dimension of life that transcends that which we know—and that we are responsible to ensure that our acts resonate with what this higher reality represents. The idea of a higher order of transcendent Masters is relevant here. Sufism makes reference to the idea of an order of Masters that watches over the world and assists in its evolution; J. G. Bennett refers to this group as the Masters of Wisdom. Such an order is akin to an exalted version of the chivalric orders (such as the Knights Templar) that were intended to ensure not only the physical well-being of those whom they served, but to help them grow and evolve.

Whether an individual embraces the literal reality of such an order or simply sees it as an ideal worthy of emulation, it provides an individual—particularly one with larger-than-life influence and appetites—with a frame of reference that gives him the passion to refine himself, as opposed to dissipating his energy in pursuits that build nothing of consequence.

Some SX Eights use their artistic passion as a source of inspiration. In *Looking for Richard*, SX Eight Al Pacino pours his passion for Shakespeare into a commentary on why Shakespeare matters—which he does by interspersing scenes from *Richard III* (where he plays the evil Richard III to perfection) with man-on-the-street interviews, expert commentaries, and actors' discussions. Pacino also gets a few of his friends (Alec Baldwin, Kevin Spacey and Winona Ryder) to play other key *Richard III* roles.

You'd think a film like this might be boring, but it's not. That's where the driving energy of the SX Eight comes in: Pacino's charisma and incredible passion for Shakespeare grabs the watcher by the lapels and drags him right into the middle of the action; no person watching could possibly think of *Richard III* as boring after watching Pacino and his pals in action. He's also good at picking interesting people for the interviews; one of the most articulate commentators is a homeless man who shares Pacino's passion for Shakespeare. *Looking for Richard* is a great example of an SX Eight at his charismatic best, both when playing a role and being himself.

Yul Brynner is an example of an SX Eight from a previous generation. Brynner was the quintessence of an SX Eight: powerful, charismatic, and fierce. He was like a man from another time, a time of invading hordes and warrior kings. I recently saw the 1960s flick *Taras Bulba*, where Brynner played a Cossack leader so convincingly that many reviewers said it was a role he was born to play. Other powerful Yul Brynner roles include the King of Siam in *The King and I,* Pharoah in *The Ten Commandments,* and the relentless robotic gunslinger in *Westworld*. But the most powerful role I ever saw him in was an anti-smoking commercial he made several months prior his death from lung cancer in 1985 for release after his death:

> *Now that I'm gone, I tell you, don't smoke. Whatever you do, just don't smoke.*
> *If I could take back that smoking, we wouldn't be talking about any cancer. I'm*
> *convinced of that.*

I was stunned when I saw that commercial: I'd never seen a celebrity give this kind of message, especially a glamorous star like Yul Brynner. To see a man who was so powerful admit his weakness, in hopes of saving lives, was a real testament to the idea that our greatest power often lies in our ability to admit our weaknesses.

Another positive example of an SX Eight is Cesar Millan, *aka* the Dog Whisperer. On his TV show of the same name, he shows us how (in his own words) to "rehabilitate dogs and train people." He also shows us something else: how an SX Eight can use his energy to correct a less-than-desirable situation.

The desire to set things right is strong in all Body/Gut types. While the One sense of justice is impersonal and abstract, and the Nine sense of justice is based on the desire to promote peace and harmony, the Eight sense of justice is deeply personal and tangibly embodied. And it's most passionately expressed in SX Eights, where it can sometimes turn into the desire for vengeance, especially when the Eight experiences some action as either a personal betrayal or a betrayal of his most deeply-held beliefs.

Culturally, most of us favor the kind of justice we see at Nine or One more than Eight. We're taught that justice is something which ought to take into account the needs of all parties (the Nine approach) or to be based on impartial principle (the One approach). But clearly, there has to be a place for the Eight's more personal and hands-on "take" on justice; Cesar Millan's work provides us with one example of such a model.

On *The Dog Whisperer*, he uses a highly personal approach to introduce balance into a situation in which the energy is out of whack. The focus is always on how to set things right, rather than where to assign blame or how to punish wrongdoers (whether canine or human). Cesar is fond of reminding people that animals live in the moment, not in the past or future (which is why a shift in our personal energy can instantly effect a change in our pets' behavior). When we remain in the moment, our focus is on what we can do to bring ourselves and our environment into balance (rather than past injustices or future problems).

So far, all the SX Eight examples I've cited have been males. That's because it's harder to find clear-cut examples of female SX Eights, especially ones that aren't a bit cartoonish (e.g., *Xena: Princess Warrior*). Whatever the recent rhetoric about women's rights, it's still something of a cultural taboo for a female to look too viscerally powerful, which is why most of the females playing macho roles are more likely to be another type (e.g., Linda Hamilton in *Terminator II: Judgment Day* is an SP Four; Sigourney Weaver in *Alien* is a probable Three playing a counterphobic Six; and Sandra Bullock as the bus driver in *Speed* is a 7w8). The female characters portrayed are powerful, but not nearly so powerful, say, as the characters typically portrayed by Yul Brynner, John Wayne, or Al Pacino.

The clearest definitive example I could find of a SX Eight is Queen Latifah, whose first album—*All Hail the Queen*—tells us that here's a female who bows down before no one, male or female. Her talent as a hip-hop artist earned her the chance to get into film, but she's still a relative newcomer, so she's only recently begun to land major roles. In 2006, she got the lead in *Last Holiday,* as a shy woman who throws her shyness to the four winds after being diagnosed with a fatal illness and deciding to "live a little" before she dies. As she blossoms, she shows us a female Eight in her full glory. By the time she discovers that the doctors made a mistake and she's actually not sick, she's become a completely new person. (From an enneagrammatic point of view, we could say she was formerly an Eight leaning into her Nine wing, but actually "living" as a Five, her connecting point, until she realizes that time is short and decides to embrace her Eightness.)

Cat Cora of TV's *Iron Chef America,* Sharon Osborne of 2010's *Celebrity Apprentice,* and Tyra Banks of TV's *The Tyra Banks Show* and *America's Next Top Model* also seem like probable SX Eights, but it's a little hard to tell for sure, because female SX Eights often lack the directness of their male counterparts (perhaps because of the cultural taboo mentioned above). They are more likely to wield power indirectly, drawing on their connecting point of Two as a way of appearing to seem less influential (more like the power behind the throne). The difference is that, while a Two is content to remain behind the throne, the Eight wants eventually to sit on it—but often in a way that doesn't reveal the full extent of her influence.

There's a seductiveness at SX Eight—especially among females—that's like a larger-than-life version of the seductiveness we see at Point 2. Witness the theme song of Tyra Banks' *Top Model,* which asks us, over and over again, "Do you want to be on top?" The tone is sexually suggestive and slightly mocking, but also inviting. Tyra is challenging young women to be bold, not timid, in pursuing their dreams. (For evidence that she's really an Eight, check out the Internet video clip where Tyra loses her temper on camera with a contestant, in order to jar her out of a defeatist attitude.*)

Bobby Flay is one of my favorite male SX Eights, because he has just the right combination of tough-and-tender to make him a great entertainer. He plays two very different roles on Food Network programs: one as an Iron Chef (on *Iron Chef America*) and one as a cheeky challenger (on *Throwdown with Bobby Flay*). As an Iron Chef, he seems to lean into his Nine wing, looking appropriately menacing as he stands motionless and cross-armed during the opening credits. He has no trouble looking like someone who could eat you for breakfast. But he actually seems to have more fun on *Throwdown*, where he gets to act more like a Seven, showing up unannounced and trying to make other peoples' signature dishes! (Like *Dinner Impossible's* Robert Irvine, he likes to talk about his "mission"—and gets his orders in a sealed envelope.) Although I never used to like cooking shows, these high-stakes cooking competitions provide an interesting arena for watching Eights demonstrate their mastery.

It's worth mentioning, by the way, that the whole Iron Chef concept really captures the essence of the SX Eight ethos. It's no surprise that it was conceived in Japan, where they still take things like chivalry and the martial arts very seriously. The Japanese version seems more intense: both the Iron Chef and the challenger look like they're going to fight each other to the death. The American version is considerably more tongue-in-cheek, but still manages to be the most dramatic cooking competition on American TV.

¤ ¤ ¤

Social Eight themes. If SP Eights are rugged individualists and SX Eights are charismatic adventurers, SOC Eights tend to be a little less rugged and "in your face" and a little more socially engaged. They're usually better able to adapt their energy to the needs of the social situation (and more interested in doing so).

Point 8 is the place where we master our ability to work with power; the social arena concerns people. So when we bring the two together, we find themes related to

---

* To locate the video clip, just enter "Tyra's tirade" on any web browser.

statesmanship, military strategy, national and global policy, the governing of nations, the organizing of cartels, extended families and family networks, international organizations, multinational corporations, neighborhood gangs and gang networks, and large-scale organized crime (especially the Mafia). This is the natural home for webs of influence, whether created for good or ill.

Charlie Wilson's War shows us a SOC Eight who starts off as a guy who likes to throw his weight around, but ends up using his influence more responsibly (almost in spite of himself). He reminds us a little of Oskar Schindler, although Schindler as a Three is more interested in impressing his companions; as an Eight, Wilson just wants to enjoy himself in a splashy way—literally. At the start of the film, we see him sitting in a hot tub surrounded by sexy babes. The time is the early 1980s. Wilson is a U.S. Congressman (played by a portly-looking Tom Hanks) partying in Las Vegas, having a fine old time. He's obviously no angel.

But after visiting a huge refugee camp in Peshawar, Wilson is moved by the starving families and children who have lost their limbs after picking up Soviet land mines meant to look like toys. Wilson decides to promote the cause of the Afghani freedom fighters in Congress; he's joined in his efforts by CIA operative Gust Avrakotos (Philip Seymour Hoffman), another tough-but-tender guy dedicated to fighting the Soviet invasion of Afghanistan. The two team up to supply the Mujahadeen with modern anti-helicopter weapons, using all manner of behind-the-scenes maneuvering to get the job done. Julie Roberts plays yet another Eightish character (fellow Texan Joanne Herring) working in cahoots with Wilson and Avrakotos to support the cause.*

Although Wilson is successful in his efforts to raise funding—the film shows him honored for his almost single-handed efforts on behalf of the Mujahadeen—his efforts to secure funding for rebuilding post-Soviet Afghanistan don't meet with the same success. We all know what happened after the Soviets were ousted and the

---

* This film shows us a good example of the Type 8 ethos that goes with the state of Texas. I lived there for several years and can attest to the big-heartedness of the people (as well as their stubbornness and independent-mindedness).

Taliban took over, a scenario characterized by the real-life Charlie Wilson in this way: "These things happened. They were glorious and they changed the world....And then we f--ked up the end game."

The Deer Hunter is a more intimate SOC Eight film that focuses on the special bond between six deer-hunting buddies in a small industrial Pennsylvania town. Robert DeNiro (the Eight) is the leader of the group, whose ideal is to take down a deer with just one shot. Three of the group (played by DeNiro, John Savage, and Christopher Walken) wind up in the military and find themselves in the jungles of Vietnam, where they're captured by the Viet Cong and subjected to sadistic treatment, including forced games of Russian Roulette. DeNiro manages to take the gun and shoot his captors, escaping with one buddy (Savage) but not the other. Later, evidence surfaces that the friend he left behind (Walken) is still alive and living somewhere in Saigon. So DeNiro goes back to find him. When he does, he discovers that his friend (hopelessly deranged from his experiences in the war), now plays Russian Roulette for money; the only way to get to him is to once again to play the game. He does, but it's his friend who loses; he dies in DeNiro's arms, symbolically reunited with the group through DeNiro's efforts to save him.

Many SOC Eight films are about major-league powerbrokers, such as rulers, generals, and heads of powerful groups, e.g., *Elizabeth* (about Elizabeth I's uncompromising rule of England and her refusal to marry, a refusal that allowed her to retain the throne); *MacArthur* and *Patton* (each about a WWII SOC Eight general who ran into trouble with his superiors); *Stalin* (about the notorious Soviet dictator who wiped out millions to satisfy his craving for personal power); *Hoffa* (about the disappearance of Teamster boss Jimmy Hoffa); and *The Godfather* and other mobster films (about the exercise of power by private syndicates who compete with governments for power and privilege). *The Last King of Scotland* is one of the more recent films documenting the exploits of a tyrant, Idi Amin, whom we see through the eyes of a naive young Scottish physician flattered by Amin's attention. By the time the doctor realizes the full extent of Amin's depravity, it's way too late—and he pays dearly for his lack of understanding. (Although the storyline is fictionalized, the portrayal of Amin as a genocidal maniac is all too realistic.)

Dr. Bahasaheb Ambedkar is an inspirational film that gives us a positive example of the SOC Eight subtype. Dr. Ambedkar could either have been a SOC Five or SOC Eight, but he clearly played a SOC Eight role in shaping the modern state of India. (Among his accomplishments is the writing of the Indian Constitution.) One reason it's hard to pin down his type is that he was born a Hindu Untouchable during the early part of the 20th century, when to be in that caste often meant a life of total poverty and ostracism from Hindu culture. (Traditionally, Untouchables cannot eat with others; no one will touch them, interact socially with them, or rent them a room because they're considered to be inherently unclean.) The social stigma of the caste is so strong that it can be hard to separate its influence from the influence of personality.

Before Ambedkar was born, his uncle, who lived the life of a spiritual renunciate, told his father that he would be a famous person who would change the world. So his family was motivated to make sure he received an education. Despite the fact that he turned out to be a brilliant scholar, he was often treated poorly by other people because of his caste. With the help of a liberal-minded Maharajaha, he was sent to both Columbia University and the London School of Economics. He ultimately earned a Doctorate in Law, Society, and Political Science.

When he returned to India, to repay his college debts, Ambedkar joined the civil service, but was once again stymied in his attempts to get established. In England and America, nobody cared about his caste, only his intellect and dedication. But in India, he couldn't even find a place to stay; nobody would rent him a room. At work, he was disrespected by the other civil servants, even his own employees. When he tried to start a business, things went well until his caste was discovered; after that, nobody would do business with him. Finally, he eventually found a job as a lecturer at Sydenham College in Bombay, where he began to gain recognition for his outstanding scholarship. From there, he went on to become politically active in the struggle to secure civil rights for members of his caste and to publish scholarly articles on many legal and political topics. During the struggle for Indian independence, he often fenced politically with Gandhi, whom he felt behaved condescendingly towards his caste; Ambedkar wasn't interested in sentimental rhetoric but wanted hard and fast legal protections for Untouchables in the new Indian State. Once independence was achieved, he became head of the committee to draft a new Constitution. He is now known as the father of that Constitution. Shortly before his death from diabetes in the mid-1950s, he converted from Hinduism to Buddhism, having stated that he did not want to die an Untouchable.

The film is a moving tribute to a man who dedicated his life and his intellect to the betterment of his people, but never managed to entirely eliminate the scourge of the caste system or its devastating effects on lower-caste Indian peoples. But he did manage to leave a lasting positive impact on Indian culture, symbolizing the kind of statesmanship that is the highest and most refined expression of SOC Eight motivation.

Film producer Tracie Norfleet is a more down-to-earth example of a SOC Eight. Tracie was a contestant on Chef Novelli's 2009 reality program, *Chef Academy*, where students try to perform well enough to earn a diploma as a culinary school graduate. Although Tracie loves to cook, her job keeps her pretty busy. So she hadn't planned on participating in the show after hearing about it from a friend of the casting director. One night, she was at her friend's house and the casting director was there, too—and he wanted her for the show. Not only did she successfully graduate from the academy, but she was asked by Novelli—who obviously noticed her executive abilities—to be Head Chef on the final dinner prepared by the contestants for influential food critics.

Tracie was agreeable (although not particularly eager, since taking charge is what she does all the time as a producer). But she seemed to have no problem taking the reins of control, despite the obvious irritation of some of her fellow students, who weren't used to taking orders from a peer. Fortunately, like most Eights, she's got a pretty thick skin. So she managed to take charge despite the challenges involved.

What was harder for Tracie was admitting how much the experience actually changed her. The first change was her decision to stop smoking (so she could smell the food better). She didn't volunteer—Novelli asked all the smokers to quit. In typical Eight fashion, she didn't make the commitment until she was sure she could keep her word. The second change was a shift in attitude towards the people she films ("Being in their position, I feel a bit more empathy towards them when they don't get their stuff right"). She also says she's learned how to "trust her gut and keep on tasting."

She summed up her experience with Novelli like this: "I hate to use stereotypical expressions like, 'He's changed my life!' But Goddamit, he *has*. And it sort of pisses me off!"

These examples show us a side of SOC Eights that has nothing to do with dictators, gangs, or Mafiosi. The reason we see so much focus on negative archetypes is that they do of course exist—and they have the power to make such a big negative impact on peoples' lives. But whatever has a big negative potential has an equally big positive potential; it just may not get as much media attention. However, the positive examples are out there, both in film and in real life. By seeking them out, we gain insight into the nature of power, especially how to use our power in a way that supports other people (rather than exploiting them).

Type nine –
the storyteller

Kind words are the music of the world.
– F. W. Faber

NINES ARE ARGUABLY the kindest type on the enneagram. They have a mildness to their character that makes them very approachable and easy to be around. This is probably why they often get along with all the other eight types—and why they are often dubbed Mediators by enneagram writers. Their ability to remain impassive in situations where other people tend to react gives them a better-than-average ability to help warring groups find common ground. Ironically, most Nines don't particularly like to play a mediating role; they'd rather be somewhere else when arguments crop up. But once they manage to overcome their aversion to conflict, they're among the best peacemakers around.

Calling Nines Storytellers emphasizes their creative potential as individuals rather than their role in relationship to the needs of others. While it's great that Nines can serve as Mediators, Harmonizers, or Devotees, these roles tend to benefit other people more than the Nine herself.

Nine is often said to be the prototype for all the types: the basic blueprint from which all the rest are derived. When the nine types are seen from a fixation-oriented perspective, Point 9 is seen as the original fixation. But from a transformational point of view, Point 9 is the place of origin for each new life cycle. And that's why young

Nines often start out in life with a kind of uncommitted quality and an uncommon receptivity towards experience. It's through their experiences (and especially their relationships) that they move from a place of blank potential through the cycle of individuation, learning something at each step along the way. When they arrive back at Point 9, they have the benefit of all the experience accumulated from each of the other eight points on the enneagram circle. At the end of the cycle, Point 9 represents the place of assimilation: the place where all that has been learned is assimilated and integrated into what is already known.

So Point 9 is a place of overlap, where the beginning and the end meet. It's the place that straddles both sides of the enneagram circle, which is probably what accounts for the ability of Nines to see everybody's point of view. It also accounts for the ability of Nines to "merge" with all nine types: to blend in with the energy of the people around them. But when we speak of merging, this implies that the Nine is actively doing something to create this merging. But Nines seldom do much of anything other than being receptive (it's Twos who are more likely to actively try to create harmony in their relationships). At times, Nines can actually be too receptive, which is why it's important for them to learn how to maintain psychic boundaries and resist being receptive to people who may not have their best interests at heart. This is one of their main challenges.

Point 9 connects to Points 3 and 6. One way to think of Point 9 is as "Point Neutral"; from there, we can move forward to activity (Point 3) or back to receptivity (Point 6). Nines connecting to Three can get themselves moving, which helps them to get things done. But they have to be careful to do this in a way that relies less upon routines and more upon conscious awareness. Nines connecting to Six can feel more alert and motivated, because the anxious energy at Six can "spike" awareness, acting like a pitchfork that gives a little shock—a shock that penetrates their placid exterior. While this kind of awareness can initially seem alarming (because the fear takes them out of a nice, steady-state feeling of "okayness"), it can help them break

TABLE 19-1.
TYPE NINE: THE STORYTELLER

DREAMY, IMAGINATIVE, EASY-GOING, STEADY, APPRECIATIVE, NATURE-LOVING

THREE Connection brings energy, initiative, ambition, work ethic, drivenness
SIX Connection brings focus, mental acuity, skepticism, nervousness, anxiety

EIGHT Wing brings deliberateness, stability, centeredness, patience, big-picture outlook
ONE Wing brings precision, attentiveness, discipline, tension, detail-orientation

Other Labels: Dreamer, Harmonizer, Pacifier, Peacemaker, Facilitator
Challenges: apathy, lethargy, repressed anger, irritability, stubbornness, passive aggression

SUBTYPES		
Self-preservation	**Sexual**	**Social**
A R C H E T Y P E S *Practical Person, Patient Endurer, Steady Worker, Sensible Detailer, Nature Lover, Unassuming Doer, Contented Putterer, Appreciator of Small Things, Enjoyer of Routines, Person of the Land, Wandering Nomad, Natural Herdsman, Itinerant Crop Picker, Member of the Tribe, Cowhand, Gardener, Herbalist, Manual Laborer, Sidekick, Peasant, Servant, Serf*	*Idealistic Dreamer, Spinner of Tales, Fantasy Writer, Mystical Devotee, Wistful Soul, Lover of Love, Tabula Rasa, Forgiving Companion, Enjoyer of Pleasure, Nature Worshipper, Meditator, Animal Lover, Surrendered Lover, Personal Valet, Devoted Servant or Retainer, Accepting Listener, Receptive Friend, Gentle Helper, Massage Therapist, Body Worker, Natural Healer*	*Willing Participant, Community Member, Natural Mediator, Calm Harmonizer, Blender of Energies, Dispassionate Go-Between, Patient Peacemaker, Consensus Builder, Family Counselor, Unassuming Facilitator, Unintentional Networker, Activity Coordinator, Team Coach, Athletic Referee, Gentle Pacifist, Low-key Leader, Cooperative Team Member*
F I L M **T H E M E S** **Ordinary people** persist despite many troubles (*The Gods Must be Crazy, The Magnificent Seven/The Seven Samurai, Sounder, Heartland, The Milagro Beanfield War, Himalaya, Coal Miner's Daughter, One Day in the Life of Ivan Denisovich*) **Passive person** finds out what he really wants in life (*The Accidental Tourist, Pleasantville, Cider House Rules, The Graduate, Moonlight Mile, The Shipping News*) **Ordinary life** is rich with treasure (slice-of-life flicks like *The Straight Story, Harry & Tonto,, It's a Wonderful Life, The Trip to Bountiful, At First Sight, Ladies in Lavender*) **Animal teachers** remind us of what really matters in life (*The Bear, Free Willy, The Incredible Journey, Sea Biscuit, March of the Penguins*) **Coming of age** experiences transform children into young adults (*The Blue Lagoon, The Man in the Moon, The Yearling, Fly Away Home, Secondhand Lions, Where the Red Fern Grows*)	**Magical/mystical side** of life is celebrated (*Willy Wonka & the Chocolate Factory*, early *Harry Potter* films, *Big, The Chronicles of Narnia, The Hobbit, K-Pax, Cocoon, Lost Horizon, FairyTale: A True Story*) **Plucky young competitors** win our hearts (*Karate Kid, National Velvet, The Black Stallion, Akeelah & the Bee*) **Childhood innocence** inspires & rejuvenates us (*Little Buddha*, Shirley Temple flicks, *Oliver, A Christmas Carol, The Diary of Anne Frank*) **Gentle or innocent romance** brings sweetness into life (*The Notebook, Murphy's Romance, Heartsounds, The Magic of Ordinary Days, Sarah: Plain & Tall, At First Sight, The Blue Lagoon, The Ghost & Mrs. Muir*) **A mysterious event** changes lives (*Agnes of God, Bernadette of Lourdes, Picnic at Hanging Rock, Bee Season*) **Deeper mysteries** are revealed through spiritual practice (*Spring/Summer/Winter/Fall, Why Has Bodhi Dharma Left for the East?*), experiences in nature (*Nell, Little Big Man, Whaler-ider, Walkabout*), ritual (*Baraka*) or unusually intense experiences (*Beyond Rangoon, Lord of the Rings*)	**Humble spiritual practitioners** acquire widespread influence (*Seven Years in Tibet, Kundun, Gandhi, Maharishi Mahesh Yogi: Sage for a New Generation, Darshan: The Embrace*) **Congenial group projects** inspire & fulfill (*Greenfingers, Calendar Girls, Young@ Heart, How to Make an American Quilt, Buena Vista Social Club, The Cup*) **Peace lovers** take a stand against war (*Sergeant York, Friendly Persuasion, Gandhi, The Conscientious Objector*) or fighters discover peace is better than war (*All Quiet on the Western Front, The Burmese Harp*) **Harmony-seeker** tries for peace at any price (*sex, lies, and videotape; Neville Chamberlain, Appeasement, and the British Road to War* [book]) **Unassertive person** learns how to lead or speak up for others (*Pleasantville, Cider House Rules, The Mahabharata, Mr. Smith Goes to Washington*) **Ordinary heroes** stand up for what they think is right (*The Hiding Place, Weapons of the Spirit, Pay It Forward*)

out of long-standing patterns of automaticity and get in touch with what they actually want out of life.

Although the center of Point 9 may be a neutral place, as we move towards the wings, we feel effects of the fire on either side. Nines with an Eight wing have a quality of imperturbability that can make them seem distant or impassive, but when sufficiently roused, they can become surprisingly belligerent and "in your face." They don't like sudden change and cannot be forced to do things against their will; they defeat their opponents by acquiescing but passively resisting. When passive resistance doesn't work, they may go on the offensive, like Eights. But when contented, they have a very grounded quality that makes them attractive to individuals who are less grounded and in need of stability. Like Fives, they're observant, but they tend to be more tuned into nature and natural cycles.

Nines with a One wing are more active, irritable, and restless; they often have an "antsy" quality that needs to be channeled into physical activity, especially activities that take them into natural settings. One of my friends with this wing likes to spend one day a week doing habitat restoration; she also hikes and canoes. But One-winged Nines can become especially tense or anxious when confronted with personal decisions. They're also more likely to distract themselves from anxiety by getting busy with some project. Once engaged, they easily get lost in the details of a task and lose track of time (where Nines with the other wing will simply "forget" stuff they don't want to think about).

Nines tend to be cooperative children who don't give much trouble to the adults in their lives, although they occasionally surprise people with a sudden and unexpected stubborn streak around things that really matter to them. It's actually a good thing that they have this streak, because they need to occasionally remind other people (and perhaps themselves) that they have definite preferences and cannot be treated as doormats. Nine children need to be drawn out and encouraged to think for themselves, not simply to go along with the wishes of strong-minded others.

Searle identifies four Nine genres: fantasy, magical realism, sword and sorcery, and fairy tales. All these themes are related; and they definitely point us to the imaginative, storytelling nature of the Nine. They also point us to the escapism that is possible at this place on the enneagram, escapism that enables us to remain in an undifferentiated state of consciousness (instead of moving out into the world where we can have the kind of experiences that facilitate individuation). The waking up needed at Point 9 involves the movement away from fantasy into action, so that an individual progresses to Point 1, Point 2, and so forth, all the way around the enneagram circle. (This doesn't mean that Nines have to abandon their childlike spontaneity or love of fantasy—just that they have to avoid using fantasy as an escape.)

There are a number of other genres we can identify at Point 9: slice-of-life themes, inspirational themes, nature themes, coming-of-age themes & themes involving waking up, stories about the power of innocence & receptivity, themes involving peace and peace-motivated social action, stories about passive resistance, stories involving musical themes (especially music that unites and harmonizes, e.g., *We Are the World*), themes involving healing and wholeness, and morality tales about the price of passivity. The common thread in all these themes is the role of harmony in daily life and how to remain in harmony in a way that does not prevent us from individuating.

When we're children, we're able to accept our lives as they are because we know nothing else. When we begin to grow up, we become aware of other possibilities in life, which can make us dissatisfied with our current lot in life. Growing up means we also have to deal with complexity, make decisions, and live with the consequences of what we say and do. And this explains the archetypal tendency at Point 9 to remain innocent (to keep life so simple and uncomplicated that we never have to grapple with its stressful uncertainties and complexities). It also explains why many people of all types idealize this state of innocence: because it represents a time in life (like childhood) or a state of imagined consciousness (like enlightenment) that doesn't require us to be aware of life's limitations and our own limitations as human beings.

It's always easier to live within limitation when we don't know what we're missing. Once we start waking up, limitation seems much more painful. But if we refuse to become conscious, this is like symbolically remaining at Point 9 on the enneagram forever and never moving around the circle, never making the Hero's Journey.

So the task at Point 9 is to avoid getting too attached to the known and familiar, too comfortable in our routines. Complacency can lull us to sleep like Dorothy and her friends who fall asleep in the field of poppies on the way to the city of Oz. Fortunately, for most of us, this kind of complacency doesn't last very long; something in life prods us awake and makes it impossible to go back to sleep again.

¤ ¤ ¤

SELF-PRESERVATION NINE THEMES. This subtype focuses our attention on the ordinary in various ways, showing us both its happy moments (*The Straight Story, Harry and Tonto*) and its trials (*Coal Miner's Daughter, One Day in the Life of Ivan Denisovich*). There's often an emphasis on nature and our relationship with it (*Walkabout*) or what animals can teach us about life (*March of the Penguins, The Bear, Winged Migration*).

And it's at SP Nine that we see the theme of waking up and become aware of ourselves as individuals (*The Accidental Tourist, Pleasantville, Moonlight Mile*). The problem of identity was a big one for the Sixties generation, which is probably why 1967's *The Graduate* became such a big hit—because it so poignantly captured the mood of the times by following the trials and tribulations of a recent university graduate who hasn't the foggiest idea about what he wants out of life.

Benjamin Braddock (a youthful Dustin Hoffman) is a young man without a future. (As one online account put it, "his face has a blank, expressionless, enervated, zombie-like look.") Returning to his parent's house after graduation, all he does all day is loll around his parents' pool, killing time—that is, until he's lulled out of his complacency by the amorous advances of the wife of his father's business partner, Mrs. Robinson (Anne Bancroft). Although he initially resists, her persistence pays off, and they begin an affair at a local hotel.

Although Benjamin enjoys the sex, the seaminess of the affair soon gets to him, and he begins to wake up: while he might not know exactly what he wants in life, this sure isn't it. But the real wake-up call comes when Mrs. Robinson's daughter (Katherine Ross) returns from college. He's pressured by his own parents to ask her out, and discovers real love for the first time. Finally, he knows exactly what he wants: to marry Elaine.

Of course, the situation is a mess; Mrs. Robinson wants him gone, and he blurts out the truth of the affair to Elaine, afraid she'll hear it from her mother. But at some point it looks like things might work out—until Elaine's parents swoop her up and take her off to Santa Barbara to marry someone respectable.

So the big question is: Does Benjamin love Elaine enough to fight for her? It turns out he does. But he has a series of obstacles to overcome before he can have his heart's desire, including hopelessness. He arrives too late at the wedding, just as she's about to kiss the groom. In a very famous movie scene, we see him standing in the church loft, pounding on the glass while crying out her name, utterly beside himself. It's in that moment that everything changes. And it changes because Benjamin knows what he wants and is 100% committed to going after it.

The Graduate is the ironic title of a film that presents us with a protagonist who has garnered the highest honors in his educational career and yet obviously knows nothing about himself, other people, or the world. The only thing he knows is the fake world of his parents and their friends (one of whom suggestively whispers the word "plastics" in his ear as a promising field). It's his love for Elaine that catapults him out of this sterile world and into real life.

Moonlight Mile is a newer version of a similar story made about 30 years later, which also features Dustin Hoffman, this time as a father whose daughter has died, leaving him and his wife, Susan Sarandon, with only his future son-in-law

Nate (Jake Gyllenhaal) for company. (Ironically enough, Hoffman is now the parent who represents the forces of convention.) Although both parents are more well-meaning than the adults in *The Graduate*, they somehow can't seem to help but want to take on Nate as a "daughter substitute," which he in his grief initially allows. But in the long run, Nate does the same thing that Benjamin did thirty years before: he wakes up, asserts himself, and becomes his own man.

Harry and Tonto and *The Straight Story* are slice-of-life films that show us another side of SP Nine: the ability to appreciate the joys of ordinary life. They both feature older gentlemen who have done a lot of living. As a result, they know how to appreciate life's small pleasures. But they're not quite done with living just yet. In *Harry and Tonto*, Art Carney plays an elderly New Yorker whose building is condemned, thus forcing him to move to his son's house in suburbia. This doesn't work out too well, so Harry decides to take off on a cross-country odyssey with his cat, Tonto, where he meets up with all sorts of interesting characters.

In *The Straight Story*, based on the true story of Alvin Straight, an elderly Iowan in frail health wants to make peace with his terminally-ill brother. The only problem is that his brother lives 300 miles away and Alvin has no money and poor eyesight, so he can't drive a car. So he decides on an audacious plan: to ride his old lawn mower to visit his brother, sleeping in fields along the way. His journey, like Harry's, is necessarily leisurely, both because of the nature of the journey and the vicissitudes of old age.

Straight is played by veteran actor and stuntman, Richard Farnsworth. Like Straight, Farnsworth had to move slowly, because he had terminal bone cancer and was in a lot of pain at the time of filming. His own real-life situation brings depth to Straight's Iowan odyssey.

In *The Accidental Tourist*, we see what happens to Nines who fall into the habit of passively going through the motions of life instead of actively living it. Macon Leary (William Hurt) is a writer of travel guides for reluctant business travelers. The purpose of the guides is to minimize the impact of foreign travel, so it will seem as though the traveler never really left home. As one of Macon's readers remarks to him, "Traveling with *The Accidental Tourist* is just like traveling in a cocoon."

And that's exactly the problem: the theme of the guides is not too different from the theme Macon is actually living out in his own life. Although he's recently lost a son to a random act of violence, he somehow doesn't seem to feel the shock of his son's death. His wife (Kathleen Turner), however, is devastated, which is why she decides to leave him, observing that she's beginning to become like him, withdrawing from life. He protests that it's not so bad. But she disagrees, saying that "there's something so muffled about the way that you experience things, it's as if you were trying to slip through life unchanged." He protests that it's not true; he says he "endures" and tries to "hold steady." But she knows otherwise and departs, leaving him alone in their rambling old house.*

Fortunately, fate intervenes to open a window in Macon's life. First he meets Muriel (Gina Davis), an unconventional but attractive veterinary technician. Macon is so emotionally unresponsive that he doesn't even realize that Muriel is flirting with him. Then he has a dream about his son, who says he's not really dead (unlike his dad!). Next, Macon breaks his leg in a way which forces him to love return to live with his humorously quirky family, so he's no longer alone. Then Muriel says she wants to help him with his dog problems (the dog is aggressive with strangers), and he reluctantly agrees.

The rest of the film explores Macon's gradual awakening, mostly because he's falling in love with Muriel . Things get lively when his wife (seeing his resurrection) gets interested in resurrecting their marriage. Now Macon has to do the most difficult thing in the world: deciding what he really wants and pursing it wholeheartedly.

◻ ◻ ◻

---

* In real life, Kathleen Turner is a Three and plays this part as a Three leaning heavily into her Four wing, because of grief. For a Three whose grief has finally put her in touch with her deep feelings—perhaps for the first time—the decision to go numb would be a disaster.

SEXUAL NINE THEMES. Although SX Nines are typically low-key, the energy of this subtype is full of mystery and subtle intrigue. It bespeaks another dimension of life which we do not fully comprehend. So the themes most obviously associated with this subtype are the ones that Judith Searle mentions: those involving magic or fairy tales (*The Chronicles of Narnia, The Hobbit, The Lord of the Rings,* and early Harry Potter films*) and magical realism (*Willy Wonka & the Chocolate Factory, K-Pax, Big,* and *Cocoon).*

But there's more to this subtype than fairy tale magic: there's *real-life* magic, mystery, and synchronicity. And fortunately, there are films that take these subtle dimensions of life seriously—films about nature mysticism (*Baraka, Whalerider,* and *Walkabout*), religious mysticism (*Bernadette of Lourdes* and *Agnes of God*), and mysterious experiences associated with youthful purity and receptivity (*Picnic at Hanging Rock,* TV's *Psychic Kids,* and *Bee Season*).

Bee Season shows us how easy it is to overlook ordinary mysticism in the search for something grander and more prestigious. It's about a family where all but one of the family members have mystical tendencies. But the only person officially recognized as spiritual (mostly by himself) is Saul, the father (played by Richard Gere). Saul is a self-absorbed Jewish professor of religious studies, who prides himself on his special knowledge of Jewish mysticism and the Cabala. He's also a Three with intellectual pretensions who not only overestimates his own abilities but underestimates everybody else's—especially his family's. When his very ordinary-seeming daughter Eliza (a Nine) starts winning spelling bees, he's delighted, especially when he realizes she does it via some sort of mystical apprehension. To him, this is a sign that she's destined to be the esoteric practitioner that *he* always wanted to be. So he begins to tutor her in Cabalistic lore, to the exclusion of all else. She allows this, but only because it's the first time he's ever paid any real attention to her. Meanwhile, the wife and son begin to drift off into their own

---

* I'm distinguishing early from later Harry Potter films because the earlier ones have a more innocent, Nine-like aura while the later ones are darker and more fear-inspiring (bringing in more SX Five and SX Six energy).

worlds, but Dad is too self-absorbed to notice. It's only after Eliza calmly and deliberately misspells a word at the National Spelling Bee Finals that he begins to realize that the mystical path is something private and personal, not a trophy for public display.

Another SX Nine theme involves the power of innocent love and how it can bring something wonderful into the world. In *The Blue Lagoon,* two children are marooned on a desert island with a crusty old seaman who teaches them basic survival skills before succumbing to the effects of too much grog. They grow up in an idyllic setting, innocent of the ways of the world. As teens, they grow irritable as hormones rage, but eventually they discover how to resolve the problem. But they're surprised when their "solution" produces a baby!

While the film isn't terribly deep nor the acting memorable by 21st century standards, its images are primordial and the cinematography breathtaking: seeing the young lovers in paradise evokes the image of Adam and Eve before the Fall. But of course they don't remain in paradise forever: at the very end, they're rescued. And this rescue will obviously take them out of their simpler world of easy survival and into a world of greater social complexity.

It's easy to idealize the world of *The Blue Lagoon,* because the scenery is so breathtaking. But it's a good thing the film was made prior to the kick-off of the 21st century TV hit *Survivor,* because such idealized images wouldn't have the same impact they did in 1980. Diehard *Survivor* fans know that spearing fish is not really effortless and that sleeping on the floor of a tropical hut is fraught with perils. (The actors in *The Blue Lagoon* look better after six years on the island than *Survivor* contestants look after one month!)

The back-to-nature idea is a beautiful ideal, but one that must give way to something else, because no one can remain in a state of innocence forever. Even before their return to civilization, the *Blue Lagoon* couple discover that life isn't all peaches and cream (or bananas and coconut milk). They'd been told as children never to go to the other side of the island, because the Boogie Man lives there. As young adults, they discover why: it's because natives from neighboring islands use the site for human sacrifice. (Even in paradise, we can never completely get away from the Shadow.)

At First Sight shows the loss of a different kind of innocence. It's about what happens to Virgil, a Nine-ish blind man (Val Kilmer), who falls in love with a sighted woman. When we first see Virgil, he's a gifted massage therapist who's apparently content with his life in a small mountain community where he gives massages at the local resort. He falls in love with Amy, one of his clients, who's an ambitious architect from the Big Apple (a probable Three). She eventually talks him into getting an operation that might restore his sight.

The operation is technically a success, but he can't see properly because he lacks any reference point for sight. The sudden explosion of visual percepts produces sensory overload. (The story is loosely based on an actual case study of Oliver Sacks, so these perceptual problems are real, not imaginary.)

The film focuses on how Virgil makes the painful transition into sightedness and gains greater self-understanding and independence along the way. But as his simple life becomes more complex, so does his relationship; the couple begins to experience problems that foreshadow a breakup. But at least he has his sight, right? Not quite. The effects of the operation turn out not to be permanent. He is gradually going blind.

By now, Virgil's once-quiet life is thoroughly shaken up. He can't go back and he can't go forward. Retreating from NYC to his home town, he gets to really know his sister for the first time. He mends their relationship and comes to terms with his situation. Returning to New York, he finds he can live as a blind man without the need to retreat from life. He sums up his journey like this:

> As a blind man, I think that I see a lot better than I did when I was sighted, because I don't really think we see with our eyes. I think we live in darkness when we don't really see what's real about ourselves—or about others, or about life....when you see what's real about yourself, you see a lot. And you don't need eyes for that.

In Hallmark's *The Magic of Ordinary Days*, we see another kind of awakening, this one involving a move not *into* the city, but *out* of it. At the film's start, we see an elegant young Denver woman with gloved hands on a train; it looks like the 1940s. Where is she going, and why? We soon find out that she's become pregnant out-of-wedlock. To save the family from shame, her father has arranged for her to marry a farmer in rural Colorado.

Given the times, she meekly accepts the arrangement, but is disheartened to find herself married to a farmer in a house without a phone that's eight miles from the nearest neighbor's. Previously an anthropology graduate student, she initially feels like a fish out of water. But she gradually discovers that life in the country is not as tiresome as it first appears. She meets both friendly neighbors and Japanese internees who used to be students at UCLA with whom to share ideas. When she starts finding arrowheads on the property, she realizes it may have anthropological treasures waiting to be unearthed. But most surprising is the way she gradually falls in love with her husband, who shows himself to be capable of a kind of sensitivity she didn't expect from someone with his background. (For example, when he learns that she loves anthropology, he goes out and buys a book on it, secretly studying up, so he can talk with her about something she loves.)

Her husband's attentiveness to her needs and obvious efforts to make her feel at home bring the kind of magic into her life that she never experienced before. Gradually, something unlikely transpires: she not only falls in love with her husband, but also his way of life.

Although this kind of theme can easily become overly-sentimentalized (focusing too much attention on the "Hallmark moments" in life), *The Magic of Ordinary Days* does a particularly good job at demonstrating the power of love to bring forth the very real seeds of magic that exist in everyday life; similar films include *Sarah: Plain and Tall* and *Anne of Green Gables*.

Beyond Rangoon tells the story of Laura Bowman, a vacant young woman (Patricia Arquette) touring Burma with her sister. We soon discover the reason for her emotional flatness: the horrific murder of her husband and son. Her lack of interest masks her inner pain. When Laura's passport is stolen, she has to remain behind in Burma.

Her inner journey begins when she witnesses the courage of female Nobel Peace Price winner Aung San Suu Kyi, who leads a peace march against the military dictatorship ruling the country. Soon after, Laura leaves the capital, embarking on a rural odyssey which is both spiritual and emotional. It's not an easy journey (because she gets caught up in the sufferings of the people and the violence of the brutal 1988 crackdown against the pro-democracy movement). But in seeing the suffering of others—and their courage and willingness to go on—she gains the strength to go on herself.

At one point, when she's having dinner with a group of students who have welcomed her into their home, she discovers they've all suffered great hardship because of their pro-democracy activities: "Looking around that table, I realized that they'd all been injured by fate. But they could still laugh. They all seemed so strong, perhaps because they were able to share their grief." Realizing she's not alone in her grief gives her the courage to heal.

(This film, based loosely upon a true story, had a positive effect on the pro-democracy movement in Burma. Soon after its release, Aung San Suu Kyi, who had been under house arrest, was released; in a BBC interview, she thanked the film's producers for telling the world about what was happening in her country.)

¤ ¤ ¤

SOCIAL NINE THEMES. If SP Nine is the place of ordinary life and SX Nine is the place of harmonious union, SOC Nine is the place of social communion. It's where we come together for the sake of coming together—for the simple joy of being with others. It's also where we begin to understand our relationship with the world: how to participate in something bigger than ourselves while still remaining an individual.

This theme of becoming an individual while also developing a social conscience shows up in many coming-of-age films, which are often about young Nines. Two of my favorite coming-of-age films involve real-life Nine Toby Maguire as a young person trying to find himself and his place in the world. In *Pleasantville*, Maguire plays a teenager who fantasizes about asking girls out on a date but actually spends all his time lost in re-runs of *Pleasantville*, a TV series cheerily reminiscent of *Father Knows Best* or

Leave It to Beaver. When a quirky TV repairman (Don Knotts) gives him a TV remote that transports him and his twin sister (Reese Witherspoon) into the happy but bland world of Pleasantville, the two teens end up assuming the identities of the two kids on the show, Bud and Mary Sue.

Initially, the town is in black-and-white (symbolically reflecting the over-simplified lives of its inhabitants). It's clear that the townspeople are sleepwalking through life, never changing, growing, or reflecting deeply on anything. As normal teenagers, "Bud" and "Mary Sue"—finding the ongoing blandness unbearable—begin to stir things up. As people wake up, the town changes: one day, a single rose in the Pleasantville park turns red, signaling a significant change in the town: its inhabitants are beginning to wake up. Each time a person crosses a crucial threshold in consciousness, he or she becomes full-color instead of black-and-white.

But for some reason, Bud doesn't change. He remains a black-and-white caricature. At first, this doesn't bother him. But as time passes, he can't help but wonder why he's left out. He's been helping others to change but can't seem to help himself.

Meanwhile, not all the citizenry of Pleasantville are happy about the changes in the town; a rift develops between people who are black-and-white and those who are in full-color. Ordinances are passed against using real colors to paint and signs begin to appear in shops saying "No Coloreds Allowed."

About this time, Bud sees his adoptive Pleasantville mom (who is now in color) being harassed by a group of belligerent black-and-white youths. For the first time in his life, he gets involved and stands up for somebody else's rights, making the bullies back down. Afterwards, she throws him her makeup mirror so he can see what's happened: he's no longer black and white. Bud goes on to assume a leadership role in fighting for the rights of people to expand their horizons, becoming the voice of social conscience for the town. When he eventually returns to his real life as David, he's no longer the unfocused kid he was when he left.

In *The Cider House Rules*, Maguire plays Homer Wells, a young man whose entire life has been spent at an isolated orphanage in the Maine countryside during the

1930s and 40s. Dr. Larch, the aging doctor who runs the place (Michael Caine), delivers the babies of women who want to put them up for adoption. But he has a secret and illegal vocation as well: performing illegal abortions on humanitarian grounds. He teaches Homer everything he knows about both delivering babies and performing abortions. But Homer is against abortion; he's not willing to assist Larch in performing these procedures.

Homer is also not as interested in "doctoring" as Dr. Larch would like; Larch is an aging SOC Seven who's grooming Homer to be his successor at the orphanage and is not above forging a fake medical certificate so Homer will have formal credentials for that purpose. (That's one reason we know Larch is a Seven—he's unconventional in his thinking and only cares about what he perceives to be the welfare of his charges, not the dictates of an unenlightened society.)

But Homer doesn't want a medical degree on a platter. He wants to see the world— or at least more of the world than just the orphanage. So when the opportunity presents itself, he hitches a ride to the Maine Coast, where he sees the ocean for the first time. He works in an apple orchard with a group of itinerant black pickers whose inability to read means they can't decipher the rules posted on Cider House barracks.

Homer likes the simplicity of his life as an apple-picker, but things gradually get more complicated. First he falls in love, but it's with a woman whose fiancé is off to war. This experience helps him begin to realize that life can't be lived simply by referring to hard and fast rules. Later, he discovers that the daughter of the apple-picking foreman is pregnant—and unfortunately, the baby is her father's. Homer knows he needs to break his own rules, and performs a compassionate abortion. Soon after, he discovers that Dr. Larch has died.

So Homer returns to the orphanage to assume the care-taking role that Dr. Larch prepared for him. At some point before returning to the orphanage, we see him reading the last of the Cider House rules, all of which turn out to be pretty trivial and irrelevant. Neither he nor the pickers need such pre-set rules: what they need—as one picker remarks—is to learn how to *make their own rules every day*. That's the point of the story. And it's also a focal point at SOC Nine, the place where we learn how to take personal and social responsibility for ourselves.

One of the social groups most associated with SOC Nine is the musical group, especially the choral group, because choral singing is an activity where people come together to literally create harmony. But even a seemingly tame activity like group singing can wake us up, as Bob Cilman and Judith Sharpe found out after establishing the choral group Young At Heart in 1982. It was originally designed to be a recreational activity for seniors at the Walter Salvo House, a housing project for the elderly in Northampton, Massachusetts. At the start, the chorus performed old vaudeville songs, something they liked and knew how to do. But one night, one of their members, Diamond Lil, stood up and performed Manfred Mann's *Do-Wha-Diddy*, bringing the house down. A new genre was born: an elderly chorus specializing in rock, punk, and disco songs.

The film *Young@Heart* follows their rigorous rehearsal schedule prior to two performances, one in a nearby prison and the other in the local concert hall. We watch the singers (aged 81–92) struggle good-humoredly with strange lyrics and bizarre rhythms, determined to persevere. Their perseverance plays off; the concerts are wonderful, despite the sudden deaths of two of their long-time members . At the jailhouse concert, we see hardened criminals cry while listening to a solo of Bob Dylan's *Forever Young*; one wonders whether the concert might have the power to change their perspective on life a little.

The idea is not so far-fetched; *Greenfingers* shows us exactly how criminals can be transformed by activities that allow them to see life from a new vantage point—in this case, the vantage point of gardening. Not surprisingly, the action takes place in England, a place where gardening has a special place in peoples' hearts. The film is loosely based on the real-life story of a convict group who become sufficiently skilled to produce a winning entry for the Hampton Court Palace Flower Show—probably the most prestigious gardening competition in the world .

In *Calendar Girls,* another adaptation of a real situation, English matrons raise money for the local hospital through an innovative approach: posing nude (tastefully, of course!) for their annual calender. In *The Cup* (yet another film based on a true story), we see a community of Tibetan monks, some of whom are just teens. When one youthful monk is caught sneaking out to watch soccer at the local tavern, instead of punishing him, the older monks allow him to procure a satellite dish so the entire community can watch the 1998 finals between France and Brazil. In the documentary *Buena Vista Social Club*, a group of elderly but talented Cuban musicians are re-assembled to revive interest in traditional Cuban music. And in *How to Make an American Quilt,* a group of older women congregate to construct a marriage quilt for a younger woman while reminiscing about their lives. (It's not a true story, but it certainly could be!)

It's interesting that so many of these SOC 9 stories involve people who are middle-aged or older. Even *The Cup*—which features a teenage protagonist—takes place in a community where the median age is well over 30. Acquiring a little life experience appears to take the edge off our conflicts and helps us see past them, so that when we come together, we don't just do so to get something done, but to experience a sense of communion with a group, an effort, or an energy larger than ourselves.

When we start out in life, we experience a sense of union with all life, but this is because our consciousness is not yet differentiated. During our teens and twenties, we acquire the ability to think independently. As we age, we discover how to combine the two: how to be an individual while connecting with something greater than the self. As Sufi teacher Llewellyn Vaughn-Lee puts it, the oneness we experience as we mature "is not the undifferentiated oneness of unconsciousness...rather, it is the oneness that reveals our individuality within the whole and shows how our unique note belongs to the symphony of life."*

Knowing that we are truly connected with life—and that *we will always be connected with life, no matter what*—can give us the courage to step out of unconsciousness at Point 0 and begin the journey of individuation. It's because we are always within the

---

* *Working with Oneness*, p. 44.

circle of wholeness that we can allow ourselves to try new things, to make mistakes, and to learn. It's an important lesson not only for Nines, as all of the stories in this chapter reveal, because it's when the Nine stands up for herself as an individual that life really opens up for her. Instead of feeling less connected with herself, other people, and nature, she actually feels *more* connected—more in tune with everything around her.

But the lesson of individuality-in-oneness is also for all the types: the more we discover our uniqueness, the more we discover how much we are the same—and how minor are the divisions that create the illusion of separation.

20

Epilogue

The only journey is the journey within.
– Rainer Maria Rilke

WHEN I FIRST BEGAN this book, I didn't know how it would end. All I knew is that I wanted to write a book that would help people locate themselves in life, probably because I spent much of my youth feeling that I didn't know who I was or where I belonged. I tried to model myself after people I knew, but that didn't work very well. Then I used the trial-and-error approach of trying out various jobs, lifestyles, etc., to see what felt right. This worked but was not very efficient. Also, it was often a painful way to learn.

I remember seeking a job once as a fry cook when I didn't really feel all that committed to the work. The interviewer picked up on my ambivalence and asked me, "What is it that you really want to do?" The question stunned me; nobody had ever asked me that in an interview. I tried to come up with an answer, but it must not have been very good because I didn't get the job. I got other jobs from less discerning employers, but none of them offered much in the way of long-term prospects. Even if they had, it wouldn't have done me much good. I needed to understand some things about myself first.

When I found the enneagram, I found a tool for self-understanding. It helped me make sense of patterns in my life and in the lives of others—to see the import of the roles we play, the paths we walk, and the archetypal themes that we enact in our lives. Enneagram work helped me feel more self-accepting, confident, and relaxed about living. I realized that a lot of things I'd looked upon as character flaws were tendencies that are natural for people of my type. As a Four, it's natural for me to notice what's missing in a situation, especially what's missing emotionally. It's also natural to look for signs of approval from others (because I'm an image type) and to hide feelings of emotional vulnerability (because I'm the "never-let-'em-see-you-sweat" SP subtype). Being an SP Four also means I am most productive working on my own, and doing creative work in a physically attractive environment (either at home or in an equally compelling location). That's why working in offices so often shut me down.

What a relief it was to understand how natural these tendencies are, and to let go of the need to beat myself up for being the way I am. What a relief to know that I didn't need to be like my parents (a Six and a Three). I'd been trying to model myself after them, and it just wasn't working.

How many of us have done the same—adopted a model for living that's based not on our inner nature but on the models we inherited from friends, family, or our culture? It's easy enough to do. Unless we have an alternative model—the kind we might get from studying a system like the enneagram.

It was great to let go of those models and find ones that better fit my personality type. Once I stopped being so self-critical (connection to One) and trying to be more defensively extroverted than I really am (connection to Two), I started noticing little things about myself that I really liked.

Enneagram work also made me more genuinely tolerant of other people. Although I'd embraced tolerance as a virtue (at least in my mind), real tolerance was hard for me, because I secretly believed that my point of view was the best! I thought, "If only everybody would just be authentic, the world would be a better place." I felt the same way about beauty and artistry; if everybody cared about them the way I did, life would be better.

Both these sentiments may be true, but everybody is not a Four, and the world would not be a better place if populated solely by Fours. All the types have something to contribute.

While the enneagram can't solve all our problems in life, it *can* enable us to see them from a new perspective: less as limitations and more as opportunities for growth. It can also help us discover our path in life, especially when we understand how each of the nine core motivations can be expressed in three different subtype arenas. We then have 27 potential blueprints for development, each of which has many diverse archetypal themes and sub-themes to explore. My focus in this book has been on pointing out these archetypal themes/subtypes, to give the reader a jumping-off point for further explorations.

But my focus has also been on providing a rationale for seeing the enneagram from what I call the Positive Enneagram perspective. By *positive*, I don't mean "nicey-nicey"; I mean seeing the glass as half full instead of half empty. The idea is to learn how to take a positive approach in negative situations—not by denying, ignoring, or hating the negativity, but by *working with it*. That's what Jungian Shadow work and Hillman's soul work is all about, and that's why the book's subtitle alludes to a *soul* perspective.

Darkness is all around us; it's inside of us, too. We can't really get away from it. But we don't actually have to. Instead, we can use it to grow. I recently had a dream that brought this home in a rather forceful way:

> *I'm with friends in a dark manor. In an old trunk, I discover a treasure, which is like the philosopher's stone. But I have to get away from the evil character who lives in the manor. As the dream goes on, the atmosphere of fear and dread continues to build. Finally, a man begins to chase me, determined to kill me by stomping me into the mud. I am so scared and confused that I don't resist. I let him stomp on me. I look up to see the evil character sitting on a wall, laughing in a horrible way. He looks like the devil.*

When I woke up from this nightmare, I was shaking with fear. All I wanted was to forget these images and think about something else. But I realized this was a bad idea; these energies were inside of me, and I needed to understand them.

After I regained my wits, I realized two things. One was that it's a risky move to steal from the devil, even when what you're taking doesn't really belong to him! The second is that the devil defeats us not by chasing us himself but by creating so much fear and confusion that we lose our bearings and allow ourselves to be defeated.

I learned something else from that dream, because I worked with it using the Jungian technique of active imagination (dialoguing with the dream character in an effort to bring about a sense of psychic resolution). For this to work, I had to let go of the "good versus evil" idea, so I could work with the dream in a non-reactive way. I cleared my mind, and tried to focus on integration rather than opposition.

But it didn't quite work. The figure snarled, "You're not going to integrate *me*!!!"

So I backed off.

Next, I saw myself throwing its face far away into the woods, where it burst into a flame, creating a big cloud of black smoke. This was the dualistic solution: to throw the devil as far away as possible so I didn't have to think about it.

But I wasn't really happy with this idea; I knew this wasn't a satisfactory solution. So I waited, trying to decide what to do next. I decided to meditate, and soon saw myself getting down on my knees (in my mind's eye) and praying for purification. When it felt right, I envisioned the devil figure once again. Then I respectfully asked the dream character whether I could approach it.

The answer was yes. To move towards the figure wasn't easy, because it radiated a repellent energy. But I put aside these feelings and tried to avoid reacting. I was surprised when horror began to give way to pity. While I didn't exactly like this character, I couldn't help but love it. Not because it was lovable, but because it needed love so badly.

I communicated my wish to hold this being in my heart. It was suspicious and did not agree. But it did nothing unpleasant, either, so I just stayed there with it for a while. Later, I realized I didn't need to integrate this energy, just to neutralize my reaction to it. That way, it no longer had the power to terrorize and defeat me.

¤ ¤ ¤

A DREAM LIKE THIS can be disturbing. Because it occurred in deep sleep (and would perhaps be called a night terror), I was strangely groggy when I awoke, even though I was terrified. But my grogginess made me receptive, so I could engage in the active imagination exercise described above.

Shortly afterward, I had another dream in which I saw a white peacock descend into a pitch-black cellar. When it opened its wings, it illuminated the darkness. The wings looked like tendrils of Belgian lace.

Dreams like these attune us to our inner world, where we find both wonder and horror. Doing active imagination and sharing dreams with others can help us attune to the realities that exist beyond the narrow band of ego consciousness that we experience every day. Enneagram work also gives us an approach for becoming aware of inner realities, especially our core motivation. Knowing the 27 subtypes provides an even finer-grained understanding of who we are and what path may suit us.

My approach in this book has been to look at the enneagram from an archetypal perspective, a perspective that allows us to experience ourselves as players in life's larger drama. Although there's always a risk associated with envisioning life from a dramatic perspective (because it can create a sense of hubris), the danger is diminished if we realize that we're not the central character in life's drama, but just one of a very large cast of characters!

As I noted in Chapter 10, there's a natural drama in life that has nothing to do with personal self-aggrandizement; it's the kind of energy that enabled J. G. Bennett to call his cosmological work *The Dramatic Universe*. This drama has a quality of tautness or tension that focuses our awareness (that brings us to *attention*—that helps us *attend* to what we are doing). It's something we naturally experience when deeply absorbed in creative work or focused on a difficult but intriguing mental problem. It's also what we experience when we attend a truly spellbinding dramatic performance. This is the drama that brings something truly splendid into life, even if it's just for a passing moment. It can light up that moment in a way that can last a lifetime—and can bring real magic into the world.

This kind of magic isn't just for stage and screen, it's for real people living real lives. It's available for everyone because it comes from the archetypes—literally, the *arch-* or *"big" types*—associated with each enneagram type and subtype. These archetypes give us the energy to "live big," whether we're a public personality like Oprah or someone shelving books in the library. As always, it's not what we do but *how we do it*—and whether how we do it fully embodies who we are inside. When the work flows out of our inner motivation, there's no difference between ego and essence—or between *dharma* and drama. The two become one in a way that allows us to be fully present in life. And to bring into the world a special gift that is ours and ours alone.

I have a young friend Csilla who was looking forward to Christmas. I asked her, "What do you want from Santa?" She told me that Santa is really Daddy. I was a little sad to hear her words; my little friend was growing up. But Csilla wasn't sad, because she'd been told by Mom in a loving way. Then she lowered her voice and told me not to tell her four-year-old brother about Santa yet. I said it was wonderful that her Daddy loved her so much that he wanted to fulfill all her dreams, just like Santa. I also said that just because Santa isn't real, it doesn't mean that magic isn't real—that it just looks a little different that we might expect.

As Csilla grows up, I hope she'll always remember to look for the magic in life and not get fooled into thinking it's not real. I hope all of us will. It's not that easy to see the magic in life once we're all grown up. But Rumi did it, and he left some beautiful poetry encouraging us to do the same. Finding life's magic is a stepping stone to discovering Rumi's One Thing—discovering the one thing in life that really matters for each of us. When we find it, we'll understand the meaning of "following our bliss." We'll discover what it means to finally come home to ourselves.

Cited sources

Adrienne, Carol. *The Purpose of Your Life: Finding Your Place In The World Using Synchronicity, Intuition, And Uncommon Sense*. New York: Eagle Brook, 1998.

Almaas, A. H. *Facets of Unity: The Enneagram of Holy Ideas*. Berkeley: Diamond Books, 1998.

Bennett, J. G. *The Dramatic Universe, Vols I–IV*. Bennett Books, dates vary.

Bennett, J. G. *Enneagram Studies*. York Beach, ME: Sam Weiser, 1990.

Berets, Ralph. "Changing Images of Justice in American Films," *Legal Studies Forum*, 20(4), 1996, reprinted by permission at http://tarlton.law.utexas.edu/lpop/etext/lsf/berets20.htm.

Berne, Eric. *Games People Play*. New York: Grove Press, 1967.

Bernier, Nathan. *The Enneagram: Symbol of All and Everything*. Brazilia, Brazil: Gilgamesh Publishing, 2003.

Blake, A. G. E. *The Intelligent Enneagram*. Boston: Shambhala, 1996.

Campbell, Joseph, and Bill Moyers. *The Power of Myth*. New York: Anchor Books, 1991.

Caplan, Marianna. *Halfway Up the Mountain: The Error of Premature Claims to Enlightenment*. Prescott, AZ: Holm Press, 1999.

Carroll, Lee, and Kryon. *The Journey Home: The Story of Michael Thomas and the Seven Angels*. Flagstaff, AZ: Light Technology, 1997.

Castaneda, Carlos. *The Teachings of Don Juan: A Yaqui Way of Knowledge*. Berkeley: Univ. of California, 2008.

Chernick-Fauvre, Katherine. [*Enneagram*] *Instinctual Subtypes*, unpublished workbook. Available from Enneagram Explorations at www.enneagram.net.

Cloninger, Robert. *Feeling Good: The Science of Well-Being*. New York: Oxford Univ. Press, 2004.

Combs, Allan, and Mark Holland. *Synchronicity : Through the Eyes of Science, Myth and the Trickster.* New York: Marlowe & Co: 1996.

Condon, Thomas. *The Enneagram Movie and Video Guide: How to See Personality Styles in the Movies.* Portland, OR: Metamorphous Press, 1999.

Czikszentmihalyi, Mihaly. *Flow: The Psychology of Optimal Experience.* New York: Harper, 1990.

Dalai Lama, "Laws of Dharma, as told by the Dalai Lama," www.indianexpress.com/ie/daily/19971225/35950683.html.

Davenport, Gloria. "The Subtypes Revisited." *Enneagram Monthly* (Part 1, May 2001; Part 2, June 2001; Part 3, July/Aug. 2001).

de Becker, Gavin. *The Gift of Fear: Survival Signals That Protect Us from Violence.* New York: Dell, 1997.

Edinger, Edward F. *Ego and Archetype.* Boston: Shambhala, 1972.

Efross, Walter. "Owning Enlightenment: Proprietary Spirituality in the 'New Age' Marketplace," *Buffalo Law Review,* 51(3), 2003.

Eliade, Mircea. *Image and Symbols: Studies in Religious Symbolism.* Princeton: Princeton Univ. Press, 1991. Cited in *The Symbolic Quest* by Edward C. Whitmont, 1969/1991, p. 76.

Epstein, Mark. *Open to Desire: Embracing a Lust for Life.* New York: Gotham, 2005.

Fox, Matthew, and Rupert Sheldrake. *The Physics of Angels: Exploring the Realm Where Science and Spirit Meet.* San Francisco: Harper, 1996.

Goldberg, Michael J. *Travels with Odysseus: Uncommon Wisdom from Homer's Odyssey.* Tempe, AZ: Circe's Island Press, 2005.

Grimes, Ronald L. *Deeply into the Bone: Re-Inventing Rites of Passage.* Berkeley: Univ. of California Press, 2002.

Hillman, James. *Anima: An Anatomy of a Personified Notion.* Woodstock, CT: Spring Publications, 1985.

Hillman, James. *Re-Visioning Psychology.* New York: Harper, 1977.

Hillman, James. *The Soul's Code: In Search of Character and Calling.* New York: Warner Books, 1996.

Holden, Robert. *Happiness Now! Timeless Wisdom for Feeling Good Fast.* Carlsbad, CA: Hay House, 1998.

Hollis, James. *What Matters Most: Living a More Considered Life.* New York: Penguin, 2009.

"Interview with Oscar Ichazo." *Enneagram Monthly,* Nov. & Dec. 1996.

Interviews with Oscar Ichazo. "Breaking the Tyranny of the Ego." Interview of Oscar Ichazo by Sam Keen. New York: Arica Institute Press, 1982, pp. 3–24.

Johnson, Robert. *Balancing Heaven and Earth: A Memoir of Visions, Dreams, and Realizations.* New York: HarperCollins, 1998.

Johnson, Robert. *Inner Work: Using Dreams and Active Imagination for Personal Growth.* New York: HarperCollins, 1986.

Jung, C. G. *The Development of Personality (Collected Works of C. G. Jung Vol.17).* Princeton: Princeton Univ. Press, 1981.

Jung, C. G. *Memories, Dreams, Reflections.* Recorded and edited by Anniela Jaffe; trans. by Richard and Clara Winston. New York: Vintage Books, 1989.

Jung, C. G. *The Red Book: Liber Novus.* Edited and introduced by Sonu Shamdasani; trans. by Mark Kyburz and John Peck. New York: Norton, 2009.

Jung, C. G. *The Structure and Dynamics of the Psyche (Collected Works of C. G. Jung Vol. 8).* Princeton: Princeton Univ. Press, 1970.

Jung, C. G. *Synchronicity: An Acausal Connecting Principle;* trans. by R. F. C. Hull. Princeton: Princeton Univ. Press/Bollingen, 1973.

Jung, C. G. *The Undiscovered Self.* New York: Signet, 1957-58.

Koestler, Arthur. *The Act of Creation.* New York: Arkana, 1964/1989.

Koestler, Arthur. *Janus: A Summing Up.* New York: Random House, 1978.

Koestler, Arthur, and Alister C. Hardy. *The Challenge of Chance.* New York: Random House, 1974.

Kornfeld, Jack. *A Path with Heart: A Guide Through the Perils and Promises of Spiritual Life.* New York: Bantam, 1993.

Kripal, David. *Esalen: America and the Religion of No Religion.* Chicago: Univ. of Chicago Press, 2007.

Lakoff, George, and Mark Johnson. *Metaphors We Live By.* Chicago: Univ. of Chicago Press, 1980.

Lane, Beldon C. "The Power of Myth: Lessons from Joseph Campbell." Available at http://www.religion-online.org/showarticle.asp?title=171.

Lilly, John, and Joseph E. Hart. "The Arica Training." In *Transpersonal Psychologies,* edited by

Listening Is an Act of Love: A Celebration of American Life from the StoryCorps Project. Edited by Dave Isay. New York: Penguin, 2008.

Charles T. Tart. 329–351. New York: Harper & Row, 1975.

Maitri, Sandra. *Spiritual Dimensions of the Enneagram: Nine Faces of the Soul.* New York: Tarcher, 2000.

Melchizedek, Drunvalo. *The Ancient Secret of the Flower of Life: Volume 2.* Flagstaff: Light Technology, 1998.

Mother Teresa, Come Be My Light: The Private Writings of the "Saint of Calcutta," edited by Brian Kolodiejchuk. New York: Doubleday, 2007.

Nachmanovich, Stephen. *Free Play: Improvisation in Life and Art.* New York: Tarcher, 1991.

Naranjo, Claudio. *Character and Neurosis: An Integrative View.* Nevada City, CA: Gateway Books, 1994.

Naranjo, Claudio. *The Enneagram of Society: Healing the Soul to Heal the World.* Nevada City, CA: Gateway Books, 2004.

Naranjo, Claudio. *Enneatypes in Psychotherapy: Selected Transcripts of the First International Symposium on the Personality Enneagrams.* Prescott, AZ: Hohm Press, 1995.

O'Hanrahan, Peter. *Enneagram Work,* unpublished workbook. Available from the author at 1442 A Walnut Street #421, Berkeley, CA 94709, POHanrahan@aol.com, www.enneagramwork.com.

Ouspensky, P. D. *In Search of the Miraculous.* New York: Harcourt, 2001.

Palmer, Helen. *The Enneagram.* San Francisco: Harper, 1988.

Pullinger, Kate. "Soul Survivor: Women Directors' Special." Available at http://www.rickross.com/reference/general/general329.html.

Rhodes, Susan. "The Circle, Triangle, and the Hexad." *Enneagram Monthly* (Part I, Oct. 2007; Part 2, Nov. 2007).

Rhodes, Susan. "The Enneagram and Ken Wilber's Integral Philosophy." *Enneagram Monthly* (Part I, Nov. 2006; Part 2, Dec. 2006).

Rhodes, Susan. "The Enneagram from a Systems Perspective." *Enneagram Monthly,* June 2008.

Rhodes, Susan. "Let's Depathologize the Enneagram!" *Enneagram Monthly,* Oct. 2006.

Rhodes, Susan. *The Positive Enneagram.* Seattle: Geranium Press, 2009.

Rhodes, Susan. Website: www.enneagramdimensions.net.

Riso, Don R., and Russ Hudson. *Wisdom of the Enneagram: The Complete Guide to Psychological and Spiritual Growth for the Nine Personality Types.* New York: Bantam, 1999.

Rumi, Jalalauddin. *The Essential Rumi,* Coleman Barks, trans., with John Moyne. Edison, NJ: Castle Books, 1997. Also reproduced at http://unfoldyourmyth.wordpress.com/2008/01/30/unfold-your-own-myth/.

Sansonese, J. Nigro. *The Body of Myth: Mythology, Shamanic Trance, and the Sacred Geography of the Body.* Rochester, VT: Inner Traditions Int'l., 1994.

Sardello, Robert. *Love and the Soul: Creating a Future for Earth.* New York: HarperCollins, 1995.

Searle, Judith. "The Gap at the Bottom of the Enneagram." *Enneagram Monthly,* Sept. 1997.

Searle, Judith. *The Literary Enneagram.* Portland, OR: Metamorphous Press, 2001.

Searle, Judith. "Story Genres and Enneagram Types." *Enneagram Monthly,* Part 1, Oct. 1998; Part 2, Nov. 1998.

Searle, Judith. Website: www.judithsearle.com.

Segal, Suzanne. *Collision with the Infinite: A Life Beyond the Personal Self.* San Diego: Blue Dove Press, 1996.

Seligman, Martin. *Authentic Happiness: Using the New Positive Psychology to Realize Your Potential for Last Fulfillment.* New York: Free Press, 2002.

Shaw, Idries. *The Commanding Self.* London: Octogon Press, 1994.

Sikora, Mario. "The Subtypes at Work, Part I." Available at www.mariosikora.com/subtype-sartpt1.html.

Tarrant, John. *The Light Inside the Dark: Zen, Soul, and the Spiritual Life.* New York: HarperCollins, 1998.

Vaughn-Lee, Llewellyn. "Dreams: Reconnecting Us To The Sacred." Available at www. huffingtonpost.com/llewellyn-vaughanlee/dreams-reconnecting-us-to_b_427339.html.

Vaughn-Lee, Llewellyn. Website: www.goldensufi.org.

Videohound's Golden Retriever 2009. Farmington Hills, MI: Gale Cengage, 2008.

Wadia, B. P. "The World of Archetypes," *Theosophy,* 11(4), 1923, pages 160-167. Reproduced at http://www.teosofiskakompaniet.net/BPWadiaSecretDoctrineStudies4.htm.

Wheatley, Margaret. *Leadership and the New Science.* San Francisco: Berrett-Koehler, 2001.

Whitmont, Edward C. *The Symbolic Quest: Basic Concepts of Analytical Psychology.* Princeton: Princeton Univ. Press, 1991.

Wilber, Ken. *Eye of the Spirit: An Integral Vision for a World Gone Slightly Mad.* Boston: Shambhala, 2001.

Wilber, Ken. *Integral Spirituality: A Startling New Role for Religion in the Modern and Postmodern World.* Boston: Integral Books, 2006.

Wilber, Ken. *Spirituality, Ecology, Spirituality: The Spirit of Evolution.* Boston: Shambhala, 2000.

Wilber, Ken. *Up From Eden: A Transpersonal View of Human Evolution.* Garden City, NY: Anchor Press, 1996.

Williams, Roger J. *You Are Extraordinary.* New York: Pyramid, 1971.

Wiltse, Virginia, and Helen Palmer. "Hidden in Plain Sight: Observations on the Origins of the Enneagram." *The Enneagram Journal.* International Enneagram Association, II (1), 2009.

Cited films & TV shows

NOTE: *At the beginning of each chapter that discusses the life themes for Types 1 – 9 (Chapters 11 – 19), there is a* **summary table** *that lists typical life themes associated with each subtype, along with films exemplifying this theme in some way. Each film is listed below, along with the year of release and the subtype(s) associated with it. To see its theme(s), consult the applicable summary table. (For a more details on themes, see my website: www.enneagramdimensions.net/archetypes_of_the_enneagram. pdf.)*

12 Angry Men (1957) – soc 1

1984 (1984) – soc 5

2001: A Space Odyssey (1968) – sp 5

21 (2008) – soc 5

24 (TV) – sx 6

300 Spartans, The (1962) – soc 6

88 Minutes (2008) – sx 6

9 to 5 (1980) – soc 2

911 (2002) – soc 6

A Beautiful Mind (2001) – sp 5, sx 5, soc 5

A Christmas Carol (1984) – sx 9

A Home of Our Own (1993) – sp 8

A La Place du Coeur (1998) – sp 2

An Absence of Malice (1981) – sp 3, sx 3

An Officer & a Gentleman (1982) – soc 8

A Paralyzing Fear: The Story of Polio in America (1998) – soc 6

A Rumor of Angels (2000) – sp 4

A Star is Born (1976) – sx 7

A Tale of Two Cities, A (1935) – soc 7

An Unreasonable Man (2006) – soc 1

A. I. (2001) – sx 2

About A Boy (2002) – sx 7

About Schmidt (2002) – sp 6

The Accidental Tourist (1988) – sp 9

The Adventures of Huck Finn (1960) – sx 7

The Adventures of Robin Hood (1938) – sx 7

The Adventures of Sherlock Holmes (1939) – sx 5, soc 5

African Queen (1951) – sx 1

Agnes of God (1985) – sx 9

Aimee Semple McPherson (2006) – sx 1

Akeelah & Bee (2006) – sx 9

Alfie (1966) – sp 7

Alice Doesn't Live Here Anymore (1974) – sp 2

Alice Neel (2007) – sp 4

All About Eve (1950) – sx 3

All Mine to Give (1956) – sp 1

All Quiet on the Western Front (1930) – soc 9

All This and Heaven, Too (1940) – sx 2

Amadeus (1984) – sx 4, sx 7

Amazing Grace (2006) – soc 1

Amazing Race (TV) – soc 3

American Chopper (TV) – soc 8

American Princess (TV) – soc 1

America's Next Top Model (TV) – soc 3, soc 4

Amish Grace (2010) – sp 1

Analyze That (2002) – soc 8

Analyze This (1999) – soc 8

Anastasia (1956) – soc 4

Animal House (1978) – sp 7

Apollo 13 (1995) – soc 3, soc 5

Armageddon (1998) – soc 8

Around The World in 80 Days (1956) – sx 7

Arranged (2007) – sx 2

Artemesia (1997)– sp 4

At First Sight (1999) – sp 9, sx 9

Atonement (2007) – sx 1

Australia (2008) – soc 1

Australian Princess (TV) – soc 1

Awakenings (1990) – sp 5, soc 5

Babette's Feast (1987) – sx 1

The Babe Ruth Story (1948) – sp 8

The Baby Dance (1998) – sp 3

Back to The Future (1985) – sx 7

The Bad News Bears (1976) – soc 3

Bambi (1942) – sx 6

Baraka (1992) – sx 9

The Bear (1988) – sp 9

Bed of Roses (1996) – .sx 3

Bee Season (2005) – sx 9

Beetlejuice (1988) – sx 7

Being John Malkovich (1999) – sp 4

Bernadette of Lourdes (1962) – sx 9

Beyond Rangoon (1995) – sx 9

Bible, The (1966) – sx 1

Bicentennial Man (1999) – sx 2, sx 3, sp 5

Big (1988) – sx 7, sx 9

The Big Picture (1989) – sp 6

Bill & Ted's Excellent Adventure (1989) – sx 7

Billy Crystal flicks – sp 6

Black Narcissus (1947) – sx 1

The Black Stallion (1979) – sx 9

Black Widow (1987) – sx 2

The Blue Angel (1930) – sx 2

The Blue Butterfly (2004) – sp 5

The Blue Lagoon (1980) – sp 9, sx 9

The Blues Brothers (1980) – sp 7

Bollywood/Hollywood (2002) – sp 2, sx 2

Book TV shows (TV) – soc 5

Born Rich (2003) – soc 7

Boys Town (1938) – soc 6

Brazil (1985) – sx 5

Breaking Away (1979) – sp 3

Broadcast News (1987) – sx 3

Broken Glass (1996) – sx 3

Buena Vista social Club (1999) – soc 9

The Burmese Harp (1956) – soc 9

Butch Cassidy & the Sundance Kid (1969) – sx 7

Butterfly (1999) – soc 1, soc 6

Cabaret (1972) – sx 7

Cake Boss (TV) – soc 8

Calendar Girls (2003) – soc 9

Camilla (1994) – sp 1

Captain Blood (1935) – sx 7

Capture of the Green River Killer (2008) – soc 1, sx 5

Castaway (2000) – sp 3

Chariots of Fire (1981) – soc 1

Charly (2002) – sp 5

Cheaper by the Dozen (1950) – sp 6

Cheech & Chong's *Up in Smoke* – sp 7

Chef Jeff Project (TV) – soc 8

Chilly Scenes of Winter (1979) – sx 6

Chocolat (2000) – sp 7

Chronicles of Narnia (2005-2008) – sx 9

Cider House Rules (1999) – soc 7, sp 9, soc 9

City of Angels (1998) – sx 4

City of Joy (1992) – sx 2, soc 2

Cleopatra (1963) – sx 8

Clueless (1995) – soc 3

Coal Miner's Daughter (1980) – sp 9

Cobb (1994) – sp 8

Coco Chanel (2008) – soc 4

Cocoon (1985) – sp 1, sx 9

The Collector (1965) – sp 5, sx 5

Colonial House (2004) – sp 1

The Conscientious Objector (2004) – soc 9

Contact (1997) – sx 6

Cool Hand Luke (1967) – sx 6

Crumb (1994) – sp 5, sx 5

The Cup (2000) – soc 9

Czech Dream (2004) – sp 3, sx 7

The Da Vinci Code (2006) – soc 5

Damage (1992) – soc 5

Dancer in the Dark (2000) – sx 4

Dangerous Beauty (1998) – sx 8

Dangerous Liaisons (1988) – sx 3

Das Experiment (2005) – soc 6

David & Goliath (1961) – sx 6

David & Lisa (1962) – sp 5

The Day the Earth Stood Still (1951) – sx 5,
soc 8

The Dead Poets society (1989) – soc 7

Decoration Day (1990) – sp 1

The Deer Hunter (1978) – soc 8

The Deliberate Stranger (1986) – sx 3

The Devil Wears Prada (2006) – soc 4

The Devil's Advocate (1997) – sx 3

The Diary of Anne Frank (1959) – sx 9

Dinner: Impossible (TV) – sp 8

Dirty Dancing (1987) – sx 1

Disclosure (1994) – sp 3

The Dog Whisperer (TV) – soc 8

Dogtown (TV) – soc 2

Donahue (TV) – sx 3

The Donald Trump's Apprentice (TV) – sp 8

The Dorothy Day Story (1996) – soc 2

Doubt (2008) – soc 1

Dr. Bahasaheb Ambedkar (2000) – soc 5, soc 8

Dr. G: Medical Examiner (TV) – sp 3

Dr. Jekyll & Mr. Hyde (1932) – sx 1

Dr. Who (TV) – sx 5

Dr. Zhivago (1965) – sx 4

Dragnet: The Movie (1987) – soc 1, soc 6

Driving Miss Daisy (1989) – sp 1

Dumbo (1941) – soc 4

Dust & Illusions (2009) – soc 7

E. T. (1982) – sp 5

East is East (1999) – sp 2, sx 2

Educating Rita (1983) – sp 7

The Elephant Man (1980) – soc 4

Elizabeth (1998) – soc 8

Ellen [DeGeneres Show] (TV) – sp 7

Darshan: The Embrace (2006) – sp 2

Emeril (TV) – sp 8

Empire of the Sun (1987) – sp 3

Enchanted April (1992) – sx 1

The Endless Summer (1966) – sx 7

Erin Brockovich (2000) – soc 6

Excalibur (1981) – sx 8

Extreme Makeover: Home Edition (TV) – soc 2

Fahrenheit 451 (1966) – sp 5, soc 5

FairyTale: A True Story (1997) – sx 9

The Family Man (2000) – sp 4

Far & Away (1992) – sp 3

Fargo (1996) – sx 5

Fatal Attraction (1987) – sx 2

Father Goose (1964) – sp 7

Father of the Bride (1950) – sp 2

Fearless (2006) – sx 6

Fiddler on the Roof (1971) – SP 2

Fight in the Fields (1997) – SOC 6

The Firm (1993) – SOC 3

Fitzcarraldo / The Burden of Dreams (1982) – SOC 7

Flash of Genius (2008) – SOC 7

Florence Nightingale (1985) – SP 2

Flowers Uncut (TV) – SOC 2, SOC 4

Fly Away Home (1996) – SP 2, SP 9

Footloose (1984) – SX 1, SP 7, SOC 7

Fountainhead, The (1949) – SOC 1

Four Weddings & a Funeral (1994) – SOC 2

Free Willy (1993) – SP 9

The French Lieutenant's Woman (1981) – SX 4

Fried Green Tomatoes (1991) – SOC 2

Friendly Persuasion (1956) – SOC 9

From the Heart of the World: The Elder Brothers' Warning (1991) – SX 9

Frontier House (2002) – SP 1

The Fugitive (1993) – SOC 1, SX 6

Gandhi (1982) – SOC 9

Garbage Warrior (2008) – SP 7, SOC 7

Gaslight (1944) – SP 6

Georgy Girl (1966) – SOC 4

The Ghost & Mrs. Muir (1947) – SX 2, SX 9

Ghost (1990) – SX 2

Ghost Dog: The Way of the Samurai (1999) – SX 8

The Ghost and Mrs. Muir (1947) – SX 2, SX 9,

The Girl with the Pearl Earring (2003) – SP 4

Girl: Interrupted (1999) – SX 4, SOC 4

Gladiator (2000) – SX 8

The Glass Menagerie (1987) – SP 2, SOC 4

Glory (1989) – SP 1, SOC 1

The Godfather (1972) – SX 8, SOC 8

The Gods Must Be Crazy (1981) – SP 9

Gone With The Wind (1939) – SX 8

Good Morning Vietnam (1987) – SX 7

Good Will Hunting (1997) – SX 8, SOC 8

Goodbye, Mr. Chips (1939) – SOC 5, SOC 6

Grace is Gone (2007) – SOC 6

The Graduate (1967) – SX 2, SP 9

Graham Kerr's Galloping Gourmet (TV) – SP 9

The Grapes of Wrath (1940) – SP 1

The Great Debators (2007) – SOC 3

The Great Escape (1963) – SOC 3

Great Imposter, The (1961) – SX 3

The Green Mile (1999) – SP 8

Greenfingers (2000) – SOC 9

Groundhog Day (1993) – SP 6

Guy's Big Bite (TV) – SP 7

Hair (1979) – SOC 7

Hancock (2008) – SX 3

The Handmaid's Tale (1990) – SOC 1

Hanoi Hilton (1987) – SP 8

Harry & Tonto (1974) – SP 9

Harry Potter (early films) – SX 9

Harry Potter films – SX 5, SOC 7

He's Just Not Into You (2009) – SX 2

Heartland (1980) – SP 9

Heartsounds (1984) – SX 9

Heat (1995) – SOC 8

Hercule Poirot films (1970s +) – SOC 5

Hester Street (1975) – SP 3

Hideous Kinky (1998) – SP 1, SX 4, SOC 7

The Hiding Place (1975) – SOC 9

High Noon (1952) – SX 8

Himalaya (1999) – SP 6, SP 9

The Hobbit (2011) – SX 9

Holmes on Homes (TV) – SP 8

Holy Smoke (1999) – SX 4

Hoosiers (1986) – SOC 3

Hostage (2005) – SP 6

The Hours, (2002) – SP 4, SX 4

House Hunters International – soc 7

House of Cards (1992) – sp 2, sx 5

House of the Spirits (1993) – sx 4

How the West Was Won (1963) – sp 1

How to Make an American Quilt (1995) – soc 2, soc 9

How to Succeed in Business Without Really Trying (1967) – sp 3

I Remember Mama (1948) – sp 2

In America (2002) – sp 2, sx 4

In Pursuit of Happyness (2006) – sp 3

The Incredible Journey (1963) – sp 9

The Independence Day (1996) – soc 8

Indiana Jones & the Temple of Doom (1984) – sp 3

The Insider (1999) – soc 6

Interview with a Vampire (1994) – sp 3

Into the Wild (2007) – sx 4, sx 7, soc 7

Invasion of the Body Snatchers (1956) – sx 5

Invincible (2001) – sp 8

Iron Chef /Iron Chef America (TV) – sp 8

Isadora (1968) – soc 4

It's a Wonderful Life (1946) – sp 9

Jane Austen Book Club (2007) – soc 2

Jerry Maguire (1996) – sx 3

Jesus of Nazareth (mini-series, 1977) – sx 2

Joan Baez: How Sweet the Sound (2009) – sp 4

John Brown's Holy War (2000) – sx 1

The Joy Luck Club (1993) – soc 2

Judge Judy (TV) – soc 1

Judgment at Nuremberg (1961) – soc 1

Julia (1977) – sx 6

Julie & Julia (2009) – sp 2, sp 7

Karate Kid (1984) – sx 9

The Killing Fields (1984) – sp 6

The King & I (1956) – sx 1, sx 8

Kinsey (2004) – sx 5

Kiss of the Spider Woman (1985) – sx 1

K-Pax (2001) – sx 9

Kramer vs. Kramer (1979) – sx 3

Kratatoa: The Last Days (2006) – soc 8

Kundun (1997) – soc 9

LA Law (TV) – sp 3

Ladder 49 (2004) – soc 6

Ladies in Lavender (2004) – sp 9

Last Holiday (2006) – soc 1

The Last King of Scotland (2006) – soc 8

Laurel Canyon (2002) – sp 1

Les Miserables (1997) – soc 1

Lifestyles of the Rich & Famous (TV) – sp 7, soc 7

Lilies of the Field (1963) – soc 7

The List of Adrian Messenger (1963) – sx 7

Little Big Man (1970) – sx 9

Little Buddha (1993) – sx 9

Little Women (1949) – sp 6

Lonely are the Brave (1962) – sx 7

The Longest Day (1962) – sp 8

Looking for Mr. Goodbar (1977) – sx 2

Lord of the Rings (2001) – sx 9

Lost Horizon (1937) – sx 9

Lost in La Mancha (2002) – soc 7

Lost in Translation (2003) – sp 4

Love Story (1970) – sx 2

The Luzhin Defense (2000) – sp 5, sx 5

Macarthur (1977) – soc 8

The Magic of Ordinary Days (2005) – sx 9

The Magnificent Seven/The Seven Samurai (1960/1954) – sx 8, sp 9

Magnolia (1999) – sp 4, sx 4, sx 8

The Mahabharata (1989) – soc 9

Maharishi Mahesh Yogi: Sage for a New Generation (1968) – soc 9

Man for All Seasons, A (1966) – soc 1

Man in the Moon (1991) – sx 2, sp 9

Man of La Mancha (1972) – soc 7

The Man Who Would be King (1975) – sx 7

Manic (2001) – soc 4

Marathon Man (1976) – sx 6

March of the Penguins (2005) – sp 9

The Martha Stewart Show (TV) – soc 2

Mask (1985) – sp 7

Masters of Reception (TV) – soc 2

Maxed Out (2006) – sp 3

Maya Lin: a Clear, Strong Vision (1994) – sp 4

Mayflower: The Pilgrim's Adventure (1979) – sp 1

Meetings with Remarkable Men (1979) – soc 5

Michael Palin's Pole to Pole (TV) – sx 7

The Milagro Beanfield War (1988) – sp 9

The Miracle Worker (1962) – sx 2, sp 4

Missing (1982) – sx 1

The Mission (1986) – sx 8

Mommy Dearest (1981) – sp 2

Monty Python films 6 – sx 7

Moonlight Mile (2002) – sx 7, sp 9

Mork & Mindy (TV) – sx 7

The Mosquito Coast (1982) – soc 7

Mother Teresa of Calcutta (2003) – sx 2

Mr. Holland's Opus (1995) – soc 3

Mr. Smith Goes to Washington (1939) – soc 9

Mrs. Brown (1997) – soc 6

Mrs. Doubtfire (1993) – sp 2, sx 3

Murphy's Romance (1985) – sx 9

My Big Fat Greek Wedding (2002) – sp 2

My Brilliant Career (1979) – sp 3

My Fair Lady (1964) – sx 1, soc 1

My Left Foot (1989) – sp 3

My Name is Bill W. (1989) – sp 1

National Lampoon's Vacation (1983) – sp 6

National Velvet (1944) – sx 9

Nell (1994) – sx 9

Neville Chamberlain book – soc 9

The New World (2005) – sx 4

Norma Rae (1979) – soc 6

Not Without My Daughter (1991) – sp 2

Note by Note: the Make of Steinway L1037) – sp 1

The Notebook (2004) – sx 9

The Nun's Story (1959) – sx 1

Nurse Edith Cavell (1939) – sp 2

October Sky (1999) – sp 2

Of Human Bondage (1934) – sx 2

Off the Grid: Life on the Mesa (2007) – sp 7

Officer & a Gentleman, An (1982) – soc 8

Old Yeller (1957) – sp 6

Oliver (1968) – sx 9

On Golden Pond (1981) – sp 1

One Day in the Life of Ivan Denisovich (1970) – sp 9

One Flew Over the Cuckoos' Nest – sx 6

One Minute to Nine (2008) – sp 2

Oprah (TV) – sx 3

Oprah's Big Give (TV) – soc 2, soc 3

Ordinary People (1980) – soc 3

The Other Side of the Mountain (1975) – sp 3

Our Town (1940) – sp 6

Out of Africa (1985) – sp 4

The Outer Limits (TV) – sx 5

The Outlaw Josie Wales (1976) – sx 8

Out-of-Towners (1970) – sp 6

The Paper Chase (1973) – soc 1

Paper Moon (1973) – sx 7

Patriot Games (1992) – sp 6

Patton (1970) – soc 8

Paula's Home Cooking (TV) – sp 2

Pay It Forward (2000) – soc 9

Philadelphia (1993) – soc 1

The Philadelphia Story (1940) – SOC 2

Philip Johnson: Diary of An Eccentric Architect (1997) – SOC 7

The Piano (1993) – SX 1, SX 4

Picnic at Hanging Rock (1975) – SX 9

Pleasantville (1998) – SP 9, SOC 9

Pollock (2000) – SP 4

Pregnant Man (2008) – SP 7

Pretty Woman (1990) – SX 6

Priest (1994) – SX 1

Primary Colors (1998) – SOC 3

The Prince of Tides (1991) – SX 6

Prize Winner of Defiance, Ohio (2005) – SP 2

Project Runway (TV) – SX 4, SOC 4

Protocol (1984) – SOC 2

The Quiet Man (1952) – SX 8

Quincy (TV–1970s) – SOC 1

Rabbit-proof Fence (2002) – SOC 1

Radiant City (2006) – SP 3

Raging Bull (1980) – SP 8

Rain Man (1988) – SX 5

Ransom (1996) – SX 6

The Razor's Edge (1984) – SOC 2, SX 4 , SOC 4, SP 5, SOC 5, SX 7

Real Women Have Curves (2002) – SP 2

Rebel Without A Cause (1955) – SOC 4

Red Badge of Courage (1951) – SX 6

Red Dawn (1984) – SOC 6

The Red Violin (1998) – SP 1

Reds (1981) – SOC 1

Regarding Henry (1991) – SOC 3

Renaissance Man (1994) – SOC 7

Rescue 911 (TV) – SOC 6

Resurrection (1980) – SX 6

Revolutionary Road (2008) – SX 4

Richard Simmons' Sweatin' to the Oldies (1980s) – SOC 2

The Right Stuff (1983) – SX 3, SOC 6

Righteous Kill (2008) – SX 8

Risky Business (1983) – SP 3

Robin Hood (1938) – SX 7

Rocky (1976) – SX 3

Romeo & Juliet (1996) – SX 4

The Rosie O'Donnell Show (TV) – SP 8

Safe (1995) – SP 4

Safe Passage (1994) – SX 6

Salem Witch Trials, The – SX 1

Sampson & Delilah (1949) – SP 8

Sarah: Plain & Tall (1991) – SP 6, SX 9

Saving Private Ryan (1998) – SP 6

The Scarlet Letter (1994) – SOC 4

The Scarlet Pimpernel (1934) – SOC 6

Schindler's List (1993) – SOC 3

Scrooge (1970) – SP 1, SOC 6

Scouts to the Rescue (1939) – SOC 6

Sea Biscuit (2003) – SP 9

The Searchers (1956) – SX 8

Secondhand Lions (2003) –SP 9

Selling New York (TV) –SP 3

The September Issue (2009) – SX 1, SOC 4

Sergeant York (1941) – SOC 9

Serpico (1973) – SOC 1

The Seven Samurai (1954) – SX 8

Seven Years in Tibet (1997) – SOC 9

sex, lies, and videotape (1989) – SX 5, SOC 5, SOC 9

Shackleton's Antarctic Adventure (2001) – SP 8

Shadowlands (1993) – SX 3, SP 5

Shakers: Hands to Work, Hearts to God (1984) – SP 1

The Shawshank Redemption (1994) – SOC 5

The Shipping News (2001) – SP 9

Shirley Temple films (1930s) – SX 9

The Shootist (1976) – SX 8

Silence of the Lambs (1991) – sx 5

Sir Gawain & the Green Knight (1973) – sx 8

Sisterhood of the Traveling Pants (2005) –
    soc 2

Six Degrees of Separation (1993) – soc 3

Skins (2002) – sx 8

Sleepless in Seattle (1993) – sx 2

Something's Got to Give (2003) – sx 7

Somewhere in Time (1980) – sx 2

Son-rise (1979) – sp 5, sx 5

The Sons of Katie Elder (1965) – sx 8

The Sopranos (TV) – soc 8

Sorry, Wrong Number (1948) – sp 6

The Sound Barrier (1952) – sx 7

The Sound of Music (1965) – sx 1

Sounder (1972) – sp 9

The Spanish Prisoner (1993) – soc 3

Spartacus (1960) – sx 8

Spiderman (2002) – soc 6

Spring/Summer/Winter/Fall (2003) – sx 9

Stalin (1992) – soc 8

The Stand (1994) – sp 8

Stand & Deliver (1998) – soc 8

Star Trek (TV) – sp 5

Star Wars (1977) – sx 7

Starman (1984) – sp 5

The Station Agent (2003) – sp 5, sp 7

Steel Magnolias (1989) – sx 2, soc 2, sp 6

The Sting (1973) – sx 7

Story of the Weeping Camel (2003) – soc 9

The Straight Story (1999) – sp 9

Strictly Ballroom (1992) – sx 1

Summer of '42 (1971) – sx 2

Summertime (1955) – sx 1

Superman (1978) – sx 6, soc 6

SuperNanny (TV) – soc 3

Survivor (TV) – sp 3

Sweet Charity (1969) – sx 2

Swing Kids (1993) – soc 1

Take Home Chef (TV) – sp 7

Take Kerr (TV) – sp 7

Take the Lead (2006) – sx 1

The Talented Mr. Ripley (1999) – sx 3

Taras Bulba (1962) – sx 8

TED: The Future We Will Create (2007) –
    soc 7

Temple Grandin (2010) – soc 5

Ten Commandments (1956) – soc 1

Terms of Endearment (1983) – sp 3

The Thorn Birds (1977) – sx 3

Three's Company (TV) – sp 7

Throwdown with Bobby Flay (TV) – sp 8

To Kill a Mockingbird (1962) – soc 1

To Sir with Love (1967) – soc 7

Tom & Viv (1994) – soc 4, soc 5

Tootsie (1982) – sx 3

Top Chef (TV) – soc 4

Top Gun (1986) – sx 3

Top Hat (1935) – soc 2

To Sir with Love (1967) – soc 7

Touched by an Angel (TV) – sp 2

Touching the Void (2003) – sx 7

Tough as Nails (TV) – soc 8

The Trip to Bountiful (1985) – sp 9

The Truman Show (1998) – sx 3

Tucker: a Man & His Dream (1988) – soc 7

The Turning Point (1977) – sx 4

Turtle Diaries (1985) – sp 5

Twelve O'Clock High (1949) – soc 8

The Twilight Zone (TV) – sx 5

The Tyra Banks Show (TV) – sx 8

Ugly Betty (TV) – soc 4

The Ugly Duckling (1931) – soc 4

United 93 (2006) – sx 6, soc 6

Unrepentant: Kevin Annett & Canada's
    Genocide (2007) – soc 1

The Unsinkable Molly Brown (1964) – sp 8

Uptown Girls (2003) – sp 1, sp 7

The Verdict (1990) – soc 1

Vertigo (1958) – sx 6

Vincent & Theo (1990) – sp 4, soc 4

Wait Under Dark (1967) – sp 6

Walkabout (1971) – sx 9

Wall Street (1987) – sp 3

Wallenberg: a Hero's Story (1985) – soc 3

War of the Worlds (1953) – soc 8

Warren Miller skiing flicks – sx 7

The Way We Were (1973) – soc 1

Weapons of the Spirit (1987) – soc 9

West Side Story (1961) – sx 4

Westward Ho the Wagons (1956) – sp 1

Whalerider (2002) – sx 9

What About Bob? (1991) – sp 6

What Dreams May Come (1998) – sx 4, sx 7

What Not to Wear (TV) – soc 3

When Harry Met Sally (1989) – sx 2

Where the Lilies Bloom (1974) – sp 1

Where the Red Ferns Grows (2003) – sp 9

White Oleander (2002) – soc 4

Why Has Bodhi Dharma Left for the East?
    (1989) – sx 9

Why We Fight (1940s) – soc 6

Willy Wonka & the Chocolate Factory (1971) –
    sx 9

The Winslow Boy (1999) – sp 6

Witness (1985) – sp 1

Wizard of Oz (1939) – sp 2, sx 4, sx 7

Woodstock (1970) – soc 7

Woody Allen flicks – sp 6

Workaholic (1996) – sx 3

Working Girl (1988) – sx 3

The World of Buckminster Fuller (1974) –
    soc 7

The World's Strictest Parents (TV) – soc 4,
    soc 8

Xena: Princess Warrior (TV) – sx 8

The X-Files (TV) – sx 6

The Year of Living Dangerously (1982) –
    sx 6

Yearling (1946) – sp 9

Yentl (1983) – sp 2

Young@Heart (2007) – soc 9

Appendix

Narrative type & subtype test*

The test is designed to help you determine your type and subtype. Some people will instantly recognize themselves somewhere in these descriptions; many will not. But everybody should be able to narrow down the possibilities to a manageable number. Further exploration will allow you to eliminate the remaining possibilities.

Instructions: On the following pages are nine categories labeled *Type a* through *Type i*. Each category includes four paragraphs: a general type description followed by three subtype descriptions (the latter are in *italics*). See the key at the end to see which descriptions go with each type/subtype.

---

* I also have a subtypes test that just focuses on subtype arenas (independent of type); it's now available in *The Positive Enneagram* or on my website: www.enneagramdimensions.net.

Type a

I'm a high-energy free spirit with a lot of imagination and ideas. I enjoy many different activities and like to devise new ways of doing familiar things. Because I don't enjoy repetitive routines, I need many creative outlets to avoid boredom and feelings of restlessness. Although I have a talent for picking up new things quickly, it's harder for me to sustain long-term interest in a single activity, project, or job. When the task is dull, my mind tends to wander; I seem to crave mental stimulation the way some people crave food. Intense feelings can be hard to digest because I'm something of a mental butterfly who functions best when there are no heavy emotions to drag me down. Most of the time, I like to keep things light, which makes me an entertaining guest and witty companion. I'm a jack-of-all-trades and know how to think on my feet. And I'm accepting of other people and customs, so I can usually make new friends easily. My challenge is to finds ways to channel my restless energy into worthwhile activities, so I don't spend all my time chasing after rainbows.

SUBTYPE ARENAS

1. *I thoroughly appreciate the finer things in life—things like gourmet food, fine clothes, exquisite wines, and other pleasures that give life its zest. So I employ my diverse talents to seek out work that allows me to indulge my passion for The Good Life. I particularly value my home environment, because home and family give me a place to "ground" my busy life full of stimulating activities. To me, home isn't just the place I live, but an environment designed to feed the senses—a space that's not only comfortable but artistically stimulating. And family isn't just my blood relatives, but the friends and acquaintances who share my interests. It's fun to make my house a gathering place where people can eat, hang out, and share ideas. While I appreciate my ability to enjoy the good things in life, I realize that it's possible to become over-attached to sensuous and psychological pleasures in a way that makes me feel somehow entitled to the latest gadget, best wine, trendiest jeans, etc. My challenge is to develop the discernment to tell the difference between wants and needs, so I can better appreciate the good things that I already have.*

2. *I want to experience everything the world has to offer—especially peak experiences in life and love. I tend to be "lucky in love," and seldom lack for companionship. When I meet someone new, that person totally fascinates me; I want to know everything about him or her. But this intense fascination usually doesn't last forever: once the novelty of the relationship wears off, I tend to find my interest waning. The same thing can happen in other areas of my life, making it hard to do anything long-term, even pursue a career path. I love to travel and can adapt to uncertainty pretty easily. I also have a talent for overcoming language barriers and finding help wherever I go. So it's easy for me to fall into the life of a wanderer, always seeking out new experiences in new places, especially those off the beaten path. But sometimes I feel that I'm missing out on something in life and would like to know what it's like to "go deep" instead of always "going broad." Spiritually, I seem to slip into altered states more easily than most people. But I can find it more difficult to cope with the demands of a regular religious or spiritual practice.*

3. *Ideals matter a lot to me, especially ideals in the service of some great vision for the future. I'm always thinking about the possibilities for a better life, a better environment, a better world. When these ideas blend together into a single, powerful vision, I can be completely swept up by it, which is why I'm sometimes able to sacrifice everything—even my freedom—to make my vision materialize. It's because of this optimistic faith in my dreams that I'm capable of attracting others to them, although I don't often seek out a leadership position because of my egalitarian nature. When my dreams actually begin to materialize, I tend to find myself looking beyond them, imagining what lies over the next hill. I enjoy being the "point" person on any project, always looking ahead, allowing others to work out the practical details of the current plan. This approach gives me the freedom to constantly stretch my imagination, which I thoroughly enjoy. But as I mature, I'm beginning to understand how satisfying it can be to carry out my plans in a more systematic fashion, translating them step by step from vague imaginings into concrete realities.*

Type b

In everything I do, I strive for perfection. While I may not always succeed in being as perfect as I'd like, the goal of perfection ennobles my acts and dignifies my life. It represents an ethical ideal to which I can aspire, a polestar that helps me stay on course in life, so I don't lose track of important values. It also gives me backbone and helps me excel at tasks that demand a high degree of self-discipline, precision, and concentration. When I truly succeed in satisfying my own exacting standards, I can feel very pleased with the results of my effort. But much of the time, the goal of perfection is not easy to attain. It's hard to completely live up to my internal image of how I ought to look, feel, and act. At times, I can feel bitterly disappointed in myself, despite the reassurance of family and friends. So I have to be careful not to let the "shoulds" in my life make me overly frustrated or self-critical—and even more careful not to project them onto others. While many people need to learn how to work, I need to learn how to play—to laugh, relax, and let go of my desire for control. Seeking out regular opportunities for recreation allows me to worry less and experience greater joy in life.

SUBTYPE ARENAS

1. *I'm a sensible person with a self-reliant, pioneering attitude towards life. Although I like a space to call my own, my material needs are modest when compared to those of other people, because I value functionality more than fashion; fancy cars and homes seem like a waste of money. In any event, I'd rather save up and pay cash for most things than go into debt; I also try to avoid dubious investments. Given the choice, I'd rather be my own boss than work for somebody else, especially if I have to turn in shoddy work just to meet some deadline. It's important to me to work at a pace that allows me to turn out a high-quality end product, so I can feel satisfied with the results. As far as family goes, although I'm not exactly warm and fuzzy, I'm an honest and decent person who takes family responsibilities seriously: those closest to me know I'll always be there for them when they need me. But I'm a bit too tense to feel comfortable with emotional displays, so it's not easy for me to express affection directly. I'd rather make something with my own two hands or perform needed services as a way of showing affection towards those I love.*

2. *I have an intense, potentially explosive personality. I've been told by others that I seem charismatic, magnetic, or passionate. But I don't feel especially complimented because I find my inner intensity hard to manage. It's something I have to constantly monitor and contain, so it doesn't leak out unexpectedly. Sometimes there's so much energy inside me that I feel like a pressure cooker. When the pressure is too great, I sometimes explode. When this happens, I can feel quite ashamed, especially when there's no justifiable reason. My blow-ups most often happen around close friends or partners, because I'm concerned for their welfare. When they do things that seem wrong-headed to me, I naturally get upset. I can also feel possessive of partners or jealous of their relationships with other people. As a result, real intimacy can be elusive. So I often end up channeling my passion into causes I believe in or ideals I embrace; I can get very involved because I'm willing to work hard to bring about positive change. If I follow a spiritual discipline, I'm drawn to paths that offer inspirational guidance within a structured approach. While my spirituality is a deeply private matter, I seem to have the ability to mentor others and exercise leadership as a spiritual or inspirational guide.*

3. *I'm a formal, reserved person with refined tastes. I tend to maintain a certain distance with people I don't know well, which is why I sometimes give the impression of being cold or unfeeling. I am definitely not unfeeling. However, it does take time for me to warm up to others because of my natural reserve. So I prefer relating to people outside my immediate circle in a setting in which social roles are clearly defined and people adhere to them in a congenial manner. Within the impersonal structure of such systems, I can function quite comfortably, without experiencing the kind of painful self-consciousness that creates uncertainty or tension. However, my preoccupation with standards, ideals, or principles can lessen my tolerance for human foibles, including my own. It can also get in the way of relationships both at work and at home, especially if I start thinking of myself as having loftier ideals than the people around me. So it's especially important for me to remember to balance the "ideal" with the "real," so I don't needlessly alienate professional colleagues or deprive myself of opportunities for intimacy.*

Type c

Emotional authenticity, depth of experience, and artistic integrity matter lot to me. I value the deeper dimensions of experience and would find it impossible to live only on the surface of life. That's why it can be easier for me to handle intense situations that allow me to experience life's meaning than those that involve mechanized routines or the exchange of empty pleasantries. More than most people, I often feel a deep sense of longing or dissatisfaction, as though something subtle is missing from life—something elusive yet precious. When I try to express these feelings, most people don't seem to understand what I'm talking about; they look away, make a joke, or change the subject. Their lack of understanding can make me feel emotionally isolated. Often, the best thing to do is to pour my energy into creative work—work that can communicate my inner experience through some kind of artistic medium (acting, writing, dance, art, or pottery). Alternatively, I enjoy doing ordinary things in a non-ordinary way. Because my inner life can be more compelling than my outer life, I have to remember to "come up for air" from time to time, so I don't lose track of family, relationships, or other things that matter.

SUBTYPE ARENAS

1. *I'm an independent individualist with a lot of creative energy. Although I appreciate my friends, I like to make my own way in life and need to spend time alone on creative pursuits. Although I'm sensitive to criticism, I seldom allow other people to see that side of me; I try to keep it well-hidden from casual view. As far as my environment goes, I'm particular about both its comfortability and its aesthetics. Light, color, balance, harmony—I notice these things and value their ability to create a rich, vibrant space. Being trapped in an environment that's ugly, plastic, or otherwise impoverished is positively painful. As a result, I tend to travel like a gypsy, bringing from home whatever I need to create a comfortable home-away-from-home. In the same spirit of enrichment, there are times when I'm willing to take a chance, in order to experience life in a deeper, more authentic way. Sometimes the course I follow can look risky to other people, but I have this way of seeing survival as more symbolic than physical at times. Physical security doesn't always mean as much to me as the chance to be a spiritual or artistic pioneer.*

2. *I'm a naturally high-strung, emotionally sensitive individual with an artistic temperament: I have the nerves of a thoroughbred and a temper to match. So my personality attracts some people and turns others off. It also gives me the ability to be 100% committed to artistic projects I take on or causes I embrace; I can also be a fierce competitor. But even when I'm at my fiercest, criticism from others is still painfully difficult to take, especially when it's personal. Even so, I'm attracted to intense intimate relationships, but often find them hard to handle, which is why I "blow hot and cold" at times. I can also be moody and irritable, especially if things aren't going well. But I also bring tremendous passion to my relationships; I am definitely not a steady-state, middle-of-the-road type of person. Spiritually, I can be like a moth to the flame, attracted to unusual or extreme paths that take me deeply into the Unknown. When I'm committed to a path, I'm totally committed. So I tend to hold back nothing. For this reason, it's critical for me to cultivate discrimination, so that the path I choose is truly a path with heart.*

3. *As part of my search for authenticity, I seek out group activities with a creative, transformative, or activist focus. But my acute awareness of myself as an individual can make it difficult for me to completely mesh with the rest of the group, in part because of my ability to read the moods of other people, even when I'm not trying to. Whether I like it or not, I can always tell when people are being less than genuine in their comments. When I detect a discrepancy between what people are saying and what they're actually feeling, it's hard to keep from pointing this out, even when I know my comments won't be appreciated. It's helpful for me to learn how to use a little tact and patience instead of direct confrontation. When I can curb my desire to speak out and try to work more behind the scenes, I often discover that it's possible to be true to myself without alienating the people around me. In any event, it's usually easiest for me to function in intimate groups that value honesty and cooperation. Then I can often relax and participate, instead of constantly needing to jump into the role of critical commentator.*

Type d

I'm a warm, friendly individual who likes to spend time with other people. Because relationships are important to me, I make them a priority in life. As a result, I'm willing to do more than my share to make new friends, maintain existing friendships, or offer assistance when people need help. I'm attracted to work that allows me some kind of social interaction, such as teaching, the helping professions, charity/volunteer work, or organizing social events. And I'm the original "soft touch" when it comes to picking up strays, whether animal or human. Although I get overcommitted at times, I can't seem to say no when I see someone who needs help. So I really need to learn how to set appropriate boundaries when it comes to serving others—and to set aside more time for myself, so that I can enjoy my relationships instead of letting them control my life. Despite my sincere interest in other people, I have to admit that my desire to embrace the helper role stems in part from my own need to gain love and appreciation for my efforts. So it's important for me to learn that I don't need to be the perfect giver in order to be worthy of receiving love.

SUBTYPE ARENAS:

1. *More than anything, I enjoy taking care of the people who are closest to me. It's a joy, not a burden, whether it means cooking their meals, doing their laundry, or caring for them in other personal ways. Family is important to me, and I love to have my friends and family close by, so I can play a tangible role in their lives. Home is also important, because it's the place where people gather for meals and holidays. I like my home to be the hub of activity and try to create an environment that seems inviting. When new guests come over, I often try to find out their likes and dislikes in advance, so I can make their visit memorable. And when buying a gift, I want to make sure it's something the receiver will really enjoy. Of course, this desire to serve other people makes me a little nosy at times, because I can't help people out unless I know what they really need. Even so, I realize there are times when I need to give them a little more space, so they don't feel overwhelmed by my attention. My challenge is to nurture people when there's a need for it and to cut the apron strings when the time is right.*

2. *The lure of romantic love is strong for me. The fun of attracting an appealing partner, the ritual of love and courtship, the seductive play between the opposites—these are the kind of romantic experiences that get my juices flowing and make my head spin. So starting a new relationship is pretty exhilarating. But once the relationship gets past the initial stages, and the romantic "high" wears off, that's when the real work begins. It can be hard not only to push through my own disappointment as I start to discover my partner's flaws, but to realize that he or she is discovering mine. I'm often afraid that the romantic image that originally attracted my partner's attention won't be enough to sustain that interest over time. It can be hard to believe that my partner could love me just for myself, rather than for what I'm willing to sacrifice for the relationship. Spiritually, I have a deeply devotional nature; I'm attracted to paths involving love and surrender. It's easier for me to relate to an approach which is more personal than abstract, and more service-oriented than ascetic. As with love, I have to be careful not to give myself away so completely that I neglect my own development as an individual.*

3. *I thoroughly enjoy participating in groups, especially social groups. I'm a great social organizer who knows how to create social functions that really "click." But I'd usually rather serve as an informal or behind-the-scenes facilitator than as a recognized leader. I'm usually very effective in this informal role, because I'm extremely attentive to the needs of those around me. So it's not unusual for the people I work with to rely completely on my help, especially in crunch situations. And with leaders who are unsure of themselves, I can sometimes step into a very responsible though hidden role, directing things from behind the scenes, like the "power behind the throne." In any event, when I work for someone, I'm so committed to justifying their faith in me that it can be very hard to delegate key tasks, even when I'm exhausted. I need to learn how to offer support without working so heroically that I lose the ability to relax and enjoy the fruits of my success. I also need to cultivate the kind of self-confidence that enables me to step out of the background and into the limelight, assuming a more upfront leadership role when the opportunity arises.*

Type e

I'm a blunt talker and straight-shooter who doesn't mince words. I tell the truth and respect those who do the same. But I have no use for phonies or people who try to manipulate me. I like everything to be out on the table, so I know what's going on. I realize that some people don't like that kind of directness; they might even find it intimidating. I'm not trying to scare anybody, that's just how I am. Sure, I can blow up at times, but it is doesn't last long. I have some strong points, too. First, I'm a person who gets things done. I'm not lazy and have tons of endurance. Second, I honor my commitments. Honor is a big deal with me, and I wouldn't be much of a person if I didn't live up to my personal code. Third, I have the strength to look out for people who really need my help. So when I see innocent people getting hurt, I step in and stop it. Of course, this sometimes gets me into trouble because I tend to act first and ask questions later. Life works better when I can manage to stay calm, slow down, and think before I act.

SUBTYPE ARENAS

1. *I'm self-reliant, independent, and protective of those I love. I keep my personal business to myself and make sure that my family has what it needs to be strong and independent. That's how I show my love—by being a good provider and protector. It's easier to show my love that way than with words. Words are cheap; I don't really trust them. It's actions that matter. All the same, I sometimes wish I could let down my guard a little, but that's tough to manage, because I need my private space. If I give it up, I might not be able to get it back. At least that's how it seems. To me, it's common sense to stock up on supplies and find ways to safeguard them, in case of emergency. It also makes sense to buy based on practicality, not image or fashion. So I don't understand people who can be suckered into buying things just to maintain appearances. Although I'm generally calm, don't mistake my calmness for weakness; I have the strength of will to take action against those who try my patience. But I generally don't seek out trouble; I'm a good neighbor and dependable friend, just so long as you respect my boundaries.*

2. *I'm a powerful "warrior" type with a fiery temper and full-bodied appetites. I love taking on new challenges that push me to the limit, just so I can test my strength and indulge my appetite for adventure. But although I can definitely be a tough customer, when it comes to love, I have another side of me that I don't show most people—a tender, vulnerable side that just melts when I see a lost child or people victimized due to no fault of their own. I'd secretly like to find a partner who can appreciate this tender part of me—someone truly worthy of my love, who I can honor and cherish forever. I'm rather like a knight errant in the old stories; the books about courtly love must have been written for people like me, because for all my intensity and focus on the physical senses, there's something inside me that aspires to an image of love that is completely idealistic. I secretly long to embody the purity and deep sense of honor that I feel inside. Spiritually, I'm drawn to strenuous paths that test my resolve and demand my respect.*

3. *As a natural leader with good social skills, I can create calm in the midst of chaos and get things organized and moving in the right direction. It's nothing I learned in school, just something I know—an instinctive ability I have to size up people and take command in dicey situations. Because I "walk the walk," I can inspire people to follow me even when the situation is really tough; some of my best moments have been during accidents, emergencies, or on the battlefield. I'm capable of making hard decisions that require strength of character. Because of my resolve, I always have allies to help me out of jams. And because I know how to watch my back, I don't often get blind-sided by opponents. But I make enemies sometimes, because I'm not always good at pulling my punches, especially in situations requiring a lot of tact and diplomacy. I'm not good at working for leaders that I don't respect or carrying out orders that don't make sense. So my challenge is to know when to be quiet and be patient, rather than losing the chance to change the situation over time.*

Type f

I'm an upbeat, goal-oriented individual who works hard to be successful in life, whether success means advancement at work, credibility as a consultant, or being the perfect parent or partner. I see obstacles as challenges to be overcome, and I enjoy overcoming them. At the same time, I'm a multi-tasker with the flexibility to adapt to changing situations and deadlines, so I tend to push through difficulties when others get bogged down. I see time as a commodity, and I know how to use it efficiently. I'm also good at accepting feedback and making improvements for the future: if I listen today, I can excel tomorrow. However, I'm such a good adapter that it can sometimes be hard to succeed at the kind of things that require a more heartfelt, subtle, or unconventional approach. It can also be hard for me to devote the kind of time to personal relationships that they really deserve. If I'm honest, I'll admit to seeing time spend away from work as time wasted. But it's sometimes difficult to be as honest with myself as I'd like, because my success in life depends so much on my talent for maintaining a positive, "can do" self-image.

SUBTYPE ARENAS

1. *I'm a Type A personality with a lot of drive and determination. When I have a goal in life, I work hard to achieve it, not allowing anything to get in my way. While I hate to think of myself as materialistic, I have to admit that financial security means a lot to me. It's not just about the money—it's about having a tangible sense of who I am, as reflected by what I've accomplished and the financial security I provide for myself and my family. It may seem like a small thing to some people, but to me, it's a way to feel solidly grounded in life. But my focus on material security makes it hard to stop working; there always seems to be something more to do. This preoccupation can make me a workaholic at times. My challenge is to know when "enough is enough"—when to shift gears and spend some time on the kind of things that can't be measured, like relationships, recreation, or being in nature. But to do that, I'd have to let go of a role that makes me feel really secure in life. It takes more courage than people realize to step away from the satisfying role of "successful achiever" and into a role that isn't all about work.*

2. *I feel a personal sense of destiny that pushes me to scale the heights in whatever I do. It's as if there's a spotlight on me all the time, and I'm giving everything I can possibly give—all in order to become a superstar in my line of work. So I'm very aware of myself: aware of the image I project and its effect on other people. I always strive to be attractive, whatever it takes—and I usually succeed because I'm willing to go the extra mile to make the most of my assets. I also have a lot of personal magnetism and the kind of natural flair that attracts positive attention. It doesn't matter whether I'm in a one to one relationship or in a large group; I know how to make the right impression. But because I project a larger-than-life image, it can be hard to live up to that image in a real-life relationship where my partner wants to know the person behind the persona. So it's important for me to know the difference and learn how to shed that persona when I come home at night. Spiritually, my challenge is similar: I need to learn how to break though my tendency to outwardly play the role of sincere seeker (but without seeking any deep-level change), so I can experience genuine spirituality instead of a not-quite-genuine facsimile.*

3. *I'm a savvy politician with a good grasp of organizational management. So wherever I start in an organization, I soon rise in rank, often achieving a top spot in a relatively short amount of time. My positive vision, willingness to work hard, and ability to mobilize a team make me an asset wherever I go. I'd rather take a leadership role than work behind the scenes. And I don't mind high-profile jobs, because I like the opportunity to take charge, showcase my work, and meet other people who are also high achievers. So I'm willing and able to take on the kind of responsibility that upfront leadership requires. As I make my way to the top, I have to remind myself not to climb so fast that I fail to learn the business properly; otherwise, my knowledge is likely to be "a mile wide and an inch deep." I also need to avoid allowing my ambition to override my good judgment, so that my actions remain ethical. I don't want to inadvertently step on people, just because I'm so focused on my goals. Otherwise, once I reach the top, I may lack both the knowledge and support I need to be an effective leader.*

Type 9

I'm a vigilant individual with a sixth sense for danger. I get nervous in new situations and have a hard time relaxing until I'm certain that my negative imaginings are very unlikely to happen. While my inner radar is good at detecting real dangers, it also generates enough false alarms to make me doubt myself and my abilities. So I have to be careful not to let my imagination run away with me if I don't want fear to either paralyze me into inaction or to trigger the kind of counterphobic response that is rash or overblown. Rationally, I understand that many of my fears are unlikely to materialize; even so, they seem quite real. I notice that humor is often the best antidote for anxiety; it not only takes the edge off my tension but also improves my ability to tell the difference between real and imagined dangers. Although my heightened sensitivities are not always easy to handle, they do give me a healthy skepticism, a keen eye for deception, and the ability to notice potential problems before they arise. They also allow me to appreciate the stabilizing benefits of family, friendship, and community-based organizations.

SUBTYPE ARENAS

1. *Home and family mean a lot to me. So it's a priority to find a family-friendly place to live that's both safe and affordable. I also like to host friends and family at my place, especially people I've known for a long time, so I'm often more willing to spend my savings on my home than on consumer goods or travel. When meeting new people, I like to go through family, friends, or organizations in which I'm involved. I tend to defer to authority, although I can feel a little rebellious if I think I'm not being treated fairly, especially at work. But all and all, I'm a conscientious employee who's able to comply with the requirements of the workplace. Although I can worry too much about things going wrong, when a real crisis strikes, I'm often surprisingly calm and collected: now that the worst has happened, I can channel all my nervous energy into put things back in order. Despite my anxiety, I also seem to have an inner reservoir of courage that's there for me at times when I really need it. I just need to find a way to tune in to that part of myself more often, so my nerves don't overcome my common sense.*

2. I'm very committed to overcoming my fears, whether they're personal, social, or physical in nature; I find it easier to face them head-on than pretend they don't exist. As a result, I often find myself involved in situations that test my courage in some way. Although the courage I cultivate is real, it's based more on sheer determination than innate strength. I have to keep pushing myself forward in order to avoid falling into a state of fearful paralysis—at least that's how it seems to me. My attitude towards love is similar: companionship is something for which I yearn, and I'm willing to muster up the courage to seek out the partner I desire. Once I'm in a romantic relationship, it's easy for me to over-idealize my partner (because of my determination to avoid uncertainty and to ensure the success of the relationship). I'm attracted to work that is mentally-absorbing (like research, technology, or other work requiring a logical approach); and I seek out hobbies that allow me to overcome fear while having a little fun. Spiritually, I'm drawn to forms of worship that allow me to gain a semblance of inner peace, despite my own anxieties and the chaos of life.

3. I'm a responsible, dependable person who enjoys being active in civic affairs. I understand the value of tradition and enjoy participating in service organizations of people who share my beliefs and values. I especially admire selfless servers like firefighters, police officers, or military personnel, so I try in my own way to make some sort of contribution to the larger community, even when it requires some kind of sacrifice on my part. Although I don't necessarily strive for a leadership role, my commitment and diligence often earn me more responsibility than I bargained for. While I sometimes wonder whether I'm up to the task, once I take it on, I'm often surprised to find that I have more executive ability than I imagined. While I don't really think of myself as charismatic, I'm a conscientious organizer who knows how to enlist support and get things done. Whether as a leader or participant, it's satisfying to be involved in efforts that make a genuine contribution to society while also allowing me to develop supportive ties with other participants.

Type h

I'm a naturally accepting person who gets along with most people. I have a kindly disposition but a tendency to have trouble with finishing up the projects I start. It's not that I'm lazy, but that I tend to get distracted by intervening events. I function better when I follow the cycles of nature rather than having to rush through the day. So it's not surprising that time management can be a problem, given the busy pace of modern life. I try to adjust, but if things get too hectic, I may need to dig in my heels and stop responding to outside demands until I get caught up. Structured activities (like a regular job) can help me organize my time, but they can also create the kind of groove that easily turns into a rut. When that happens, I need to find some way to get unstuck, so I'll seek out something that can give me the motivation to change, whether that motivation comes from inspirational stories, new friends, or new activities that change my outlook on life. What really matters is that I discover how to be more aware of myself and what I really want in life, so I can actually fulfill my dreams instead of just talking about them.

SUBTYPE ARENAS

1. *I'm a real homebody who enjoys puttering around and organizing my stuff, although I sometimes spend more time just shifting things around than really getting organized. I'm attracted to collecting things, so clutter can be a problem, although it may bother other people more than it bothers me. I also feel at home in the natural world, so I enjoy activities like gardening, walking, or being with animals. And I can also enjoy indulging myself with small pleasures, like tasty snacks. So I have to be careful to take care of myself, so I don't slip into bad habits that may be hard to break. My steadiness and patience make me a good parent; I instinctively know how to relate to small children and to allow them to do things in their own way. On the other hand, it's easy to allow my family to completely define my life and to somehow forget my personal needs in the process. As far as work goes, I'm good at jobs that require a steady hand, but I can find deadlines, office politics, or direct criticism stressful, so I seek out work situations that are harmonious and try to ignore conflict situations whenever possible. I enjoy life more when I get myself moving, eat the right things, and block out regular periods for self-development.*

2. *I'm a bit of a dreamer who enjoys getting lost in the depths of my own imagination. I have an innate sense of oneness with life, and often feel a spontaneous sense of connectedness with everything around me. I have a childlike sense of romance, and love to be inspired by stories that others might call silly or sentimental. I also enjoy fantasy or magic, and like to bring magic into the world in some way, through stories, songs, poetry, or dance. If I don't create it myself, I can at least appreciate it in the books I read or the films I watch. When I fall in love, I fall completely—and this makes me vulnerable, because it's so easy for me to see my partner as some sort of fairy tale prince or princess. It can come as a shock to discover that real-life partners can be both more wonderful and terrible than I ever could ever have imagined! While it's not easy to wake up to this kind of reality, it helps me to see the difference between the kind of magic that is sheer fantasy and the kind that can survive my real-life experiences. Spiritually, I have a mystical streak and sometimes tune into dimensions beyond the five senses. I'm attracted to paths that provide a natural bridge between my ordinary life and the worlds beyond it.*

3. *I enjoy participating in groups, doing things that brings people together like hiking, singing, or working on group projects. When conflicts arise, I initially try to look the other way, even though my impartial nature makes me a natural mediator. I find it less stressful to play to role of participant, without the pressure of having to take the lead, sort things out, or help the group make decisions. It's such a pleasure to simply blend in, especially when things are running smoothly. However, when they're not, I can eventually get annoyed and decide to step out of the ranks and actively help people resolve their differences. If necessary, I might even take charge, especially if I'm the obvious person for the job. Although I don't see myself as a natural leader, people tell me they like the way I organize things, probably because I'm not very egocentric and like to enlist the talents of everybody involved. It's the sort of approach that usually creates a harmonious group. My success in this arena may encourage me to take the initiative more often and help me overcome my natural aversion to assuming a role that requires a lot of assertiveness or decision-making.*

Type i

As a reflective person with an inventive mind, I like to think deeply about things in life. My mind naturally seeks to understand what is going on around me, so I'm an alert observer of people and situations. I'm also good at taking in a lot of data and then sorting it out to make sense of what I see. As a result, I spend a lot of time alone, in my own mental world. But I also enjoy being with other people, just so long as I can avoid feeling overwhelmed by the situation. When there's too much outer input in too short a period, my circuits seem to become overloaded. When this happens, I need to retreat into a quiet space so I can recharge my batteries. The other problem in social situations is that I'm not very good at small talk. While I don't mind conversing, I'd rather talk about deeper things that require a certain amount of reflection (and perhaps research). Once I've thought a lot about something, I usually have definite opinions, if anyone cares to draw them out. But other people usually have to take the first step, unless I'm in a group that I know very well. In public gatherings, I often become a silent observer, unless I have a special role to play (perhaps as an instructor, photographer, or technical advisor).

SUBTYPE ARENAS

1. *I'm a self-contained, sensitive individual with reclusive tendencies. Having a personal, private space means a lot to me, because it gives me somewhere to put my stuff, gather my thoughts, and work undisturbed. It's important that other people respect the physical boundaries I set, because if they don't, it's hard for me to really trust them. At the same time, I can often accumulate the kind of miscellaneous stuff that tends to pile up over time, creating my "castle walls." So I often need a nudge from friends and family members to get rid of things I don't really need, although I tend to resist their efforts (at least initially) because it's so stressful to having my personal space invaded. I also need encouragement at times to get out of the house and become more physically active and socially involved. But leaving the security of home can seem like a daunting prospect, because it's like stepping beyond an invisible barrier into a different world. Since it can take a lot of initiative to get me past that barrier, it's good to have outside interests and friendships that are compelling enough to pull me out the door.*

2. *I'm a intense but introverted individual with a vivid imagination. I have an active inner life and a need to find some sort of creative outlet for my ideas and inspirations. I'm also strongly motivated to seek intimate companionship with a partner or trusted friend with whom to share ideas. But it takes a lot for me to trust someone enough to invite them into my inner world, because not many people can accept my little quirks and idiosyncrasies. Despite my desire for intimacy, I don't want to open up to people who might betray my trust. So the desire for openness competes with the desire to remain hidden, producing emotional conflict that can be painful. I don't often meet people on my wave length, so it means a lot to have at least one special confidante with whom I can share my innermost thoughts, speculations, and hidden desires. Even so, there are some still parts of myself that I don't share with anybody. Spiritually, I'm attracted to spiritual or esoteric paths that are deep, philosophical, and possibly shamanic; the path I pursue is likely to be unconventional in nature and to involve more secret or solitary practices than social interaction.*

3. *My thirst for knowledge is never quenched, especially knowledge esteemed by the larger academic or social community. I study life with detached but focused curiosity, detecting meaningful patterns that other people don't necessarily notice. Such patterns fascinate and intrigue me. Although I'm more motivated to study what personally interests me than to follow current cultural fads and fancies, whatever I study, I'm likely to acquire a high degree of expertise, whether as an academic with advanced degrees or a dedicated amateur. I'm motivated to share my understanding by taking on some kind of educational role, whether as an author, educator, or researcher. The products of my work are more likely to be more scholarly than popular, and I'm more likely to teach at an advanced than an elementary level. I appreciate getting formal recognition for my work, both because it gives me a recognized role to play in the larger culture, as well as a means for establishing relationships with professional colleagues.*

KEY

TO ENNEAGRAM TYPE AND SUBTYPES TEST

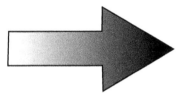

(see also next page)

Para.	Type	Type Descriptions
a	7	**The Improviser:** lively, enthusiastic, energetic, quick, interested, receptive, appealing, funny, inspiring, forward-looking, persuasive, restless, mentally active, experience-oriented (see Ch. 17)
b	1	**The Perfecter:** intent, hard-working, formal, self-disciplined, reserved, critical, corrective, thorough, precise, detail-oriented, principled, serious, careful, judging, reserved, ethics-oriented (see Ch. 11)
c	4	**The Deep Sea Diver:** sensitive, intense, verbally-gifted, authenticity-focused, individualistic, emotional, empathic, original, artistic, self-conscious, dramatic, self-critical, depth-oriented (see Ch. 14)
d	2	**The People Person:** nurturing, supportive, outgoing, friendly, warm, engaging, accommodating, helpful, attentive, receptive, eager, interactive, affectionate, people-oriented (see Ch. 12)
e	8	**The Master:** strong, grounded, blunt, powerful, controlling, concrete, assertive, magnetic, dominating, ruling, unapologetic, self-possessed, staunch, personal exemplar, power-oriented (see Ch. 18)
f	3	**The Self-tester:** energetic, outgoing, achieving, pragmatic, positive, confident, assertive, optimistic, goal-focused, versatile, adaptable, prestige-seeking, multi-tasking, success-oriented (see Ch. 13)
g	6	**The Steward:** sharp-eyed, watchful, careful, protective, defensive, responsible, conventional, cautious, monitoring, skeptical, shrewd, loyal, traditional, safety-oriented (see Ch. 16)
h	9	**The Storyteller:** practical, receptive, unassuming, imaginative, dreamy, companionable, peace-seeking, agreeable, implacable, facilitating, unresisting, harmony-oriented (see Ch. 19)
i	5	**The Puzzle-solver:** shy, sensitive, introverted, detached, reflective, sharp, penetrating, incisive, intellectual, observant, systematic, deep, esoteric, shamanic, expert, concept-oriented (see Ch. 15)

Type	Subtype Descriptions
1	**B – The Perfecter** 1. SP ONE (The Detailer) *industrious, exacting, disciplined, tidy, stern, strict, serious, precision-oriented* 2. SX ONE (The Crusader) *tense, focused, forceful, ascetic, critical, inflamed, impassioned, cause-oriented* 3. SOC ONE (The Lawmaker) *principled, refined, reserved, high-minded, mannerly, appropriate, rule-oriented*
2	**D – The People Person** 1. SP TWO (The Matriarch) *warm, affirming, sympathetic, helpful, eager, inquisitive, all-enveloping, nurture-oriented* 2. SX TWO (The Romantic) *affectionate, emotional, pleasing, sexy, romantic, seductive, intimacy-oriented* 3. SOC TWO (The Diplomat) *friendly, facilitating, supportive, diplomatic, organized, gracious, friendly, event-oriented*
3	**F – The Self-tester** 1. SP THREE (The Pragmatist) *energetic, determined, ambitious, hard-working, practical, efficient, materially-oriented* 2. SX THREE (The Superstar) *charming, attractive, charismatic, winsome, image-building, attention-oriented* 3. SOC THREE (The Politician) *adaptable, confident, assertive, glib, outgoing, team-building, prestige-oriented*
4	**C – The Deep Sea Diver** 1. SP FOUR (The Artisan) *original, persevering, frank, soulful, dauntless, independent, symbol-oriented* 2. SX FOUR (The Dramatist) *high-strung, moody, intense, competitive, creative, extreme, artistically-oriented* 3. SOC FOUR (The Critic) *shy, self-conscious, emotionally sensitive, thoughtful, tasteful, refined, critique-oriented*

Type	Subtype Descriptions
5	**I – The Puzzle-solver** 1. SP FIVE (The Archivist) *shy, detached, observant, secluded, compartmentalized, privacy-oriented* 2. SX FIVE (The Wizard) *odd, quirky, unusual, intriguing, mysterious, intimate, confidentiality-oriented* 3. SOC FIVE (The Professor) *curious, exploratory, deeply-delving, multifaceted, shamanic, knowledge-oriented*
6	**G – The Steward** 1. SP SIX (The Family Preserver) *warm, protective, familial, steadfast, loyal, careful, nervous, security-oriented* 2. SX SIX (The Scrapper) *skeptical, ambivalent, uncertain, unpredictable, idealizing, defensive, risk-oriented* 3. SOC SIX (The Guardian) *dutiful, responsible, obedient, conventional, respectful, community-oriented*
7	**A – The Improviser** 1. SP SEVEN (The Bon Vivant) *Appreciative, celebratory, enthusiastic, sensuous, lifestyle-oriented* 2. SX SEVEN (The Trickster) *high-flying, spontaneous, entertaining, zany, fascinated, freedom-oriented* 3. SOC SEVEN (The Visionary) *forward-thinking, activating, inspirational, futuristic, innovation-oriented*
8	**E – The Master** 1. SP EIGHT (The Weight Lifter) *strong, stable, calm, earthy, concrete, plain-spoken, survival-oriented* 2. SX EIGHT (The Knight) *magnetic, hot-tempered, protective, powerful, chivalrous, honor-oriented* 3. SOC EIGHT (The Leader) *fair, magnanimous, broad-minded, kingly/queenly, even-handed, leadership-oriented*
9	**H – The Storyteller** 1. SP NINE (The Comfort Seeker) *unassuming, puttering, stuff-collecting, boundary-seeking, comfort-oriented* 2. SX NINE (The Mystic) *merging, emerging, mystical, receptive, nature-loving, union-oriented* 3. SOC NINE (The Cooperator) *participatory, cooperative, peace-seeking, facilitating, harmony-oriented*

Index

NOTE: Only those films and TV shows mentioned in the text are included in the index. For a complete list (including films listed in Tables 11-1 through 19-1), please see Chapter 22.

This index is also available online at www.enneagramdimensions.net/archetypes_of_the_enneagram.pdf.

Lightning Source UK Ltd.
Milton Keynes UK
UKOW05f0604101017
310697UK00003B/139/P